GRIT

GRIT

A Family Memoir on Adversity and Triumph

© 2018 Jeff Moyer

All rights reserved

1st Edition

jeffmoyer.com

Published by Music from the Heart
Chula Vista, CA

ISBN 978-0-9675768-0-0

Cover Design and Photo by John Kyle Moyer
Cover Illustration by Jessica Will

Table of Contents

DEDICATION

To the steadfast hearts of Mark, Bonnie, Jane,
Jack and Louise

Brother, Sister, Grandma; Dad and Mom

BAKED IN THE CAKE

PLEASE FORGIVE THE UNEVEN MARGINS IN THIS
BOOK. THE BOTTOM MARGIN IS UNNECESSARILY
WIDE AND THE TOP MARGIN IS SQUEEZED. THE
BEST MINDS AT KINDLE DIRECT PUBLISHING
AND MICROSOFT WERE UNABLE TO OVERCOME
MICROSOFT WORD'S ABSOLUTE DICTATES
CONCERNING MARGIN SIZE WHEN PAGES ARE
NUMBERED. A WIDER TOP MARGIN WOULD HAVE
INCREASED THE NUMBER OF PAGES.

Preface

Memoirs abound detailing the remarkable lives of authors with disabilities. Each has added to the recent tectonic shift in public consciousness concerning the meaning of disability. My own life's relationship to disability began with the silent realization, at the age of five, that I could no longer see my sister's soap bubbles floating in Cleveland's torpid summer air. Two weeks later my brother Mark was born with a severe cognitive disability. These twin vectors shaped and directed my life's trajectory. Each of us who lives with disability finds themselves on the long road leading to our difference becoming wedded within us as a multi-faceted fact of our normal life.

This book takes the reader on my family's odyssey that is our braided arc from victims to victors. These word journeys will take you through moments of unbearable heartache, down savage state institution's corridors and through a historic demonstration that changed American and ultimately world disability history. These vignettes also include tales of true life humor, dogged advocacy, sweet barrier surmounting victories and some seminole moments within american Disability Rights and assistive technology history. It will share one family's travails with severe cognitive disability, epilepsy, institutionalization, progressive blindness, progressive hearing loss, cancer of the mouth, throat and lungs, facial disfigurement, extreme vocal impairment, and an undiagnosed Attention Deficit Hyperactivity Disorder. And yet, although my family has endured more than its fair share of losses, the universal truths told here are about the heart's Phoenix of resilience, the fire of advocacy, the pride of accomplishments and the buoyancy of humor.

My own path has touched truly historic moments including being the troubadour for the 1977 San Francisco Section 504 Demonstration. In addition I performed at the U.S. Senate following the 1990 signing of The Americans with Disabilities Act. I penned a civil rights provision to the the Highway Bill of 2006 authorizing a department of transportation evaluation of a seminal type of assistive technology. But most important to me were the more humble actions required to establish a supported living home for my younger brother Mark.

In these pages I present, for the first time, a new paradigm for thinking about those with cognitive disabilities (and all disabilities) and describe becoming a kidney donor to save the daughter of a friend. I am

9

blessed with a good memory and have only realized the full meaning of my life by writing, editing and re-editing these pages.

I hope that you find GRIT of value.

Chapter 1: The Beginning

Double Trouble

It was early July in 1954. I sat next to my mother on the glider swing on the front porch of our modest wood frame house. I loved the porch and this rare moment to sit with my mother, without my sister or father requiring any of her attention. She knew the baby was restless and asked if I wanted to feel the tiny baby move, with great awe, I laid my small hand on her swollen belly, I felt a movement as if a fish had flipped within her. The realization that my little brother or sister was swimming around inside of her thrilled me with a wonder I had never known. The smoke from her cigarette curled around us creating the familiar acrid sting of cigarette smoke mingled with her perfume. She sipped from her gin and tonic and smoke slowly in the hot July evening.

My mother spoke about how busy she would be when the baby came and how she would need my help, as would the new member of our family. She told me I would be a big brother, and I felt that I was approaching an important role—one that would require responsibility that I couldn't imagine—but for which I eagerly waited.

Two weeks later, I laid gravely ill on the sofa in the living room, on the other side of the windows behind the porch swing. I drifted in and out of consciousness. I had the measles—a particularly devastating bout of the childhood disease which had left me with a critically high fever for days and had brought the doctor to my side twice. As I groggily awoke, I heard my mother speaking to my aunt in concerned, quiet tones, and I could tell by the scraps of conversation that drifted through the murky haze of fever and pain, that they were talking about me. I was too weak to speak. My body ached and felt hot, limp, and quite foreign. It was better to be asleep, so I closed my eyes and was gone.

Days later, I sat docilely on the sofa with my sister Bonnie, staring at the array of unopened presents from relatives and neighbors, that had been sent to me during my illness. I didn't remember anyone else ever getting a present because they were sick. I vaguely understood that I was recovering from a different sort of childhood disease, and I accepted that the presents were somehow justified. I knew that I had been sick in a way that I had never seen anyone else experience, and only later would I be told that I had had a brush with death.

I was five, Bonnie was seven. She begged my mother to let her blow bubbles from the light red bottle that sat amid the other gifts on the coffee table. After several pleading requests, my mother relented and said that it was time that I could be allowed outside and that together, we could sit on the porch and blow bubbles. It took all of my strength to walk onto the porch and collapse onto the glider. Bonnie happily unscrewed the top of the glass jar and dipped the plastic bubble wand into the pink viscous fluid. She gently blew through the circular opening, and I could see bubbles stream from the wand, then disappear as bubbles do, but, I thought, way too quickly. I mentioned to Bonnie that there was something wrong with the bubbles since they all broke right away. She had no idea what I was talking about. Bonnie reported that the air was full of bubbles. I could picture them floating magically in the still, summer heat. I could imagine them in my mind, but I could not see them. I chalked it up to an unknown category of experience. It didn't make sense to me, but as I sat weak and listless, I also didn't have the energy to try to figure it out.

On August 8, 1954, a few days after the mystery of the bubbles, I was feeling stronger and had begun to return to our family's cozy routines. But, that day, all attention swirled around my mother. A swift alignment of people and roles was demanded, for Mom to get to the hospital and for Bonnie and me to be taken care of. I didn't know why, but there was no happiness or eager anticipation coloring the excited and intense activity. My maternal grandmother, Mama Smith, arrived, and my parents left. Mama Smith explained that the baby was arriving early and that nobody was quite ready. But I knew my responsibilities as a big brother were about to commence and that, early or not, I was prepared to take on my important new role within the family.

I awoke early the next morning fully expecting my father to be home with news of the birth, but he was not there. My father was still at the hospital. Downstairs, my grandmother silently gave me my cereal and milk. She stood at the sink with her back to me, and I could hear her quietly crying. When I asked her what was wrong, she seemed unable to speak. I finished my breakfast, went outside, climbed onto the porch swing, and waited for my father. His car pulled into the driveway; I slid off the glider and moved to the top of the stairs that led to the front walk.

I couldn't wait to hear from him all the details and feel his strong arms around me as together we would talk about the new baby and whatever was to happen next. But Dad walked grimly up the stairs; a hard expression I didn't recognize had set his usually friendly face into a scowl. He didn't look at me. My five-year-old face turned upward toward him, my hope turning suddenly into confusion. My father did not speak a word to me, or acknowledge me at all. He walked right past me as if I weren't there. The screen door slammed behind him, and he disappeared into the house. My father had never ignored me before. He had never failed to greet me. He would always smile and open his strong arms to lift me up. But I had just felt an unspoken and unfamiliar emotional chill shut me out. It left me standing alone and bewildered.

I knew something was terribly wrong, and as I stood alone in my father's wake, I somehow recognized that I could no longer depend on the world that I had known. The unthinkable had happened, and as I assessed my reality, I vaguely understood that I was on my own in handling the dark cloud that was suddenly engulfing my world.

Mark's Different

When my mother returned from the hospital some days later, Mark, our new brother, did not. My mother was tired, sad, and seemed to bear an emotional weight that colored everything she did and said. She sat on the sofa with Bonnie on one side of her and me on the other. She quietly and painfully explained that Mark, whom we had been allowed to name, was different. She said that he was mentally retarded and very sick. He still needed to be at the hospital for a few days, but that when he came home, we would have to be quiet and patient. Mark was going to need our help.

When Mark did come home from the hospital, the sadness did not leave my mother. It seemed to infect everyone in the family as grandparents, aunts, and uncles came to visit. Ours was a neighborhood of post-war working class families. Children of all ages filled nearly every home. I had seen families with newborn babies. Chortling and constant attention burbled throughout those happy homes as the new baby seemed to glow amid unending warmth and happy focus. In our home, there were no smiles. My mother talked on the phone with a heartache that she did not attempt to disguise. The minister came to call. He spoke to her in a quiet voice about God's will and of mysteries we cannot understand.

I had really looked forward to Mark's birth, in part because I could not imagine how my mother could muddle through the day without my company. I was about to start school, and I thought that Mark had arrived just in time to spare my mother from the unspeakable dilemma of life without a child companion. But I knew then, that as I started my new life at school, a happy resolution at home was not to be. We walked through the motions of my preparations for my first day of kindergarten, but there was no joy in the tasks. Those feelings, along with security, spontaneity, and hope itself, had been extinguished as the cloying pall of unending pain about Mark heavily cloaked our family.

Later, I quietly listened to my mother talking to a friend on the telephone. She told her friend that she thought she could have handled a physical handicap in one of her children, but not a mental handicap. Later, she confided to her brother that the hospital had offered not to feed her new son if she so chose. The doctor suggested that they could keep him comfortable, but just let him quietly die. He recommended that Mark not be brought home, but that if my parents chose to have him live, he should immediately be sent to an institution. He counseled that the attention Mark would require was so great that my parents' other normal children would suffer in the force field of Mark's extensive and unending needs. But my mother and father were stalwart and they followed their hearts. Mark was going to be part of the family. With grim determination, they clung to each other as they set out on an uncharted course. Our family's new life circumstances had begun.

Trusted

Mark came home from the hospital, and despite the emotional overtones of sadness, life settled into the ragged routines required for tending to the needs of a newborn baby. Kindergarten and an entirely new landscape of experience opened up as I stepped out on my own. Every weekday afternoon, I explored the world as an independent little person. The niggling visual incapacities I had observed that summer day, while watching Bonnie blow bubbles, continued in kindergarten, at home, and in the rough and tumble interactions with neighborhood children. An optometrist told my parents that I was pretending I couldn't see, and they believed him. I became squeezed between my parent's expectations and the real barriers presented by my diminished eyesight. Even so, overall, life seemed expansive and manageable.

My relationship with Mark was fascinating, painful, and focused. There was always an unspoken heartache about his retardation, but having a

14

new baby brother was a charming addition to my life. Shortly after he was brought home from the hospital, my mother counseled me that, like all newborn babies, the top of his skull was not yet hardened and that the "soft spot" should not be pushed for fear of damaging his tiny brain. One fall afternoon, Mark lay in his playpen in the front room, just in front of the sofa. I lay beside him on the floor, watching him through the wooden bars. My mother told me that she was going to go downstairs to do some laundry, and she asked me to keep an eye on Mark while she was gone. Finally, I had a big brother responsibility that was important; I was being asked to take care of him, alone. I was trusted with Mark, and the two of us were left on our own, with me in charge.

The late afternoon sun shone through the window in slanting rays. The vivid colors of the soft toys that surrounded Mark in his light blue sleeper presented a beautiful picture of tranquility and, it seemed to me, one of perfect normalcy. Mark didn't look different to me; in fact, he seemed like a perfect little baby, and I thought to myself–a thought that had occurred to me quite often by then–"Those doctors have to be wrong. Mark is just fine."

But my nagging curiosity about the soft spot on the top of his head wouldn't leave me alone. I reached my hand between the bars of the playpen and slowly and carefully touched the top of his head, stroking his fine, dark hair. He became fidgety and squirmed as I touched him. But I spoke to him in a soothing voice, and he stopped wriggling. He grew quiet and my hand rested on the top of his head. Like a moth to the flame, I was drawn to the danger. With gentle pressure, I tested to see if there really was a soft spot. Having a soft spot on the top of your head seemed like a fantastic and impossible notion; I thought that, like Mark's retardation, it was probably some ridiculous piece of misinformation that I could readily prove wrong. But instead of feeling firm skull under my fingers' pressure, with horror I felt soft tissue yield to my touch. I didn't press hard, but the unmistakable feeling of the soft spot was enough to convince me that my mother had been right; I had just done a terrible, unthinkable thing. I quickly withdrew my hand; the motion and suddenness of my action resulted in Mark's previous restlessness quickly ratcheting into a full-siren cry of distress which brought my mother running up the basement stairs to his aid. As she reached into the playpen to gather him up, I bolted up the stairs leading to the second floor, to the refuge of the bedroom that I shared with my sister. I was certain that I had just done Mark irreparable harm, and that my willful disregard of my mother's entreaty had caused instant and devastating damage to his little

15

brain. I felt with heartsick remorse that I had, in fact, just ensured his life's fate–the very one that I had previously convinced myself was wrong. From then on, every missed milestone, every developmental delay, and every sober parental exchange concerning Mark's failed progress sent another stinging arrow into my guilty and aching heart, for I knew that the problems Mark was experiencing were my fault.

It was late winter, 1956. Although long delayed, Mark had just learned to stand by himself, and on a snowy February afternoon, my mother asked if I wanted to take Mark outside for his first experience with snow. Even though I was fighting an inner demon, unknown to my parents, I wanted to redeem myself. This responsibility–being entrusted with Mark's care outside for the first time alone–excited me and seemed an opportunity to gain some relief for my troubled heart. So began the long process of bundling Mark and me into sweaters, leggings, galoshes, overcoats, mittens, scarves, and stocking caps. Mark, padded and stiff with the heavy clothing, was carried to the front yard by my father and was put down standing and stationary on the crusty snow of the small front lawn. As my father went back inside, I dug under the hard-packed surface and scooped up a bit of clean snow. I offered it to Mark after licking a bit myself to model the idea. His pink mouth opened birdlike, and his tongue licked the fluffy snow from my mitten.

My father had not been gone for long when a boy named Ronnie, who was eight–a year older than I–walked down the shoveled sidewalk toward us. I didn't know Ronnie well. He lived two blocks away and was one of the bullies who stalked the playground during recess, looking for someone upon whom to exert his superior strength and aggression. He wasn't wearing a hat, and his ears were red with the cold. His jacket was leather, and everything about him seemed menacing and hostile. He walked up and stared down at Mark. Mark stood unmoving with his unfocused eyes blinking in the cold air. Ronnie said, "What's wrong with that kid?"

I responded: "Nothing! He's my little brother, Mark, and there's nothing wrong with him." I burned with indignation; my desire to protect Mark and our family's painful reality smoldered within me. Ronnie jabbed his gloved hand straight out, striking Mark in the middle of the chest. Mark toppled backward, without any attempt to break his fall. He landed flat on his back, on the hard crust of the snow. As Mark fell, his terrible cry of shock, fear, and pain filled my ears.

Instinct and anger suddenly exploded, and I felt unexpected and unfamiliar rage. Propelled, I leaped onto Ronnie and showered him with a rain of wild punches, striking his head and shoulders, as I wordlessly screamed a yell of outrage and revenge. Caught entirely off guard, his hands flew up, attempting to block my punches as he stumbled backward. I continued to pound at him with roundhouse blows as he fell in a clumsy off-balance retreat. Then he regained his footing, turned, and ran down the street.

Mark continued to cry in a breathless wail. I quickly turned my attention toward this crisis of uncertain proportion. My father ran, coatless, down the steps and into the yard within moments. Without asking what had happened, he scooped Mark into his arms and hurried him back inside. I stood momentarily unmoving, then slowly walked back into the house behind them feeling confused and helpless—a swirl of emotions tied to only one bleak thought: once again, I could not be trusted.

Chapter 2: Something's Wrong

Can't See It

I really had looked forward to first-grade. My sister Bonnie was two years older than I, and I watched her academic progress with envy. While I was in kindergarten, she had been in the second-grade. My kindergarten class would walk in pairs past her classroom on the way to the gym, through the halls of Caledonia Elementary School. I would stare intently into her room and catch glimpses of the older students at their desks. The idea of having a desk, learning to write, and having books that you could read by yourself–these were goals that made me wish that kindergarten would get over with so that I could join the ranks of the seriously engaged student body.

Finally, the big day came. On that first day of first-grade, Miss Messenger walked back and forth at the front of the room, making us all understand that she was in charge and that the frivolity of early childhood was over. She was a strict woman with a tight, gray bun and a no-nonsense style. She quickly established a boot camp sergeant's control of us, as we sat meekly in the September heat, trying to make sense of this sudden shift in our fortunes.

One of the first learning activities that we were expected to perform was printing the alphabet. Miss Messenger stood at the blackboard and carefully printed each letter. We were supposed to follow her example–in turn–to print the letters on the wide-lined paper we had been given. I could get the general idea of the letters, but I couldn't see the details, other than the edge of a curved line, an angle, or maybe some sort of a tail. I raised my hand, and Miss Messenger called on me. I told her I couldn't see what she was writing on the blackboard. She moved me to the front row; it didn't really help at all. A frustrating struggle to try to see the board from the front row began.

I wanted to comply with my new seating position's obvious advantage, but I couldn't do it. After a series of exchanges with a growingly intense Miss Messenger, her higher angels kicked in. She patiently printed out a page with the whole alphabet in order, both capital and small letters, and it solved the problem. Of course, I had to listen to her very carefully to figure out what part of the letter you printed first and how the pencil was supposed to move around, to draw the whole thing.

We were also learning to read. Miss Messenger had a giant book opened on a table at the front of the room. It was a jumbo-sized, first Dick and Jane reader. Miss Messenger would show us how to sound out the words, and she would read the page of text to us, slowly moving her long wooden pointer back and forth through the lines of words. Then she would point at one word at a time as she called our names. We were expected to individually read the word out loud. She called on me. I flushed with embarrassment. I couldn't see the word. I could tell there were big pictures and what I thought were the words, but I couldn't make them out. Miss Messenger told me to just come closer until I could see my word. As the class watched me, with growing humiliation I slowly walked the short distance toward the enormous book. With each small step and with no word coming into view, I was forced to move closer and closer. I really wanted to see the words. I figured I was not doing it right–not trying hard enough. Then I was standing right in front of the table with the great book on it, and I was leaning over the table to get close enough to see the words. I finally could read when I was about a foot from the words. Laughter rippled through the room. I looked at the floor and went back to my desk. Miss Messenger didn't call on me to read from the big book again.

The nurse invited me down to her office the next day for a command performance with the same eye chart that I had failed in September. When the nurse had called after my exam early in the school year, my parents had explained to her, as they had been told by the optometrist, that I was just pretending that I couldn't see. He said I wanted to wear glasses. But now, the nurse said that she thought she might call my parents again because she thought I really needed glasses. This call from the nurse was not going to make things any easier at home. I couldn't do anything except go back to Miss Messenger's room, try to see and muddle along, grabbing whatever clues I could from what was said and the little I could see.

When we read from our books at our desks, Miss Messenger let me get as close to the book as I needed to; then I could see the big words on the page. I had to get so close my nose touched the page. But I was learning to read and write. There was an increasing problem with reading out loud because of its growing importance. By the middle of the year, we were going around the room, reading out loud from our seats a lot. Other kids would read out, nice and loud, and fast; I knew it was because they were smart. A few of the kids had trouble reading; they stumbled, and mumbled, and made mistakes, and took a really long time when it was their turn. I thought that I was smart too, but when I tried to see to read, I could only see one word at a time if it was a short word, or just part of a word if it was longer. Because I was so close to the book and it took me so long to see, I sounded like I didn't know how to read. I hated reading out loud. I really hated it.

Gym class gave me troubles, too. I liked relay races, dancing, and activities when balls weren't being thrown. But much of the time, balls were in motion: basketballs, big rubber balls, volley balls, soft mushy balls, a giant rubber ball, and small soft rubber balls. I almost always missed the catch and often was hit.

Second-grade started. To my shock and dismay, the print was a lot smaller in the books, and there was a lot more of it. We all went down for our eye tests. The nurse seemed to know that I couldn't see the eye chart this time. Again, she called my mother.

My second-grade teacher was not as strict as Miss Messenger; she quickly understood that it was hopeless for me to try to read the board. So every day, she would write down everything that she wrote on the board and give it to me in nice large printing on our wide line paper. Reading class was even worse than before, and I became practically the worst out-loud reader in the class. I knew I was smarter than that, and I would dread my turn approaching as one by one, the kids in my row, took their turns. My turn came ever closer. I would burn with shame as I struggled to see and read out loud. Just before Christmas vacation, the school nurse again tested my vision. My parents got the fourth phone call from the school about my vision.

The Piano Lesson

It was a cold winter afternoon in December of 1956, as I walked around our long block to my piano lesson. Bonnie was taking piano lessons, and my mother and both grandmothers played. Music was a regular part of our family's life; I was thrilled to be joining the world of musicians. The week's assignment, "March of The Fairies", had been a difficult piece to master. Written in the key of D, with two sharps–two hands with changing chords for the left hand, and individual notes blending into two hand chords–it really took some practice to memorize the piece.

I had begun piano lessons when I was six and now, at nearly eight, I had been at it for a year and a half. I felt proud of my months of work and this week's accomplishment, but as I trudged up the flight of stairs to Hendershot's Studios on the second floor above Fred's Bakery, I also felt the familiar upset, churning stomach that always accompanied my session with Crandall Hendershot. He was a Cleveland celebrity, being the organ accompanist for a local daytime women's exercise show whose star, Paige Palmer, referred to him as "Uncle Cran". He always got one opportunity during the show to smile into the camera to do his signature Adam's apple bow tie wiggle; he had done it for me upon our first meeting, but there was no bow tie wiggling during my lesson.

I liked the gentle piano teacher. I loved to be learning the instrument that required so much attention and practice, and which filled the hours that I had open to me, while baseball and other sports occupied the boys in the neighborhood. But I dreaded going through the lesson pretending I could see the music. That pretense had been required from the beginning, but every lesson demanded more and more struggle to repeat Mr. Hendershot's playing–dredging the notes from what I could hear and repeat–rather than assessing the score and playing, with the seeming magic that eye/hand alchemy provided.

Two years earlier, I had sat in the examination chair of an optometrist who shared a common waiting room with my Dad's brother, Uncle Chuck. He had just opened his first dental office, adjacent to the optometrist. My parents' concern about my visual problems had led them to take me to this stranger's optical office for evaluation. I sat and looked at pictures and shapes as the clinician divined the truth of the situation. His declaration, having examined my eyes and assessed my performance on the battery of pre-literate visual tests, was that I was pretending I couldn't see. He expertly explained to my parents that I wanted to wear glasses and that I was trying to convince them that my vision needed correction. They were counseled to be firm and told that I would quickly outgrow my obsession with eyewear. The school and the piano teacher had been enlisted as allies in the adult world's united confederation that, together, would break me–once and for all–of my hard-headed campaign to wear spectacles.

During the first lesson, as I leaned close to the open piano book straining to see the little black notes on the music staff, Mr. Hendershot put his hand firmly on my shoulder and pulled me back from the open book. He told me that he had been warned that I was going to try to fool him, but that he would have none of it. So week after week, I sat ramrod straight, a proper eighteen inches from the music, and pretended that he was right. He played, I concentrated and listened hard. I would then attempt to repeat his instruction, and measure by mangled measure, we would go over the week's piece until blessedly, the hour would be over, and I would walk home exhausted.

Afternoon by afternoon, my mother would patiently repeat the exercise. As I sat, a sighted boy's distance from the sheet-music, she would, note by note, tutor my mastery of the week's lesson. She must have wondered at my slow, albeit dogged, playing ability. It was tedious and drawn out work for both of us. Then, with the week's piece memorized, I would go back to Crandall, where another, yet more difficult piece was waiting for me, requiring the increasingly complex and gut-wrenching demands of pretending that I could see, since everyone was convinced that I was pretending that I could not.

That winter afternoon, although I was proud and excited about my accomplishment in the learning of "March of the Fairies", I knew that I was going to be presented with some colossus of a task within the pages of the second-hand piano book my sister had finished two years before.

I sat in the small waiting room shared by Crandall and his brother Sheldon, who taught clarinet and saxophone. Unlike Crandall, his brother was a loud, bombastic teacher, and I would always hear him yelling during my lesson at his hapless students, as they squeaked and honked their way through their hour long ordeals. Today he was in full bull-moose mode, hollering at a child who I pictured cringing under the lash of his tongue. I was already tense, and his anger made whatever sense of accomplishment I had felt quickly drain into the sinkhole of fear.

Crandall's studio door opened. The girl, whose lesson had ended, hurried through the waiting room. Mr. Hendershot told me to come in and to prepare for the day's lesson. As I walked into his piano studio, he excused himself. I took off my heavy winter coat, and I set my lesson book on the piano's music rack, and then sat waiting on the well-worn piano bench. Mr. Hendershot returned, quietly closed the door, and at his direction, I launched into "March of the Fairies". I played it at the peak of my ability, making only one mistake. As the last chord rang out, I waited for his praise. "Very good," he said absently, as he turned the page in the useless book. I was crestfallen. I wanted praise, and a prolonged analysis of the quality of my playing, and a chance to forestall a little longer the task soon before me. But

22

Crandall had bigger plans for the hour before us. He ceremoniously announced that today I was going to begin sight reading. He tapped the beginning of the two pages of music in the open piano book and said, "After a year and a half of lessons, you are ready and should be able to sight read the music, so please begin."

I felt the shaky bottom drop away from my fragile house of cards, and the sickening freefall of tumbling consequences begin. I weakly told him that I would like him to play the piece first. He said no, that it was time that I demonstrated my ability to play by sight reading the music. I couldn't speak. My gaze fell downward. I heard the clock ticking on the wall, and I could hear the blood pounding in my ears. I sat, frozen at the piano, my hands unmoving, waiting for my ears to give them, as always, some rudimentary musical clues about what they were supposed to do. Crandall sternly told me to play. He said it didn't need to be perfect, but to play what I saw on the page before me. Without raising my eyes from the piano keys, and burning with shame, I meekly said that I couldn't see the music. He was silent. He asked me to confirm that I really could not see the music. In an even quieter voice, I repeated my confession with the heaviness of one guilty of a terrible lie, discovered by an authority figure long deceived. He rose from his chair, walked to the window to gaze into the gathering darkness of the street below. With his hands clasped behind his back and still facing the window, he flatly and with a grim finality announced that, if I really couldn't see the music, there was no way that he could continue to teach me. He told me that the lesson was over, as were all future lessons with him. My parents would not be charged for this final, aborted lesson. I said nothing. I numbly stood, put my winter coat back on, picked up the piano book, and, for the last time, walked out of Hendershot Studios.

I put my stocking cap and gloves on in the waiting room, and I walked down the hall and down the unheated wooden staircase. As I began my long, cold walk home, my heart pounded, and my mind raced, knowing I would have to face my father. He had threatened me many times with dire consequences like putting splints on my elbows, so I couldn't bend my arms if he again caught me holding the Sunday funnies close enough to see them. Whenever he came into the room, I would startle with fear, snap back from whatever I was struggling to see and pretend that I could see at a normally-sighted distance. This awful development, this stripping away of the thin masquerade that kept my life working—such as it had—was ending. Another adult's judgment, although reflecting the truth, was about to crash through the veneer of the stage-set of my life. I knew my love/hate relationship with piano lessons had ended, but I couldn't anticipate what was to follow.

As I walked along, I trembled from an inner foreboding, and I felt very alone. My bleak reverie ended when my mother stopped her car and honked. She had been running an errand prior to picking me up. I opened the door and climbed heavily inside. My mother would be easier to tell than my father. Knowing something was wrong, she asked me what had happened and why I wasn't at my piano lesson. I knew that my mother's world was really hard. Mark's severe retardation was resulting in the normal little milestones and pleasures of early childhood being denied to her. I hated to add to her burden, but this was unavoidable. I told her the whole story, about never having been able to see the music, learning to play by imitating her and Mr. Hendershot. I told her that he had said that he wouldn't teach me anymore. As would become her pattern, when given bad news about my vision, my mother said nothing in response. We drove home, and I walked inside, putting the worn, red, dog-eared book in its usual place on the piano. It was never to be opened again. I went upstairs and laid on my bed feeling defeated. I suppose that my mother told my father. Nothing changed, and nothing was said to me about the matter. Repeated calls of concern had come from the school nurse and my second-grade teacher. Now Mr. Hendershot had created the tipping point. An appointment was scheduled with a pediatric ophthalmologist.

Why Not?

My mom told me that I was going to see a real eye doctor. So, over Christmas vacation, we drove to the ophthalmological office that would become my semi-annual destination for the next ten years. Dr. Kazdan was a handsome, quiet man who smelled of pleasant cologne and breath mints. He put several different eye drops into my eyes which stung, made them hurt, and made my close up vision blurry. After the drops took effect, he began the exam. Dr. Kazdan got really close to me. The little bright light on the lens he peered through shone harshly into my dilated pupils. My eyes now hurt like anything, but he told me repeatedly what a good job I was doing, and that he wanted me to hold on for just a little longer as he continued to slowly explore my retinas. The exam was long and brutal. Dr. Kazdan put a big mechanical lens machine in front of my eyes. The thing was metal and cold, as I was told to look through the eye holes. He took lenses from a fine wooden cabinet and held them one after another in front of my eyes. I couldn't read many of the letters on the eye chart across the office, so he asked if the letters became any clearer as he moved the hand-held lens into one position after another. When he was convinced that a specific lens would help, he would snap it into position in the large, stationary machine through which I peered. It was always a clearer or not clearer answer that was required. Sometimes it was obvious and I could see the black letters, or part of them, more clearly. Sometimes, it was just hard to tell. Then, I had to hold my breath and just guess. The eye chart evaluation also took a long time, and I focused with extreme concentration. I tried to give the right answer but feared that there would be no magic through this strange optical divination.

I was giving up thinking that I might actually be able to see any better. After the exhausting exam, I was taken into the waiting room, while Dr. Kazdan talked to my Mom alone. I picked up one of the children's magazines, with big dark print, but my vision was hopelessly fuzzy from having my eyes dilated. I was sad that this doctor wasn't really going to be able to help me. I could tell from the examination, and how little of the eye chart I could see, that there was no use expecting things would get much better, although I knew I was going to get glasses. I sat alone and felt the dead weight of disappointment. Mom came out, and we went downstairs to the optical company where I, at age seven, would pick out my first pair of glasses frames.

Dr. Kazdan told my Mom that he didn't know why I couldn't see. He said that either I was the world's greatest child actor (after all, I'd been acting this thankless part perfectly for years), or something was happening that he could not explain. Although I needed glasses, they weren't going to help me see normally. After two weeks, the glasses came in and we drove down to have them fitted. I could see more clearly through the new sophisticated black and streaked gray frames I had selected. Things weren't out of focus anymore, but, as I had expected, I could still not see most details, just as before. No one understood, and I could not see nor explain the small moth holes in my visual field.

Dr. Kazdan decided to pursue an intensive and thorough evaluation, trying to determine why I couldn't see. So, one Monday morning in February, my Mom packed my pajamas, bathrobe, slippers, and toothbrush, and took me to the hospital for admission to undergo a week of tests.

The first couple of days the hospital stay wasn't too bad. The first morning, I was allowed to walk around in my street clothes within the public areas of the pediatric ward. I was taken to the crafts room, where there were a few other kids who generally didn't seem sick at all. I met a boy my age, also in for tests, and I instantly liked him. His name was Ray and he had been there for some time. He wore a bathrobe and pajamas. He suggested that I add ginger ale to my urine specimens. Ray said it made the nurses get real excited. There wasn't anything in the crafts room I could see to do so I didn't go back. There was a television set on the wall between the two beds in my room, but it was too far away for me to see. I really did like the personal radio that was pinned to the pillow, though. I could get WHK, my favorite rock and roll radio station, and I could listen to it whenever I wanted, with the volume turned way down.

I would turn eight in two weeks. For those five days, I lived in the hospital room with a boy about my age. He was really sick. He was there when I got there and was still there when I left. I never learned his name. I don't think that we ever spoke. He never left his bed, even to go to the bathroom which was located right off our room. Late Monday morning I was told to get into my pajamas before lunch, and I hung my regular clothes in the closet. I had my first hospital meal and I sort of liked having my meals brought to me on a tray in bed. On Monday afternoon, I was taken in a wheelchair to the x-ray lab for lots of "pictures" of my head. I didn't want to ride in the wheelchair, but they insisted.

On Tuesday afternoon, I had a brain wave test. The nurse used a hard, dull syringe full of glue to stick each electrode to my head. The electrodes were little round things with trailing wire that was going to get plugged in someplace. The nurse said it would give the doctors information about the electrical impulses in my brain. It took a long time to get all of the electrodes properly glued on, and the process hurt a little. When I was all wired up, she slowly led me to a special hospital bed. I was wheeled into a darkened room, and the electrode wires were all plugged in someplace behind the bed, and then the nurse left. The same nurse spoke to me through a speaker in the ceiling. She told me to stay very quiet, but not to fall asleep. I was not to think of anything. She said to just keep my thoughts still like a blank piece of paper. I laid there in the semi-dark for what seemed like a long time. My mind raced, trying to stop all those thoughts that kept me from thinking nothing at all, like the nurse had instructed. But I kept thinking of blank paper, sheets of blank paper, rolls of blank paper, and newspapers with nothing written on them. I thought about blank paper a lot. It was genuinely stressful to try to clear my busy little-boy mind. The test was finally over, and I supposed I did well enough because the nurse didn't say I had done it wrong by being unable to think of nothing at all. But I guessed that she knew that my mind had not been blank because the electrodes must have been buzzing. She took a fine tooth comb and worked and worked to get all of the electrodes off and to scrape the dried glue out of my short hair. My scalp was sore and really itched, but I got to keep the fine-tooth comb, which I thought was pretty neat.

Back into the wheelchair and back to my room. All week, groups of serious, white-coated doctors would march in, a couple of times a day, and they would pull the sheet curtain between my bed and that of the sick boy. I would hear them talking quietly to him and to each other, and then he would moan and cry as they did whatever they were doing. He got lots of attention; none of it seemed to be good. I felt sorry for him but was really glad it wasn't me that all of that painful stuff was happening to.

Every morning, a nurse would put a thermometer, slick with Vaseline, up my behind to take my temperature. I hated it and didn't understand why they couldn't put one in my mouth, instead, like my Mom did. On Wednesday morning, Ray came in and we talked about what had been going on for each of us. He laughed and suggested that I take the anal thermometer out when the nurse left the room, heat it up by putting it on the radiator, and then stick it back before the nurse read my temperature. He said it really made them run around. However, the radiator was on the other side of my roommate's bed. Besides, putting a really hot thermometer into my rear-end didn't sound like a very good idea.

After lunch on Wednesday, a nurse walked in. Without a word she put a tray loaded with metal and glass jars, and vials bristling with needles, down on my bedside table. One particularly nasty looking, big, glistening, silver hypodermic needle jutted toward me. I told her that she had made a mistake—the boy in the other bed was the sick one, and I was just there for some tests. So she glanced at a clipboard and said that this tray was definitely for me. Then she left. I stared at the ghastly hypodermic needle, thick and long, and looking like it was going to be used for something I couldn't imagine, but absolutely did not want to experience.

About an hour later, after I had been given plenty of time to study the horrible display of diabolical medical instruments, and had worked up my fear and dread to a fever pitch, a grim doctor and an unsmiling nurse came into the room and flanked my bed. The doctor wore a blue smock and walked directly to the fearful tray. The nurse wore green and white and came around to the other side of my bed. Without any explanation, I was commanded by the nurse to roll over on my side toward her. She suddenly

27

pulled down my pajama pants to my knees and jerked my pajama top up to my shoulders. The nurse grasped me under the knees and behind my head in sort of a wrestling hold. The doctor, who spoke broken English, began to wipe off my back and spine with cold alcohol, preparing me for the ordeal of a lumbar puncture–a spinal tap.

The procedure began abruptly. It was painful in a way that I had never experienced pain. Shocking jolts shot through my back, and just when I thought it couldn't get any worse, it did. I screamed and screamed the entire time. The doctor barked orders at the nurse and she yelled at me to quit struggling. I would temporarily stop but would start again at the next onslaught of needle-driven pain. I don't know how long the spinal tap lasted–perhaps for forty-five minutes or an hour. Then the nurse strictly told me that I couldn't move at all until the next day, or I would get a terrible headache.

Finally, it was over, and they left. I lay limp and exhausted, with a burning ache throughout my back. I laid as still as I could, afraid to even turn on my radio. I suffered the aftermath of the procedure alone and felt a bewildering disorientation, not knowing why I was being put through this misery. The nurse, who brought me my dinner, disapprovingly said that children all over the pediatric ward had heard me screaming. She cranked up my bed a little so I could eat. But lying back in my bed, I couldn't really see my dinner tray. I groggily opened the cardboard carton containing my milk and poured it onto the bottom of the glass that sat upside down on the tray. The milk splattered all over the tray and onto my bed, soaking my pajamas. I only realized that the glass was upside down after I had emptied the carton and felt the cold wetness. My dinner was swimming in cold milk, and I was soaked and miserable. I ate the soggy, milk-soaked food. When my mother and father came to visit later that evening, Mom helped me, as I painfully changed into dry hospital pajamas, while the nurse stripped and changed the bed. Everyone was concerned about the required movement necessary to get into dry pajamas and dry bed clothes.

Thursday morning I still hurt but was beginning to feel like I was not going to get the dreaded headache. Then, after lunch, a new nurse brought the same tray of cruel needles and vials in and set them, once again, by my bed. I told her in a shaky voice that I knew there was a mistake since I had my spinal tap the day before. She patiently explained, in a soothing voice, that there had been some mistakes, and they hadn't done it correctly. I was going to have to have another spinal tap right then. I started to cry. Instead of leaving, she held my hand and quietly talked to me. She explained that I needed to help, and if I could stay relaxed it wouldn't hurt so much. She compared it to pounding nails into concrete vs. soft wood. She said that putting needles into my spine was like that. The nurse explained that if I could keep my back muscles relaxed, the needles would go in more easily, and it wouldn't hurt as much. She said that she would be there and that she could help me stay relaxed if I worked with her. Minutes later, when a different doctor began the procedure, the nurse held me gently in position while she bent close to me and asked me to respond to one question with multi-part answers after another. She kept me talking non-stop, as a steady string of questions was rapidly asked, requiring responses demanding concentration. I wanted the process to work; I wanted to stay more relaxed although the pain was still terrible. The kind nurse asked me to recite the alphabet frontwards and then backwards, to recite it without vowels, to count to one hundred frontwards, backwards, then by fives, tens, twenties, and so forth. My voice rose in pitch, speed, and volume as I rapidly, and with all the focus I could muster, responded to her queries. The spinal tap dragged on, but I didn't scream that time. I will never forget the skill and compassionate understanding of that wonderful woman.

On Friday afternoon I was discharged. I said goodbye to Ray who was also getting ready to leave. The next week the doctor phoned and told my parents that, after consultation with some other specialists; they could definitively say that I did not have a brain tumor. That had been his worst fear. I returned to school. A new understanding had taken root among the adults in my world. The experts' conclusion was that I apparently really could not see normally, although the test results did not disclose the cause.

My father, however, was a hard sell. I don't think he could believe that such a loss was befalling his eldest son. His denial was very strong. He tried to help me every way he knew. It was as if he would will it to be so. Dad observed that it looked like I could see just fine—most of the time. There were regular disturbing mishaps that might have given weight to Dr. Kazdan's belief in the legitimacy of my seriously reduced sight.

For example, the summer before the hospital stay, when I was seven, I ran my bike head-on into a fine old tree growing in the path of the sidewalk down the block. I had been given a sturdy, second-hand, little orange bike and I was exploring. I was on a solo bike ride, venturing down an unfamiliar stretch of sidewalk. I didn't see the tree dead ahead or the abrupt curve in the sidewalk that led around it. Suddenly, I was hitting the tree. My face and hands were scraped and bruised, and my bike's front handlebars bent out of alignment. Dad straightened the handlebars and trued the front wheel. It was a most confusing time for me. I wanted to see, really tried to see, but most of the time I felt like I couldn't see when it really mattered.

Cub Scout Baseball

Before the hospital stay, Dad would get quite angry with me for continuing what he thought was my stubborn charade. My new eye doctor had no diagnosis; my limited vision was a complete mystery to him. Further, there was no information provided to my parents concerning what I could or could not see. This lack of information let my Dad believe that I could be included in and succeed at softball. When Cub Scout baseball began, I was going to play. I had never played baseball on a team before, but it always looked like fun. So with a vague optimism I hoped that the ball wouldn't come my way very often, that good luck would happen, and that I would get by. Regardless, I didn't think I had a choice. In 1957, my world, as an eight-year-old, would require participation in Cub Scout baseball. It was inevitable. Everybody who was in my Cub Scout pack was put on a team, so we were all going to play—a rough mix of ages, abilities, and limitations. My first season was about to begin.

All teams were named after Indian tribes. I was on the Iroquois team, and my Dad had volunteered to co-coach. My father was a natural athlete—strong and muscular—a champion gymnast in high school. At thirty-five, he was still capable of Olympic-grade feats of skill, strength, agility, and balance. One afternoon, while walking by a high, gymnastic bar at our community park, Dad did a hand stand from the top of the high bar, then a full circle, and a flipping dismount. He grasped one of the uprights supporting the bar and, with great exertion, extended his body parallel to the ground. He was amazing and awe-inspiring. I could hear Dad on the phone with the other father who was sharing the coaching responsibilities. I saw him writing out the names of the other boys on the team. I knew he was writing in his clean, manly script, and I felt a pride and excitement about his involvement and leadership. I wasn't very good at baseball; in fact, I was really bad at it. I couldn't see the ball until it was a few inches away, if I saw it at all. When our neighborhood boys played backyard baseball, I was expected to bring my father's catcher's mitt, fielder's glove, and softball. But

30

I was worthless as a player, so I just watched. My visual field was damaged in a moth-eaten way. There was a big blind spot in the middle of my right eye, but lots of smaller ones, too. But I couldn't communicate that. If the ball was coming, in the middle of a blind spot, I wouldn't see it unless it grew larger than the hole in my vision.

There were no practice sessions in the short and inclusive Cub Scout baseball season. One cool, late-spring evening, Dad drove me to the first game at the softball field behind Caledonia Elementary School, where I was a second-grade student. All of us Iroquois milled around one bench, and the Shawnee team, our first opponent, milled around the other bench, across the weedy softball field. We all knew each other from school and the Cub Scouts, and we excitedly talked in twos and threes as we flexed our baseball gloves, punching their pockets. Some of the guys had worn, broken-in gloves, but mine was new, and I was still trying to get it to move easily. I could see better out of my left eye, and my brain factored this in, as I proved to be a left-handed thrower and a right-handed batter. My Dad stood talking to the other coach as they both wrote on their clipboards. Dad called out last names and told each boy what position he would play. My heart was pounding with excitement and anticipation, and pride for my Dad being in charge.

My name was called last, and I was told that I would pitch. Pitch? I didn't know how to pitch! My throwing was lousy. I couldn't catch. Disbelieving, I stood, with my new baseball glove hanging limply at my side. A coin was tossed; the Shawnees were at bat, and we were taking the field. As my teammates ran to their positions, the other Dad tossed me the ball. I didn't see it. It hit my glove, quite by accident, and rolled back toward him. He flipped it to me again; this time it hit my chest. It stung, and I rubbed the burning ache with my free hand as I walked toward the ball rolling away from me. This time, he walked over and handed it to me. The other guys were in their positions, and the game was just waiting for me, the pitcher. I walked to the mound, and with a sense of pending calamity, began the game. I threw the ball in the general direction of home plate. I couldn't distinctly see the batter or the catcher, not to mention that I really did not know how to throw a baseball accurately. I think the soft ball hit the ground short and far to the side of the waiting batter. As it rolled, the catcher ran and retrieved it from the dirt in front of the backstop. He threw it back. The ball bounced on the ground in front of me and hit my shoulder. I walked after it. Now, my chest and my shoulder really hurt. But, worse than the physical pain, was the stinging rash of embarrassment I could feel crawl into

31

my face. I felt trapped in a spiral of impossible expectations. Instead of picking up the ball, I kicked it by mistake, and it skittered somewhere between first base and home plate. So it went.

Once or twice I actually caught the ball, I think, after a panicked juggling action. My throws were wild–wide or high–or grounders. I had absolutely no control over where my throws went. I walked two guys, and my body hurt in numerous places from being struck by the ball. The third boy hit a pitch that somehow was within the strike zone; he scrambled to first base and was safe. The ball had sailed over my head and bounced wide of second base. The second baseman fielded the ball and threw it to the boy playing first base, but the batter had already tagged first and the ball was thrown back to me. Another four wild pitches and the tired catcher no longer ran after the ball. With that walk, the kid on third base scored. My father walked out to me and said, "Let's try you at second base instead." I felt relieved that I was being taken off the mound, but I was tense knowing that any position was going to involve certain, although not constant, inevitable failure.

Grandma Jane, my Dad's mother, was divorced from Grandpa P.C. and was seeing a guy named Lefty, who had played professional baseball for the Cleveland Indians, decades before. I liked Lefty. He and Grandma Jane would babysit for Bonnie, Mark, and me on Saturday nights. Like my Dad, Lefty was also very athletic and gave me special attention which I craved. He had quietly watched the first game; he was justifiably concerned that the ball might hit me in the face and injure me since I obviously could not catch it. So Lefty went to a sporting goods store and presented me with a glasses protector. I had never seen one; it was an odd-looking thing that resembled half of a catcher's mask, consisting of a padded leather frame with a black wire cage protecting the eyeglasses. It was held in place by elastic straps that went over and around my head. My parents quickly endorsed the glasses protector; I was now required to wear the awful contraption for all baseball games. It made me really stand out and drew unwanted attention from every other boy.

Two nights a week, for six long weeks we played, as my father futilely tried me in nearly every field position. Finally, Dad decided that right field held the least opportunity for disaster. But, regardless of how far away I was from the action, I had to wear the cage over my glasses–a ludicrous piece of safety wear, I thought–for the far reaches of right-field. Once assigned to right-field, I hoped that if I played really deep, where the parking lot started, the ball would never come to me. As I ran past the other outfielders, I yelled that I would get the long ones. During the unending minutes that ensued, I entertained myself trying to kick dandelions out by their roots and seeing if there were any interesting rocks lying on the weedy uneven ground.

I felt like I wasn't really in the game. Sometimes I pretended that I could see it. I would strike the pose of one intently watching the action. I'd plant my hands on my knees, as I'd seen baseball players do on television when they were concentrating on the infield, although I couldn't see anyone at all. Once the ball was hit really hard and it came rocketing and bouncing along the ground right toward me. I heard everyone yelling at me, but I didn't see the ball until it was about six feet away. After it bounced past me, I ran into the parking lot looking for it, but I had no idea where the ball had rolled; I wandered back and forth among the parked cars in vain. After an excruciatingly long time, one of the dads came out to retrieve it. He handed me the ball, and I wildly threw it back in the direction of the unseen game. Naturally, play had come to a complete stop. With the ball's return the game resumed, moving right along again without me. I had developed a good toe down kick that was working pretty well on the dandelions. Then I heard my father calling really loudly. He yelled that it was my turn at bat; I hadn't even seen that the sides had changed.

I walked hurriedly toward the infield though I wanted to run. I had run out, but I couldn't run back. I felt sick and stiff-legged, like I was moving in slow motion. I walked past the other team's stock-still outfielders, second baseman, and pitcher. I was certain that all of the parents and both teams were staring at me, although no one said a thing. My shame was complete; I tried to fight back the tears, but I had begun to cry. Tears streamed down and wet the leather of the padded glasses cage that now made me feel like an even more absurd spectacle. A buzzing sound filled my ears, and I was so close to vomiting that I could taste it.

My father took my glove, handed me the bat, and I faced the pitcher. I swung late and wildly at the first three pitches and then slumped back to my team's bench. I walked past my teammates, sat down on the far end of the long worn plank, dropped my glasses protector in the dust, and studied the heavy, smooth, round, metal head of the bolt that secured the bench. No one spoke, including my Dad, which wasn't unusual. We never talked about the baseball team or my complete inability to play. But two nights a week, in silence, after dinner, we would drive to the playground parking lot, and I would go through another gut-wrenching miserable baseball game, wearing the tear-stained glasses protector.

Dad's Hope

My parents had received bad news in August from Dr. Kazdan. He reported that I had lost more vision in the months since his initial exam the previous December. The doctor counseled that, although he did not understand the cause of my visual deterioration, the reality of it could not be denied. He recognized the rareness of my condition and ultimately wrote about my case for a professional journal.

I had begun third-grade in September. Now, in late October, school had settled into a focused routine. I liked my pretty, young teacher; in fact, I had a hopeless crush on her. As had become the pattern, she happily wrote out for me all board work. At home, I could feel that my parents were treating me a bit differently. Their denial had turned from shock into a sort of deeply muffled anguish, as the complexities of Mark's retardation, and my deteriorating vision created grief upon grief. But acceptance about my vision had taken root.

My favorite time of day was evening after Mom had washed the dinner dishes, with Bonnie and me taking turns drying them. Our homework would then be completed. Our pattern for that special time of day was, I suppose, a pretty normal part of regular, comfortable family life. Every other evening, my sister and I would take our baths–taking turns being first to use the bath water–a carryover from the deprivation of the depression, and my grandparents' pre-indoor plumbing, rural roots. After Mark went to sleep, we all would put on our pajamas, robes, and slippers–relaxing while watching television together. One of my Dad's previous jobs in the late forties had been selling early televisions, and we had been the first family on the block to have a set. But in 1957, TV's were commonplace. It was the golden age of family-oriented, feel-good television programs such as *Mr. Peepers, Topper*, and *Circus Boy*. Mark went to bed pretty early, and we would enjoy a tranquil, stress-free zone of TV programs, snacks, and down time.

It was during just such an evening's television reverie that Dad went into the kitchen to prepare bowls of ice cream, with selected toppings, for the four of us. A couple of years before, he had added a half-bath, off of our kitchen, at the back of our small wood frame house. I chose it, rather than walking upstairs to the house's original bathroom. It seemed like quite a luxury. My Dad busied himself dishing out the ice cream into the four, colored aluminum bowls that we had gotten over a period of weeks, with fill-ups at the Sunoco gas station, where my young, married student Uncle Norman worked. I was passing back through the kitchen when my Dad said he had something to tell me.

My Dad never spoke to me in such a way, and I stopped with eager anticipation, wondering what matter of consequence was waiting to present itself. My Dad wore a lightweight, steel-blue bathrobe with white piping around the collar and cuffs, moccasin slippers, and yellow pajamas. His back was turned to me as he dug into the carton, filling the bowls with the three flavors of Neapolitan ice cream. Bonnie liked chocolate and vanilla–it was strawberry and vanilla for me. As he worked, the impressive muscles of his shoulders flexed under his night clothes. He stopped and stood erect, although he did not turn around. He said, "Jeff, Grandma Jane and I have been talking. You know, Grandma Jane, you, and I have the same color eyes." We all had very dark brown eyes, a vestige of a Native American ancestor, and the source of considerable family pride. Dad turned to face me and continued to speak, "We decided that we would both give you one of our eyes." He stopped talking. My mind raced with the giddy possibility of seeing normally and the guilty thought that my sight would come at the cost of my Dad and grandmother losing an eye. A long moment passed, and I could see Dad's shoulders shake.

His handsome face was twisted in torment and sorrow. He squeezed his eyes shut, and he choked back a sob as he said, "But the doctor said it's impossible. An operation wouldn't work. He can't do it–I can't help you, I can't help you." With that simple finality, he wrapped me in his strong arms and held me, as he sobbed a deep and bottomless cry. I began to cry, too. Dad wept and shook. I had my arms around him as well–a futile attempt to comfort him. There was no comfort for either of us. We stood in that moment of impossible mutual desire to ease each other's grief. We embraced in love and helplessness. Standing in that modest kitchen, I sensed the moment's timelessness and poignancy. No other words were spoken. We both dried our tears, and my Dad turned back to finish the ice cream preparation by adding chocolate, butterscotch, and cherry sauce, as requested. I went back into the living room and settled on to my place on the floor, very close and to the side of the TV set. A new concession to the reality of my ruined vision was that I was allowed to sit as close as I needed to see the screen. I sat at an angle so as not to block anyone else's view. My Dad brought us our ice cream, and we relaxed into the last show before school- night bedtime and the end of our evening together.

Chapter 3: A Hard Summer

The Stallion

When I was ten years old, there was no place that held more pure magic for me than Wally and Orpha's farm. Born and raised in Tennessee, they were horse people complete with Western clothes, real cowboy and cowgirl drawls, and style. My Dad and Wally had worked together in the early fifties and, along with two other co-workers, formed a foursome that held regular picnics and parties for each other's families. Gatherings were held, round robin, but every summer we would go to Wally's farm, twice, for a wonderful afternoon of fresh corn, hamburgers, and riding horses.

On Memorial Day, 1959, Mark was not quite five; but at ten, I was trusted to be Mark's protector and guardian. The four families gathered. Mark had no peers to play with, although it is unlikely that, if there had been kids his age, any of them would have played with him, due to his severe disability. We all sat down at picnic tables, and the kids were served glasses of pop as the adults began to drink their first beers. I was happily talking to Kathy, a pretty girl my age, and was enjoying the warmth of the early afternoon and prospects of music, horses, and the picnic. The women had brought side dishes, desserts, deviled eggs, and potato chips. Mark was restless and wandered away from the group as Orpha got out her guitar and the adults began to sing. I loved the familiar sound of her guitar and the adults' sweet crooning and harmonies. I did not want to leave, but my mother had told me to keep an eye on Mark, so I reluctantly left Kathy's company and followed him, attempting to re-direct him as I caught up.

We found Wally's dog enclosure that kenneled his hunting dogs, and the puppies born that spring. The dogs crowded on their side of the chicken wire, and we scratched their noses through the fence and were licked gratefully in return. The singing was audible but faint as we left the dogs and wandered into the couple's freshly-planted garden, but there was nothing to see or do there. I had an idea, so I took Mark by the hand, and we returned to ask if we could go across the broad field to the farm's classic red barn. Smiling and squeezing my shoulder, Wally walked with us and opened the wide metal gate.

The year before, Wally had offered me a nickel if I could tackle one of the sheep in his flock. Somewhat fearfully, but not wanting to shrink from the manly challenge, I ran up to the nervous animals who bunched together as I approached. I was alarmed when one large, black-faced ewe baaed loudly at me. I turned, changing my mind about the wisdom of throwing myself among their nervously-shifting, sharp hoofs. The four men in the group, all watching from the fence rail, laughed as my courage dissolved, and I walked slowly back toward them, away from the flock. This year, as Wally swung the gate open, he teased, "Don't tackle any of my sheep!"

Mark and I crossed the broad expanse of grass and entered the picturesque old red barn. On the top floor, the hay bales gave off a sweet, dry smell; Mark and I sat for a few minutes, on a bale at the base of the graduated staircase stack that rose to the rafters. Wally's Ford tractor sat in the middle of the barn floor, inside the massive sliding door, open now to the sunny afternoon. Mark and I walked around the big machine, and I marveled at its giant back tires and high metal seat. Flies buzzed above us. There really wasn't anything to do. Bored, Mark walked back outside. I caught up with him, and together we wandered down the steep hill next to the barn and down to the stable entrance on the floor below. A doorway, about five feet wide, opened into a large room for saddling horses. We explored the open space, the tack room, and the passageway to the now empty stalls. We wandered into one of the horse's stalls but swarming, early summer flies surrounded us. Mark wildly swatted at them, making short, fear-filled yelps. Being unable to calm him, I took his hand and led him quickly back down the passageway toward the entrance.

Precisely as we were hurrying through the wide doorway to the outside, out of nowhere, Wally's golden stallion galloped down the slope behind the barn, suddenly bursting into the opening, driving us apart. I was abruptly forced against the right door jamb as Mark's slight body was pressed against the left side of the doorway. Stark terror gripped me. The horse ran so close to me that his side's stiff hair rasped my chest and face. My field of vision was suddenly blocked by the horse's massive side. I screamed, "Mark! Mark! Mark!" Simultaneously, my little brother wordlessly shrieked. It took less than a second for the horse to pound through the space, but every crashing hoof seemed to strike the ground in slow motion. My own panicked screaming rang in my ears. I was frozen with fear, knowing I couldn't protect little Mark from the deadly force of the horse's wildly churning hoofs. The excited horse powered past us, running into his open stall. I hugged Mark as he continued to scream. We moved as quickly as I could lead, out the door, up the slope, and back across the yard.

As I cradled Mark against my chest, I shuddered. We had just escaped a really perilous situation, unharmed.

Wally hurried across the yard toward us. I could see facial expressions at close range, and as he neared, he had a very worried look on his leathered face. I told him what had happened, and he apologized for the frightful encounter with his prize horse. Wally reported that the horse had jumped the fence and run directly into the barn. He said that the horse had done it before. But as we talked, I pondered the randomness of real danger and how I couldn't protect Mark from such unforeseeable peril.

Later that afternoon, Wally saddled the beautiful golden stallion to give all of us our horseback ride. He had asked me to go with him to saddle his palomino. He reintroduced me to the fine horse and helped me to overcome my fear. Following his directions, I swung into the wonderfully-tooled saddle astride his horse's back. Wally wore a tan Stetson hat, multicolored cowboy boots, and a plaid, pearl button shirt. He held the reins as the horse docilely followed him around the barnyard. The stallion was a real look-alike for Trigger, Roy Rogers' famous mount. After my earlier encounter, I felt that I was doing really well, just sitting on the now quiet animal's back, as Wally led the horse around the grassy expanse. But, in spite of my pleasure, a dark cloud hung over me from the earlier moment of terror. I was left feeling disoriented—both frightened and fortunate.

A Broken Leg

It was early June 1960. I had turned eleven in February. Mark's life at five, and the family's, had begun to change in a very disturbing way. We had moved in November 1958, to a wonderful house, three blocks from our previous home. In that first neighborhood, Mark had been generally protected from abuse. Mark was known to all, and close relationships between parents kept everyone behaving properly.

Our move had introduced us to a new neighborhood where there were few relationships, between my parents and other adults, which would have provided an extension of parental watchfulness and protection. It also seemed like the kids around Mark's age were of a different stripe. They behaved as a tribe of which Mark was not a member, but an outsider—a helpless target for their cruelty. Mark was getting older, and his high energy level meant that when he did play outside of the house, everybody in the family got a little relief. Mark was venturing out into the company of neighborhood kids, but these play encounters often ended badly.

One evening, a little girl named Annie had rung the bell and asked if Mark could come outside and play. Annie, although a year younger and a head shorter than Mark, was one of only two children who ever asked to play with him; it was with appreciation that my mother sent Mark off with his little friend. Mark went outside, and the rest of the family relaxed into individual pursuits. I was watching TV, Bonnie was doing her homework, Mom was doing laundry, and Dad was puttering in the backyard. The intoxicating, early summer evening's quiet was broken as the phone rang; a neighbor gave my mother the shocking news that Mark was lying in the street at the end of our block, having been hit by a car. The neighbor had already called for an ambulance. In an urgent voice, Mom frantically summoned Dad from the yard. She repeated the terrible news to him, and they exchanged short statements of planned action. Dad bolted through the front door and sprinted down the block while Mom got her car keys and prepared to follow him. She told us to stay put and wait for their call. A minute later, an ambulance siren screamed as the rescue squad arrived at the scene. This was the crescendo of a developing pattern, not an isolated incident.

That spring, the spiral of violence that the neighborhood children brought to bear had become relentless. One late afternoon, Mark didn't come home when expected; Mom searched, heard Mark crying, and discovered him tied by his neck to a tree trunk in a yard three houses down the block. The gang of children had been playing house. They had assigned themselves family roles, and it was decided that Mark would be the dog. They had tied Mark to a tree by his neck and then abandoned him behind the high thick bushes that hid the yard from view. The same group of children had, at another time, handcuffed Mark to a swing set, and then, again, abandoned him. On another early evening I had heard Mark's cry. I ran into the neighbor's back yard to find Mark, on the ground, being beaten by two younger boys using wooden croquet mallets. They were hitting him repeatedly as he lay curled on the ground, unable to protect himself. As I ran down the driveway, and into the back yard, Grandma Jane was close behind. As I reached Mark, she rounded the back of the house and witnessed the kid's father standing on the back porch, calmly drinking a cup of coffee while watching the entire scene. That time, Mark had been badly bruised and scratched, adding another trauma to his growing portfolio of violent abuse.

But Mark was now lying in the street. This time he was seriously injured. The neighbor who had phoned us, and summoned the ambulance, said that she had seen Mark being made to chase balls thrown into the street by older children. His lack of judgment and poor vision resulted in his running into the path of a moving car, striking the side of the vehicle. The impact threw him onto the roadway, and his right femur was badly broken. Mom followed the ambulance within which sat Dad, comforting Mark. An hour later, my father phoned from the hospital. Mark was in surgery and would require six weeks of hospitalization, in a traction cast, while his right leg began to heal.

Thus began a summer of visits by family members, holding to the hospital's limit of two visitors at a time. A few days after the accident, Bonnie and I were allowed to visit with our father, stretching the hospital's two person limit. Mark was obviously uncomfortable but overjoyed to see us. He cried and pointed to his foot which stuck out of the rigid plaster traction cast. Tension was held on the cast by straps that ran through overhead pulleys and were anchored by weights. For days, Mark had been in misery as he unsuccessfully tried to make the adults in charge understand him. The orthopedic surgeon dismissed Mark's constant complaints with the assessment that he just didn't like being in traction. But our father's judgment was different. Dad had served as a naval hospital corpsman in the Pacific Theater during World War II and held a degree in chiropractic medicine. He had not been able to start a practice after graduation because of his role as sole family breadwinner and lack of financial resources. Dad carefully examined Mark's foot and discovered discoloration and swelling on the front and heel. Taking out his ever-sharp pocket knife, Dad cut away two semi-circular sections of the cast to relieve the pressure. The sharp edge of the plaster had been slowly cutting into the flesh of Mark's foot. Dad's action exposed two ugly, deep, raw wounds about the size of eggs.

After traction, to stabilize the still healing bone, Mark came home in July, encased in a heavy white body cast that extended from his waist down both legs, stopping above the knee on the leg that was not broken. He lay on a cot in the living room during the day, from which he could watch television and participate in family life. Mark was extremely good-natured as we took turns engaging him, reading books, playing impromptu games, and helping him pass the long summer days, confined as he was in the hot, itchy cast. I convinced my mother to let me draw on the cast, and she agreed. I decorated the plaster, much to Mark's delight. Mark particularly liked my childish cowboy cartoon character, drawn on the cast covering his foot. At bedtime, Mark would be carried upstairs by dad and then brought back down each morning to resume his life on the cot. The awkwardness of Mark in the cast, and its sheer rigidity and weight made the task an effort that required our father's considerable strength.

I was a paper boy for a community newspaper that I delivered twice a week. Somehow, the editors heard about Mark's story, and they sent a photographer over to take our photograph for a human interest feature. The man with the big camera asked me to read Mark a book, so I got out my magnifier and, feeling the full flush of embarrassment, squinted at close range at a Yogi Bear Golden Book. The photographer shook his head and suggested that I hold the book back as if I could see it normally. Uncertain, I nervously complied. The camera flashed, and the photo was snapped of Mark, his hands folded behind his head, as he looked at me sitting beside his cot, as if I were reading him the book. In actuality, I never read books to him. Reading out loud was no fun for me or the listener. Instead, I would tell stories, play with puppets, do my dramatic death by Mark's gunshot, or other exaggerated play acting with Mark; but I didn't read.

Days later, as I looked at the large photo that ran, over the headline, "Boy Feels in His Bones He'll Be Late for School," I felt like a fraud. The story didn't mention either of our disabilities. Mark was portrayed as just a kid with a broken leg who was going to miss the beginning of school, the brother of a faithful paperboy. We were both wearing glasses, and Mark looked intelligent, typically-developing, and I looked very sighted. I wondered what life would be like if we were actually the boys in the story.

Finally, in late September, the cast was removed, and Mark began to propel himself, stiff-legged, through the house in a crabwalk-crawl. He had missed the first weeks of kindergarten.

Little League

Mark's and my family's lives were intertwined, but I had a separate life that did not involve him. I played miserably and was miserable playing three seasons of Cub Scout baseball, and then, when I was eleven, a broader and more serious baseball organizing principle exerted its grim magnetic pull. It was the school district-wide Little League, and I felt that I had to play. I really didn't want to. The teams used a standard hardball and, fast, overhand pitching. These factors, I knew, made my certainty of failure absolute. But I didn't think I had a choice. All of the boys I knew had signed up, and so my Dad drove me to the try-outs. It was another public embarrassment for me in a yet wider arena. I wore my hated glasses protector; I missed every catch and struck out when I had my batting try-outs. But the organizers weren't told that I really couldn't see, so I was assigned to one of the minor league teams since everyone who wanted to play was put on a team. One of my friends made one of the real teams in what was called the "major league", and he was issued a genuine baseball uniform complete with spikes, knee socks, jersey, knickers, and a woolen baseball cap. Those of us on the minor league teams were given a cheap cotton cap and a colored tee-shirt with the name on its front of the company which had paid for them.

I only played two games. The first game, I asked for right field, and I struck out without incident. Only one lone hit came to right field, but the center fielder ran after it, and I was spared humiliation. But in the second game, the coach rotated positions to evaluate his team's talent. I was assigned to third base–a frightening development. I understood that I would be in serious trouble if the ball did come to me, and I knew that getting hit by a hard ball would hurt. But I so wanted to be normal, to be a regular boy on a team, that I swallowed my fear and took my place at third base. The first half of the first inning ended, requiring nothing of me. We came up to bat. Three outs later, I had not been required to face the pitcher. As I took the field at the top of the second inning, I heard Lefty whistle, and I looked over to see my hero standing a few feet away. I was thrilled and proud that a real retired professional baseball player had come to see me play.

Lefty had moved in with us when we had moved to our bigger home in 1958. Lefty, usually worked nights. We shared a bathroom, and we would talk in the morning. I would be getting ready to go to school as he was getting ready to go to bed, after working all night at the railroad yard. During the late afternoon he would be up and working on his car or otherwise busying himself outside. He would patiently play catch with me, trying to teach me to catch the ball–a futile effort because to catch a baseball, you first must be able to see it.

Lefty's baseball career held great fascination for me, and he would talk about the violent nature of the game when he had played and the brutal racism that he and his teammates would exert on the populous of the towns they toured. I was repulsed by those stories, but I still loved the attention Lefty gave me, especially when it didn't involve trying to catch the wicked hard ball. My favorite interaction with Lefty became learning to pantomime pitch. This involved a long series of lessons as he showed me the slow, graceful, step by step movements of the pitchers of his day. First, the pitcher would glance at the runners, a methodical checking of all the active bases. Then, studying the batter, at a leisurely pace, the baseball would be snapped into the mitt a time or two. Following that, leaning forward, the pitcher would read the catcher's sign, which indicated what pitch to throw. Next came a steely-eyed checking of the runners once again and, finally, after staring coldly at the batter, winding up, lifting the leg, and pitching the imaginary ball hard and fast and of course straight and true. I had rehearsed and rehearsed the whole sequence. Lefty would appraise my progress and then correct my moves or make stylistic suggestions. He never failed to encourage me and I began to move smoothly through the routine.

But now, although I was in a real game, with Lefty's arrival, my imagination lifted me onto the pitcher's mound, and the game's progress fell away into a soft blur as I drifted into a daydream. I slowly and confidently began moving through my well-greased pitcher's moves. I was just at the point in my choreographed pitching cycle, of throwing the imaginary ball into my mitt, when I heard the crack of the batter's bat making solid contact with the real baseball. All at once, I felt my gloved hand buzz with a sharp sting. My hand snapped back with the sudden force of the accidentally-caught baseball as the line drive amazingly hit the pocket of my open glove. For the first time ever, I had actually caught a fast-moving baseball! Adrenalin flooded, my mind, scrambled with frantic urgency, and I knew I was supposed to do something. Excitedly, I grabbed the baseball out of my glove and heaved it wildly toward first base. The first batter of the inning had been walked, and he was standing on first. But, my throw went over his head, and the first baseman had to run to retrieve the ball. Our opponent's coach yelled for the runner to take second. He took off. The first baseman finally reached the ball. Watching the slowness of our responses, the coach hollered for the runner to keep going, round second and on for third. The first baseman had a terrific arm and he fired the ball back to me, but I didn't see it until it was hitting the ground and bouncing between my open legs. I turned and scrambled to follow its path. The runner rounded third and scored as I ran back and forth by the empty bleachers looking for the ball. The action of the game had stopped as everyone watched. Seeing my dilemma, Lefty walked over and kicked it toward me, and I finally picked it up and threw it, again badly, toward the pitcher. I caught a line drive and was credited with an out, but was also charged with three errors and a run.

Following my own private debacle, Lefty shouted goodbye. I was put back into right field, and the game crawled on into the afternoon. It finally ended and I rode my bike home in abject misery. But a part of me stubbornly believed that a chunk of the problem was my lack of concentration.

That evening, after supper, I took my hardball and my glove, and I went into the back yard. I hoped, grasping the last scrap of belief within me, that if I just tried harder, I might be able to see the ball. Although failing time after time, I repeatedly heaved the baseball skyward and, hearing it hit the ground someplace, found it and tried again. The last time I ever threw a baseball, I pitched the grass-stained sphere straight up into the evening sky. I suspect it was the only time I had ever thrown the baseball accurately. I finally saw the ball on its downward flight. But when it appeared, the ball was only six inches above my upturned face; I had no time to react. It hit my nose with terrific force and I fell to the ground, blood streaming from my broken nose. The pain was shocking and my misery was complete. I had failed. There was no more hope. I was a beaten boy with only cold shame for company. Going behind the garage, where I couldn't be seen from the house, I assessed my aching and bleeding nose. I sat, unable to stop the bleeding with the folded white pocket handkerchief my Dad had encouraged me to always carry. When it grew dark, I wadded the bloody hanky into my back pocket, walked back inside hurriedly through the house, hollered goodnight to my parents, and quietly joined Mark, already asleep in our room. I fell asleep, my bleeding nose throbbing.

In the morning, my alarmed mother saw the extensive dried blood on my pillow. Mom asked what had happened. I told her that I had had a nose bleed during the night, but she didn't believe me. My swollen and discolored nose required an explanation. I sheepishly admitted I had been hit by the ball while trying to catch it the evening before. Since I had not been wearing the hated glasses protector, I got the expected lecture about its necessity.

That evening's sudden and painful moment of truth had proven to me, once and for all, after three years of failure, that I could not play softball or baseball at all. I never again picked up a baseball nor put on a ball glove. Although it had been a crushing defeat, it was also a great relief to be free of my own expectation concerning an activity that was impossible. Years later, in discussion with a sighted friend from childhood, I learned that he and his athletic brother did not go out for Little League because they didn't like it. What a revelation to me. I thought that everyone played and that I had to, as well.

45

Chapter 4: Suffering and Sweet Solace

Society for the Blind

I was declared legally blind in February of 1960, when I was eleven years old. But it was six months later when the dominoes began to fall in a cascade of dramatic and life-changing occurrences. I crossed the arbitrary threshold into legal blindness, although I could still see the big E on the eye chart with my better eye. I could not read print that was smaller than the largest printing in speech balloons in the Sunday comics. To accomplish that, I had to press my eye so close to the page that my nose would get dirty from the newsprint. I had tried bifocals, two years before, in the fourth-grade, but they didn't help; nor did the various, detective-type magnifying glasses that my father repeatedly bought for me in drug stores.

One early August evening, as she was doing the laundry, my mother told me that the doctor had called and suggested that I be evaluated by the Society for the Blind. The words formed a strange and frightening image. I pictured a closed community–a society where everyone was blind. I certainly didn't feel blind, and I didn't want to be part of their society. I pictured fancy society balls, grand parties and dances, where only sightless people were invited. It frightened me, and I wanted no part of it. My mother quickly dispelled my troubled imaginings, when she said that they had just opened a new program–a low vision clinic–where I could get powerful magnifiers that would help me read.

Both of my parents worked, so it was one evening, after dinner, that my Dad drove me down to an old mansion near Western Reserve University, where the Society for the Blind was housed. We entered the quiet old house and waited off the main entrance hall, with its grand staircase. There was a giant, tactile globe, about three feet across, and with real delight, I explored the Earth's mountain ranges, coastlines, plains, and continents. I had never touched anything so tactilely stimulating and was gathering a new appreciation for the Earth's physical geography, when a nice old lady, about my grandmothers' age, came into the waiting room and sat down next to me. She was blind, or if she could see, her vision was much worse than mine. She showed me how to use a special record player that she was giving to me. It was a Talking Book machine, and it played specially-recorded records that moved very slowly, at half the speed of standard 33

1/3 RPM record albums. She played a minute of the book's first record. The reader was great and sounded like an actor. She told me I could take the Talking Book machine home, and she registered me to receive the recorded books by mail. She lent me *The Yearling* to read before the first books from the Library for the Blind would arrive. I was thrilled, and for the first time, I was able to read comfortably and independently. I loved listening to the records and being able to read books without my mother or sister having to read out loud to me. I spent the remaining summer afternoons lying on my bed and thrilling to the books, as worlds of adventure and imagination opened to me. The friendly social worker had also booked an appointment for me to come back and to be seen at the Low Vision Clinic

A few weeks later, on a Saturday morning, my father again drove me to the Society for the Blind, where an attractive young woman took me upstairs and into the Clinic. An eye doctor, after evaluating my vision, showed me lots of optical aids, and I tried out near and distance magnification systems that miraculously let me read standard print and to recognize letters well down the eye chart.

When I had narrowed down my selection to one near and one distance optical aid, the social worker took over. She patiently watched and made suggestions concerning how the wonderful magnifiers should be used. My preferred, print reading lens was a dome of solid glass, about as big around as a tennis ball, with one flat side which rested on the page. I peered through the dome of polished glass and could read the greatly magnified print. When I lowered my good eye right onto the dome, I could even read newsprint. It was thrilling. As I manipulated the "Plano-convex" lens as it was called, I discovered that, if I lifted one edge of the lens's flat plane up from the page, I could let in light and create an even more magnified image, although distorted around the edges.

The distance aid was called a monocular and looked like a classic opera glass–half of a set of binoculars. The telescope screwed onto a two piece handle–a stem that unscrewed in the middle. When assembled, the monocular balanced nicely on the handle. The social worker tied a pirate-like black eye patch around my head to block the vision from my worse right eye. The patch allowed me to focus on the telescope's magnified image. With the monocular, I could easily read much of the eye chart, down to the 20/40 line. As I swung the monocular toward her, I could clearly see my patient, pretty helper smile at me and wave. For the first time since I was a little boy, I could clearly see a person's face across a room; I reveled in my new visual power!

When I got home, I immediately experimented and was able to see the television set from the couch, relaxing, while leaning back onto the comfortable high-backed sofa. No longer would I have to sit on the hard floor, within eighteen inches of the screen. But my deep shame about my vision overrode my pleasure and new visual capability. I maintained a high vigilance against people other than my family seeing me use the new, obviously strange, scope and patch. When I would hear anyone come into the living room, I would rip the eye patch off and thrust the monocular and patch under a pillow. If a non-family member happened to be there, I would feel discovered. The family living room was not the protected clinic with the social worker's quiet encouragement–it was the world of strangers and their stilted reactions. The optical aids were the visible symbol of my deficit, my handicap-my damaged and weak eyes.

School started, and I was finally in sixth-grade, the highest grade in the elementary school. I had finally reached the long-awaited top of the heap; I was king of the mountain. Sixth-grade camp was always held the third week of the school year, and sixth-grade dancing classes began right after that. The first day of sixth-grade, my shaky self-esteem was bolstered as I considered the joys, privileges, and anticipated adventures of the upcoming year.

On Monday evening of the second week of school, my mother and I talked as we often did as she did the laundry, and I entertained myself catching glimpses of items of female underwear amid the pile of clothes on the floor. My mother said she had something important to tell me. Mom spoke quietly and carefully as if she were going to tell me something I really didn't want to hear. She reported that after my August examination, Dr. Kazden, my ophthalmologist, had said that if I continued to lose vision at the rate I had been, in another year I would not be able to read print at all. He felt that I should begin to learn to read and write Braille. Mom said that I was going to attend a new school.

The following week, I was to start attending James A. Garfield Elementary School, a school with a sight saving class. The idea was that, by not straining my eyes, my sight would be saved by reading Braille and using large print books. She said that I would get picked up by a maintenance man from our school district and be driven out to the new school that was about thirty minutes away. My heart thudded, and my breathing quickened, as I considered what I was being told. I would not go to sixth-grade camp. I would not be going to school with friends I had known since kindergarten; I was being uprooted from the familiar–my neighborhood school–my world. I was going to have to learn Braille; I was being cast out of the sighted world and into the world of the blind. Gripping fear pressed cold against me, and I felt a sickening dread.

I went back to school on Tuesday; my teachers had been told that I was leaving. I wasn't expected to do my homework or prepare for tests. My sixth-grade teacher announced on Tuesday morning that I was going to be leaving Caledonia at the end of that week and attending a new school. No one even looked at me.

A list of what would be needed for camp was passed out. Everyone else excitedly talked at once to their friends, as they read the camp packing lists. I was fading like a ghost. On Friday, all talk was about camp. The lessons that were taught were not for me. I handed in my text books and cleared out my desk. I left school that afternoon, loaded down with the year's nearly empty notebooks and other un-used school supplies. Alone, I wandered into the no man's land of dislocation, alienation, banishment.

Sixth-grade

On Monday, September 19, 1960, at the beginning of the third week of the school year, I was picked up by a friendly maintenance man in an East Cleveland School District car, for the long ride to the first day at my new school. I was nervous and heartsick about being uprooted from Caledonia. The driver made friendly conversation but despite his smiling efforts, all I could focus on was the fact that I was going to a new school where I was supposed to learn Braille, and where I didn't know a soul.

We drove from Cleveland Heights, a dense middle-class city, through newer suburban communities and into the Ohio countryside. The houses were farmhouses and far apart. We finally pulled up to a fine old, two-story school building. We were at James A. Garfield Elementary School, and the driver walked me inside and up a flight of stairs to the first floor and the principal's outer office. He told the secretary I was there to start school and he left, promising that he would pick me up at home, once again, the following day. The school secretary told me to have a seat on the wooden bench and wait. I sat down on the smooth hard pew-like bench, so similar to the "bad boys' bench" in the principal's outer office at Caledonia. I listened to the secretary's focused typing and to the sounds of the classroom

49

across the hall, where a teacher with a soft southern accent lectured to her class. I studied the rounded arm of the old worn bench, the pale green wall in front of me, and the brown paper lunch bag that sat on my legs. The school's cafeteria filled the air with the indistinct smell of the cooking of institutional food. My former elementary school didn't have a cafeteria. Whatever they were cooking didn't smell like anything I would want to eat. I thought about the years of walking home for lunch every day. I thought about my sixth-grade class and how they would be arriving at camp and what fun they must be having.

The principal, a wiry, unsmiling woman in a drab suit, finally came out of her office and introduced herself to me. I silently waited as she spoke to her secretary. She then escorted me into the classroom across the hall, telling me that Miss Stone, my Braille teacher, would come to get me in a little while.

We interrupted Miss Horvath, the sixth-grade teacher I had been listening to, in the middle of a Science lesson. Miss Horvath was a pleasant-looking young woman with wire-rimmed glasses and a round, kind face devoid of makeup. She had the plainest haircut I had ever seen on a woman and her utilitarian clothing and sturdy shoes spoke of her practical, rural life. The principal introduced me to Miss Horvath and, in turn, Miss Horvath introduced me to the class; they mumbled a greeting in unison. I was given the desk in the front row, next to the door. I watched as a girl was moved, from that most conspicuous desk to a desk in the back of the room. I sat down, and Miss Horvath continued teaching. She told me that I came in at the beginning of a lesson about how to identify some of the plants we would find on the field trip that we would be taking the following week. I felt an odd sense of being included in the "we" that she spoke about. She continued with the lesson about telling the difference between white, red, and black oak trees by the shape of their leaves, and how to recognize poison ivy and poison oak. I listened with real interest to her nature lesson. This class's field trip was going to be a hike in the fields and woods around the school. This would not be one of the grand field trip adventures to which I was accustomed–a class visit to one of Cleveland's wonderful museums or to hear the Cleveland Orchestra.

In about an hour, Miss Stone wordlessly stepped into the classroom and Miss Horvath welcomed her, and introduced us. Miss Stone quietly told me to take my lunch, since I would be with her for the rest of the morning. I obediently stood up and followed her out of the classroom. We walked, without speaking, down the old school's long hall, past other classrooms,

50

and entered the last room at the end of the hall, across from a staircase. Miss Stone said that this was the resource room, and that she would be teaching me to type and to read and write Braille there.

On one wall there hung a large typewriter keyboard chart, in front of a single mechanical typewriter that sat on a small table pushed flush to the wall. The majority of the room was taken up by the extensive Braille area. Several tables of varying heights sat side by side. But this was not just orientation. Instruction started immediately. Miss Stone began by introducing me to the Perkins Braille Writer, a simple-looking, squat, gray, metal machine with nine large keys. Miss Stone showed me how to roll the heavy Braille paper into the Braille writer and how to lock the paper down. Then she showed me the six tightly-sprung keys that were used to punch the Braille dots through the stiff paper. Three additional keys were the space key, backspace key, and paper advance. The six Braille-writing keys each had a number assigned to them, which corresponded to one of the six numbered dots within a single Braille "cell". If all six dots were punched, the resulting array of bumps looked like half of an egg carton–two lines, side by side–of three dots each. The room had the particular smell of Braille books, a unique smell common to all classrooms and libraries where Braille is stored. But even the Perkins Braille Writer, heavily built and with oiled parts, also had a new and specific, unfamiliar smell. I was being introduced to a world that I had never known existed. It demanded my attention and immersed me in a multi-sensory assault of stimulation.

Miss Stone had her own fragrance too, a heavy floral perfume that seemed to radiate in waves from the bosom of her flowered dress. Her tightly permed gray hair framed her serious face, and she spoke in a no-frills, down-to-business manner. Quite unlike Miss Horvath, Miss Stone wore a pearl necklace, big silver earrings, and pointed blue-framed glasses. Miss Stone told me to just punch any old dots I wanted, to just make some Braille on the blank, stiff paper. After banging away, I looked at the random Braille dot combinations, pale bumps against the manila-colored paper. Miss Stone said that I was to touch the Braille with my fingertips, not read it with my eyes. I told her I wasn't blind, and that I could read the dots. I held the paper within two inches of my left eye, and I could see the faint contrast of the six dots as they combined in different combinations from my experimental hammering. Miss Stone quietly took the paper from my hands and laid it on the table in front of me. Then she put my right index finger on the raised dots and showed me how I was supposed to read, sliding the pad of my right index finger across the page as my left index finger kept my place at the beginning of the line. But the tactile combinations of the six dot Braille cells were indistinguishable to me.

I began to feel a new, sinking despair. I certainly did not agree that I needed to be attending this new school, but to my shock, I realized that learning Braille was going to be very hard. I struggled through the first lesson and all subsequent lessons. Twice a day, at Miss Horvath's suggestion, I would silently rise and walk down the hall to the resource room. There, I would sit with Miss Stone, struggling with Braille, or at the large print typewriter on whose cumbersome keys I was learning to type. Typing was a much better experience, because I was genuinely enjoying developing the new skill, and because I could see the typed letters by peering through my new high-powered magnifier.

Using my optical tools, in the general classroom, was a different story. I hated the conspicuousness of the optical aids, and I would feel a prickly flush when I had to use them. During the first day in Miss Horvath's class, I discovered that I could not use my new monocular telescope from my front row seat. The blackboard was too close. I couldn't get it in focus since the minimal focal distance of the lens system was thirteen feet, and my front row seat was not that far from the blackboard. I had to raise my hand and tell Miss Horvath, and everyone else, about the difficulty. She patiently stopped instruction to have me test different desks until I found the one that allowed me to see the board. One classmate after another had to relinquish their seat to me until I found the optimal desk, and then that long suffering student had to switch desks with me. Sometimes, when the blackboard was clean, I could read her neat handwriting, and sometimes, if she had written over a smeared cloud of chalk erasures, or if the sun was shining on the blackboard, it was no use. Then I would have to raise my hand to tell her that I couldn't read the board, and she would write out whatever it was, just like my other teachers had.

There were other indignities as well. I was given large print books– unmanageably large books with pinkish paper covers held together with plastic spiral binding. I still couldn't read their print very quickly, or for very long, even with my magnifier, but it was easier than regular print. Despite their functional value, I hated them. Those pink, large print books were the final indignity. I didn't even have the same books as everyone else.

During that school year, I always got to school late and had to leave early. That was because of the schedules of the maintenance man who drove me to school, and of the bus driver from the rural district, who drove me home. I was driven home alone in a small yellow school bus, on a schedule timed for his return, to take the other special education students home. That bus driver was the best counselor I ever met. He would let me talk, and then he would agree that what I was experiencing was difficult and unfortunate. He would always find ways to encourage me. I looked forward to riding with him every afternoon.

My Braille and typing instruction came during music, art, gym, recess, and the other fun activities that helped make a social community out of a classroom.

Sometimes Miss Stone would include me in her beginning Braille class. Then I would have Braille instruction with the younger children, all of whom were totally blind. The oldest was two years younger than I was, but most of the kids were first, second, or third-graders. We would sit at the low circular table in small, children-sized chairs, and I felt ridiculous. The little ones would best me, time and again, on the Braille skills we were supposed to be mastering. I would try to sneak up on the tasks visually, but Miss Stone kept a sharp eye on me, and I was frequently reminded to touch the Braille, not read it with my eyes.

If the regular classrooms were going to art, music, gym, or lunch, they would have to walk past the resource room door, which was always open. If I was sitting at the large print typewriter, I was out of sight, but at both round tables where Braille was taught, I was in direct view. Then, with shame, I would sense the lines of students staring at me through the open resource room door. I was the only student of Miss Stone with low vision and the only sixth-grader. I felt quite alone and fearful. I didn't want to go blind, and I put up an intense inner battle of will, using the repeated behaviors of resistance, against everything that was supposed to help me. Poor Miss Stone–she put up a really good fight, but my nose nearly developed a callous from the Braille letters that rubbed against it, as I struggled to read the tactile dots with my weak, but determined, eye. I carried a Perkins-Brailler home with me regularly, for homework, but I carefully hid it as much as possible from public view. Worse than my embarrassment about optical aid use, was my loathing for the Brailler. It represented blindness–voiceless, relentless, and stalking.

Dance Class

I was beginning to get to know the students a bit, in my new school, who shared my classroom and with whom I ate lunch. I developed a tenuous

53

friendship with Richard and Bill. Their curiosity about my life, and mine about theirs, seemed to transcend the many differences between us.

The prettiest and most popular girl in the class was Lila. Her hairstyle was countrified, and even her dresses conveyed her farm life. But her yellow blonde hair, which fell in long ringlets around her shoulders, and her bright blue eyes were appealing. They cut across the city/country divide. One noon hour, as we stood in the lunchroom after finishing our home packed sandwiches or hot cafeteria meal, a knot of members of our class gathered in awkward conversation. Lila was the center of the group and was holding court, as those blessed with good looks and popularity often will. For the first time I spoke directly to Lila.

My progressive retinal disease had eaten a hole in the center of my right eye's field of vision. But the visual cortex, the largest processing center within the complex human brain, had taken over and instructed the eye to pull to the right, allowing the more intact peripheral vision to be used to gather whatever visual information it might. The resulting effect, for anyone looking at me, was the disconcerting appearance of my eyes looking in different directions. I was painfully aware of how my eyes looked, and I had begun to adapt. I wore sunglasses whenever possible, or I wouldn't look directly at the person to whom I was speaking, to avoid being reminded of my eyes' unwanted misdirection.

But that noon hour my guard was down, and I looked at Lila when I spoke to her. Lila knew she was pretty, and her ready haughtiness and obvious sense of superiority kept girls, pegged down the social ladder, meekly in their place, and kept most boys at a tentative and unsure distance. But I had spoken directly to her, and her response made me wither with regret. Following my errant right eye's gaze, she looked to her left as if seeking to see someone who everyone knew wasn't there. She looked back at me and asked, in a loud and irritated voice, "Who are you talking to? Who are you looking at?"

I stammered, "I'm talking to you." I heard my voice trail into a quiet apology as I tried to explain the mechanics behind my right eye's poor tracking. But Lila had stopped listening. Her attention had been drawn back to her admiring circle of friends, and I realized that there was no purpose in continuing. I had been dismissed, and with Lila's disdainful rejection came the unspoken judgment, for others to follow, that I was not worth talking to.

In October 1960, the sixth-grade dance class began at Caledonia Elementary. My mother received a call from the principal, a woman who had known my family for years. She offered to allow me to participate in the after school activity, even though I was no longer a student at her school. The little yellow school bus got me home in time to splash on some Old Spice aftershave and hurry to Caledonia for the after school dance class. The first day I arrived a few minutes late, and the class stopped, as the aptly named Miss Tallberg, an unusually tall dance teacher lifted the arm off the record player and welcomed me.

This was the first time in three weeks that I had returned to the community of lifelong friends, bullies, girls, and outcasts. As I walked into that gym, I felt branded and ostracized. I no longer belonged, nor had I shared the unifying experience of sixth-grade camp. That magical connection was now entirely theirs; I no longer held membership. But these were familiar individuals, one and all, and in the course of the ninety-minute class, I began to feel a meager sense of reconnection. My faltering sense of belonging was short-lived. As the class ended, and we filed out of the gymnasium, everyone else began talking with their friends and carrying on their unbroken lives. I was again alone.

The next dance class, as we moved from partner to partner, I hungrily felt the relief of kind smiles from the girls whom I had known since childhood. Miss Tallberg picked me to be her partner, to demonstrate the fox trot. She had big hair, really high heels, and was dressed as if she were going out on the town. I stood close to her as instructed, holding her hand as my right hand wrapped tentatively around her shapely hip, to rest against her back. The underside of the shelf of her impressive bosoms brushed my flat top haircut, as we moved to the box step she was teaching. I could hear stifled laughter, and I knew the other boys were glad it was me and not them. My progressive loss of vision and uprooting from the school were public events. When I moved from partner to partner in our instruction circle, I felt that perhaps some of the girls felt sorry for me. But none of them spoke with the mocking arrogance I had felt from the queen-bee of the sixth-grade at James A. Garfield Elementary.

One girl, Betty Jane, smiled at me in an open and flirtatious manner, and when I had a chance to dance with her a few steps of the cha-cha, fox trot, or jitterbug, it seemed that we both felt a special pre-pubescent attraction and delight. After the dance class, I asked Betty Jane if I could walk her home, and although she lived many blocks in the wrong direction, I happily carried her books, and before she disappeared into her house, I was gifted with a sweet smile and request to call her.

It was never easy to arrive at the dance class, walking up Caledonia's driveway early, while everyone else was in class, or making my awkward entrance a few minutes late. Although my budding relationship with Betty Jane was an unexpected pleasure, the after school class reinforced my sense of being a boy without a real community. After a few weeks, Betty Jane invited me to come over to her house on a Saturday afternoon. She lived with her mother; her parents were divorced. I didn't know anyone else whose parents' marriage was not intact, and their small duplex seemed to reflect their modest circumstances.

But her mother was friendly, youthful, and really knew how to dance. She taught us advanced jitterbug moves that had not been part of our dance class instruction, and we both quickly delighted as spins, throw-outs, and behind-the-back hand exchanges took our jitterbug dancing to a new level of sophistication and excitement. During dance class, we had little opportunity to practice since the instruction always took place in a mechanical round robin structure, ensuring that no one would be left out. But on Saturday afternoons I would arrive at Betty Jane's, and we would practice and laugh, and celebrate the sheer joy of youthful promise, dancing with a comfortable partner and perfecting the moves that became smooth with the fluid ease of rehearsed action.

In February my parents allowed me to have a birthday party, to which I invited some of the boys and girls with whom I had grown up. I put white liquid shoe polish on my white bucks, but the white got all over the sides of the pink rubber soles. So I applied red liquid polish to the soles' edges. The effect was clown-like and startling. But I was ready to dance with Betty Jane, and the last thing I wanted was for people to ignore my dancing feet. Betty Jane and I showed off our jitterbug routine, to the amazement of my former classmates. Best of all, in a game of spin the bottle, my spin stopped, pointing close enough to Betty Jane that she jumped up and grabbed my hand, guiding me out of the recreation room and into the basement's darkened laundry room. We stood for a moment, our arms around each other, and then she kissed me, and I kissed her. It was a long, hungry, and delicious entry into the mysteries of sexual exchange. We returned to the party, newly bound by our magnetic first kiss.

Back in my country school, I seemed to never be in class long enough to learn anything new. My Braille and typing instruction continued as before, and I was beginning to master beginning Braille.

One afternoon, I was sitting at the round table with the first and second-graders learning Braille at the same level that I was. I felt a smoldering humiliation whenever I was required to be instructed in that mismatched little class. As I sat struggling to discern the difference between several dot combinations, I heard my name called in a stage whisper from the hallway. I turned, and I heard the boy surreptitiously addressing me: "It's Bill!" and I realized that my own class had stopped in the hallway, in front of the resource room, on its way to music class. Lila, Richard, Bill, and everyone else, was looking at me in the children's circle. My misery saturated every thought with powerlessness.

However, as the end of the school year approached, my mother gave me great news. Miss Stone and the Cleveland Society for the Blind's children's social worker had conferred and recommended that I be allowed to start junior high back in my regular school district. I had proven so resistant to learning Braille that they agreed, with resignation, that Braille instruction be discontinued. They advised that when I could no longer read print, I would then be ready for Braille. With that news, my aching heart sang, and my shackled spirit felt a freedom that was dizzying. The rest of the school year sped by, and my attention was riveted on Betty Jane, dance class, and the upcoming, district-wide, graduation dance.

The afternoon of the graduation dance arrived, and I hurried to Caledonia. I was rejoining this group's movement into junior high. We all piled into long school buses and arrived at the YMCA for the event. The late spring, warm air wafted through the Y's open doors, and we talked excitedly with our school-friends, amid the crowd of strangers from the district's five other elementary schools.

The dance began, and Betty Jane and I danced every dance together. A jitterbug was played, and we started our routine. Quickly the dance floor cleared, and the entire room encircled us as we powered through the moves we had so long practiced and perfected. We beamed smiles of excited joy toward each other and basked in the public acclaim of the moment. We were awarded the best dancers' certificates. Within days, Betty Jane would dance entirely out of my life for good. But in that sweet moment, the pain and wrenching alienation of the sixth-grade school year came to an end.

Broken Leg Number Two

Life at home, during that marbled year of losses and liberty, was tied to Mark's suffering. Mark's broken leg had kept him from becoming a member of the kindergarten class at Caledonia. But when the cast came off, at the end of September, a decision about late enrollment had to be made. Considering Mark's limited mobility, as he began to use his legs again, it was decided to wait until he was fully ambulatory, before enrolling him in school. In mid-October our parents had gone away, for a well-deserved getaway weekend, with their best friends. The couples went to Northern Ontario, to their friends' cottage, for the annual adults-only weekend. They returned late Sunday afternoon, and that evening our family was all back together.

I was playing with Mark in the living room, as dinner dishes were being washed. Mark's leg was still stiff, but we were beginning to wrestle and play on the floor as we had, before his leg was broken, in early June. Our five-year age difference made me a strong playmate for Mark. At eleven, I was capable of lifting and manipulating his weight easily. I hoisted Mark onto my back, supporting his legs with my arms as I walked around the living room, pretending to be his horse. He always loved that form of play, and he laughed excitedly as I whinnied and jostled him, as if galloping from room to room. Then I got down on my hands and knees, and he happily climbed astride my back. I started bucking–pretending to be a bronco. It didn't occur to me, as our horseplay became more physical, that he would get hurt in any way. But foolishly I stiffened my legs, sending him careening over my head. Mark laughed as he became airborne.

He hit the floor, and I heard a sickeningly loud crack. It was followed by his terrible scream. He lay on the floor crying, a wail punctuated with terrified shrieks of pain. I stood helplessly by, as Dad pulled Mark's pants gingerly down his legs to assess the problem visually. The tone of my parent's conversation was low, urgent, and grim. Dad hurried upstairs to change clothes and get his car keys. I followed him and stood in the open door of my parent's bedroom. I nervously asked Dad what he thought was wrong. My father reported, in a quiet voice, that Mark had broken his leg again and that the police rescue squad had been called.

A swirling nausea swept over me. I ran into our bedroom and into the small bathroom, where I fell onto my knees. I sobbed in a paroxysm of prayer, disbelief, horror, guilt, and remorse. Dad was soon standing beside me and said, quietly, that I must pull myself together since there was an emergency at hand. My father finished getting ready to leave with Mark, and I stopped crying and went back downstairs and tried to entertain Mark. I hid my face behind a dishcloth and, in an exaggerated voice, attempted to act like my face's reappearance was magic. Mark watched me, laughing briefly each time, but then returned to jagged cries of pain. The doorbell rang, and Mom hurried to open it. Three uniformed policemen entered, wheeling a low gurney. When Mark saw them enter, it must have reminded him of the accident in June when uniformed men lifted him from the street into the ambulance. Mark panicked, and as he was carefully lifted onto the low bed, his cries of pain were suddenly mixed with shrill screams of fear. My weak activity as a clown ceased as I stared at the awful tableau.

This time, Mom went with Mark, and the rest of us followed the ambulance to the hospital. Grandma Jane was phoned, and she joined us. As the family waited for the orthopedic surgeon to assess the extent of the injury, I felt the shame and weight of responsibility. The doctor came out to report that Mark's leg was indeed broken–the same leg, the same bone, but a new break. This time traction was not needed. Mark returned home the next day, encased in another cast that girdled him from the waist down, this time without immobilizing the unbroken leg.

I entertained Mark, for a time every day, with puppets or toy guns. We played–to his delight–and for the salving of my aching conscience. I felt guilty in an absolute way. I knew that I had intentionally thrown him off my back. But no one spoke of it. My hell was a private one, made all the more difficult by Mark's innocence and good nature. The second cast came off, just before Christmas, ending seven months of plaster, pain, and immobility. Mark's freshly mended leg was much thinner than the other, and it had long dark hairs that had grown while the leg had been encased in casts. During the summer, the traction cast's sharp edge caused wounds that were, by December, speckled purple and yellow and awful looking. Mark's leg was stiff, and the knee could not bend. A period of slow rehabilitation through normal use began.

A few weeks later, we were all watching television one evening. Mark and I were lying on the floor sharing pretzels, served to us in a yellow ceramic bowl. Out of nowhere, Mark picked up the bowl, spun around, and threw it hard against a wall about five feet behind us. The bowl struck the wall and with the startling sound of shattering glass, exploded into many pieces. No one spoke. The moment held sudden foreboding. A new problem had just been visited upon us–Mark acting violently. My mother wordlessly cleaned up the glass and the pretzels.

The Ukulele

Music lifted me up during that tumultuous year. When I was a young child, our house was often filled with music. My mother and both grandmothers played the piano, and the blonde upright that stood in the dining room often rang out hymns and popular songs from many decades. Bonnie had three years of piano lessons and played pretty well, I thought. After my lessons abruptly stopped, I still enjoyed playing the few pieces that I had painstakingly memorized.

My father had attended college while working as a punch press operator. Upon graduation he was promoted to a white-collar job, doing time-motion studies, back on the factory floor. Dad struggled with his new management role, due to the negative impact it was having on his blue-collar friends. After considerable soul-searching, he resigned and was unemployed for several months. During that austere period my folks were forced to sell the piano, followed by my elaborate much-loved Lionel electric train layout, which my Dad had spent years painstakingly building. I silently watched as strangers moved first the piano and then the intricate train layout on two sheets of plywood out the front door.

After the piano was sold, the only musical instrument in the house was my Dad's ukulele. Dad had learned to play during World War II, and he had numerous ukulele songbooks. His playing was fluid, and his wonderful, soft baritone voice was usually complemented by my mother's sweet, alto harmonies or by the chorus of my parents' friends' voices when their social group would sing together at parties. My father played a sturdy and quite serviceable plastic instrument. It was matched by the Arthur Godfrey ukulele that I received for Christmas in 1957. I was eight. The uke came complete with a book of songs and a device that clamped over the strings which allowed one to play different chords by simply pressing one of five buttons. The spring-loaded inner mechanism would press the strings down, exactly on the correct frets, to form the desired chord. Without any real practice–presto! I was playing sweet ukulele music. I loved the little instrument that looked like my Dad's. I played it happily, learning songs from the songbook that came with the uke, until the wonderful little instrument accidentally fell and cracked. It was discarded by my mother. With that loss went my involvement with the uke until February 1960, during my first Boy Scout camping weekend, when I turned eleven.

The Scouts included boys from eleven to fourteen. The age difference made the older boys seem quite mature and grown up. Bill, one of the fourteen-year-olds, brought his uke along and entertained us with playing and singing. It was a remarkable moment of revelation for me. Here was a cool guy, who I held in some awe for his competence, confidence, age, and size, playing the very same plastic instrument, as my dad. Not only did the ukulele's cool factor suddenly increase, but it was an instrument that I could access and learn to play.

I returned from camp on Sunday afternoon, and I asked my Dad if I could borrow his uke and songbooks. He willingly consented, and I went to my room to begin to learn the chords that would turn the humble instrument into a vehicle of self-generated entertainment and accompaniment. The book included "My Darling Clementine", a song which I knew and that only had two different chords. After a couple of hours of practice, I appeared in the kitchen, before dinner, and performed my first song, really playing a stringed instrument. My parents sang along, patiently waiting between phrases as I laboriously changed chords, and then applauded at the song's end. My parents' support and encouragement was instant, and I felt a real sense of pleasure from their approval. I was hooked and soon I was learning new songs from Dad's songbooks.

But there were other songs that I wanted to learn like "Jamaica Farewell" and "Dream" from albums by Harry Belafonte and The Everly Brothers. I remembered learning to play the piano when I was unable to see piano music. Crandall Hendershot, my childhood piano teacher, had been unaware of my limited vision. I had imitated his playing by listening carefully, then picking out the matching notes by ear. I figured that I could apply the same intuition to playing the uke. I slowly and methodically began teaching myself new songs and increasing my repertoire. The more chords I learned, through the slow method of reading them one by one with my magnifier, the more range of songs I could master. Gradually the systematic logic of chord relationships and keys began to come to my ear, and my speed and ability to intuitively play new material expanded.

During the summer of 1960, Aunt Pauline, my mother's sister, came to visit. I loved Pauline and her entire family. They lived in a gracious town on Long Island, and they had a New York sophistication that always brought me new ideas about what was hip. Her children were my sister's and my ages. Buzzy and Johnny were my only male cousins my age, and visits were always eagerly anticipated. The news was presented to me that I would be going back with Pauline for a totally new experience–I was going to visit them alone. It was a real thrill to board the airplane, piloted by Pauline's husband Howard, and take off for New York. On the flight, a stewardess asked me if I would like to go into the cockpit. The experience was magical. My uncle, who was the flight's captain, sat in the middle of the cockpit. He was surrounded by the other flight crew and the vast array of controls, switches, and dials that comprised the flight deck of the United, four prop, DC-6. Howard invited me to sit in the captain's chair. As he stood, I gingerly slid into the warm leather seat, stunned at the beautiful view through the vast, surrounding windshield. Howard instructed me to turn a large circular knob slowly to the right, and the majestic aircraft made a gradual turn. I listened to the clipped communications between a control tower and other pilots on his earphones, and I felt a real awe, at the position of authority and responsibility that I saw and heard. Howard returned to the controls, fine-tuned the plane's course, and I sat for a while longer observing the quiet professionalism of the crew as they spoke to each other about the flight and made kind small talk with me.

The best part of the vacation, however, was yet to come. My parents had given me $10 to spend on my trip and combined with the money I had saved, I had a wallet that was bulging with promise. Everyone in Pauline's family was actively musical. Pauline was a talented pianist who gave lessons in their home. Howard sang in The Unitarian Church Choir. All of the kids played instruments, with high proficiency, and I found Buzzy's French horn playing very impressive.

When I told him about my playing the ukulele, much to my surprise, he showed real interest. We walked into Huntington, the quiet little town nearby, to check out the music store. There, hanging on the wall, were two matching, beautiful Harmony wooden ukuleles. We handled them with the reverence of deep-pocketed violinists appreciating available Stradivarius instruments. Buzzy saw from their dangling price tags that they cost $9.00. I had the money and decided to buy mine on the spot. The next day, with money from Pauline, Buzzy bought his. I taught him the chords I had learned, and we were quickly playing and singing together and figuring out new songs. Buzzy had a quick ear. The week was spent bonding and playing our new ukuleles. I flew home holding my treasure. Although I was not invited into the cockpit during this flight, the stewardesses were indulgent and listened to me sing and play. I owned my first instrument, and I began to imagine the real opportunities it would open.

Every fall, the Kiwanis Club sponsored The East Cleveland Talent Show, and I decided to audition playing "Jamaica Farewell". I was nervous as I sat among the other children and teens, all waiting for their turn to show their stuff. There were accordion players, tap dancers, vocalists, pianists, a guitarist, duets and quartets, and every sort of lesson-developed youthful performance I could imagine. When my turn came, I stepped to the center of the area set off for the auditions and sang the three verses of the calypso song playing my lovely little ukulele. When the letter came in the mail, that I had made the show, I was thrilled. I was going to be on stage in front of the whole community! That particular happiness came in sharp contrast to the protracted loneliness resulting from my removal from my neighborhood, sixth-grade class.

In late October, a couple of weeks before the talent show, my Mom got a call from the local newspaper asking if I could come down with my ukulele and have my picture taken for an article promoting the upcoming event. The final touches were put on my costume. I wore an unfinished straw hat that was popular at the time and was supposed to be what calypso singers wore, as they sat in the sun on the beach. The costume also included a striped shirt, also purchased on my New York vacation, blue jean shorts my mother had cut off in a ragged pattern, and rubber thong sandals. It was a cool October afternoon, and the costume was carried in a paper bag. I changed in a bathroom at the newspaper office. I shared the photo with a barbershop quartet of beautiful high school girls. We posed with me sitting on the floor, gazing up at the four pretty girls in their Roaring Twenties-style costumes. They leaned on their canes and smiled benevolently down at me. When the photo and article ran on November 10, the day before the show, I was lying in my bed, confined with a full-blown case of mumps. The illness puffed my neck and cheeks and made swallowing very painful. But my physical suffering paled compared to the loss that I felt, at not being a performer in the annual talent show.

The next year, my Dad helped me put together an even better act. He had taught me many songs from his youth including "Five Foot Two", a fast and demanding, classic ukulele standard that I learned from his songbooks. Dad helped me string three 1920's favorites together into a medley. My costume was a borrowed candy-striped blazer, bow tie, and straw boater hat, and I was billed as "Oh Uke Kid". As I stepped onto the center of the stage and was hit by the blinding spotlight, my light-sensitive eyes began to burn fiercely. But as the pit band started playing a thrilling vaudeville back-up to my vocal and ukulele, I was filled with the new joy of musical performance and the exhilaration of being alone in front of an audience.

Stable

My vision relentlessly deteriorated throughout elementary school. Every six months, I returned to Dr. Kazdan's pristine office for the examination and eye test that documented my helpless slide. At ten, I struggled with my better eye to see the largest two lines on the eye chart: the big E and the next two jumbo letters. At eleven it was just the big E–that final mega-signpost of measurable vision: 20/200 and legal blindness. Crossing that threshold, as special education closed in, I was driven into a hard internal corner. I marshaled my will, my grit, my prayer, and my innermost determination against further decline of my severely limited sight. By sheer force of will, I was going to stop the creeping deterioration.

I was twelve in early summer 1961 when I went with my Mom for my semiannual ophthalmologic exam. The routine never varied. I would be examined, with my mother silently watching, and then Dr. Kazdan would speak to her privately. While driving home, she would relay the doctor's report to me after a few minutes of silence–always at the same place on the drive home–and always spooling out the bad news that my vision had gotten worse. Mom's report closed the circle because I already knew that I had lost more vision. I dreaded that confirmation of my continual downward spiral and how it would impact my parents, especially my Mom. I knew the bad news would load fresh heartache onto my already heavily burdened parents. But on that warm, late morning, I was to hear a different declaration. Mom told me that Dr. Kazdan had reported that my vision had not gotten worse; miraculously, it had stabilized!

My elation was momentary. Dr. Kazdan, and now my mother, added a dark caveat and draconian new life rules. Although the doctor still couldn't diagnose my mysterious disease process, he speculated that I could lose the remainder of my vision if I were struck in the head. He also thought many activities were no longer safe since my vision was so limited. Therefore, he directed my parents to forbid me from engaging in any potentially risky activities including diving, wrestling, football and, most catastrophically, bike riding. I had been spared what had seemed like the inevitability of blindness, but frightening vulnerability loomed, paired with a stunning cluster of boyhood losses.

Two years before, with saved paper route money matched by my parents, I purchased a beautiful, black, three-speed English "racer" bicycle. It was a Raleigh–sleek, serious, and unique among all of the bikes in my neighborhood. It had tan handlebar grips, a matching leather seat, and a behind-the-seat bag, setting off the shiny black fenders and frame. It even had a friction-driven headlight and tail light. I felt proud and invincible, riding my Raleigh, if not just a little frightened by the occasional vision-caused accidents and frequent near misses. The nastiest accident was not caused by poor vision though, but by inexperience and overconfidence. One icy winter day, on my way to the barber shop five blocks away, I tried to power up a high curb by riding hard and expecting the bike to bump up onto the sidewalk, as I had seen my friends do. But the trick didn't work, and the bicycle hit the curb and came to an abrupt stop. I was thrown headfirst, over the handlebars, onto the sidewalk. My forehead hit the concrete, and I was knocked out. The results were a painful concussion and a bent front wheel. Despite its danger to me, I loved that bicycle. My most prized possession, it was great looking, elegant, and it gave me freedom and wide-ranging mobility. Now that love affair was over. I had to sell my bike and forever give up the shaky independence it provided. Alone, I was condemned to a harsh fate. Now I would walk everywhere, as my friends whizzed past on their bikes. Once Dr. Kazdan had uttered the judgment, there was no discussion. Beginning on that fateful Saturday morning, I was forbidden to ride my English racer again. With a heavy heart, I went to the garage and sadly regarded her. Now I had to find a buyer. My parents suggested a price of $25–half of what I had paid. Within days, a neighborhood boy lustfully grabbed it. He lived on my paper route, and over a series of weeks I saw my former bicycle rapidly lose its star quality. Its new owner immediately stripped the Raleigh of its fenders and leather bag. Then the kickstand disappeared. The frame quickly became dull and scraped from being dropped carelessly onto the sidewalk. I would pass it, lying on its side, in front of the drugstore across the street from his house. Seeing it, my heart would ache as I witnessed its battering and neglect. Simultaneously, during that period, I had begun to breathe a little easier with the relief of not going blind. Yet a chilling fear stalked close behind. An errant blow to my head might throw me into certain, complete blindness.

So in spite of my heartache about the new constraints on my activities, I complied with the limitations placed on me. In July, Boy Scout

Camp began. I was only going for one of the two weeks because I had not sold enough cookies, light bulbs, and fertilizer to pay for both weeks of camp. That seemed like enough, anyway, since I had a love/hate relationship with the Boy Scouts. Our troop was a ranked gang, where *Lord of the Flies* bullying made up much of the scout experience when adults weren't looking. Anyone who was vulnerable was the target for mean spirited mischief–including me. I never retaliated.

Camp started, and my usual tent mate and I shared a tent with a large open front side. A center wooden ridge pole crossed the front of the tent, allowing the canvas front to create a shady awning, held aloft by poles, ropes, and stakes. When the tent's front wall was raised, exposure to open night air made summer nights more comfortable. The July weather had been dry and hot. After one evening's campfire, I used the outhouse and brushed my teeth at the camp pump. I sat on my cot changing into my pajamas when another scout crept in with a fire bucket. A red bucket stood in front of each tent, to be kept full of water in case of fire, a new camp safety provision. He whispered that it was Brad's bucket and everyone was pissing into it. Poor Brad wet his sleeping bag regularly. He always tented alone, and nearly every morning Brad would spread his flannel sleeping bag over the peak of his one-man tent to dry and air out. The sleeping bag, wet or dry, smelled of urine. Everyone in the camp knew of Brad's unfortunate problem, and I felt sorry for him. We were both low on the social totem pole, and Brad and I occasionally spent time together outside of the Scouts. I refused to participate in the community mischief. Having collected my tent mate's contribution to the mean spirited prank, the perpetrator ran off to continue to fill the bucket with troop urine.

A few minutes later, he snuck up and returned Brad's fire bucket–a partially full bucket of warm piss. Through his tent's opening, Brad had been observing the not-so-clandestine skullduggery. Moments after the bucket was returned, Brad reached out, grabbed the edge of the bucket and flung it hard into the night. He didn't aim, but the airborne container sailed directly toward our tent, standing a dozen feet away. The bucket rose in a low arc and hit the ground right in front of my cot where I sat in my pajamas. As the container hit, the movement of its foul cargo continued on, and I was suddenly soaked in warm piss. As was the pattern, when some misfortune befell another scout, those observing had burst into hard and raucous laughter. The entire camp was tented in an open circle and had been watching the fire bucket plot develop.

Soaked in urine, I was humiliated, angry, and, impossibly upset. I burned with an unspeakable frustration, disgust, and rage. Brad's bucket heave had made me the brunt when I had not even participated in the community's harsh prank. But I had been a silent bystander and didn't interrupt the action by telling the counselors. That never crossed my mind. In that moment, I was suddenly filled with reckless anger and desire for revenge. I jumped off my cot and ran over to Brad's tent. I grabbed the stake that anchored the guide rope for the front of it and pulled hard. The stake came out of the ground and the tent sagged. I continued to pull more of Brad's tent stakes out of the ground as his tent slumped. With defensive, retaliatory action, Brad jumped out and ran over to my tent which was standing a few feet away. Seeking the single most devastating response he could marshal, Brad was reaching up–struggling to lift the center ridge pole off its upright support–intent on bringing our tent down. I had pulled up two or three stakes from his tent, when I saw Brad about to collapse our tent.

Brad was a big-boned and heavyset kid, about two or three inches taller than I. I hollered and ran up behind him, and jerked his shoulder back as he was wrestling to unseat the ridgepole. As I grabbed him, Brad wheeled around, with his arm cocked, and struck me hard in the eye with a crushing elbow blow. I don't think he meant to hit me with such devastating effect. I felt the cracking impact; I saw a great flash of light, and I was knocked suddenly to the ground. My hands flew to my face, and I convulsed with terrible fear. I could hear myself screaming, "Oh no, I'm going to go blind! I'm going to go blind!" My face pounded with fierce pain, and my mind was crazed with the horror of the seeming inevitability of blindness. Only now, can I imagine the emotional trauma that the episode must have caused Brad and perhaps the perpetrator of the fire bucket prank.

The two older teenage counselors, responsible for our troop, rushed to the scene. By flashlight, they could see that I had been injured and would require first aid. They worriedly helped me up and assisted me as I changed into dry clothes. Then the three of us walked through the woods to the nurse's quarters as I continued to shudder and weakly cry. The kindly, gray haired nurse lived in a rustic cabin attached to the camp's first aid clinic and sick bay, with its single bed. When I got to the first aid station, the counselors left me in her concerned care. The nurse had me lie down on the narrow bed as she made a large ice pack. I held it over my eye and cheek, dulling the throbbing pain. Brad's blow had blackened my eye and extensive surrounding tissue and discoloration had already begun. My initial surge of fear and panic was now slowing to dread and shock. In less than a month I had violated the dark warning. Remorse and awful expectation came to stay.

The nurse's competent and maternal care comforted me to a degree. I heard her phone my parents. She returned to the little white room and suggested that I strip down to my shorts. She turned back the cot's bedding, and I got in, gingerly. The nurse told me that my folks would come out to pick me up in the morning. With a lead-heavy heart, I drifted to sleep.

Mark and First-Grade

Mark and I had shared a bedroom, from the time he was moved from a crib to a bed. Our bedroom was two distinct places for me, with very different emotional tones. When I was alone, the bedroom was my place of refuge, solace, and pleasure. It was where I could lie on my bed on Sunday afternoons and listen to Talking Book records, or clip my crystal radio to the radiator by my bed and listen to WHK–Cleveland's top rock and roll station. I decorated the wall beside my bed with my pennant collection. Pennants had been gifts, and my purchases, as favored souvenirs from Boy Scout adventures, family vacations, and major league games. The wall was festooned with my ever growing collection, carefully arranged in varying patterns, depending on the number of pennants I had to display.

When Mark was there, that room was a place of conflict and emotional upheaval. When I would bring friends home from school and we would go there to play, Mark almost always burst through the closed door, interjecting himself into our activities. I couldn't get him to leave me alone. I didn't like being impatient and embarrassed by my little brother. I felt anger marbled with guilt and resentment. But sharing a room with Mark wasn't easy, even when friends weren't involved. One Saturday morning, I awoke with stinging points of pain on my arms and legs. Mark stood by my bed. He had quietly climbed onto my bed and pulled the thumbtacks from all of the pennants he could reach. He methodically lined up the thumbtacks tightly around me with the points sticking up. Every time I moved at all, I got pricked and I had to holler for my mother to come rescue me from Mark's painful picket fence of tacks. I have no idea what had motivated him. He wasn't angry or mean spirited–he was just Mark.

Mark's congenital disability was also developing new manifestations. One early morning, when he was five, I was awakened by a frightening, unfamiliar sound coming from his bed. He was jerking violently in short slamming motions and choking with a tight, irregular gurgle. I raced out of the room to get my parents. They threw their clothes on and Dad wrapped Mark in a blanket, still in the throes of the seizure. My parents rushed him to the hospital where he was diagnosed with epilepsy.

Mark's cognitive limitations were obvious and severe. We lived next door to a softhearted and friendly woman who taught kindergarten at Caledonia Elementary School. In consultation with my parents and the principal, she had seen to it that Mark would be allowed to attend her kindergarten class in spite of his disability, which would have ordinarily excluded him from enrollment. His first year in kindergarten had begun mid-year due to his two broken legs. Mark was not successful in kindergarten, cognitively or socially. Our neighbor protected him at school, and our mother walked him to and from the classroom door picking him up at the end of each half-day class. Mark repeated kindergarten. Everyone hoped that another year might result in his gaining on missed developmental mile markers. However, Mark had made no progress. Although Mark was not a good candidate for first-grade, he could not again be held back. A year older, Mark was already taller and stronger than the other children.

In September 1961, Mark began full day classes as a first-grade student. We lived within a fifteen-minute walk from the school. Mom recruited neighborhood kids in Mark's class to walk him to and from school each morning, and again in the afternoon after lunch. They were paid five cents for each walk. Mark was eager to please and universally friendly, but his overbearing overtures toward other children were not well received, and the best that could be expected was that he would be tolerated by the more generous and understanding of his peers. First-grade held greater expectations of attentive classroom behavior than had kindergarten. Mark's limitations instantly became irritants and distractions. His neighborhood age-mates also began to show fatigue with their protector responsibilities. Mark walked home alone, more than once.

One cool day in early October, a few weeks after school had begun; Mom became concerned when Mark did not arrive home at the usual time for lunch. After a few worried minutes, she walked briskly toward the school. The new community library stood on the corner of the street, down the block from the school. As our mother rounded the corner of our block, she could see the broad expanse of the library lawn, one street away. There stood Mark, crying fiercely, helplessly soaked to the skin by the cold spray of the library's automatic sprinkling system. Every time he tried to run off

69

the lawn and away from the cold water, one of the boys in the ring of bullies, that surrounded the lawn, would run at him and force him back into his torture. My mother screamed his name, the boys scattered, and Mom ran to his rescue. Furious and broken-hearted, she hugged Mark to her and walked him home, as he shivered, sobbing inconsolably. That day, at the age of seven, Mark's school life ended. He refused to go back to first-grade that afternoon or ever again. Mark became a boy without a future, a child with no hope of education. Our parents grappled with the grim knowledge that unless some alternative was found, all of Mark's days were going to be spent at home.

Mom had recognized her need for a life that did not revolve around Mark. She had enrolled in a shorthand course and had borrowed typing drill books from the library, dusting off her secretarial skills, dormant for years. Within weeks, she was a Kelly Girl–a member of a temporary job placement service–and soon she was working full time at Nela Park, General Electric's flagship research and marketing center that happened to be on a beautiful campus of wooded hills at the end of our street. With Mark not attending school, child care was needed. Grandma Jane had a retired friend who gladly accepted the full-time job as Mark's caregiver, and who became a fixture in our home. The small woman's quiet and patient nature was a perfect fit for Mark's high energy and need for understanding. Every day, Dad or Mom would pick her up before they went to work and return her home at the end of the day. The new routine worked well enough. The winter months were particularly peaceful, since Cleveland's hard winters resulted in little interaction between young children.

But Mark's solitude and lack of interaction with anyone except the meek and mild babysitter, gave him an abundance of energy and a deep desire to play with me at the end of every school day. During my year-long purgatory at James A. Garfield Elementary, I struggled with my social isolation and with my rock-ribbed rejection of Braille. I would arrive home and trudge up to our second-floor bedroom and drop onto my bed, hoping to spend the remainder of the afternoon alone, listening to a Talking Book or my radio. I wanted to escape to a different place-alternative and imaginary. No sooner would I close the door against my life's jangling pathos, then would Mark come running up the stairs and burst into our bedroom, wanting my attention. Sometimes I would impatiently engage him for a few minutes and then dismiss him by pretending to sleep, or by announcing to him that I just didn't want to play. At other times, I would refuse to engage with him at all. If I did reluctantly play, any activity would do. Sometimes, I would use my bare hands as puppets, giving them different voices. There was always the old standby of pretending to be shot by Mark. When all else failed, I would hide behind a pillow or my own hands, and then "magically" reappear–always eliciting peals of laughter, shouts of excited joy, or happy bursts of anticipatory giggles. Sometimes my emotions could bristle with selfish irritation at what seemed like the extraordinary requirements Mark forced on me. But I could also soften, with the realization of the difference that a little attention from me could make in his otherwise lonely life.

As my vision loss had progressed, and as Mark's world became smaller and crueler, I would repeat my same nightly prayer: a beseeching plea to God's mercy, which I had been taught was great. I considered the dual assaults of my progressive blindness and Mark's battered life to be too great a burden for one little family. I would bargain with God by offering to sacrifice my eyesight in exchange for Mark's intellectual healing and ascension to normalcy. The prayer always ended in the same painful summary of outrage: "Not both of us! This isn't fair!" My vision continued to deteriorate and Mark's plight deepened.

Seventh-grade

The decision had been made, due to my resistance to learning Braille, to return me to my neighborhood school district. As a result, in September 1961, I began my first year at Kirk Junior High School. Caledonia Elementary was all white, but had students from families with a broad spread of incomes–from working poor to very wealthy. Among Caledonia's diverse neighborhoods was Forest Hills, one of the most exclusive areas in Cleveland. But Caledonia was one of six elementary schools, all of which fed into Kirk Junior High. Kirk students also came from an even lower economic rung. Overall it was a diverse range of students that included WASP's, black kids, and many from East Cleveland's pocketed ethnic communities: German, Italian, Hungarian, Polish, and other Eastern European enclaves. But ethnicity, race, or economic background predicated nothing. There were toughs, jocks, musicians, and excellent and gifted students, among all of Kirk's subgroups. But Kirk's hard core kids were really tough. Their spiking testosterone levels made the place a testing ground for anyone with something to prove, especially as the informal power hierarchy was shaking out early in the school year. On the first day of seventh-grade, a short, muscular, aggressive, and threatening African

American guy, backed by four of his lieutenants, assailed me with demands for money. I weakly said I had none–a lie–and the kid closed in, throwing me against the lockers and threatening me with a beating. He punched me several times as I cowered, falling against the lockers. I dug a quarter from my pants pocket and gave it to him. He struck my shoulder hard with the flat of his hand, snarled a threat, and marauded down the hall.

Frequent fights–real beatings–took place in the woods near the school. I would lower my head and hurry by, hoping to be quickly past the chance of harm.

The stalking neighborhood bullies I had endured in elementary school had become an increasing threat. Among the worst were Doug and Bruce, identical twins. They lived down the street, across a gradual divide between the nice houses like ours and smaller, less comfortable ones. At the far end were two-family houses crowded onto small lots. The twins' double-family house was on my paper route. It was set very close to the sidewalk, creating a narrowing personal danger zone. Twice a week I delivered the community newspaper and every two weeks collected from my customers. Doug and Bruce were always hanging out on the street and sidewalk in front of their house. They hassled anyone they chose, who dared to walk through their territory. In cold weather, they wore shabby, stained brown work jackets with a company name stamped on the front and the back. Doug, the meaner, had menaced me twice before. I had always been able to talk my way out of the potential fight. It was through such dangerous encounters that I first applied the judo of psychology. I had learned that bullies often need a supporting posse. If I was lucky, the presence of witnesses gave me an audience to use, in my strategy to avoid the dreaded blow to the head.

It was a cold Saturday in February 1962, as I made my way slowly down the block, collecting from my hundred and sixty-five customers–a process that took two, tiring three-hour rounds to complete. Doug defiantly blocked my way. I stopped and he stepped in, so close even I could see the hard glint in his ice blue eyes. Bruce drifted out of view. Doug radiated malevolence. A heavy shock of brown greased hair flopped across his forehead, and his teeth shown in a gum chewing snarl. He held my gaze as he verbally mocked my poor vision and unwillingness to fight. He called me a coward. His gloved hands never stopped packing a snowball that he had worked into a hard, polished, glassy ball of ice.

His jeering taunts were cold and unrelenting. As always, I began to flatter his physical prowess and attempt to defeat his aggression by pointing out that anyone could beat me up since I couldn't see to fight back; but there

72

were no onlookers and, my words had no effect. He kept interrupting, obviously enjoying my seeping fear. A sudden sharp impact punched my left eye. An ice cold pain and shocking pressure had come from out of nowhere. Bruce had packed an identical ice ball. At short range, it slammed into the side of my face, forcing hardened ice against my eye, behind my glasses. A flash of bright red light burst within my vision, and pain seared my temple, eye, and nose. I froze–motionless, eyes gripped shut, not knowing what had happened until the nature and cause of the pain became clear. I reached up and took off my glasses, and pulled the puck of ice away from my eye socket. I heard again the ever present, now internal, entreaty not to be hit in the head or eye. I was helpless. I stifled a cry and held my breath, but uncontrollable tears flowed. I tightened my face and clamped my mouth against any sound; my eye hurt with an impossibly severe ache. I waited; eyes squeezed shut, for them to do whatever they were going to do next. My face stung with numbing cold and pounded with pain. By then, Bruce had walked back across the street from the place where he had delivered his blindside attack. Doug had kept me stationary with his bullying sidewalk block, while Bruce had taken unhurried aim. Bruce, a milder soul in general, was obviously shaken by the result of his missile's impact and asked several times if I was all right. Doug watched silently. With a quaking voice, I said that I wasn't supposed to get hit in the head because I could go blind. But I forced out that I thought I was okay, wiped the ice and tears from my face with my gloves, and put my glasses back on. Gratefully, I noticed no change in my vision. The thugs let me pass and wandered silently into the street, aimlessly seeking another focus for their joint, toxic attention. I quit the paper route a few weeks later. After four years, I was tired of the long hours of delivering and collecting, but I also wanted no more confrontations. Such things, however, were out of my control.

Every year Kirk Junior High's faculty put on a carnival. The prized trophy was a brightly colored wooden stick, about two feet long with a smooth, beveled, milled handle. The sticks, which we called canes, could only be won at a hoop toss booth, requiring nominal skill. I had never been good at any games requiring hand/eye coordination, but, somehow, I gently flipped the wooden hoop at just the right arc, and it clattered onto one of the prized canes. I was jazzed–I had a cane! I went looking for my friends, who had gone into another section of the gym. I was walking alone, on a narrow staircase, when a tough Italian kid muscled into me, grabbed my cane, and walked quickly outside. I impulsively followed him and, as I gradually closed the distance between us, I unabashedly asked for the return of the cane. The thug led me outside, well beyond the school. We were followed closely by his knot of hangers-on. When we reached the broad expanse of the football practice field, he stopped, wheeled around, and told me that I was full of shit. He flatly said that this was his own cane, but if I wanted it, I could fight him for it. He loudly smacked the cane into the palm of his hand repeatedly. He wanted to fight, and I recognized that he might use the stiff wooden rod as a weapon. I spoke in a trembling voice and explained that I couldn't fight because I could go blind if I got hit in the head. Using my junior high psychology, I suggested that I would be easy to beat up since I couldn't see and couldn't fight. I said that his prowess might be better demonstrated on a more fitting opponent. He was silent as the words sunk in. I stated that although any one could beat me up, I was sure that he was a very good fighter. His posse stood immobile, considering this new and strange dilemma for their leader. After a long silence, he threw my cane back to me. It bounced off of my chest and rattled to the ground. I picked it up, walked through his circle, and back into the noisy gymnasium.

But it wasn't just the bullies that made Kirk so difficult. Junior high was functionally exhausting. As I searched for each new classroom, in the day's rotation of classes, I would have to read door numbers. That required standing six inches from the door and staring at the small numbers for some time, as I scanned back and forth, catching scraps of information with the patchy vision in my lousy left eye. Early in the year, I would approach each teacher and explain that I had low vision, and could not read the board without a telescope. They also needed to understand that the telescope couldn't focus any closer than the third seat from the front of the classroom. There, I would have a chance of reading the board. I would also ask not to be required to read out loud, although that classroom activity was seldom required. Everyone had gym class twice a week. Most guys carried a gym bag on those days, containing their tennis shoes and gym clothes. However, I always carried a gym bag whether or not I had gym that day. It contained my books and my hidden optical aids–the leather case with the monocular telescope and its two-piece, screw together handle, an eye patch, and the heavy, crystal ball-like, thick Plano-convex magnifier. I felt embarrassed and conspicuous using my optical aids. I would feel the curious or mocking stares from the other students, particularly during the first weeks of school. When I thought that the other students were absorbed in their work, I would sneak the monocular out of my bag and peer through the wonderful lenses and mirrors that brought the world close enough to see. I appreciated the telescope and magnifier's functionality, but I hated being a public spectacle.

An older student had been assigned to read to me during the period after lunch. But this was not just any other student. Joan was my reader, one of the prettiest girls in the ninth-grade. Two years older than I was, Joan was in my sister's class, and I was delighted to have such an attractive and popular girl serve as my reader. This was going to be great. We were given the Social Studies office, during one of the lunch periods. I sat at the office's oak desk, in the narrow room, while Joan used a table at a right angle to the desk as she read my day's work aloud. She was the first person, other than my mother or sister, to read to me, and her personal style and general allure made me relax and absorb her reading with full concentration.

Early in the school year, Connie was added as my evening reader. I had known Connie since early elementary school. She was paid by my parents to come over every evening and read my homework assignments to me. Connie was a good student, and she quickly became a great help in my tedious and time-consuming process of learning through listening. She would quiz me for upcoming tests, and together we spent every school night pouring over the textbooks and notes that underpinned our academic world. Joan and Connie were my friends and invaluable bridges to learning. Their services began a pattern that would last throughout my formal education.

Thank you, Mrs. Delaney

In September 1962, eighth-grade began. I had two student readers, Connie and a new reader at school. They were meaningful accommodations to my vision loss, but I still had to read visually for much of my studying, class note taking, and for test taking. I crawled along as I had previously, my face touching the paper, straining to see through my thick magnifier, and squinting at the blackboard through my monocular.

From the first *bonjour*, we spoke absolutely no English in Mrs. Delaney's French class. She observed my struggle to read, without comment, after my first day's explanation of my visual limitations. During the second week, Mrs. Delaney spoke to me in English for the first time. Assigning the class silent work, she asked to see me in the hall. Once in the privacy of the empty hall, Mrs. Delaney quietly asked if it was painful for me to read. I was stunned. No one had ever asked me how it felt before, and her concern touched me. She asked if there wasn't a large print version of the French textbook. I had been required to use large print books in sixth-grade, and I was repulsed by the idea of their introduction in the caldron of junior high. But, I told Mrs. Delaney, truthfully, that my mother had sought large print books and learned that there were no large print editions available for any of my required texts. Mrs. Delaney paused and asked if there was such a thing as a large print typewriter. I had one at home that was virtually unused. I preferred to struggle with my mother's standard size print typewriter. Through the tortured logic of damaged self-image, small print made me feel less conspicuous. Little did either of us know the magnitude of what was forming, as Mrs. Delaney's personal commitment.

As Mrs. Delaney requested, the following week my father drove me, with the recently dusted, large print typewriter, to junior high; together we lugged the heavy old manual up to her third-floor classroom. Seeing the typewriter's bulk, she asked us to take it directly to her car. From that day on, Mrs. Delaney typed a separate large print version of all materials needed in her class, every vocabulary list, assignment, board notation, test, and most incredibly, the entire text book.

Every Monday morning, she would discretely slip the giant stack of papers containing the week's work onto my desk. The sheets were double spaced and French accent marks added by hand. When the large-print typewriter ribbon became faint, I really fought to read. Then my progress on tests slowed to a crawl. Noticing my additional difficulty, until the ribbon was replaced, Mrs. Delaney began printing over every letter on the page with a black pen. It was as if she were going to WILL me to see, by the sheer grit of her persistence. I took the sheets home and was able to study vocabulary lists, articles, pronouns, verb conjugations, and all matters French.

When it came time for tests, Mrs. Delaney would pass out purple, mimeographed sheets that had been reproduced from mimeo masters reused year to year, and then she handed her one of a kind, large-print masterwork to me. At first she would slip me the bundle of the weeks papers surreptitiously, but eventually with a flourish. My new champion had flair and attitude, eventually flaunting the papers for all to see before she dramatically swept them onto my desk. Her actions dared anyone to comment or mock. It became a badge of honor to have the thick stack of French to study–hand crafted by Mrs. Delaney. Her typing filled many notebooks and contained a complete low vision French course. Studying language requires precise reading, and her provision of accessible text provided me with the ability to succeed, pulling my study of French from the jaws of nearly certain failure. I was never more than an average French student, but Mrs. Delaney was a teacher who had made a singular and monumental commitment to my education. The following year, in ninth-grade French, Mrs. Delaney repeated her over the top efforts. I can't imagine how many hours she must have spent typing my materials on her own time. It was not required, and she was not recognized in any way for that Herculean undertaking. I am not certain that I ever fully expressed my gratitude. I have been unable to find her today to thank her properly. So instead, for the world to hear, and from the bottom of my heart-thank you Mrs. Delaney.

Chapter 5: Black Hole

The Decision

In early January 1963, my parents received a phone call from the state Board of Corrections, the state agency that managed Ohio's institutions for individuals with mental retardation. The agency also oversaw Ohio's prisons and roads. The month before, my parents had completed the required paperwork for Mark's institutionalization. Beginning that process triggered an indeterminate waiting period. Our parents had spoken to the intake worker at a state facility in Cleveland. She sold the idea to them–Mark would receive education, learn a trade, and be safe from bullying since he would live among others of his own "kind". Much sooner than expected, the January call informed them that a bed had "opened" at an institution in Columbus, one hundred fifty miles away. This was the only opportunity. If they turned this placement down, there would be no others offered. They were given less than a week to decide. They quickly planned to drive down, to take a tour, in preparation for Mark's move to Columbus.

The following Saturday, Mom and Dad were given the parents' tour of the Reception Center, a newly-constructed, pleasant and sun lit receiving center, where new residents stayed for the time required to assess their intellectual ability. But, by mistake, they were also led through a standard ward area where fifty adults languished, without activity, in horrifying conditions. Yet, in spite of the misery they witnessed, our parents had no alternative. Mark had no friends and no hope of schooling. Worse, the violence toward him by neighborhood kids was relentless and increasing. Mark had also begun to act out with occasional bursts of violent and oppositional behavior–undoubtedly a consequence of the brutal thuggery he endured. The road ahead promised isolation, danger, and unhappiness. Mark's explosive outbursts cast a long shadow on the family's future, as our parents imagined what would happen, as Mark would grow older and stronger.

After Mom and Dad's harrowing exposure to the reality in Columbus, we sat at the dinner table, in the early January evening's darkness. Bonnie and I were told that Mark would be moving in two days. We ate in heartsick silence. After dinner, my mother began to methodically label Mark's clothes, as she had been directed. I watched her working on the kitchen table, printing Mark's name and assigned number, with indelible ink, on every article of his clothing. This was the same table at which she had worked tirelessly, attempting to teach Mark to print his first name. Her face was a mask of tension, and her mouth was set in a tight line. During the next day—Mark's final twenty-four hours living at home—we lived every routine for the last time. He had a toy box with a padded lid covered in red vinyl, with a cheery circus elephant pattern. Mom removed the toys and carefully stacked all of Mark's clothing inside.

On Monday morning, January 14, 1963, everybody was up and getting ready to leave. Bonnie and I were going to school—Mark was going away forever. I said goodbye to Mark, and just before I left for school, I watched Dad back his white 1963 Pontiac Catalina out of the driveway and slowly drive away with Mom and Mark.

I came home from school and went to my bedroom. Mark was gone. For the first time in my life, I had my own room. I lay back on my bed and felt the guilty pleasure of being free of the responsibility of having Mark share my space. In my solitude, I listened to the familiar hissing and clanking of the steam radiators. Mom and Dad had not yet returned from their terrible trip, nor had they shared what they saw in that overcrowded ward in Columbus. There was no way for me to know then, the terror and sorrow that Mark would endure in that ghastly and depraved place. I was not experiencing my parents' spirit-bowing heartbreak or the fiery guilt of committing their youngest child to a state institution. That day marked a turning point in all of our lives. The crush of that granite, heavy burden had begun. He was only eight years old when he went into that prison, and he had done nothing but be born with a profound difference.

We were aware of private institutions, but my parents said that they would cost as much as perpetual enrollment at Cornell University. I didn't know how much Cornell would cost, but I suspected that it was very expensive and that there was no question about our family's inability to afford such an option. It was known that Rosemary Kennedy, President Kennedy's sister, lived in such a private institution. The only real choice we had was The Columbus State Institution for the Mentally Retarded. My mother said, with a shudder, that when you entered the grounds, passing through the high iron fence, a large concrete sign read, "Columbus State Institution for Morons, Imbeciles and Idiots". The decision my parents were forced to make, held devastating outcomes for them, as individuals, as well.

Alcohol became the anesthetic that bludgeoned their remorse, as they slid nightly into slurred oblivion.

FOR THE CRIME OF BEING DIFFERENT

For the crime of being different,
For the crime of being slow,
For the crime of not quite fitting in,
We sentence you to go -
Where you will be with others
Who are also of your kind-
Far, far away from city lights -
Out of sight and out of mind.

The sentence is quite final,
There can be no appeal,
You have no right of protest,
No defense nor free man's bail.
Within the institution,
Away from prying eyes
Drugs and brutal tedium
Will become a way of life.

Through the power of the people
And in the wisdom of the State,
We sentence you to go away,
And live your star-crossed fate -
Perhaps in time these walls will fall
These prisons will be shunned
But 'til that time this sentence stands,
The State's will shall be done.

For the crime of being different,
For the crime of being slow,
For the crime of not quite fitting in,
We sentence you to go -
Where you will be with others
Who are also of your kind.
Far, far away from city lights -
Out of sight and out of mind.
© Jeff Moyer 1988

First Visit

Mom and Dad signed the papers; Mark became a ward of the State of Ohio, and he was remanded to The Columbus State Institution for the Mentally Retarded. No trace, that Mark had ever lived in our home, remained. His clothing and his toys had vanished. Beginning then, a new, powerful heartache snaked constantly through our family's days. Relatives handled it in different ways. Uncles and aunts shook their heads and uncomfortably voiced platitudes, and words offering cold comfort. They repeated the doctor's grim counsel, at Mark's birth, that it would be better for the rest of the family if Mark were sent away. We deserved a normal life, they mumbled half-heartedly. Mom's parents, Mama and Daddy Smith, said it was God's will. Grandma Jane worked in a drugstore, but during her time off, Mark had been her first priority. She cried and begged my folks to change their minds. She offered to quit her job and take care of Mark full time. That was a hopeless and impossible proposal. Grandma Jane was nearing retirement and old age, and her eventual passing made her offer a temporary solution at best. Her emotional pressure created constant friction, as Mom and Dad mounted a bitter defense supporting their unwanted, impossible decision.

The institution's policy was that "settling in" required a six week period without any family interaction. During that time, there was no communication from Columbus and no relief from the gloom that shrouded our home. Mark, like all new residents, was living temporarily within The Adjustment Center, the new and modern building that contained the sleeping rooms, eating area, and diagnostic facilities that had become the complete extent of Mark's new world.

On the first Saturday in March, my parents, Grandma Jane, and I drove the one hundred fifty miles to Columbus, to visit Mark within the confines of the Adjustment Center. Bonnie had a Saturday job at Woolworth's and was unable to go. The long drive followed State Route 1, the asphalt truck road to Columbus. We went to the institution's administration building, at the center of the cluster of mammoth brick buildings, on the vast grounds. The blackened old buildings were all three stories tall, and the institutional green hallways smelled of strong disinfectant and urine.

We found the small office that served as the portal for family contact, divided by a low wooden half wall. A plain young woman sat at a desk behind the barrier. Dully and officiously, she found Mark's index card, and handed it to us with instructions to bring it back at the end of the visit. She gave us directions to the Adjustment Center. We were allowed to bring food and toys and were permitted to visit for a half hour. We walked to the Adjustment Center where we were met by a staff member who led us into the small visiting room, furnished with half a dozen cold metal chairs and a sturdy gray table.

We sat down and Mom and Grandma Jane began unpacking the sandwiches, green grapes, potato chips, cookies, milk, and coffee that they had brought for our lunch. In a few minutes, Mark was brought in. His appearance was shocking; his previously neat hair was now shaggy and unkempt. Normally lean, he was starkly thin. When he saw us, he began to cry inconsolably and was gathered in my mother's arms. She cried too, as did Grandma Jane. When Mark saw Grandma Jane, he fell into her waiting arms and continued sobbing. He was very hungry and ate a great deal. We each took turns forcing the happy talk that filled the minutes, creating the appearance of normalcy in the midst of this horribly abnormal scene.

A brief thirty minutes later, the same staff member who had ushered Mark into the room opened the door and told us the visit was over. She asked us if we would like to briefly see where Mark lived. We followed her down a long hallway. The sleeping area was like a small barracks, with perhaps eight beds, with lockers between them. There were large scale cartoon characters high on the wall. Mark was furtive as we stood for the long moment, taking in the room. High windows let in the gray light of late winter. Mark was told to say goodbye to us. He again began to cry, this time with a panic that sent chills down my back. The staff person restrained him and told us to leave quickly. We walked back down the long hallway to the parking lot, with Mark's anguished screams echoing behind us. The drive back to Cleveland was silent. My mother bit her lower lip and smoked one cigarette after another. My father, stone faced, also chain smoked as he drove. Grandma Jane sat in the back seat with me and quietly cried. The drive to Columbus would always be a hard one. It took three and a half hours, and there was only one restaurant. Roadside rest facilities were crude, half-walled, multi-stalled outhouses.

A couple weeks after our first visit, we were notified that Mark's diagnostic period was over and that he had been moved to a regular, euphemistically-called "cottage". It was decided that Grandma Jane and I would make this first visit. After the long drive, we went directly to the institution's reception office. This time, Grandma Jane would have none of the directives given by the woman behind the low wall. We were told to have a seat and that someone would bring Mark to us. Grandma Jane said she wanted to see where Mark lived. She demanded to know where the building was that housed her grandson. She was relentless and, reluctantly, the woman gave us directions–through the inner hallways, to the adjacent institutional building.

We walked up an inside staircase. The gray granite stairs each had four deeply rounded depressions, two per side, worn into the stone by the shuffling feet of unbroken generations of institutionalized souls, going to and from meals. We walked to the third floor and knocked on a heavy metal door, with chicken wire embedded within a thick, glass panel. After several knocks of increasing force, a white clad attendant rattled a large ring of keys and opened the door's heavy lock. We were led into an enormous room, with two rows of shabby, iron frame beds crowded along opposing walls. Fifty boys, about Mark's age, saw us and rushed at us. They hugged us, grabbed us, and swarmed from every side. My mind staggered. It was foreign, overwhelming, and frightening. I repeatedly scanned the pressing throng of children, and then I saw him. There was my brother. Mark was three rings of boys back, his arms reaching toward us-one boy among fifty. His cry was lost in the din of shouts, wordless grunts, and raw exclamations of unmet human need. Somehow we extricated ourselves and Mark from the unwashed throng of boys and were led by the attendant to a bleak narrow room for family visits.

This time, Mark was not wearing his own clothes. He was dressed in threadbare, stained rags, and he wore a pair of old, scuffed leather shoes we had never seen before. His hair was filthy; he had the wild and greasy look of a child from a third world orphanage. We dressed him in his own clothes. We had settled into grim understanding, when his clothes had been shipped back to us, when he was moved from the Adjustment Center. After Mark had changed clothes, we sat, while he hungrily ate the lunch that we had brought. Grandma Jane clipped his fingernails and toenails, and I played the manic part of the entertainer forced into joyless service. I recognized the need to try to help lift the moment, through sheer force of will.

When we left, Mark again screamed and was roughly restrained as we made our exit. Again, my grandmother cried all the way back to Cleveland and repeated shreds of her futile offer to quit work and take care of Mark.

Taking the Stage

As I began seventh-grade, my casual friends were all the guys with whom I had grown up. They were all athletes. Kirk Junior High School had Varsity and Junior Varsity sports year- round: football, basketball, and then track. I walked the two miles to school with those guys, all of whom played after school sports. But I walked the long walk home alone every afternoon. I really wanted to belong after my sixth-grade dislocation at James A. Garfield Elementary School.

Seventh-grade presented social barriers in my class schedule as well. Decisions the school administration had made, concerning the conditions of my enrollment, had created ongoing separateness. Due to the school's fear of my being injured or assumptions about my not being able to do the work, I was not allowed to take Wood Shop, Print Shop, Metal Shop, or Mechanical Drawing. I was allowed to take Gym, but many of the activities in gym class were impossible. Anything involving fast moving balls was terrifying: I did not play football nor baseball but attempted volleyball and basketball. I was afraid of wrestling since it held the possibility of a blow to the head, but I was cut out of so many gym activities that I chose to wrestle anyway, in spite of the risk. The young gym teacher paired me, in my 139 weight class with Eugene, the tough muscular kid who had thrown me up against the lockers, demanding money on the first day of school. The gym teacher slapped the mat, signaling the start of the match. I'll never forget Eugene's hateful snarl and hypnotically churning arms. He moved like a cougar, hard-muscled and menacing. In a flash, he lunged violently, threw me onto the mat, and quickly pinned me. Powerless, my body was jerked over my shoulders and head, wrenching my neck. So it often went.

Sports and manual arts provided an informal male initiation and rite of passage. Since I joined no sports teams and took no shop classes, I was not included in the circle of other boys' experiences and friendship

85

connections. I wanted to belong, as all kids do, but I seemed to be in a world quite apart.

Junior High did offer exposure to the organized arts including theatre and musical groups. In seventh-grade, I had my first experience with Student Theater. The whole school attended performances of plays produced by actors from the eighth and ninth-grades. I loved the plays and admired the older students on stage. They memorized their lines and then so confidently and convincingly became the characters they portrayed. In the safety of the darkened auditorium I would sneak out my monocular to watch the players on stage. The male lead, two years my senior, was one of the serious actors. He was confident and self-directed, and I looked up to him. I silently wondered if I could ever be like him. I wanted to join the ranks of those performing actors, striding under the stage lights.

Eighth-grade began with the predictable routines that had been laid down in seventh, but I was a year older, and new opportunities began to develop. A couple of weeks after the beginning of eighth-grade, it was announced that anyone wanting to audition for a part in the fall play should report to the auditorium after school. I gathered my books and jacket from my locker and found a seat in the auditorium, with a few dozen other hopefuls, waiting to audition. The high arched windows were open to the football practice field, and I could hear the yelling of coaches, and the grunts, and the crack of shoulder pads and helmets, as the football team practiced their punishing plays. The previous year, I had walked past football practice every afternoon and felt emptiness about not being allowed to engage in that rough and tumble tumult. That afternoon, with the quiet expectation of the audition at hand, I hoped that I was opening the door to a new kind of identity, as a performing member of the stage community. Mr. Martin, the direct and thoughtful drama teacher, walked to the center of the wooden stage, stopped, and spoke to us in a strong voice, telling us how auditions would work. In small groups, we would be given scripts, assigned parts, and then be directed to read a scene from the play on the spot. There wasn't much to it, only reading out loud with ease, comfort, believability, and poise. My heart thudded heavily, and my hopes sank. I couldn't read out loud fluently, or even at a normal rate. My limited vision had made reading out loud one of my greatest fears and embarrassments, since early elementary school. Now my lack of that very visual ability was going to exclude me from a thing I really wanted and believed I could do. Reading aloud was an exercise in both futility and misery.

Mr. Martin had instructed us to put our names on his clipboard. In small groups, he called the names of those who had signed in. I had not, being too ashamed to so publicly demonstrate my limited vision. I would have had to find the clipboard, get out my magnifier, press my face to the clipboard, figure out where to write and write my name, knowing I would not be able to stay on the line, and then try, nonchalantly, to find my seat. Auditions began. Mr. Martin read the lines of any missing character. Absorbed and nervous, I observed a whole range of theater craft. I waited.

Finally, hours after the auditions had begun; I sat alone in the darkening auditorium as the last students left the stage. Mr. Martin glanced at the clipboard and then at me. He asked if I had signed in. I said no. I asked to talk to him. I walked down the center aisle and approached the stage. I wasn't sure we were alone so I spoke in a quiet voice, not wanting to be overheard. With the old familiar shame rising within me, but driven by burning desire, I told him that I really wanted a chance but had low vision and couldn't read out loud very well. I promised that if I got a part, I would be much better after I learned my lines. Mr. Martin told me to walk up onto the stage. He handed me a script and said to do the best I could. My cheeks burned. Certain that failure would follow I pulled the thick magnifier out of my back pocket and lowered my face to the page. I haltingly stammered and slowly and poorly read the part I was given, as Mr. Martin filled in all of the other characters' lines. After a few excruciating exchanges, he asked if there was any way to make the print bigger. I told him that I had a large print typewriter, but that Mrs. Delaney, my French teacher, was using it. He said he would talk to her. He spoke to me in a relaxed manner, like a kindly uncle. Mr. Martin said that he would consider my audition, based on factors other than my sight reading ability, and that I should come back in a few days when the cast would be announced. He put his hand on my shoulder and thanked me for coming to the audition. I left feeling the warmth of renewed hope.

On the prescribed afternoon, everyone who had auditioned gathered in the auditorium after school. With background thumps and cracks of football practice, Mr. Martin read the new cast of the play: *Mrs. McThing*. I had been given the part of Poison Eddie Shellenbach, the lead comic villain. It was a wonderful part. Mr. Martin handed out the dog-eared scripts to the cast, handing me a Mrs. Delaney-esque, thick crisp stack of white typing paper, containing my large print script. The script was generated from the mechanical, large print typewriter that he must have borrowed from Mrs. Delaney. He had, no doubt, spent numerous long hours pounding on the stiffly-sprung machine to create my accessible script. Like Mrs. Delaney, Mr. Martin understood my extraordinary needs, and he was not afraid of the mountain of humble, extra work necessary to meet them. Although I barely knew him, I saw a teacher worthy of admiration. Mr. Martin had lost several fingers in a World War II explosion. I learned in later life, when we had become friends, that he had typed that script with one finger.

Play practice was part study hall, when one was not required on stage, part social hall as we whispered to others not actively engaged, and, of course, under Mr. Martin's direction, part intense interaction with the other actors as we learned our lines, our blocking, and how to react to the other characters in the play. New friendships developed and old ones deepened as we slowly became unified. We melded into one cohesive group: actors, stage crew, prompters, prop handlers, and the others who would make the magic of the play come alive for the audience. After play practice, I would walk home with other cast members. We tended to be the oddballs and lone-rangers that didn't have a broad circle of friends. But we had become a group unto ourselves. I recall walking past the football practice one evening, and thinking that I no longer felt the longing I had, to belong to the team. I now belonged to a different team.

I spent hours at home memorizing my lines, with help from Connie, Bonnie and Mom. The goal was not only to master my own lines but also to know the other characters' lines. We were responsible for our own costumes, and I managed a rough approximation of a gangster's outfit. My Dad lent me a fine white silk tie, for my navy blue shirt. I added my striped sports coat and my narrow-brimmed Alpine hat. The resulting ensemble gave me the look of a teenage mobster on a budget.

The play was performed for the school, after lunch, and for the community the following evening. The afternoon that I first stood on stage, under the lights, in costume, with a live audience of silent students sitting in the dark beyond the stage lights, I felt a sense of wonder and belonging. My limited vision was invisible, and I was participating in a group activity that took courage, concentration, teamwork, and long weeks of focus. I was succeeding. I felt a sense of freedom and happiness that I had never known.

Ninth-grade

Ninth-grade began in the fall of 1963. The burgeoning pattern of junior high was fully established, and I was singing in the choir, getting leads in plays, and participating in student council. I had developed some avoidance strategies to hide my low vision. I continued the pretense of acting as if I could see and had learned to look down while walking in the halls, in order to avoid actually missing a girl's smile, and being misunderstood because of my lack of response. But, with my practiced downward gaze, I hoped that they would conclude I was lost in thought.

I returned to The Cleveland Society for the Blind's Low Vision Clinic and this time discovered a miniature, silver telescope more powerful than the opera glass monocular from a few years earlier–ten times magnification compared to six power. I liked the stronger scope because I could see greater detail with it and because it could be completely hidden within my closed fist. My convoluted logic was that although it would appear strange to be looking at the blackboard through my fist, it was more acceptable than using a big optical aid, thereby admitting low vision. The stronger scope was more demanding in its requirements and quite tricky to use. I still needed to be more than thirteen feet from whatever I was viewing. During a class when I couldn't get a clear focus on the board, I discovered that if I unscrewed the eyepiece and held it absolutely steady with my thumb and first finger, slightly away from the remaining mirrors and lenses, I could focus inside of the thirteen feet focal boundary, which gave me more flexibility concerning where I might sit in the classroom. It was very hard to do though, and I had to hold my hand absolutely still without moving either piece of the telescope. Being able to read the board also depended on several other factors outside of my control: harsh fluorescent lighting, the teacher's handwriting, blackboard erasures, sunlight, time constraints, and content all could have devastating effects. Even under ideal circumstances, the actual portion of the blackboard that I was viewing was very small. It was much smaller than with the bigger, less powerful monocular. The combination of the absolute demands of the optical system's steadiness and the small target zone resulted in very slow blackboard reading and note taking.

That fall, I had moved into a surprising position of modest leadership. I campaigned for, and was actually elected, vice president of Student Council. All officers enjoyed the prestige and honor of working behind the sales counter at Kirk's bookstore. We would take turns selling pencils, pens, erasers, paper, Kirk book covers, and such, from behind the bookstore's caged wall. Students would cue up in the long bookstore line, before school and during lunch periods. A friendly and popular Civics teacher and Student Council Advisor oversaw our area. The bookstore was like a chummy clubhouse with a very select membership.

But I was carrying on a very tense and difficult masquerade. Always embarrassed about reactions to my misdirected right eye, I would glance at each customer and look quickly away. Transactions usually required making change. I strained to identify the coins without holding them too close to my face. Guessing what had been handed to me resulted in ongoing mistakes. I had not yet figured out how to identify coins by touch. In short, the job was error filled and nerve wracking. I concocted an elaborate rationale that I presented to the other officers working the bookstore. I suggested that it would be more efficient if we worked in pairs: one interacting with the customer and the other (always me), filling the order. My fellow officers (and friends) must have recognized my plight because they agreed to my plan without comment. I was very grateful for their help and support.

Ernie had become my friend over the course of junior high. He had two older brothers, and together they had amassed a wonderful collection of 45 RPM records. That resource and his initiative led to the very cool job of disc jockey at the YMCA Friday night dances. Ernie needed a second guy, to free him from the turntable to dance, so he invited me to work for him. I eagerly agreed to the wonderful opportunity. Every Friday after school, we would go to his house and then to the record store where Ernie would buy five new records, at a dollar apiece. The disc jockey job paid ten bucks a week. Five went to keeping his collection fresh, and then, three to Ernie and two to me.

Every Friday, we would lug his record collection to the Y and set up for the dance. We sat on a low platform, within a square of collapsible, long tables. We positioned the microphone, records, and turntable against the wall. Guys and girls would come up and lean on the tables, asking for specific songs–requesting a ladies' choice–or just to visit. That social proximity allowed me to identify the girls with whom I wanted to dance.

Before I became one of the disc jockeys, it was really difficult. I would slowly walk around, as casually as possible, approaching everyone as closely as I dared, straining to identify who was who. That was a stomach churning task, but I forced myself because I loved to dance. But working with Ernie as disc jockey, the problem was solved. We would take turns announcing. That was my first experience working at a microphone, and I thoroughly enjoyed it.

Like nearly everyone else, my social activities were the most important element in my school life. Scholastics required extraordinary attention and were fraught with exceptional difficulty. The visual tasks of math had always been rigorous, but in ninth-grade they became much more demanding. Algebra was the class, and Mr. Faulkenstein was the teacher. He did not seem to like teaching and seemed to dislike nearly all students. I certainly felt that he didn't care for me very much. On the first day, he challenged me about my need to use the small silver telescope. For the first time, I could sit at the back of the room and still see the blackboard. Mr. Faulkenstein wrote with a clear neat hand and never erased, which made reading his board notations possible, with my telescope, from the back of the room. The higher the power of magnification, the smaller was the viewing area. Mr. Faulkenstein could not understand why I chose to sit far away if I saw so poorly. As I struggled to read and take notes, with my face pressed to the desk, he would shout at me to wake up, and I would stutter out an explanation, feeling a mix of shame and anger at his affront to my way of seeing.

I was in his class after lunch on Friday, November 22, 1963. He had just handed out a test to everyone, and we were settling into the chore of its work. A girl in the class, who had been working in the principal's office, came in a few minutes late and asked Mr. Faulkenstein, in a trembling voice, if it was true that President Kennedy had been shot. I remember his strict and cold response. He flatly responded that we were to pay attention to the test. A murmur rippled through the class, which he squelched with another enjoinder to get back to work, which we did. A few minutes later, an announcement came over the public address system. The principal somberly reported that the President had been assassinated and that school was dismissed. The test remained half completed; Mr. Faulkenstein scowled as we handed him our incomplete tests and left the classroom.

Mr. Faulkenstein kept his eye on me. Just before Christmas vacation, I gave him the opportunity he needed to exercise his particular form of rough justice. My seating position at the back of the class was heady. Never before had I been in that outer sphere of the teacher/student relative gravity, and I took advantage of it. I wrote a note to one of my friends and passed it to the guy next to me to pass along. Mr. Faulkenstein saw the note leave my hand, and he intercepted it. He unfolded the paper, read it silently, and then read it aloud. He had me. As I gazed at the blackboard through my monocular, he suddenly filled the telescope's field of view. Staring unblinking down at me, his laser beam cold blue eyes burning, he ordered me to stay after class for a swat.

Most of the men teachers kept paddles—two-foot long wooden boards with handle grips for the purpose of delivering stinging corporal punishment as deemed necessary. I had never been swatted, but the fear of the experience riveted my attention throughout the remainder of the class. After everyone else had filed out, Mr. Faulkenstein gripped his oaken plank and slapped it menacingly into the flat of his hand. He told me to bend over and grip the side of his desk. I did as I was told and, without fanfare, he delivered a quick and hard blow to my buttocks with the paddle. It stung like fire, and I picked up my books and walked out, not wanting to give him the satisfaction of a reaction. I felt like I had been initiated into the ranks of the bad boys—the fraternity of those who knew the sting of the paddle, the real pain of punishment. From then on, I used my telescope with defiance, in Mr. Faulkenstein's class, quietly daring him to question the veracity of its necessity. But I never again passed a note.

First Holidays

The first year that Mark was gone, he remained at The Columbus State Institution from January until late November. The Wednesday before Thanksgiving, our parents drove to Columbus to bring Mark home for the holiday weekend. They arrived back at around 4:00 p.m., just as I arrived home from school. Mark's presence, back in the house, was stressful for everyone, but we all played our roles and pretended that all was well. But all was not well. Ten months in the confined, cramped, barren, and violent environment had changed him. Mark exploded into the house, full of a frantic energy that was startling and unsettling. He ran from room to room, floor to floor, then nervously settled in front of the television to watch the local children's programs before dinner. Grandma Jane arrived, and Mark ran to her crying. His attention was temporarily focused on the toys she had brought for him and her smiling talk. Dinner was served, but Mark was unable to sit still long enough to eat much. He bolted from the table and ran out of the room. Mom followed him to try to coax him back to the table, but he became difficult. The evening was spent handling Mark's resistance and oppositional behavior.

My little brother needed a normal haircut and a thorough bath. As per our monthly visits, he also needed to have his fingernails and toenails cut. Mom and Grandma Jane gave him a bath and shampooed his filthy hair. He was put to bed rather early, and he fell heavily to sleep. Despite the early hour, we were all emotionally exhausted from Mark's demanding behavior.

The next day was Thanksgiving, and Mark's intensity had lessened. However, it would bubble up episodically, and I sensed his anger roiling just under the surface. Grandma Jane and Dad's brother, Uncle Chuck, and his family were going to come over for Thanksgiving dinner. It was early afternoon, and Mark and I were settled in front of the television set to watch the parade. The front door opened, and Uncle Chuck, Aunt Simi and our cousins, Kit and Susie walked in. They all greeted Mark in upbeat, excited voices. Without warning, Mark bolted up the stairs. I ran after him. He ran into our bedroom and violently slammed the door in my face. I opened the door and quickly stepped in. Mark was trembling and breathing heavily. With a sudden motion he pulled off his glasses, folded the earpieces down, and gripped them with both hands. Then he broke the glasses, snapping the nosepiece and both temple pieces in one sudden flex of his nine-year old hands. He threw the broken glasses onto the floor. Then, without a pause, he reached down and grabbed the bottom of his heavy oak bed frame.

Mark was a slight little boy, but I was about to witness an unbelievable and alarming demonstration of his astonishing strength. With a superhuman burst of energy, he flipped the entire bed into the air. I stood within a foot of the bed, on the opposite side, and I saw the fully made mattress, box spring, and four poster bed frame, flip upside down in mid-air, land back on the floor where it had stood, but now, completely upside down. The bed hit with an incredible crash, narrowly missing me. My parents bolted up the stairs as I ran around the bed and took Mark into my arms. He sobbed. I was holding him as our parents burst into the bedroom to stare dumbfounded. Mark's crying was inconsolable, and my mother took over, holding and rocking him back and forth in her arms as he wailed. The look on my mother's face was unrelenting anguish, frustration, and pain. I helped Dad right the bed. Then we walked heavily downstairs. No one asked what had happened. The one question everyone did ask was if Mark was all right. I answered that he was, although I knew it was not true. Nothing was all right. Eventually, Mark came back downstairs. We tiptoed through the rest of the day, no one talking about the earlier eruption or the emotional pain burning in every heart. The rest of the weekend was spent in the awkward dance of faux normalcy, and on Sunday my parents drove Mark back to Columbus. They said that when he recognized the institution, he began to scream in horror.

Christmas was a repeat of Thanksgiving's tension and difficulty, but with gifts. At the end of Mark's several days of Christmas vacation, his new clothes and toys were bundled up for the long drive. But this time, Mark understood that the trip home had been a brief reprieve from his new life behind the locked doors of The Columbus State Institution for the Mentally Retarded. Throughout the torture of the hours driving back, he screamed, kicked, and hit with terrible ferocity. He was returning to prison. The new clothes and toys, each labeled in indelible ink with Mark's name and number, were left in the Administration Building, along with Mark, who was restrained by an attendant as he struggled, screamed, howled, and violently sobbed. The gifts were never seen again.

My parents drove silently back to Cleveland. Dad said that Mom wept the entire way home. When they arrived, Dad grimly swore that he would never put Mom through that torture again. He flatly said that Mark would never again come home, and in the eighteen remaining years of his incarceration in Columbus, Mark never spent another night on the outside. Christmases and Thanksgiving dinners were quieter during those years, but we all knew that Mark was spending that day suffering, away from his family and in a world without holidays.

In 1998, on the day before Christmas, Mark and I were sharing a quiet afternoon in my home. I asked him what he remembered about Christmas in Columbus. Mark's memories were usually a jumble of impressions that he could not sort, concerning time or circumstance. Answers usually could not be relied upon for their veracity. But this time, he responded with a five-word summary which, without a doubt, gave a vivid and terribly sad account, accurate, and touching on many notes in his chord of memory. Mark said, "The boys beat me up."

Madcap Mom

The fires of protracted suffering, and the cold water of necessity, tempered Mom's fierce love. She led a life of constant sorrows, but she

94

somehow found the flexibility and grounding to incorporate humor into our everyday life. Cousins looked forward to family get-togethers and said that her zaniness reminded them of Lucille Ball. Mom loved costumes and theme parties, for which she could let her imagination and creativity run wild. She had a wonderful ear for mimicry and she could take on an exaggerated persona to great comic effect. She could sing in a faux operatic style and boom out send-ups of pompous characters, which never failed to please.

Mom's brother, Norman, lived nearby, and they often spoke on the phone. Cut from the same cloth, they would occasionally prank each other with vocal disguises, attempting to draw the other into an unknowing conversation, using their pretend personas. One evening, Mom answered the phone, and a man's nasal voice introduced himself as the new head of a church committee. Believing it was Norman, Mom immediately responded to the caller with one of her pretentious put-on characters. The caller hesitated and then carried on. He asked if Mom would be willing to serve on the church's new committee. I could hear her end of the conversation as she enthusiastically offered to co-chair the committee and suggested some absurd gala they might undertake. Well into the conversation, Mom recognized that it was not Norman on the line but, in reality, a most befuddled church member. She did co-chair the newly established committee.

Dad was on the road two, or even three weeks, each month, and during those long weeks, Mom would soldier on with work and family routines as a single parent. One evening, when I was fourteen, I was watching television in the living room, when I heard Mom call from upstairs. She asked me if she could borrow my guitar. Perplexed, I took my instrument upstairs and handed it to her through the door to my parents' bedroom. She thanked me and closed the door. Having no idea why Mom would want my guitar, I returned to my program. A few minutes later, Mom called from upstairs and asked me to come to the staircase. As I did, from the second floor came the sound of Mom chordlessly strumming my guitar and singing "Dominique", a popular song of the day, recorded in French. As I stood looking in disbelief at the staircase, down Mom came, high stepping and continuing to sing in a very funny voice, in her best remembered high school French. The staircase gave her the stage for a perfect dramatic entrance, and she had asked me to come close in order to see the moment of comic theater. I could first see her kicking legs wearing Dad's black knee-high dress socks, then her long Navy blue bathrobe, my guitar, and, finally,

95

the crowning glory of her costume. "The Singing Nun" had recorded the song, and Mom had taken a white bath towel and fashioned a nun's wimple around her face and head. Her comic interlude was really hilarious, and we stood face to face, laughing uproariously at her impromptu performance. Many comedians know lifetimes etched with tragedy. Mom's humor was, no doubt, deepened by that root. Regardless, it provided many moments of relief and uplift to our reeling family.

Parents' Decline

When Mark was institutionalized in 1963, my dad was forty-one and my Mom was thirty-nine. I turned fourteen the February following that dark day in January when Mark was moved to Columbus. Mom and Dad had always had an active social life, primarily connected to three other couples, the men having all worked together in the early fifties. Regular parties rotated from home to home. When it became our turn, dishes of chocolates and party mix would be set out, along with shrimp and cocktail sauce–an extravagance otherwise not present in our modest lives. Drinks would be poured, and soon the couples would be singing old standards in three part harmony, accompanied by Dad's ukulele or Orpha's guitar.

But, from the time Mark was institutionalized, a slow change crept over my parents as heavy drinking became a regular evening activity. My parents would arrive home from work at about 5:30 p.m., and the first drinks of straight gin or vodka on the rocks would be poured. They would drink until dinner and then until bedtime. Parties, once celebrations, began to end badly. Dad frequently became too drunk to drive, or even walk without assistance. Mom, on those miserable outings, would silently drive us home. Her drinking, behind closed doors, kept pace with my Dad's, but in social settings, she was able to put on the brakes and maintain her ability to function.

Holidays were the worst. One Christmas afternoon, we were celebrating at the home of their best friends who lived right down the street and who were members of my parent's tight social circle. I was busy playing a new board game with my sister and their daughter, Kathy, when my mother quietly told us to get our coats. She was visibly upset and told us to get in the car. We said a quick goodbye to Kathy, put on our coats and walked outside in time to see the host and his adult son struggling to get my Dad up the basement steps and into the car. Dad was so drunk that his head

96

lolled backward and his legs buckled. They held the car door open, and Dad fell through the door and onto the front seat. Mom drove the few blocks home. My mother and I somehow got Dad up the stairs and into their bedroom where he passed out. It was 3:00 p.m. on Christmas afternoon. Variations on this became a depressing repeated tableau of all holidays.

Every four weeks, either my parents or Grandma Jane would drive to Columbus to visit Mark. I went every month. The reality of those visits was so harsh, the circumstances within which Mark existed so unbelievably depraved, that we would be emotionally bludgeoned by the experience. When my parents arrived home after those Saturday ordeals, stiff drinks (they drank nothing but stiff drinks) would be poured immediately upon walking back into the house. I watched them with growing concern and despair. Their social world shriveled. Their circle of friends became distant. I suffered my own embarrassment and shame for their drunkenness.

Connie was my evening reader throughout junior high. On school nights she would arrive at around 7:00 p.m. to read for two hours. Connie lived three blocks away, and in mild weather she would walk to and from the house. But when Cleveland's weather was inclement, her parents would drive her to our house. Initially, my father would drive her home. One winter night, Connie arrived in the midst of a heavy snow. By the time she was getting ready to leave, the snow was really coming down, and driving winds made walking miserable. Several inches of new snow had made sidewalks difficult. My father told Connie that he would give her a ride home. It was obvious that Dad should not be driving. His speech was slurred and thick. Connie hesitated and gave me a furtive glance. She responded that it was not necessary and she would just call her folks but my father insisted. With an obvious stumble down the few stairs to the back door, and with a forceful injunction to Connie that startled both of us; he walked out into the weather to get his car. Connie's looked turned woeful and she put on her scarf, coat, and mittens, following Dad into the storm. I was angry, ashamed, and very confused by my Dad's behavior. He became difficult when he drank heavily, and I found myself, more and more, trying to anticipate his moods. I would attempt to humor him the best I could, but his truculence made my efforts futile. A few minutes later, with relief, I saw Dad's car pull back into the snow-filled driveway. But the incident's trauma had lasting results. After that evening, Connie always arranged to have her mother pick her up.

I went to my Uncle Norman and Aunt Marinda, who lived nearby and poured out my heart to them, sharing my concern about my parents' drinking. They responded with an airy dismissal. My uncle told me that their drinking was within normal range, and my folks just enjoyed a drink now and then. But the fact was that they drank heavily every night. My father bought full cases of vodka and gin. Every evening he emptied a quart of vodka, while my mother managed to put away one-half to two-thirds of a bottle of gin. On Sunday evenings, Dad would go to the garage and smash the week's collection of empty bottles into small pieces in a heavy metal trash can. I suppose that Dad must have been ashamed about nosey neighbors or trash collectors seeing how much had been drunk in the Moyer household that week. The sound of breaking glass was a familiar and dark weekly reminder of the volume of alcohol they consumed.

Mark's ghastly circumstances inflicted wounds that festered on my parents' hearts. My brother was moved to a third floor ward, accessible only by a stark black fire escape made of spaced iron slats. One could see the ground through the open gaps of the stairs and landings. My mother was terrified of heights. She would always tremble from the savage emotional trauma, amplified by her required climb up the fire escape and across the final landing, with the ground visible thirty feet below. I remember her slow and terrified steps, as she forced herself to face one of her deepest fears, in order to endure fresh horror and heartbreak. Early on in Mark's institutionalization, he had begun to show the signs of raw physical violence. Deep scratches on his face, neck, and arms, bruises in shades from purple to green and yellow, black eyes and split lips were constant testaments to the violence of his daily life. Filthy hair, absent personal hygiene, and threadbare, stained clothes from a common bag, were always shocking. In a ritual transformation, Mark would change into his clean clothes, and properly fitting shoes that we had brought. Finally, he would put on a watch, ring, and sunglasses. We would leave the institution and go to a local restaurant where he would hungrily eat, gobbling his food. The speed suggested the demands of the lawless congregate meals he endured. Sometimes a new toy would be purchased before he would be driven back to the locked ward. There, his own clothing would be stripped off to be taken home. His rightful clothes would be exchanged for the hideous rags that were his institutional "uniform". Whatever gifts we had given him would be stolen within a matter of a day or two. We all felt a terrible helplessness about Mark's situation that continued to deteriorate even further over time. My relationship with my parents was worsening too, as the distance between us gaped, with their nightly drunken spiral into oblivion.

My father's drinking had a more negative impact on his relationship with me than did my mother's. His personality changed when he drank, and the harsh emotional distance that resulted, created alienation for me that added to my overall sense of disconnection from a normal, predictable life. One evening when I was fourteen, my Dad made me stand at one end of our kitchen as he stood at the other. My mother stood, cooking at the stove in the middle of the kitchen. Dad told me to look at him. I complied. But he responded angrily that I was not looking him in the eye, and in an even more demanding tone, Dad commanded me to look him in the eye. "I *am* looking at your eyes, Dad," I replied.

"No, you're not!" he bellowed, "Look at me!"

"Dad, I *am* looking at you," I pleaded.

My father became even more drunkenly insistent, loud and hard. I knew that it must have seemed to him that I was not looking him in the eye. Strangers often made that mistake. But this was my Dad. Convinced that I was intentionally avoiding eye contact, Dad lectured me about the importance of looking another man in the eye. He stated that in the business world, avoiding direct eye contact was the mark of a liar. Mom stood at the stove, drinking, cooking, and saying nothing. His anger and accusation, and Mom's quiescence, made me feel alone, without family support when it mattered. Once again, I was on my own, being harshly lectured about an attribute that was misunderstood–something I hated and could not control. Such episodes widened the distance between my father and me. I vaguely understood that my folks drank to numb the unrelenting guilt and the pain of Mark's circumstances. I could imagine that they felt something like distraction–not relief–but a numbing of the fierce emotions that ravaged their days.

As the dismal cycle of their drunkenness deepened, our home life narrowed into an ever-more isolating darkness. My parents' dependence on alcohol blotted out all other possibilities, ending their previous social life and crushing any semblance of normal family life. They sat wordless, evening after evening, drinking, smoking, and staring at a stupefying stream of situation comedies, variety shows, and movies. Most evenings, after my homework, I would join them watching television. One evening, I walked into the kitchen to get a snack, during a commercial break in the program we were watching. My Dad had gone into the kitchen a minute before, to pour himself another glass of vodka. There stood my father with the upended vodka bottle in his mouth. His throat worked in long gulps as he downed the straight liquor. He saw me and silently went back to shakily pouring another tall glass of vodka on the rocks for himself.

Evenings never varied, and mornings had become grim and silent exercises in dull routine as my parents prepared for work, both red-eyed and painfully hung over. They wordlessly arose, smoked the day's first cigarettes, showered, dressed for work, and drank black coffee. My father's handsome face was bloated, and a red rash of broken blood vessels blotched across his cheeks and nose. My folks and I became strangers. The one thing that united us was enduring the punishing reality of Mark's hell.

All of us knew that the institution was a brutal prison. I increasingly felt the stirrings of outrage–the fire of the advocate–burning within me. I wanted Mark to have a better life. Once, I asked my mother why we didn't just get Mark and bring him home. Mom said, through a tight grimace, that the State representative had warned her that the door swung only one way– that Mark could be taken out–but once out, he would never get back in. Mom told me that she knew she couldn't handle Mark's outbursts, and she didn't want to saddle Bonnie or me with Mark's care when she and my father were gone. The tension in her voice made it clear that there could be no further discussion on the matter. My parents held down their jobs, drank themselves into unconsciousness every night, and suffered the unending grief and sorrow that only those in their hideous life circumstances could understand.

Chapter 6: Force Fields

The Well

In 1965, I turned sixteen and joined the community that had been calling out to me for years. I had been learning folk songs since I was ten and borrowed Norman and Marinda's copy of *Calypso* by Harry Belafonte. At eleven, I had been given a Kingston Trio album. My early ukulele repertoire included many of their songs, and pop hits of the day, along with standards taught to me by my father.

When I was thirteen, my musical perspective shifted dramatically when I first heard traditional blues. *Van Ronk Sings* opened that dimensional door. My cousin Kit, Uncle Chuck's daughter, three years older than I, introduced me to that record and many others. When I put the needle down on that album, a compilation of traditional, hardcore blues, I was transfixed and transported. The album's songs had overwhelming power–howling lyrics and driving, inconsolable guitars. The song's stories were of wandering, junkie's misery, unfaithful lovers, motherless children, and death by vigilante. Dave Van Ronk's voice of suffering spoke to me. I bought the album and began to learn the songs such as "He Was a Friend of Mine", "Cocaine Blues", and "Tell Old Bill". The heartbreaking pathos of those songs gave me an expressive outlet for the real pain of my own life. For Christmas, Uncle Chuck's family gave me *The Times They Are a Changin'*, an early Bob Dylan album. After beginning with the uke at age eleven, I graduated to the guitar at fourteen. But my first guitar lessons ended immediately. The instructor said that he couldn't teach me if I couldn't see to read music. I applied the same method I had used for learning the ukulele– learn the needed chords and, by ear, figure it out.

I would take the bus downtown on Saturdays and hang out at the Prospect Musical Instrument Exchange. It was an old time, Vaudeville-era music store. I would occasionally play different guitars, but I always bought something: finger picks, guitar strings, harmonicas, and *Sing Out* folk song magazines that I couldn't read. But I did struggle through one song, learning the lyrics and chords for "Mail Myself to You", a funny Woody Guthrie song. When I was fifteen, my father drove me downtown to that store. I wasn't going to look. I was going to buy. My Dad paid for a handsome twelve-stringed guitar. I learned to play it in a Lead Belly, fingerpicking style, using a Pete Seeger instruction record. Pete's audio instruction was slow and clear, and although there was an accompanying book, I didn't need it. By 1964 I was taking weekly lessons from a very hip guitar teacher and guitar maker, who taught from his front room and guitar workshop, in Cleveland's college bohemian neighborhood.

Mom supported the lessons and encouraged the pretense of my budding independence. She would park a few doors down from the instructor's shared house, so I could appear to be arriving on my own. I learned a lot of fingerpicking technique and I thoroughly enjoyed brushing up against the artists who shared the instructor's home. A few Lead Belly songs were added to my growing repertoire. Dylan records introduced me to the idea of playing guitar and harmonica at the same time. Bonnie bought me a harmonica brace and harmonica for Christmas, when I was sixteen, and I began the long process of learning to play guitar and harmonica simultaneously. For years, I had been listening to and ludicrously attempting to imitate Dave Van Ronk's rough and ragged, whiskey and tobacco, dried voice.

New music rushed in. My friend's college-age siblings had numerous folk records. We listened to and learned to play the songs that were becoming folk revival standards. My buddy played banjo and I played guitar as we sang in his recreation room. I found songs and styles that better matched my teenage voice and some that communicated passion for social change. Other protest troubadours like Tom Paxton, Buffy Saint Marie, and Phil Ochs played songs that addressed issues of real social consequence, and I began to learn and sing their ballads and stirring anthems. I was always ready to play for family and friends, and I continued to enter the annual Kiwanis talent show. Grabbing at any opportunity to perform, I began to share my own compositions. Music was a big part of my life. Civil Rights and social change were in the air and in the songs.

At Shaw High School where I attended tenth-grade, and where my sister Bonnie would graduate, folk music appealed to only a few of us, who relished our little folksy subgroup. We called ourselves individualists and lived the lonely life of the offbeat. I identified with young people working for causes that bettered the conditions of the downcast. Young civil rights workers were taking high-risk action that I could only imagine. Then, in early 1965, The East Cleveland Congregational Church opened The Well, an integrated urban coffeehouse and gathering place. Rev. Dewey Faggerburg, a Caucasian activist and visionary clergyman, paired talents with Cleo Malone, an African-American community organizer and lay minister. Together they established The Well. It brought together teenagers and adults from Cleveland's urban and sprawling suburban communities. The church's congregants volunteered as "servants" at The Well–located in the racially charged, changing city of East Cleveland. A friend told me about having gone one evening with his older sister and I was immediately interested. The next Friday night, instead of dressing for the high school dance, in white jeans, madras shirt, and penny loafers, I decided to go to The Well. I put on my blue jeans, denim work shirt, and new, very artsy leather sandals. I told my folks that I was going to The Well. They had heard of the coffeehouse and both opposed my going. But The Well exerted a strong magnetic pull. I aligned, like a compass, to its politics.

On that spring evening at age sixteen, I declared my independence from my parents' control. I defied their wishes and, despite their objections, told them that I was going to The Well, anyway. I walked the three miles, into inner city East Cleveland, to spend my first evening at the coffeehouse. When I returned home, after midnight, having been dropped off by a new friend, my mother met me at the door. She was sober and concerned, and we sat in the kitchen and talked about The Well and what my experience had been. I told her that I had found a kind of community there that I had never known before. From that first evening, I knew that I was going to make the place my first independent social home. My parents must have recognized that I was not going to be denied. They reluctantly dropped their objection.

It was a long walk, but it was easy to find. The Well was located on busy Euclid Avenue, in a narrow storefront, squeezed between an art theater and a bar. On weekends, the place would be packed. It was decorated in bohemian chic–six foot-high tan burlap panels and flat black upper walls and ceiling. Track lighting completed the little place's beat mystique. Fifty plastic chairs were grouped in fours around square cafe tables, and a small bar-style counter, with a few stools, divided the tiny work area from the public section of the room. Only coffee and, sometimes, stale doughnuts were served as refreshments. Coffee was thirty cents if you had it. If you didn't, the servants would take whatever you had or nothing at all. You could get anise added for a nickel. The place was an interracial, intergenerational, and interfaith melting pot. It was always crowded with friendly people of all ages, including senior citizens, working age people, and young adults. But the majority of The Well's weekend evening patrons were always searching teenagers.

Young people from all over Greater Cleveland, who identified with the ideals of racial harmony, Civil Rights, the anti-war movement, and the burgeoning folk scene crowded the place. We filled the tables, stood in the back, and even sat in the front display window. We mingled joyfully and were carried on the hormonal tide lifted by the free love movement of the sixties, our budding independence, and the opportunity that the place gave us to meet and establish new friendships. The Well was the beginning of many a fleeting and serious romance. Being a folk singer and songwriter gave me a certain allure with the girls, which provided a real boost to my self-esteem.

Coffeehouses were all about interpersonal communications and performances, and many of us went ready and eager to play and sing, recite or read. Folk music and poetry provided The Well's primary creative media. Among The Well's regulars were d. a. levy, (who chose this lower case presentation of his name), Cleveland's well-known beat poet, and Bill Miller, an excellent, wisecracking, blues harmonica player. Every half hour or so, Cleo Malone would call for quiet and it would be time for one of the structured "Speak Out" sessions. Then, one of us would have the complete attention of the crowded coffeehouse. A musician would play three songs, or a poet would read his or her poems, or a political discussion would begin with someone's political statement. Guitar cases were always lined up along the walls. Anyone interested in speaking out or performing would sign up with Cleo. The Well did not require any activities demanding high visual acuity. Sitting and talking at cafe tables was easy and safe.

Oh, how I wanted to be hip! I drank coffee, the only beverage available, and I decided that smoking cigarettes would be a chic addition to my overall coffeehouse persona. I performed songs by my musical heroes and my own freshly penned work. Not only had I found my social home as my latter day "beat" identity took root, but an interested and empathetic audience for my early songwriting. When I performed, my music was well received and I was encouraged to continue. I began to be asked to perform at church services conducted by Rev. Dewey. He would speak frequently at suburban white churches, and he would take me along to provide the music. Dewey had marched with Dr. Martin Luther King, Jr., and a large portrait of the Civil Rights leader hung above his desk in his church office.

On an early Sunday evening in May 1965, shortly after I had begun going to The Well, I met a pretty girl named Cathy, whose father had accompanied her to the suspect coffeehouse. Cathy was graduating from Brush, a suburban high school. In comparison, I was a lowly sophomore, with two more years of high school ahead of me, but love knows no such boundaries. Cathy gave me her phone number before they left, and we soon began to talk frequently on the phone, and to plan dates, going to The Well. I would hitchhike the five miles to her home and then take the bus with her, back into the city and the coffeehouse.

We dated all that summer. Some of our dates involved my going to her home for dinner. We would often listen to records, and I would always take and play my guitar. I thought that I could hide my low vision from her. Only after a couple of tense weeks, when I was getting past the initial uncertainty of young romance, did I quietly admit the extent of my limited vision. She offhandedly told me that she had known from the beginning that I could see very little. I felt relieved but a bit confused, since I thought that I had been carrying on the perfect masquerade as a sighted guy.

That summer, my parents told me that we were moving from Cleveland Heights, where we had always lived, to Lyndhurst, an entirely new community and school district. Through an ironic twist of fate, we moved to a small ranch house not far from Cathy's home. My teenage love affair and new bonds at The Well softened the social dislocation of being uprooted two years before graduation. I would attend the same high school from which Cathy had just graduated. For a few weeks, before Cathy started Ohio State, I happily walked to her house every day.

In late August our first summer ended, and Cathy moved to Columbus to begin her collegiate life. I miserably enrolled as a junior at Charles F. Brush High School. Although our ongoing relationship was reduced to letters and weekly phone calls, once a month I would board a Greyhound bus on Friday after school, to visit Cathy for the weekend. I disliked Brush High School from the start, but I consoled myself waiting for the monthly weekends with Cathy or for typical weekend evenings spent at The Well, where I felt like I was at home, alive, and validated as a musician.

A Valid Test

In the fall of my junior year the Pre-Scholastic Aptitude Test, (PSAT) was given, a prerequisite for the SAT, required for anyone intending to apply to college. On a Saturday morning, I lined up with the throng of nervous classmates as I anticipated the ordeal. I hated the visual demands of all tests, but, particularly standardized tests, because of their impossibly small print. I would frantically crawl through the timed, pressure-packed reading exercise, but always too slowly, peering through my magnifier, face flat on the table. My neck and good eye would ache, and by the end of the timed exam, I would know with sinking despair that, once again, I had not finished all of the questions and that those left blank would be marked by the merciless scoring machine as wrong answers.

But there I stood; ready to again engage in the impossible visual race against time. I had my magnifier in my jacket pocket, and I anxiously waited for the cafeteria doors to be opened. Then, the rush of students hurried to select a seat. Students generally gathered among friends for moral support, but my requirements were different. I quickly assessed the room's lighting, looking for a seat as far away from the glaring fluorescent fixtures as possible. Unlike the vast majority of people with low vision, who require additional light for maximum visual performance, I did best in low glare, high contrast lighting. This was impossible in the harsh fluorescent glare of the cafeteria. The hard wash of bluish light presented the worst possible type of illumination for me.

I settled on a table by a wall away from the windows and waited. Before the tests were distributed, we were given a new type of long, narrow, optical-scan answer sheets that would be scored by a machine. They necessitated marking numbered, multiple choice answers exactly within the prescribed lines of tiny, low contrast, light blue, dotted boxes. I despaired when I saw the dense answer sheets that required exacting, visual targeting. The tests were passed out, face down on the tables in front of us, and we were told by the proctors not to turn them over until instructed. An army of frowning teachers prowled the cafeteria, insuring that no cheating would occur. The order was given, the stop watch was started, and hundreds of tests were instantly turned over, hitting the cafeteria tables with a chorus of flat slaps, followed by complete silence as every student began the focused rush against time.

I quickly figured out how to hold my free left hand in order to block the overhead light, allowing me to read as my left eye pressed against the cold glass of the Plano-convex lens. I started reading the questions and laboriously searching for the tiny place to mark my answers. It was excruciatingly slow going. My neck quickly developed the familiar ache from curling forward into my craning, contracted reading pose. More than once I realized I had entered the answer in the wrong dotted box, and I lost more precious time as I erased and slowly raced on. My left eye unrelentingly throbbed, but I kept doggedly reading, with the certainty of how far behind I was falling. I could hear other students flipping page after page in their test books. I heard them finish, one by one, push in their chairs, and leave the tables as monitors gathered their answer sheets, pencils, and test books. I was aware that I was fretfully working, among a dwindling few still taking the test. Time was called, and we were ordered to put our pencils down onto the tables.

With powerless resignation, I reviewed the answer sheet, one-third unmarked, documenting the point at which time had beaten me back from demonstrating my knowledge. I stared at the scribble of pencil marks and erasures that filled in the rest of the narrow page. I wondered if I would have some of my correct answers marked wrong because of my inability to fill in the boxes neatly or because of the smear of erasures. I knew for certain that the empty one-third of the test boxes would all be scored as wrong answers. My eyes burned. I walked away from the PSAT with a heavy heart and squinted as I wandered out into the brilliance and ocular pain of the Saturday mid-day. I walked slowly home and thought about the test and its impact on my chances of getting into college.

The scores came back and I was in the forty-ninth percentile in Math, and forty-sixth in English. I read my scores and I stung with the bitter injustice of the situation. I felt frustrated, blocked, and the very real pressure of the necessity to find a way to demonstrate my true scholastic stuff. This was just the ramp up to the SAT, the big time testing ordeal. It was the bellwether all colleges and universities–scrutinized as the true measure of an applicant's academic mettle. I decided to talk to Brush's college counselor.

Miss Kingsette was an intelligent, unsmiling, short, gray-haired woman with absolute power of the pen concerning college application recommendations. Through her secretary I made an appointment and then tensely sat before her and showed her my test scores. I demonstrated how I had to read with my magnifier and explained how difficult and slow it had been for me to read the test booklet and to mark the answer sheet. I told Miss Kingsette how unfair I thought the testing process itself had been for me. I implored her to help me find an accommodation that might give me an even chance with the dreaded, but required, upcoming SAT test. Miss Kingsette grimly read from my open folder on her desk, considered my PSAT scores and then my overall academic record. "You're an average student and your PSAT score is average," she intoned with a hard finality. "Why would you expect to do any better on the test than this?" I argued that, because of my partial blindness and my complete lack of accommodations, I had not had an even playing-field in classes. She stared, silent and unmoved. I pressed forward, without any encouragement. I asked if there weren't some sort of special test arrangement for legally blind students. She was still silent. I continued pleading. I asked if the test couldn't be read to me.

107

Finally, with begrudging resignation, she looked away and told me that there was a large print test that could be specially ordered that also allowed for extended time. I was thrilled and nearly jumped up with the news. I eagerly asked her if she would please order the test. She wasn't happy about it, but she did agree to order the special edition test. When the SAT test was scheduled, I didn't file into the cafeteria with the other students. When my large print version arrived, testing days were arranged. I was excused from classes, over a period of two full days. I sat in an inner administrative office and, still reading through my magnifier, took the large print test. Not only could I read the test-books, but there also was an easy to fill in, large print, answer sheet. This time, unlike the PSAT, I was able to read and answer all of the test questions.

When the scores came back, I had received a 687, or 98th percentile in Math and a 593, or 96th percentile in English. I felt vindicated and proud. The day I got my scores, I waited, after lunch, in Miss Kingsette's outer office, with my results in hand. When I was called in, I handed her my test results and she studied them. Remembering her admonishment about my ranking as an average student and my average test scores, I asked her if she had ever seen a student score higher on the SAT, than their academic capability. After a long moment of silence, she said no. I told her that I was capable of much better work than I had been able to accomplish and that I could succeed in college if I only had the assistance I needed. I took the opportunity to tell her that I wanted to attend Antioch College in Yellow Springs, Ohio, a bastion of liberal thought and social action. She said she would consider endorsing my application, depending on my grades at semester's end. She reminded me that Antioch required a 3.0 GPA. I knew that my midterm grades had to shine. I left her office feeling quietly victorious.

Open Sore

Circumstances, concerning Mark's life within The Columbus State Institution for the Mentally Retarded, were not amenable to advocacy on his behalf. Direct, personal communication from the Institution was nearly non-existent. The only communication came in the form of the unfailing monthly bills for Mark's "care". Since 1958, Dad had worked as an on-the-road industrial machine salesman. Beginning when Mark was seven, Mom had worked full time as a secretary at General Electric. After Mark was sent away, I was told that it took nearly all of my mother's General Electric salary to pay the income-adjusted bill. The Ohio Bureau of Support, which was responsible for State institutions and State prisons, applied a sliding scale to family income for institutional maintenance. My folks' double income resulted in the pegging of their bill at the highest monthly rate. In actuality, in even the most rudimentary ways, our family could not support Mark's basic childhood needs.

Mark's was one of the fifty, narrow, iron bedsteads, lined side by side, on opposing walls, in the cavernous sleeping room. No more than a foot separated the shabby cots–sagging mattresses supported by stretched wire and springs. The heavy iron beds looked like they belonged in a third world prison. Grandma Jane asked at the administration building about how to arrange for the purchase of a new mattress for her grandson. She was told that she couldn't just replace Mark's mattress–she would have to replace all fifty. Grandma Jane worked behind a cosmetic counter in a drugstore. The only solution offered was the impossible. She could not afford to purchase fifty new mattresses. Mark was not going to receive any special treatment.

Community clothing was similarly drawn from a common collection of completely worn out, poor quality, stained, and ill-fitting rags. Attendants would randomly pass out clothes with complete disregard for size. Shoes were, also, horribly worn, ill-fitting, and random. They were all a rough, light gray or tan, having been scuffed beyond all identifiable color. There was no right of privacy. Attendants stole all new clothing. Mark never could hold on to any of the articles of family provided clothing. New clothes and shoes would disappear into the black of the institution's theft hole. The Columbus State Institution for the Mentally Retarded was a place of aggregate misery on a dumbfounding scale, as well as an inept, apathetic, and faceless bureaucracy.

On a cold January evening, an unexpected call startled my mother. The State worker informed Mom that all family visits were being suspended. The institution was quarantined with an outbreak of hepatitis. Mark was very sick and bedridden in the institution's pathetic, emergency-only hospital ward. Absolutely no family visitation would be allowed. Mom's voice trembled as she repeated the news. Two weeks later, Grandma Jane sat with us at the supper table and worried aloud about Mark and the dearth of communication since the call about the hepatitis lock down. Family telephone inquiries had disclosed only that Mark was still in the institution's hospital. Finally, we learned that he had been released back to his ward. Additional weeks of worry crawled by. We received a phone call in late March, telling us that the quarantine had been lifted. We were again permitted to visit. Mom, Dad, and I immediately planned to visit the next Saturday. Three months had elapsed since Mark had had any family contact. This was the longest time that had ever passed between visits. Someone made the depressing trip to Columbus every month.

That Saturday's three and a half hour drive bore the additional dread of what we would find in the wake of the medical crisis. Mark was, as always, overjoyed to see us. But he labored under a bludgeoning dose of Thorazine, a commonly used heavy sedative. His emotional affect was thick and deadened. The hepatitis had left Mark very thin and with the yellow pallor of that punishing disease. The institution's crowded and filthy conditions had been a fertile breeding ground for the virulent contagion. We redoubled some cleanliness precautions. Before we got into the car to go to lunch, we would thoroughly wash Mark's hands in the administration building's public restroom. We also always washed our own hands, both before lunch and at the end of the visit.

Visiting always involved bringing Mark's own clothes and shoes. He would sit on the edge of his narrow bed, on the threadbare and stained bedspread, to peel off his state-provided rags, before he dressed in the clothes we had brought. As we waited, the fifty other boys and teenagers who were captive on the ward swarmed us–hugging, clutching, and grasping at us with desperate community hunger for physical contact. The attendant would separate us from the throng, and we would leave with Mark dressed in his clean regular clothes and shoes. The heavy door would be locked behind us, and we would walk back down the black iron fire escape from the third floor. How Mom suffered, trembling like a bird, on that required walk up and down the fire escape! Once we were at the bottom of the black metal staircase, we walked down the sidewalk, along the huge building, toward the passageway that led through the administration building and into the parking lot.

But this time, as we walked, Mark was painfully limping. When we got to the car, Dad sat Mark in the back seat and drew his pant leg up, exposing an angry open sore on his left shin. The crusted wound was swollen and festering. It was obvious that the injury had not received any medical attention. We drove to a shopping center nearby, containing a drugstore and the restaurant where we would eat. While Mom, Mark, and I stayed in the car smoking, Dad purchased the first aid supplies necessary to

110

clean, salve, and dress the wound. Dad's medical training was put to use as he attended to Mark's swollen, infected shin.

We went to lunch, as we always did, at a family hamburger chain; but a wordless tension stiffened every moment. Then, it was back to the ominous, three story, brick human warehouse that held floor after floor of identical fifty-bed and fifty-chair wards. Mom questioned the attendant about Mark's wound. Her query was blandly but directly answered. Maybe Mark had fallen, been pushed, or thrown down the fire escape. The circumstances were not clear. Mom asked about whether Mark had received any medical attention. The attendant didn't know. There were no records. Mom showed the bag of giant Band Aids, gauze pads, antibiotic cream, and adhesive tape to the noncommittal attendant and pleaded with him to see that Mark's wound was cleaned and dressed daily. The bag was taken, but the worker's apathy suggested that there was a low probability that the medical supplies would be used for Mark. We said goodbye and painfully pulled away from Mark's desperate, anguished grip. The heavy metal door clanged as it locked behind us. Mark was left, pressed against the locked door, crying in hopeless despair. The cold reality was that we were powerless.

Godman Guild Settlement House

Cathy and I kept our romance alive against substantial odds. She was enrolled as a college freshman at Ohio State University, as I lived out my sentence as a humble high school junior. When I would go to Columbus for the weekend, I would stay with friends of hers in their off campus student apartments, sleeping on the floor. Cathy and I would grab whatever moments of privacy that her dorm hours and the circumstances of the apartment might provide. We always went to see Mark. The visits were fleeting. On Sunday afternoon, I would board the Greyhound or stick out my thumb on the freeway on-ramp heading north.

It would be another goodbye to independent, collegiate Cathy. Although it promised its own limitations, I was looking forward to Cathy's return to Cleveland for the summer and the chance to see her regularly, with the inherent equilibrium that her return to her parents' home might offer.

But in the spring of 1966, Cathy told me that she was going to stay in Columbus to attend summer school in her declared major, social work. This was a gloomy development, but I didn't need to ruminate on the change

111

in my fortunes. Cathy was resourceful. As part of her summer school program, she was going to be doing an internship at The Godman Guild Settlement House that served Columbus's near north side. She suggested that I move to Columbus for the summer, to work with her at the Settlement House. There was a job for me as well. We were to work in place of two VISTA volunteers, Volunteers In Service to America, who had failed to show up for their community duty. Already-planned inner city projects were assigned to us. I had decided to study social work in college as well, so I explained to my parents that this was an opportunity to gain some first-hand experience in the field. My beleaguered folks did not have the energy to oppose the idea. Perhaps it was because I would be earning my own way and because I had become such an independent teenager. They allowed the plan to develop without objection.

Cathy and I would be working in two inner city, racially mixed, poor neighborhoods, attempting to turn two vacant lots into community supported play areas tagged "Tot Lots". Already working there on Saturdays, Cathy had convinced her supervisor at the Settlement House to hire me as well, for the standard $18.50 per week. It was at the beginning of the summer, before my senior year of high school. My parents drove me, my clothes, guitar, Talking Book Machine, tape recorder, bedding, and a box of kitchen essentials to Columbus.

Cathy had helped me find a little apartment, in an old subdivided Columbus house, near campus. The job's meager pay was not quite enough to cover my expenses. My apartment was $50 a month. That left me $6 a week for groceries. I supplemented my poverty level income with money earned, working evenings, as a human subject for The Air Force and Ohio State Psychology Department. I rented a bicycle for the summer–an act of considerable defiance of the doctor's judgment, enforced six years before– that had eliminated bicycle riding from my life experience. I rode that bicycle everywhere, and I felt free, although nervous, considering the many near misses and direct hits that plagued my bike riding.

The summer's real magic was the work through The Godman Guild Settlement House. The work itself was very meaningful, and I began to engage in the life of social action that drew me in and inspired me. During spring quarter, as a precursor to our summer's work and as part of her internship, Cathy had managed to organize Saturday clean-up activities during which junk and trash had been hauled away from the vacant lots. She even got a construction company to donate railroad ties and sand. Large sand boxes were constructed and kids began to congregate at the simple play areas. Two days a week, we would arrive at each of the two lots to conduct day long supervised playgrounds for the neighborhood children. We would intentionally meet the children's mothers, and Cathy would attempt to talk to them about volunteering to help organize an ad hoc network, that we hoped would continue the Tot Lots as co-ops after the summer.

We also hoped that our efforts and the Tot Lots might bridge the color divide, weaving the neighborhood more closely together. The neighborhood residents were universally poor. Mr. Freid, the Settlement House's director, suggested that the Tot Lots might provide a focus for community organizing and improve both the well-being of the children and the racial harmony of the community. We met with Mr. Freid once a week to discuss our work. I suggested that music might also be useful in bringing everyone together. Mr. Freid agreed that I could give it a shot, so we talked up the community music evenings with the children and their parents.

On Wednesday evenings, I would balance my guitar behind my bicycle, and Cathy and I would ride our bikes across town to the Tot Lots. The musical evenings began on the playground vacant lots but quickly moved onto one of the neighborhood front porches. I sang and encouraged others to join in singing selections from my repertoire of folk songs, drawing on the spiritual-based Civil Rights songs that I had learned from records and at The Well and demonstrations. I would lead the singing, playing my guitar and harmonica. The spontaneous community music evenings did draw both black and white neighbors together. At times, scores of adults and children would stand on the sidewalks and front lawns, crowding the porches of the homes that were the centers of the music. I would stand on the walk leading to the porch and lead the music that joined the community's voices. Occasionally, other guitars or a mandolin would appear, and the instrumental accompaniment would swell. Mr. Freid spoke several evenings about available Settlement House resources. We wanted to create some lasting community momentum. Within the racial tension of that place and time, we accomplished some short term goals. We brought mothers and children together and did produce some remarkable and energetic evenings of harmony and good will.

There were several children who we came to know, as they immediately became regulars, playing every day on the Tot Lots, whether we were there to supervise or not. Two such kids were T.T., age five, and Sister, his seven-year-old sibling. T.T. would often greet me as I arrived on my rented bicycle, showing me a strand of barbed wire, bullet, broken glass, or other menacing artifacts that he had found in the sand of the Tot Lot. On music evenings, T.T. and Sister would move around the crowd, telling everyone that we were their friends, taking real pride and ownership in their familiarity with us, as I conducted the evening's entertainment. Sadly, the Tot Lot ideal of a safe and organized place for children to play did not survive into the fall. I ran the final musical evenings, and we had our farewells with the children with whom we had fallen in love. We disengaged from the neighborhoods, and the fragile dream collapsed.

Cottage Concerts

During that summer in Columbus, I took full advantage of my proximity to Mark. Occasionally, on her afternoon off, Cathy would join me for my weekly visit. The trip required taking the High Street bus from campus, downtown to the state capitol, and then transferring for the long and sad bus ride down Broad Street. The Broad Street bus rattled past the chilling Ohio State Penitentiary, The Columbus Arena, and past miles of offices, houses, and shopping centers. It continued into the eastern outskirts of Columbus, where the sprawling wooded expanse of Mark's institution was located. The bus stopped across from the main gate. Then we walked between the stone pillars, into the forbidding, high, iron fence, and up the long driveway to the cluster of grim institutional buildings. With or without Cathy, I would make the trip every week. I always took my guitar, and I would play for Mark and the fifty other boys with whom he lived, behind the ward's heavy locked door. The institution euphemistically referred to the bleak wards as "cottages".

A couple of times that summer, I arrived when Mark and his ward-mates happened to be outside for a brief respite from their dismal, overheated confinement. Those days, I put on my unscheduled and uninvited concert, sitting under the trees that bordered the sidewalk, across from their three-story, foreboding institutional building. I would unpack my guitar among the protruding tree roots, on the hard packed, weedy earth, and sing to Mark and the other children as they gathered around.

One afternoon, Mark's cottage happened to be sharing the outdoor space with a cottage of younger girls. I was singing and playing, when a tiny girl, perhaps five years old, walked up to me–spellbound by the music. Her ill cut, dirty, brown hair clung in greasy strands to her face and neck. Her unblinking, pale, blue eyes stared in wonder at me, and her mouth opened in a little, pink "O" as she reached out her tiny hand to touch my guitar. She

114

was painfully underweight and wore a thin rag of a dress in a pattern of small faded blue flowers. Hundreds of institutional washings, in coarse detergent, had left the dress a dull, yellowish gray. The innocent wisp of a child stood transfixed. I stopped singing but strummed softly as I smiled and quietly spoke to her. She touched my guitar and stared at me. There was a fleeting moment of sweetness that passed between us, and then from behind her, a matron barked a hard edged command for her to get away. The child was lost in her moment of awe as I heard the attendant bellow, with greater intensity, to get away from me. The battle-axe suddenly closed on the waif, as she harmlessly stood unaware. The woman's thick hand grabbed the cloth at the shoulder of the child's dress. With a violent jerk, the attendant pulled her off her feet, throwing her hard onto the gnarled tree roots that rose above the grassless dirt. The helpless girl opened her mouth and wailed a thin and pitiful cry of pain and shock.

The middle aged woman was stocky and wore a bleached white uniform, designating her as one of the institution's attendants. She had a grandmotherly appearance, with wire framed glasses and a helmet of gray tight curls. She towered over the little child and screamed down at her. The woman bellowed that she had told her never to touch anybody. Then, the brutal woman turned toward me and smiled, as if I would understand and appreciate her maintenance of order. In a friendly and matter of fact tone, she patiently explained that the girl had to learn how to behave. I was stunned and sickened by the violence, but couldn't figure out how to help the child. I recognized that I could do nothing about the endemic abuse of that awful place. I was afraid, that if I confronted the attendant, it might result in retribution toward Mark after I had gone. Mark and everyone else imprisoned there, were subject to such ugly acts of random brutality on a daily basis. As the little girl was dragged back to her unit, weakly crying, I tried to return to the music. A few minutes later, the attendant for Mark's cottage announced that it was time for the boys to climb the iron fire escape–back into the airless prison of their barracks. As I said goodbye to Mark and prepared to walk back down the long drive to the bus stop, he clung to me, trembled, and cried deeply.

When I went on visits with my grandmother or my parents, we would always take Mark away from the institution for a restaurant meal. But since I didn't drive, I could only visit within the confines of the institution. There was a small commissary, staffed by women who also lived at the institution. Burgers and other simple food, coffee, and soft drinks could be purchased. During my summer in Columbus, I began to take Mark to the commissary for a meal or a cup of coffee and a cigarette, at the conclusion of my musical visits.

I started smoking when I was sixteen, and cigarettes had been given to Mark by the staff, at nine years old, as a behavior control incentive. Once a tobacco addiction had been developed, behavior could be manipulated, using cigarettes as reinforcements. I was seventeen, and Mark was twelve that summer. We would sit in a worn booth at the commissary, and Mark would wolf down a hamburger. He was always hungry. We would always drink coffee and smoke my cigarettes. It was quite strange to see my little brother smoking cigarettes, but everything about the institution was tilted toward the perverse.

Visiting for an afternoon every week, I became a recognized part of the daily life of the cottage. As I became acquainted with the attendants, they would sometimes share shocking information with me. One afternoon, one of the attendants told me that Mark had a problem with masturbating in inappropriate places. I considered the completely public space within which Mark lived. It consisted of two cavernous rooms and a doorless, public, toilet/shower room, without any dividing walls. I wondered where an appropriate and private space could be found. Apparently, everyplace was inappropriate.

The next year, the Columbus State Institution came up with a plan to control Mark's, and I suspect others, natural inclination toward masturbation. Mark began to be injected regularly with female hormones. His arms and legs lost all of their hair, and his nipples became swollen and purple. As Mark moved further into puberty, his beard began to develop, patchy and thin, unlike the thick and full family beard pattern. Mark's body was permanently altered by that medically sanctioned, chemical castration. His genitals turned permanently black from the chemical engorgement.

During that summer of 1966, I became an integrated part of Mark's brutal and barren world. I took my Talking Book record player to Columbus and played my folk music records, as well as the few Talking Books I had received from the Cleveland Public Library before I left. One of the books that I listened to was *Of Mice and Men*, by John Steinbeck. The novella tells the ghastly stereo-typed tragic story of two depression era, migrant ranch hands named George and Lenny. Lenny has a cognitive disability and loves soft animals. But, as might be expected, he isn't aware of his own strength. George loves Lenny and protects him, and offers them hope, by telling a story about how it will be when they buy their own place. He tells Lenny the story–time and again–always reassuring and comforting him with the recited vision. After a period of drifting, the men are hired on as ranch hands. Predictably, Lenny inadvertently kills the flirtatious daughter-in-law of the rancher who hires the men. Lenny suffocates her as she struggles to free herself from his embrace. George knows that Lenny will be captured, and hung for the accidental murder. To save his friend this horror, he takes him to a pine wood and begins to tell him the familiar story. In the middle of the tale, George slips a revolver from his pocket and shoots Lenny in the back of the head, in what might be called a mercy killing. The book's dark conclusion dropped to my core like a lead sinker. I read the short book two times through and struggled with the apparent truth it contained. I couldn't avoid the misguided conclusion that if one truly had mercy in his heart, he would kill a loved one, as a means of freeing him from his irresolvable suffering.

During the next weekly visit to see my brother at The Columbus State Institution, after I played guitar and sang for the boys in Mark's unit, I took him, as was our pattern, to the greasy little commissary for our routine. Then, I did something I had not done before. I led Mark away from the institutional buildings and onto a low rise dotted with pines. We sat on the ground beside each other in silence, experiencing the quiet and calm of the wooded slope. I thought about taking my brother's life as George had in the book. I pictured buying a pistol, in one of the pawn shops I had seen, in the inner city neighborhoods within which I was working. I imagined carrying the pistol with me in my jacket pocket or guitar case. I gazed at my little brother sitting quietly in his medicated stupor, and I wondered if I could pull the trigger and bring an end to the impossible, unending suffering and brutality of his life. My heart ached for some resolution to his plight–some answer that could release him from his very real hell.

I imagined the shot ringing out, the attention that would be drawn to us, and how I would stay with him, holding his body until I was arrested and he was carried away on a stretcher. I pondered my years in prison and the end of all other possibilities for my life. Then I thought of my parents and grandparents, and the terrible grief that the entire ordeal would bring crashing down on them. I came to the conclusion that if I had any real courage, and if my family hadn't been in the picture, such an act of mercy would be the right thing to do. What would befall my family bothered me, but I was primarily afraid of the consequences that I would personally face.

117

I put the idea away. In the final analysis, in my youthful mind I decided that my cowardice was stronger than my mercy.

The summer ended and I returned to Cleveland. The following October, I was visiting Cathy for one of my regular weekends and we decided to pay a visit to the depressed neighborhoods where we had sown so much of our hope and belief. The afternoon air had the cutting sting of autumn's chill as we stood looking at the little vacant lot where children had happily played just weeks before. A discarded and stained refrigerator, with its door removed, lay on its side. Rusty bed springs and other trash now blighted the open lot. All of the sand was gone from the sandbox, and in its place were scattered fast food wrappers and beer bottles.

A low cloud cover cast a dull light on the dismal scene, when the sound of T.T.'s bright voice cut through our reverie. We turned to see T.T. and Sister bound through the front door and down the front porch steps of their house across the street and run to greet us. T.T. was wearing a tee shirt and shorts, and Sister wore a thin summer dress. The children shivered as they simultaneously and excitedly spoke to us. Then T.T. exclaimed, "Sister, show them your hand!" Sister held up her left hand. Her middle and ring finger were completely gone, leaving a shocking gap between her first and little fingers. She shyly smiled at us as if she was showing off a new puppy. T.T. answered our shocked silence by blurting out, "Sister got her hand caught in the washing machine's wringer." I thought about her mother and how frequently she was drunk or not at home during the days of our community organizing effort. I wondered what terrible circumstance had led to this sad result. I could feel my heart being broken in a new way.

We had become a part of their lives for a brief summer. We had believed that we were going to make a difference for them, and somehow leave them safer and cared for, in the fabric that the neighborhood was going to weave around them. But instead, the Tot Lot had quickly reverted into a convenient dump and eyesore. Sister's life had taken this course. She was subject to real neglect, which must have been some sort of factor in the loss of her fingers. It was cold. We were comfortable in our warm woolen coats, while those children shivered without jackets. In my limited, youthful experience, I wondered what difference social work could really make. I doubted that I could bear the heartache of getting close to those countless souls who would suffer beyond my ability to help them. My experience, over that last summer, had profoundly affected me. The combination of my growing social activism, leading of group-involving music, and first-hand

118

knowledge about how bad things were on the street and within the institution, began to knit a pattern in my life. It changed me forever.

Senior Year

It was the fall of 1966. I was beginning my second and senior year at Brush High School. Brush had only two distinct student identity groups: collegiate and greasers. The collegiates were, as the name suggests, college bound boys dressed in white Levis, madras shirts, and penny loafers that were the preppy uniform of the day. Their hair was worn in crewcut, flattop, or Princeton hair styles. Collegiate girls wore straight bangs, flips, or ponytails, cardigan sweaters, solid color blouses, and pleated skirts.

Then there were the greasers. Greaser boys wore longer, slicked back hair that often reflected an oily sheen. They wore highly polished pointed shoes, peg-leg pants, white dress shirts, and black leather jackets. Greaser girls' hair was uniformly big and stiffly sprayed. The look was achieved by a technique called ratting. They tended to wear more seductive clothes such as shorter skirts and tight sweaters. Their black leather jackets matched their boy friends'.

I didn't fit into either group. My identity had sprouted in the weedy counter culture. Blue jeans were not allowed by school dress code. I wore whatever I thought I could get away with: blue work shirts, turtlenecks, vests, desert or engineer boots, and black jeans. Senior year I often wore a neck tie with my work shirts. I was generally ignored by the collegiates, but the greasers found mocking me to be a source of constant sport.

The school's dress and hair code was standard for the period; hair that touched the ear or collar, or sideburns below mid-ear, was strictly forbidden. The assistant principal often spotted me trying to slip my violations under his radar. In the crowded hallway between classes, he once pulled me out of the flow of students and challenged me concerning the length of my hair and sideburns. My sideburns were definitely longer than allowed. I defiantly explained that I was acting in Community Theater and my character demanded the look I was sporting. Along with The Well, The Muse Theater Group was another outlet for my creative nature and the cause for many late weekend nights. The administrator ordered me to leave school right then, and to come back with my hair properly trimmed, or face suspension. I was to report to his office the following morning.

Run-ins with him were ongoing, as were constant verbal and physical assaults by the greasers. I would frequently be tripped in the hallways, have insults thrown at me in the cafeteria, or have my books punched out of my arms while walking down the stairs. Once, in a study hall, as I sat cramped over my magnifying glass, struggling to read a textbook, a hand shoved the back of my head, hard, and my face–inches above the desktop–hit the wood with a hard thunk. When I looked for the culprit, only studying students were sitting around me, with the exception of the girl next to me, who stared open mouthed–in shock at the act of aggression she had just witnessed.

Brush High School was hard. But the shining light of leadership, and being recognized for my true nature, overcame all of the struggles. One teacher, Mrs. Kresge, recognized in me something that she must have seen through the elevated vision of a great teacher. We had long talks, and she suggested that I establish a new student club: The Council on Human Relations. And so it was that I spread the word about this new after school student organization, and the Council on Human Relations came to life. Mrs. Kresge was our sponsor, and we brought speakers to Brush who addressed such timely and critical social matters as race relations. Cleo Malone, the black lay-minister who ran The Well, was one speaker and students were invited to my inner city coffeehouse–where my truer identity lived and breathed.

During my senior year, we connected with Glenville High, the high school my parents and their siblings had attended during the thirties and forties. It was now in an African American community. We developed the idea of a Student Exchange Day, during which a cadre of willing (and brave) students attended classes at each other's schools. I provided an introductory presentation for the Glenville students. A round table discussion after school concluded the day. But nothing could change the fact that these students were plunged into a school environment where the glare of racists and the murmured epithets created a toxic brew in contrast to our good will.

Mrs. Kresge helped me create an invaluable community of support; my presidency of the club was truly a position I valued. Such teacher's gifts often are given well beyond their responsibilities, and the seeds they plant bear fruit they will never know. Like Mrs. Delaney and Mr. Martin, Mrs. Kresge cannot now be thanked, but her smiling face hangs in my hall of memory, among the good and the selfless educators that truly blessed my years in school.

But the mechanics of school were monumentally difficult before P.L. 94-142, now the Individuals with Disabilities Education Act. I would

120

have benefited from the same simple accommodations I had received in earlier grades such as readers for study in school and test taking. My scholastic life involved the strain of telescope and magnifier use, and the evening reading sessions with the honor student who read to me at home. I also spent many long hours weekly, listening to reel after reel of volunteer readers, doggedly plowing through the dull tomes of my textbooks. The recorded tapes were of varying quality, but even the most inspired readers never failed to put me to sleep, as I listened endlessly to the hypnotic drone of the dense material. Recorded books were unavoidably read with a hypnotic rhythm. I knew tapes could lull me to slumber, even at my most vigilant and alert times.

My senior class load was jam packed with reading assignments. The sheer volume of the assignments demanded hours of nightly reading through listening. I seemed to always be behind. I would struggle with my magnifier or have my reader pour over Cliff Notes and attempt to help me master basic plot development for classics that I had not found time to read. Mr. Hill, my English teacher, had a sour disposition and despite my obvious disability, enforced a uniform standard of expectation for all of his students. His tests were always hand written on the blackboard in small, tight script that would fill all of the room's blackboard panels.

I was approaching mid-year finals, when two powerful forces of relationship and college planning drew me into their intense gravity. I was about to break off my longstanding relationship with Cathy, ending nearly two years of poetry-rich romance, sexual discovery, and emotionally wrenching triangulation. We stewed in constant conflict as she tried to balance her affections between me and an ongoing string of other, generally older, men. The end of my hope for a real, committed relationship with Cathy also dampened my interest in attending Ohio State. Cathy, my familiarity with Columbus, and proximity to Mark had been the main drawing points, along with its affordability and relaxed GPA requirements. But without Cathy, I didn't want to go to OSU, although I had applied.

I focused on Antioch College in Yellow Springs, the school that really held my interest. Antioch appealed to me because of its liberal history and reputation, its small size, and its work-study program which, I hoped, would allow me to pay the private tuition during alternative quarters, by doing paid fieldwork. But to be considered for enrollment, an overall 3.0 GPA–a B average–was required at senior mid-term. At the beginning of my senior year, my grade point average was 2.9. I was barely below the required 3.0. My work in Senior English had not been great, and I was facing the mid-term final with a C+ average in English. The term paper and final exam counted for a great deal of the final grade. I calculated that, if I got an A on both the term paper and the final, I would get an A- for the term. Combined with my other anticipated grades, I would be able to pull my GPA to 3.0. a standing that would make me eligible for admission to Antioch. The razor thin margin along which I skated had my full attention, and I studied like never before for the English final. My term paper was my very best work and I felt certain that I would gain the desired A for the substantial effort.

Final exam week in January came with fresh snow. Midmorning of the day of my English exam, I walked to the high school. Blinding sunlight reflected mercilessly from the field of harsh dazzling white. My terribly light sensitive eyes burned with pain, but worse was the concern I felt about the time it would take for my eyes to accommodate to the indoor lighting of the school where I would soon have to perform at my visually limited best. The capacity for the eyes to adjust, from one light level to another, is called light accommodation. The nature of the damage to my retina resulted in my eye's severe light sensitivity and my accommodation time being much longer than normal.

Other students walked into the building without stopping. I knew, with sinking despair, that it would take my eyes several long minutes to get used to the indoor lighting of the school–minutes during which I could see nearly nothing at all. I entered the school and waited inside for my eyes to cooperate and accommodate to the lower light levels, so that I could see enough to walk down the hall to the classroom. All I could see was blackness like a darkened movie theater. The hallway was clearing, and I decided to press on before my eyes had time to adjust. I slowly picked my way down the corridor to my English classroom, straining against the fear of bumping into another hurrying student.

I entered for the ninety-minute test as Mr. Hill was giving instructions. Mr. Hill had written the one hundred fifty questions in his smallest script on all of the chalkboard panels. I knew that my task was Herculean. I had to unscrew the small, ten-power telescope and hold the two segments perfectly aligned in my left hand in order to get a clear focus on the board from my front seat in the classroom. I always sat in the front because of Mr. Hill's tiny handwriting. Every time I would read a question, and then write the answer on my numbered notebook paper, I would have to return to the telescope, realign the touchy two parts of the lens system and, finding the sweet spot, read the next question on the board. I knew the material and left just an occasional numbered space blank for reconsideration. But as the hour and a half ticked by, I recognized with certainty that I was failing once again, not concerning my knowledge of the material, but failing to see fast enough to finish all of the test questions within the allotted time. Mr. Hill stood, called time, and the few of us still taking the test were told to stop writing. I had only completed question one hundred and six. A full forty four questions remained blank, along with the handful of unanswered questions I had skipped. My hope for an A was falling away. Only Mr. Hill's sense of justice could breathe life back into my dream of applying to Antioch.

After the classroom had emptied, I approached Mr. Hill with my incomplete answer sheet. I showed him how far I had gotten and explained the difficulty I'd had. Of course, he had watched me since the term began, as I struggled to read the board, and he had observed daily the difficulty I had with all visual tasks. Nonetheless, his look was wooden and impassive. Mr. Hill coldly directed me to add my answer sheet to the pile on his desk. I stammered out the singular importance of that test to my college plans, but he only stared unblinkingly and repeated his instruction.

When the term papers and final exams were returned at the end of the following week, I had scored an A on the term paper, but a miserable ninety-eight out of one hundred fifty on the test. I had left six of the questions blank to reconsider and had answered incorrectly on two. But every one of the last forty-four questions, that I had not had time to answer, was marked wrong. A red diagonal line was slashed through numbers one hundred and seven through one hundred fifty. I had failed the test and a large red F was emblazoned at the top of the paper. During that day's instruction, I heard very little of what was said as I followed the arc of my hopes into the dark depths of lost opportunity.

After the class, I again approached Mr. Hill. He stared at me again as he sat, his hands folded in front of him, a now hardened look on his face. He shook his head once. He stated that I had earned a C in his class, but that he would give me a C+ in light of my difficulty. He said, with icy closure, that he could not change the grade on the final or give me any other special consideration. I silently gathered my books and walked out of the classroom, feeling a sense of outrage and futility at this final impasse. There was no other avenue for appeal open to me. I had failed to finish the test. I had failed to increase my GPA. I had failed to gather enough momentum to secure a recommendation from the college counselor to apply to Antioch. My vision had again been tested and it had failed.

But, despite that bitter disappointment, through the remainder of my senior year, I felt accelerating happiness knowing that high school would soon end. Although the future was uncertain and I had no vaulted goals, the pathos and general alienation of my years at Brush High School were ending. I eagerly anticipated the release from high school's oppressive gloom. Upon graduation I would leave behind, once and for all, the gang of greasers who had bedeviled my years at Brush. On the last day of school we were released from the normal schedule at noon. I wandered among the graduating seniors who mingled on the school's front lawn. A small circle of my friends, all girls, sat on the grass. They saw me. One of them called my name. I crossed the small plaza in front of the school's broken, dry fountain to join them on the lawn. The plaza and empty fountain opened at the base of a grassy steep hillside. As I walked across the cobble stoned plaza toward my friends, I suddenly felt a sharp pain in my shoulder. A rock had been thrown at me from the hillside. Reflexively, I turned toward the fountain and another two stones struck me in the chest and the thigh. Half a dozen greasers were standing in a semicircle on the hill, each holding rocks that were now being hurled down at me. I said nothing. I really didn't know what to do. I felt outrage and fear. Several more stones hit my body, and I heard others whiz past my head and strike the plaza. I suspect that my passive, non-violent reaction must have unnerved them. Being struck by stones thrown at close range certainly did hurt. Inside I quaked with the threat of serious injury.

Perhaps my assailants were concerned about prolonging their attack, risking being seen by a teacher. But whatever the reason, the stoning stopped. With jeering insults, they dropped their remaining stones and slowly dispersed. As the crisis passed, my dread subsided that they might have struck me in the head. Living with the medical admonishment that a blow to the head could cause me to lose the remainder of my vision, I seethed with silent outrage at their thuggery. But as I turned to join my concerned friends who had observed the attack, I felt the triumphant thrill of psychological victory over the mob of bullies. The rock hurling attack came as the culmination of two years of constant ridicule and violence at their hands. I had not given them the satisfaction of any reaction throughout those two years. My response had been in keeping with Martin Luther King and Gandhi's teaching of non-violence.

124

Chapter 7: In Harness

The Price of Support

It was a cold Saturday morning in January 1967, as my Dad drove me downtown to Ohio's Department of Blind Services. After several phone calls, Dad had learned that I was eligible for financial assistance for college expenses like tuition, books, adaptive equipment, and readers through the Ohio Department of Vocational Rehabilitation Services. Dad knew downtown streets well. He spotted the multi-storied, low rise, state office building and parked his 1965, white, Pontiac Catalina in the nearly empty lot. The utilitarian building had an ancient elevator with a cage style manual door. A dour elevator operator stopped the car, exactly at our floor, using the car's brakes and years of repetitive experience. Dad searched for the office.

A serious, blind man introduced himself as Walter. He told us that he was a rehabilitation counselor and instructed my father to take a seat in the waiting room. I was led into a small office, where I was told to sit down and wait for the vocational evaluator. I was left alone. On the desk was a rudimentary, angled wooden board with geometrically shaped cutouts and corresponding wooden blocks in a tray at its base.

After a few minutes a gentleman came in, introduced himself as the evaluator, and sat down. He explained that the morning's first evaluation involved my being time tested to see how quickly I could complete the task of inserting the blocks into their correct holes. I asked what the purpose of the test was. The vocational evaluator told me that the test would demonstrate my manual dexterity–a skill necessary to work in a sheltered workshop. I felt my stomach knot, and I told him that I was going to college and that there was no need to test me concerning my ability to do sheltered work. He impatiently dismissed my assumption and stated that the purpose of the battery of evaluations was to determine what kind of work held the greatest potential for my success. He said that college was not necessarily what my future held. He returned to explaining that I needed to be thoroughly evaluated to see exactly what I was capable of doing. Then he cut off any additional discussion by taking out a stopwatch and telling me that when he said "go", I was to put the blocks in the right holes as quickly as I could. As he said begin, I used the combination of my limited vision

125

and my sense of touch to fit the blocks into their correct holes. I felt the imperative to do well, as I nervously completed the task. For the next several hours, the evaluator tested me in a variety of ways.

I was stepped through other vocational evaluation procedures, involving nut and bolt sorting and assembly. I was asked to respond to a battery of verbal tests, concerning preferences between alternative activities. My memory and reasoning, verbal and math skills, and general knowledge were all assessed. Eventually, I spoke to Walter about my vocational goal of becoming a social worker. I had decided, after the previous summer's discouraging work at The Godman Guild Settlement House, that social work would be very emotionally taxing, but I had no other idea about what I might state as my vocational goal.

When Walter and I finally walked back into the waiting area, my father asked what we could expect next. Walter said that an eye exam with their ophthalmologist was required and would be scheduled. He told us that after all of the required information was in their hands, they would make a decision. It would take several weeks before I would receive their letter. We said goodbye to Walter and rode the elevator with the silent attendant back to the first floor. We walked through the empty office building's lobby and into the harsh glare and numbing cold of the winter afternoon. As usual, Dad and I didn't talk on the way home.

Throughout those difficult years, my parents and I never spoke about my severely limited vision or its implications on any aspect of my life. After that Saturday morning, I was disoriented by the implied loss of control of my own destiny. I was in the final semester of high school, and my eighteenth birthday would be in February. I waited through the winter and early spring, as other seniors excitedly spoke about letters of acceptance and what college they would be attending in the fall.

Miss Kingsette refused to support my application to Antioch College. I received my letter of acceptance to The Ohio State University. I really didn't want to go there. I didn't hear from the rehab office until April, when I received a letter informing me that I was eligible for vocational rehabilitation services. But, if I wanted to go to college, the letter ominously continued, I would be required to attend a six-week, pre-college program that the bureau sponsored. The mandatory program was to be held at The Ohio State School for the Blind in Columbus, during the summer after high school graduation. I was dumbfounded and horrified at the prospect of this forced confinement right after high school and, worse, it was to be at the School for the Blind! Just the idea of The Ohio State School for the Blind filled me with dread. After graduation, I had planned a week on my own visiting cousins and friends in New York City, and then I had vaguely anticipated a summer rich with the pure thrill of heady freedom. This mandate was chilling. I would finally finish the drudgery of high school, only to be made an unwitting captive among other teenagers with blindness and low vision, forced to attend a meaningless sounding program.

While my high school work had suffered, I still had managed a nearly B average. I did not feel like I needed whatever this pre-college program was supposed to offer. I phoned Walter and explained that I did not need the program and requested a waiver from the rigid requirement, but Walter was unmoved. If I wanted their help with college, the pre-college program was non-negotiable. In early June 1967, I finished my last final at Brush High School and flew to New York City with a heavy heart. The vacation was to be a cruel taste of freedom before the purgatory of institutional confinement began. I spent a couple of days with my cousins at my aunt and uncle's gracious home on Long Island and then went into the big city to visit my friends.

New York City was a shock. I had harbored thoughts of moving to Greenwich Village and attempting to make it as a folk singer, instead of going to college. I crashed in my buddy's crummy, cockroach ridden, cold water, third-floor walk-up. Then, I miraculously ran into a friend, also visiting from Cleveland, and we agreed to rent a room for the remaining time before our return home. We spent two nights in a shocking Bowery hotel, sharing one bed and a dirty bathroom down the hall. The beaten down souls who lived in that depressing place had hit bottom. My suitcase was stolen, and I watched the NYPD pick up corpses from the sidewalk in the early morning light. We watched rats climb from the sewers, and I felt a fresh clarity that New York would not be my home. I returned to Cleveland and joylessly walked through my high school graduation.

The very next day, I packed my bags for the six-week program at The School for the Blind. My folks drove me to Columbus, and with resignation I was shown my room at the school. I arranged my possessions in the sparsely furnished dormitory bedroom, under the watchful eye of a residential matron, beginning my six weeks of retrograde confinement. My roommate was a very sweet and bright guy who was totally blind. As we all cautiously began to meet each other, I quickly found myself in the company of other high school grads with varying degrees of vision loss. This was an entirely new experience. Some of the others had been students at The School for the Blind, and others had been enrolled at public high schools.

127

My guitar, high-quality reel-to-reel tape recorder, and a just-released copy of The Beatles' *Sgt. Pepper's Lonely Hearts Club Band,* made me a magnet for the other students and our room became the dorm's gathering place. That summer's program held many invaluable learning opportunities that I didn't understand at first.

Valley of the Blind

I took my place, among forty teenagers, as we began the six-week pre-college program. On Monday morning, the day after all of us had moved in, the matron who ran our dormitory awakened me. She stood over my bed, shaking my shoulder and telling me that it was time to get up. I was startled by her uninvited presence in our dorm room, particularly because I was sleeping naked, as was my practice. I expressed, quite clearly to her, that it would be more appropriate if she would knock and not enter. She seemed surprised that I would take offense at her standard means of waking her charges, but she did honor my request.

At breakfast, we were all given our class schedules. As I read through my weekly assigned classes, the only one that seemed purposeful was a college level English course, taught by a professor from The Ohio State University. That college English course did prove to be well taught, demanding, with content rich and engaging; it provided a welcomed relief from the tedium of the other courses. On the other extreme, the living skills class included an insulting curriculum of telephone etiquette, personal hygiene, wardrobe selection, and basic table manners. But there was a real world element to the table manners instruction. Our table manners were silently observed and evaluated during cafeteria meals. When the on-looking instructors felt that we had mastered acceptable table manners in the open cafeteria, we were tapped to begin to take our meals with the teachers in their private eating area. I was not selected among those first few students who had been designated to enjoy the improved eating area. It was odd and disconcerting to have some of my new friends suddenly absent at meals.

I found the whole idea grating to my egalitarian sensibilities, although I silently wondered why I, too, had not been given an early nod. But shortly after the selection process began, I was privately told that I would be eating among the elite crowd in the teachers' dining room. In spite of my previous opposition to the selection program, I found myself relieved, proud, and pleased. I ate all further meals, in table clothed comfort, among

128

the hand-picked company of my peers who could deftly wield a knife and fork. A far quieter and more refined atmosphere prevailed, compared to the tumult of the student cafeteria. I felt somehow deserving of the relative luxury and select company. But, after a few days, I did ponder how quickly my moral objections had been co-opted. There were other and more profound lessons that occurred to me, early in that pre-college program.

One of my new friends was a year older and had lost most of his vision, very quickly, during his just passed freshman year of college. We hit it off right away, and we looked for opportunities to venture off by ourselves. Although also partially sighted, he had considerably less vision than I did and frequently needed my assistance. He was self-possessed and, like me, felt out of place in the program.

I reflected on the irony that his limited vision did not reduce his appeal as a friend to me. I had unconsciously accepted that my limited vision was a legitimate liability in any friendship. Although it was painful, I had always considered it quite reasonable that I would meet rejection as a friend. After all, I rejected myself. I considered my visual disability to be a huge liability. It dawned on me that, perhaps, I was really okay, just as I had assessed my new friend. I recognized that I really liked him in spite of his reduced vision. I deduced that perhaps others could like me as well. That simple, but profound, epiphany became the foundation stone upon which I began to build a more positive self-image; one that included my limited vision. Up to that moment, I had hated and been ashamed of my pathetically weak eyes. I had tried to hide my eyes' limitations. I had gone to great lengths to reject low vision as being a part of me; but during that summer program, I had the seminal experience of meeting, and liking, someone who held the very attribute that I loathed within myself. That pivotal experience began the glacially slow changing of my self-perception.

My new friend was the first individual I had ever met who had the same type and level of disability as I. We shared that identity. Years before, in sixth-grade, when I attended the school with the special education program, I met children who were totally blind, but I did not identify with them in any way. Not only were they years younger (enough of a difference for the prepubescent to feel disconnected), but they were totally blind. I had no identity with their disability whatsoever. Blindness was blindness, and it presented a terrifying eventuality as I had slowly slid towards sightlessness. Although I knew that I didn't make the grade as a sighted guy in many ways, I clung to my identity as a member of the sighted world. This new guy in the summer program was like me, partially sighted and "normal" in some undefined way. I found myself liking all the other teenagers in that program, but my older friend with low vision was my first real, disability- identity-peer.

Within the weave of the fabric of that summer's experience, came other realizations. I recognized the profound impact that living at The School for the Blind, had had on those students who had grown up within its walls. They had been isolated within the school's experience and were to my thinking, perhaps, less socially experienced than those of us who had lived in the rough and tumble of public schools and community life. Some of the classes appeared to aim at their particular needs, attempting to fill in the gaps left by years of isolation. But the School's students had a comfort level with visual disability and a camaraderie that was a product of their life experience–living where blindness was normal. In many ways, they exuded a quiet confidence, since they had a familiarity and ease with blindness itself and with the sprawling campus and routines of life there.

Those of us with low vision were not required to take orientation and mobility or cane travel classes. I wondered why this program was the first introduction to cane travel for the teenagers who had lived at The School for the Blind. I puzzled about why they had not been encouraged to master such essential independent skills before now. After all, my own independent travel skills had meant that I could hitchhike, pick up dates at their homes, albeit on foot–take public transportation, and make my way in the wider sighted world. Of course I hadn't begun to understand the tremendous difference that a little bit of vision made, compared to total blindness, when traveling in unfamiliar environments. I had what can only be called a sighted person's ignorance and conceit about the nature of my ability for independent travel. I was obtuse about the impact and challenge of blindness. I somehow figured that blind people should be able to rely on their hearing, and what I assumed was their extraordinary perception to get around.

At The Ohio State School for the Blind in 1967, those of us with travel vision were allowed to walk off campus for ice cream or to frequent the other commercial establishments near campus. My older friend and I were both over eighteen and had low vision. As independent travelers, we were even allowed to walk to a tavern for a beer, occasionally. In Ohio, in those days, eighteen-year olds were allowed to drink low alcohol (3.2%) beer; we thoroughly enjoyed getting away and relaxing outside the watchful eye of the dorm matron. But totally blind kids, regardless of their travel skills, didn't have those privileges. Only when in the company of a low vision guide, was off campus travel permitted to them. The old adage about the one eyed man being king in the valley of the blind seemed to hold true. Or, if not king, at least a desired ticket off campus.

Abuse of Power

The vast majority of the staff and instructors who worked in that program were caring and competent. They discharged their responsibilities with genuine regard for the students and took an individual interest in their well-being. There were frequent demonstrations of staff members going above and beyond their job duties to be of assistance to students. They often provided needed out-of-class tutoring, and evening and weekend volunteering for non-academic activities. The physical education teacher took a special interest in me. One afternoon, he walked through the gymnasium as I was trying to master flips on the trampoline. He stopped and began coaching me. Following that session, he gave me several additional one-on-one private classes on advanced trampoline. The English instructor from Ohio State would often stay after class if a student requested tutoring. Mobility instructors, comparably, often spent longer periods than had been planned if a student would benefit from extended sessions, learning independent travel skills. The psychologist showed particular caring and heart as he counseled us concerning our attitudes and perceptions about blindness.

But I also witnessed some of the other staff recklessly exert their inherent authority and power over the students. Institutions, that the public assumes provide an educational safe haven and a supportive or, at least, benign environment, can shelter those with ill intent. Most staff members seemed to be attracted to work with students with visual disabilities, by a genuine desire to be of service. But a few wielded their authority through controlling and sometimes cruel means. One afternoon, I was walking down the hallway when I saw the typing teacher standing, holding the half open door of his classroom. He watched a blind student walk slowly toward him. The student had a spinal deformity that caused him to lean forward. The boy was tapping with the cane in his left hand and he was trailing the lockers along the wall with his right hand, as he felt for the typing classroom door. When the student was within striking distance, the waiting teacher flung the door wide open, hitting the unsuspecting student hard in the head with the heavy wooden door. The stunned student fell backward and moaned, grabbing his head with both hands. As he rocked in pain, the typing instructor lectured him loudly. He barked that he needed to be a better traveler. The teacher sternly lectured that, in the sighted world, people would not be looking out for him. He continued that he had better take better precautions when looking for a doorway in a public building.

One afternoon, my roommate came back to our dorm room obviously shaken. He asked me if his eyes were ugly. He had slight dark scars under his eyes from radiation treatments he had received as a child. But his kind and hopeful face had sweetness and good nature that made one quickly forget the skin discoloration. I asked him why he asked about his eyes' appearance. The headmaster, an overbearing man, had stopped him as he walked in front of the administration building, telling him that he should wear dark glasses because the sighted world did not want to look at his ugly eyes. He reported that the administrator said that eyes like his were why blind people wear sunglasses. I responded that his appearance suggested that something unusual had happened to his eyes, but that they were by no means ugly.

On two occasions, staff neglect may have had devastating consequences. Every Wednesday evening, we were the only swimmers at The Ohio State University pool complex. The natatorium had four separate pools, each in its own cavernous room. One evening, one of our group who was totally blind and a poor swimmer, inadvertently wandered from the shallow end of the pool into water over his head. He instantly began to thrash wildly, yelling for help. No staff person was in our pool area. All of the school's staff who were there, and the lifeguard, were talking among themselves in the adjoining pool area. As I was beginning to swim towards the boy, the headmaster came promptly into the pool area. As he lowered the rescue pole toward the terrified student, he lectured him on taking greater responsibility for his actions. On another evening, one of the pool areas was again unattended. The lifeguard was flirting with a young female staff member. An alarmed, partially sighted student alerted him that there was a motionless swimmer lying on the bottom of the unguarded pool. The lifeguard ran, dove into the deep water pool, and pulled the unconscious student to the surface and out of the water. His vigorous rescue efforts brought the coughing and gagging student back into consciousness. An ambulance arrived, and he was rushed to the university hospital. The next day, the uninjured and grateful student returned to the program.

I learned a great deal about what goes on behind the walls of segregated schools. The best of human intent and the most base of our capacities were vividly demonstrated. My understanding about the impact of the social contract was broadening.

That summer, I visited Mark as often as I could. The combination, of my confinement at The School for the Blind, and Mark's institutionalization, made me feel blue. I took the Greyhound bus to Cleveland every weekend to be with my girlfriend, and to escape from the rigors of dorm and institutional life. Mark turned thirteen on August 9 and I visited him with my folks shortly before the program ended. I got a ride home with another student, sitting cross legged in the back of his father's open pick-up truck, with the clutter of my possessions around me. I spent three wind-blown hours on the freeway, traveling back to Cleveland. I felt the rigors and structure of that summer's experience being sandblasted away, as the summer sun heated the gritty, sand filled air that whipped constantly, as I rocked with the movement of the speeding truck.

Working

I was scheduled to enroll at Ohio State that fall, but I didn't really want to go. I needed a break from school. I was directionless and adrift. I returned from Columbus resolute in my decision not to begin college immediately. I told my parents that I had decided to withdraw from enrollment at Ohio State. I said I might consider enrolling in the newly established Cleveland State University, beginning with the winter quarter. Mom and Dad agreed to the plan, such as it was. But there was a caveat–I would have to work full time and pay rent. Mom worked at General Electric, and she suggested employment there as a possible option. She arranged an interview at the Personnel Office of Nela Park, the sprawling General Electric facility a few miles away. Nela Park was a college-like campus that included manufacturing, packaging, research, and marketing for General Electric's Lighting Division.

On the appointed afternoon, my mother introduced me to the manager of Nela's Personnel Office. Mom went back to work. After a few preliminary questions, the gentleman handed me a four-page application to complete. Sitting at a table in the interview room, I laboriously filled in the application using my magnifier, squinting with my head bent over the form. Shame burned in my cheeks as I slowly completed the application. When I finally finished, he gave my application a perfunctory glance. Then the employment officer told me that the company didn't hire "the handicapped".

His words were few, succinctly slamming the door in my face, and I silently agreed with his assessment. I wouldn't have hired me either. He told me that he would give me the name of a company that did hire the handicapped, but I really didn't want to accept that label. It was confusing. I didn't feel handicapped. My only limitation, which required substantial effort to work around, was that I just couldn't see much. Still, the name and telephone number that he handed me was my only ticket to a job. The next day I phoned the company and the local bus company, to figure out how to get to the precise downtown address. I learned what times the bus I needed ran and where to get off. It would be an hour bus ride.

The following day, I took the bus downtown. As with all such travel planning, I had to know at what stop to exit the bus, what side of the street to travel, how far down which block the building was and so forth, because reading building numbers was arduous. The next day, I found 1010 Euclid Avenue and walked up the stairs of the old factory building, to the office of City Blue Printing, or, as insiders referred to it, City Blue. I told the receptionist that I had been referred to them for employment. She gave me an application that included the standard work history section. Afraid of a General Electric type rejection, I didn't want her to see me struggling to read, using my magnifier. I asked her where the men's room was located, and I sat in a toilet stall as I slowly completed the form. I was applying for work in a factory…doing what, I couldn't imagine. Despite the company's reputation for hiring the handicapped, I didn't want to let them know I couldn't see. I would apply the same paradigm that I had always used–work harder and succeed. After nearly an hour, I walked out of the men's room and returned the completed application. The woman behind the office's desk scanned the application and noticed my recent graduation from high school. She asked if I could start work the following morning. A longtime employee was leaving; I would have one day to be trained to run her machine. The pay would be minimum wage: $1.65 per hour. I accepted.

I was excited and apprehensive as I rode the bus home. I was going to be an Ozalid machine operator, whatever that meant. But what if I couldn't see to do the work? What if I failed at this, my only shot at employment? That night I packed my lunch, but it felt different than the same routine I had completed since sixth-grade. I was about to join the working class. Early the next morning, ninety minutes before I was to clock in, I left for work dressed in my denim jeans and jean jacket, wearing my hiking boots–a leftover from my years in the Boy Scouts. I carried my lunch in a brown paper sack and felt proud to be a member of the great community of the employed.

I arrived on that first morning as an employee of City Blue and was introduced to the woman who I would replace. She was well liked and was leaving after many years of faithful service. I had one day to learn her job, running the complicated Ozalid machine. It was a hulking, 8 feet tall, specialized, copy machine of sorts that made a facsimile of original "tracings", the term for draftsmen's large scale mechanical drawings. City Blue did many things. Blueprints were there stock and trade. My department would receive jobs, to copy the tracings of various properties and machines for companies all over Cleveland and for other cities within the region. The large machine had a broad deck, onto which the operator would guide the four foot wide, precious documents, aligned atop specially coated yellow duplication paper. I had to guide the leading edge of the tracing and duplication paper into the moving rollers of the machine. With the alchemy of the papers coating, ammonia, and specialized high-intensity light, the Ozalid machine copied the tracing. The duplication paper came in two formats. It could be spooled off large rolls positioned under the machine's front work surface, or, it could be fed in, a single sheet at a time, sized to approximately match the tracing to be copied.

As the day got under way, I realized that I had thrown myself head first into a nearly impossible situation. I was going to attempt to do a job that had absolute visual requirements. The machine had ten light settings and thirty speed settings. There were three different kinds of paper, depending on the nature of the tracing to be copied. To successfully perform the job, one was required to execute a precise dance, handling valuable and easily damaged tracings. The choreographed series of tightly timed actions, feeding the unforgiving monster machine was unrelenting. The nerve wracking interaction demanded split second visual assessments and hand/eye coordination. The consequences of each decision resulted in an unending chain of sequenced success or failure. The calculus of the interactions of tracing, age and color, light setting, speed setting, paper type, and the lockjaw clamp of the machine's rollers could make small mistakes quickly become catastrophic. The day of training was truly exhausting. I understood how the machine worked, and I had an idea about how to manage the various processes required. But there were so many rapid fire visual calls to make that I knew failure would be breathing down my neck.

While the demands of the job kept me pressed against my vision's limits, some functions were simply beyond me.

The work, which I could barely see to do, required concentration and accuracy. After getting the paper roll moving by feeding it unerringly into the Ozalid, I was taught to pick up the original tracing delicately–by the top edge–from a large work table, then, to pivot and sweep it onto the moving paper. A fast alignment was required to square both side edges of the tracing with the moving paper roll. Then came the point of no return, as one guided the pristine drawing into the opening of the machine, to be caught by rollers drawing the work into the huge apparatus. If all went well, in mid process, the tracing folded back onto itself in a catch tray, away from the copy, in a vertical climb. The copied tracing would then have to be lifted smoothly, away from the shallow tray, and swept back on to a second pile of copied originals. Never missing a beat, I was supposed to then pick up the next original and place it on the moving paper, repeating the previous action. Generally, the tracings looked brand new and were a uniform four by three feet. Some of the tracings to be copied were quite old and were a smaller format. The older ones varied in the thickness of the paper, and their darkness and thickness of line. Most of the old ones were twenty-four by eighteen inches, and had obviously been taken from historic company or government archives. If the tracing stuck to the moving copy, as many of the ancient ones did, I was instructed to quickly and deftly peel the original away from the vertically rising roll or precut sheet as the copy went on to the fixing process. The ammonia spray caused some sort of chemical process that made the chemical/light generated copy permanent. Each job always involved copying many tracings. After feeding and removing all of the originals, into and out of the machine, one would have to walk to the back of the machine, where the continuous roll of finished copies would have gathered on a long work table to be cut from the roll of forty-eight inch wide paper.

Armed with a long pair of sharp shears, I was then to quickly drive the scissors precisely along the line of the exact top and bottom of the tracing copy. This involved flawless hand/eye coordination–a complete impossibility. I saw everything with ragged islands of diminished sight, amid irregular shaped blind spots concentrated in the center of my vision. I had to slowly find an island of vision by scanning, and then try to spot what I was straining to see; but I couldn't see fast enough or with enough detail to do the cutting job. I would start off well enough, being able to see the original cut into the paper, but I had a wicked left hook, and I usually sliced off the bottom right corner of the copy as I guessed where the line was, being unable to see the detail of the copied drawing across the wide paper. My slice would ruin the copy and required re-making the copy–a tedious task indeed–especially because there were so many copies that needed re-doing after my thoroughly impossible, failing performance.

There was a very patient foreman, a black guy who was incredulous when I told him I couldn't see very well. He asked aloud what I was doing as an Ozalid machine operator. He tried to teach me the technique of a straight cut that involved a precise lunge, but in spite of my best effort, I would inevitably miss the line or slash a sharp southpaw hook. He muttered to himself as he excused me from the task and finished cutting the remaining copies from the roll. The next day, he assigned the job of cutting the copies, for all of my jobs, to another very likable guy who worked at the machine next to me. He would stop what he was doing and good naturedly, although with wisecracks, come over and do that part of my job. Today it would be called a reasonable accommodation, if it were the only aspects of the job that I couldn't do. In such arrangements, I might do more copying and my coworker more cutting, but ideally we would get all of our work done. But, the fact was, I was a complete washout as an Ozalid machine operator.

More than once, I did not position the tracing squarely on the fast moving paper roll, and I remember the stomach wrenching sound of the tracing paper ripping, as it became first twisted, then accordion folded, mangled, and torn by the ever moving pinch rollers on the inside of the machine. The disbelieving and increasingly frustrated foreman would have to make a repair with wide tape, then, bring the horribly damaged and patched tracing back to me for a re-copy, as he watched, arms folded.

In the course of my days at that machine, I had seen another of the Ozalid operators take a bad copy and dramatically tear it into pieces. It looked pretty satisfying. When I similarly saw a copy that was imperfect, I, too, tore the copy into shreds. Only after I had, did I realize that I had inadvertently also torn up the original ancient tracing that had stuck to the copy. So it went.

After numerous similar costly mishaps, I was told by the foreman to see Personnel, where, after a brief interview, I was transferred to shipping and receiving. This new job was much simpler. It merely involved receiving new work, logging in the job, passing it on for completion and then shipping the completed work and original tracings to the customer. Finished jobs were wrapped in wide paper, according to precise techniques, then address and shipping labels were affixed. Unfortunately, this job also required good vision. As a result, I made several mistakes involving swapped tickets and jobs shipped to the wrong customers. The most serious was sending a rush job, via standard shipping, to the wrong customer in the wrong city.

Once again, the disbelieving foreman sent me to the Personnel Office. This time, the very kind and patient fellow told me that they would keep me on as a delivery messenger, a job they reserved for the handicapped. My mind flashed back to my interview at GE where I was told that City Blue hired the handicapped. There it was; I was being offered the very job known to the General Electric personnel officer. I knew it would be excruciating to take buses around town and then track down addresses and suite numbers. If I had had a limp, one arm, or a mild cognitive disability, the job might have been a good fit; but with low vision, it was an untenable mismatch. I respectfully resigned on the spot. During the middle of the day, I waited for the bus and wondered what possible work I could do successfully. City Blue might hire the handicapped, but they didn't have a job for me.

Cleveland State and Dismay

During the late summer of 1967, I failed in my first full-time job. I had been working at a job that I couldn't see to perform, although I was too ashamed to tell the company about my reduced sight. I had worked earnestly and applied myself diligently, but I couldn't see well enough to do the work. After I failed, I puzzled over the real dilemma of what to do next with my life and my time. I had no real marketable skills of which I was aware. Since I wasn't enrolled in college, my parents most appropriately expected me to work.

As I was considering my dilemma, I ran into a friend from high school who told me about his recently going to work at The Holiday Health Spa. It was a new idea in consumer services–a franchise, membership based, health club. I was living at my parents' home, and A Holiday Health Spa had opened nearby. My friend said that the job required no special skill other than being good with people. So I interviewed and was quickly hired as a staff exercise program specialist. I was nominally responsible for exercise routines for club members, who ranged from body builders to heart attack rehabilitants.

After I had been offered the job, I was handed a sheet of paper with an anatomical drawing that identified the body's muscles. I was told to memorize some muscle groups and reference them with customers. We wore short sleeved, white medical smocks over white shirts with neckties. My initial schedule was eleven hours of work on men's days, which alternated with women's days. Only men worked as men's program specialists, and women worked with female members. Women also wore faux medical smocks, over leotards that showed off their shapely bodies. But in spite of our ersatz professional image, we were engaging in the most blatant misrepresentation imaginable. The spa had red carpet and an extensive array of gleaming universal gym equipment, free weights, slant boards, stationary bicycles, and rowing machines. There was also a row of mechanical devices that jiggled, rotated, and undulated flabby bodies, allegedly to increase blood flow. Every wall was covered with ceiling to floor mirrors, giving the customers a constant view of their sags, bellies, and flab.

We sat behind a white counter, with a bin that held pre-printed alphabetized exercise program cards, most of which were blank. The cards were supposed to track members' workout routines. But few members used them. There was an alcoholic salesman who would come in, drunk after lunch, and sit around on the exercise benches shooting the breeze until he went for his sauna, steam-bath, and whirlpool. There were several body builders, including a runner up for Mr. Ohio 1954, who strutted the same stuff that had dazzled 'em, thirteen years earlier. All of the regular members pretty much kept to their own peculiar regiments. But, now and then, the cards would really have to be used to set up and develop a complete work out for a member. I couldn't read the cards without my magnifier and, even with the magnifier; I read the small print very slowly and not very effectively. That presented a circumstance that always led to great angst and ultimate failure in the tasks of completing, monitoring, and increasing the routines. But I rarely had to bother with them, since most members were entirely self-directed.

One afternoon, I was required to set up a cardiac rehabilitation exercise program for a new member–a civil judge. He was seventy-three years old, muscle-less, pear shaped, and had just been released from hospitalization from a heart attack. His doctor told him to "get in better shape." On his first afternoon, the judge shuffled out onto the exercise floor

139

wearing rubber sandals, a sleeveless undershirt, and baggy Bermuda shorts. Completely guessing, but under the pretense of the authority of my position, I had him pumping chrome-plated, lightweight dumb bells, doing sit ups, and other exercises that I hoped would help. When I think about the genuine liability of supervising a heart attack rehabilitation exercise program, with absolutely no knowledge, I breathe a sigh of relief that my efforts did not cause him any harm.

Our workdays included doughnut runs, lunch, dinner, taking saunas and steam baths, and working out. We vacuumed, wiped down the silver equipment and gold, plastic-padded benches and boards, and generally kept the place spotless. We were also expected to learn how to exert high-pressure sales tactics on naive guests, whom we would entice to come in for a free visit. I found that aspect of the job ghastly. I did not attempt to sell any of the multi-year contracts during my four months as an employee. Once again, there were visual requirements beyond my ability. I found the job distasteful and unethical. The manager, who knew nothing of my visual limitations, had discussed the company's interest in me as a management trainee. I declined.

Sometimes a job can teach us about a type of work that we don't want to do. That was the benefit of the Holiday Health Spa experience for me. But more importantly, college was looming as a necessity. I would have to find a career path, since I was failing at unskilled work.

I quit the spa just before Christmas and enrolled, with a sense of relief, at Cleveland State University for the winter quarter of 1968. Beginning after Christmas, my parents paid the rent on a basement apartment in East Cleveland, where public transportation was accessible to campus. I settled into my first quarter as a college student. My apartment was a mile and a half from The Well, my coffeehouse home most evenings. Cleveland State had recently been established, expanding from Fenn College, a venerable, small, urban campus. It was complicated to get to school. First a bus, then a Rapid Transit commuter train, and then another bus took me on my circuitous route to campus.

During high-school, my mother would always arrange, with the voluntary National Braille Press, to have my textbooks recorded onto reels of tape. For the first time, it became my responsibility to figure out how to get my books read to me. Fortunately, reading actually proved to be relatively easy. A hip high school friend had just moved back to Cleveland, after living in New York City for two years. We were both members of the counter culture, and his cool factor was very high. He needed the money and

140

had the time to become my reader. Every evening he would come to my apartment and read whatever the syllabus required. I settled into the grind of classes, research for term papers, and the unending studying that is the lot of all college students. The Department of Blind Services paid him to read, paid my tuition for books, and even gave me a wonderful, portable reel-to-reel tape recorder. I made the Dean's-List, for the winter quarter, and felt that I was flourishing when spring quarter started. I filed my grades with Walter, my rehabilitation counselor, whom I had first met prior to the required summer program at the Ohio State School for the Blind. Although I was still ashamed when I had to use my optical aids in class, I was able to get extended time on tests when needed, and generally felt competent as a hard working college student.

One afternoon, when I returned from classes, I got a strange telephone call from Walter, asking me to come to his office to discuss a problem. I arrived a few days later at the appointed time, and I was ushered into a conference room. Walter, who was totally blind, was seated at a table with two sighted male coworkers. The group was grim as Walter began to outline the referenced problem. I had let my hair grow long and had grown a beard, in the style of the counter culture of the sixties. Walter said that he had learned that I had "let my appearance go" and that I was giving blind people a bad name. He told me that, as a client of the Department of Blind Services, I needed to shave and get a haircut. My father and I had argued for years over my hair. The assistant principal at my high school had enforced the high school's short hair code for boys. But now I was a college student enjoying all the freedom that that license allowed. I was incredulous by this fresh affront to my personal freedom. I told Walter that I was on the Dean's-List, was held in high regard by my professors, and that I was fulfilling my responsibility as a student in full measure. Further, I suggested that my appearance was not unlike many other students. Finally, I told Walter that I did not represent anybody but myself and that I was doing that quite well. It was clear that Walter did not like my responses, but he saw no way around the stalemate. I did not comply with Walter's desires but, as spring quarter ended, I was troubled by issues of greater consequence. A mounting malevolence stalked Cleveland's counter culture. Gangs of thugs, with violent ill intent, were targeting the little shops, coffee-houses, and other gathering places. A black friend, who dared to go into a diner near an all-white neighborhood, had been beaten unconscious in its parking lot and hospitalized, with extensive injuries. I had been clubbed over the head, with a blackjack, in broad daylight, in front of the police station. I was diagnosed with a concussion. Another time, I had been hit in the back with a brick, thrown through the open window of a speeding car, as I rode my bicycle to the well. The Well, my beloved church sponsored coffee-house, was ultimately closed after the refusal of the landlord to renew the lease. Another of the church's coffeehouses had been firebombed. The owner of the building where the coffeehouse was located, who was an art dealer, also had his home firebombed; the conflagration destroyed extensive works of art. A friend who ran Cleveland's first head shop, had his arm broken by baseball wielding hoodlums, as they smashed everything in his shop.

Everywhere I looked there was dark oppression and the crumbling and crushing of the inclusive, socially minded communities that had been so much a part of the last three years of my life. Moreover, I had no career direction and no goal for my college education. The only serious career I had considered was social work. But my summer's experience, before my senior year in high school, had been disillusioning. Working with those in poverty had made me feel that a career in social work would be heartbreaking, but I was still passionate about the day's pressing social issues. A high school counselor had suggested I major in a field that I loved. The only course that I really loved in high school was speech, and delivering speeches about my convictions had been gratifying. Without conviction, I enrolled at Cleveland State as a speech major. But after two quarters of freshman courses, plus two speech classes, I pictured myself graduating with a degree in speech–a degree that would prepare me for no career of which I was aware. I floundered.

Chapter 8: Breaking Away

Cleveland's Burning

At the end of spring quarter in 1968, I gave up my own basement apartment. I moved in with a friend from The Well who lived in a basement apartment on Superior Avenue, in a fairly rough part of East Cleveland. He had offered me his extra room, open to the kitchen, bathroom, and living room. It wasn't gracious, or even private, but our mutual friends gathered there, and I enjoyed the social life the place offered.

That summer, I started two jobs. My favorite was teaching basic guitar and piano, a couple of afternoons a week, at a children's orthopedic hospital. Those lessons were a stream of consciousness experience, as I intuitively worked with every child who wanted lessons. All of the children were engaged in healing from serious orthopedic operations, or were involved in physical therapy, post-surgery. One boy was in a body cast. The cast extended his left arm from the shoulder, rotating his arm and hand toward his back. I taught him to play guitar by instructing him to perform the needed skills with each hand separately. I would provide the other hand's fretting or strumming as we went along. By the end of the summer his cast was off; while he was in rehab, he successfully combined both hands' independently learned actions, and he was playing guitar!

My other job was working at the concession counter at an art theater, two miles up a long hill from our apartment. I worked from 7:00 p.m. until 1:00 a.m., four nights a week, making and serving popcorn, pouring soft drinks, and retrieving candy from behind the glass display counter. The job was rife with potential visual mistakes that lurked within every customer interaction and fretful money exchange. But, in spite of the inevitable and highly anxiety producing failures of vision that occurred nightly, I was allowed to watch the movies from the back of the house once the crowd was in and settled. I tried to convince myself that it was a cool job, but I could see almost nothing of the movies from the back of the theater and I was very nervous throughout each evening's customer interactions.

One night in July, at about 1:30 in the morning, as I walked down the long hill back to my inner city apartment, I could smell smoke. I could vaguely see the flickering tongues of fire burning in the city below. A knot of grim onlookers stood on the sidewalk. As I passed, someone commented darkly that riots had begun and that the black neighborhood within which I lived was being burned to the ground.

I deeply believed in civil rights. The murders of Dr. Martin Luther King Jr. and Bobby Kennedy seemed to bring the curtain down on that hopeful, valiant epoch in America's and my own history. At Cleveland's memorial service for Dr. King, Dewey and Cleo spoke and I provided the music. Following the service, Cleo and I led the singing of "We Shall Overcome", at the head of the long column of mournful marchers, as we solemnly walked around the beautiful lagoon in front of The Cleveland Museum of Art, next to the church where the service had been held. The unity of the vision that had bonded us was being fractured by the urban uprisings that were exploding within America's cities. It was a time of wrenching dislocation of all our dreams. I stared in disbelief at the lurid orange fires that were burning Cleveland.

The riots were raging right down the road from my apartment. My building stood across the street from a bed of railroad tracks that crossed Superior Avenue via a concrete and steel bridge. A short distance from the bridge, in front of my apartment house, two uniformed, but unarmed East Cleveland traffic control officers had cordoned off the street with their car, by which they stood. They turned traffic back from going under the bridge behind them and deeper into the city. Before going into my building, I walked out onto the street and anxiously spoke to them about the crisis. As we spoke, one of the officers suddenly shouted with alarm. He pointed at the bridge. He had seen the silhouettes of two figures carrying rifles, running behind the low wall of the train bridge. The gunmen took positions behind the black iron, low wall on the middle of the railroad bridge. Without warning, from the darkness, the gunmen opened fire. Rifle fire cracked; bullets whizzed around us, and ricocheted off of the pavement. Fear threw all of us into panicked action. The uniformed men jumped into their car and sped south, away from the bridge, leaving me standing alone in the roadway. I was within thirty feet of my building, but it required unlocking an outer door. I was facing an abandoned gas station, directly across the street. Gripped with fear, I ran toward the boarded up gas station. Gunshots continued, and the sound of ricocheting bullets zinged off of the walls. I flattened myself behind the shelter of the derelict building, breathing in ragged gasps.

My roommate and my cat were across the street in our basement apartment; its windows and back entrance were within line of sight of the shooters on the bridge. As I listened, I could also hear the snapping menace

144

of gunfire from the east and west. This was my first encounter with life threatening danger. Right across the street was my apartment building, but I would have to get to it by carefully advancing south, down the block, cross Superior, and then move back north, on the same side of the street as my building. My roommate and cat were in harm's way; I needed to alert them, and we all needed to leave the area. My heart pounded as I prepared to run from the safety of the darkened gas station to the first inset doorway on Superior Avenue that would provide shelter. The snipers were shooting at anything that moved–any possible target of opportunity. Adrenaline surged through me, and I think I held my breath as I made my break. I ran across the gas station's concrete expanse, along the shops, to jump into the first storefront doorway. I sprinted from doorway to doorway, varying the time periods between my runs. Scurrying from the protection of one recessed alcove to another, I slowly edged my way down the empty street. I finally reached the end of the long block and, relieved, figured that I was out of range of the gunmen. There, standing in the middle of the street, were the same two uniformed, unarmed city workers. I told them that I had to return to my apartment across from the gunmen's bridge. One said that he had seen the rifle bearing rioters running on the bridge, just before they had opened fire. Woefully, they said that I was on my own. We wished each other well. Fear and loyalty propelled me as I slowly picked my way back toward my building. I ran the last long segment of the gauntlet, fully exposed to the riflemen on the bridge.

I suddenly realized that the gunfire had stopped. The ongoing crack and sputter of arms fire still sounded from further down Superior and from both the east and the west. My hands shook as I unlocked the apartment's outer door. I hurried into our apartment and woke my friend. He had fallen asleep before the riots began, sometime after 11:00 p.m. We developed a hurried plan. A woman friend of ours, who lived one block up Superior–away from the bridge and the rioting–had a car. I called her. She was awake and had been worriedly monitoring the riots and fires by sight and on television. We would immediately walk to her apartment. From there, we would drive to the safety of my parents' home. They were in Europe on a rare business convention and vacation. We grabbed a change of clothes, the cat, and her litter and food. She purred as I lifted her on my upturned forearm. We walked quickly into the smoke-filled night. We arrived at our friend's apartment a few minutes later and she drove her '65 black Chevy Coupe out of the dangerous city, into the suburbs. We lived at my parents' house for two days after the riots and followed their aftermath through

145

television broadcasts. Carl Stokes, the first African-American mayor of any American city, took all white policemen off the streets. Order was slowly reestablished. The National Guard moved in, and martial law was established in Cleveland. We headed back into the city. During the next days, we could see the boots of National Guard troops march past our basement apartment windows, and the hot summer air churned with the rumble of jeeps and military trucks. Under what had been the snipers' bridge, frightened young men sat on the back of armored vehicles, behind mounted machine-guns. National Guard troops patrolled the seething city in jeeps and on foot.

The next night, I went back to work at the art theater. I was walking home at my usual 1:30 a.m. The summer night's heavy gray fog shrouded buildings just across the street, as I approached my block—the same block which had held such danger just nights before. As I crossed the street, I was startled by the sudden appearance of a National Guard soldier. He wore a helmet and battle fatigues, and he trembled as he pointed a rifle with affixed bayonet at my midsection. He ordered me to raise my hands. He demanded, voice quaking, to know what I was doing in that neighborhood, two and a half hours past the 11:00 p.m. curfew. I told him that I was walking home from work at the Heights Art-Theater, and that I lived at the end of the block. He demanded my identification. He was about my age. We stared at each other. He eyed me warily and continued to hold his rifle trained on my belly. He was a National Guard soldier, and I was a sandal-wearing, bearded radical. His bayonet gleamed dully in the fog filtered light of the streetlamp. I asked the soldier's permission to reach into my back pocket to extract my wallet. He told me to move slowly. I did. He studied my identification. His eyes moving nervously from my draft card to me and back again. He finally announced that I could walk down the block and return to my apartment. My life, as a member of the sixties revolution that was going to change the world, seemed to be over. A jeep drove slowly past me as I opened my apartment house door, with a great sense of relief and sadness. My alienation from my city and my young life was nearly complete. The counter culture in Cleveland, as I had known it, was ending.

Farewell

I was adrift. The systematic crushing of our little, idealistic community and the urban riots that had exploded in my neighborhood made daily life grim. Combined with the undertow of ongoing family pathos, I wanted to leave. Mythical, magical California was calling my name. The allure of the road and the gravitational pull of San Francisco, promised a peaceful life among hip people. I was aching with a restlessness to put distance between myself, my parents' heavy drinking, and the bludgeoning pain of my brother's institutionalization. I needed to test myself–to see if I could really make it on my own in spite of my severely reduced vision.

I had an unread small-print copy of Jack Kerouac's beat epic, *On the Road.* It had been given to me by a friend who had returned from California. The books ideas that had been told to me of road glory were shaping my amorphous plan. One friend came back from San Francisco after the 1967 "summer of love". He reported that you could unroll your sleeping bag on the ground in Golden Gate Park for free and that you didn't need to take anything warmer than a wool shirt. He described a place that was open, free, and ready for anyone with the drive to get there. Another buddy came back, rich with stories about communes in the Santa Cruz Mountains with lovely women who had welcomed him with open arms. I wanted to leave Cleveland to have a great adventure and to find a place where I might be successful in some, as of yet, undefined way.

Leaving Cleveland was no longer a vague alternative; it was beginning to feel inevitable. I tried on various notions about places to go, but California seemed the most attainable. A friend from a wealthy family was planning to go to Nepal, to hike in the Himalayas; he invited me to go along. Although the journey would not be a permanent move, it would be a grand adventure. But when I considered the cost and my resources, I ruled that globe trot out altogether. The trip would cost a princely $1,500–far outstripping the $450 I had in savings. Moving to California, on the other hand, seemed possible. Since there was no absolute cost assigned to a cross continental sojourn, I considered it quite doable. I intended to move. It would be a total and permanent change of scene.

I wasn't just planning a visit to California; I was getting ready to move away and not come back. I waited expectantly for an unknown opportunity. I bided my time, teaching guitar at the children's orthopedic hospital and working at the art theater. A friend came by in July and invited me to go to a three-day gathering and musical happening in Woodstock, New York. He was leaving the next day, but the diversion from my mounting single focus held no appeal. I didn't like crowds, so I declined.

In late August, the opportunity I was awaiting presented itself. A friend from Shaw High stopped by. He said that he and some friends were heading to Los Angeles in a few days, driving a "You Drive It" car. I asked

147

him if there was room for me in the traveling party, and he said that he supposed that room could be made. Without any idea concerning what I would do when I got there, I began to make the hurried arrangements required to leave for California. I sold my stereo. I gave away the second-hand furniture which I had scraped together. Friends agreed to hold my record collection and other valuables. I stripped down my possessions to those that would fit in a backpack. I selected three changes of clothes, my Boy Scout sleeping bag, canteen and mess kit, a small bag of brown rice, optical aids, a copy of *The Lord of The Rings* trilogy, my father's dagger that his father had made for him as he was going into World War II, and my beloved guitar. I told my roommate that I was moving away, started to say goodbye to my other friends–and to the life I had known. I anticipated that my absurdly minimal wardrobe, including a heavy wool shirt and light wool jacket would be sufficient, along with my minimal camping gear.

My monthly visits with Mark at the Columbus State Institution for the Mentally Retarded were depressing and grim. I realized that my leaving would hurt Mark, and would place long spans of time between my visits to see him, but my own selfish desire to break out of the directionless routine of my life proved irresistible. I would walk away from my real responsibilities as Mark's brother. I was going to leave and Mark would have to be cared for by my parents, my sister, and grandmother.

I phoned Cleveland State and dropped out of school. Then I met with Walter, my rehab counselor. I returned the wonderful tape recorder that he had provided, and listened to his lecture about the mistake I was making. As always, I presented my perspective to him. We said goodbye, with the stalemate of differing viewpoints between us. As I left his office, I had untied another critical grounding rope that connected me to my life in Cleveland.

On Sunday afternoon, September 8, 1968, I found a ride to my parents' house to get a few last things and to say goodbye to my mother and my father. I had written a note to them, quoting from Kahlil Gibran's *The Prophet*. It described how the parent, like an archer, shoots the arrow of their child's life into the future, where the parent cannot travel. I folded the single sheet of paper containing Gibran's thoughts amid my own ramblings, justifying my leaving Cleveland. My friend waited in his car. My folks were watching a movie on television, and my mother was ironing. I stood there trying to figure out what to say. I went downstairs to my bedroom and gathered together a few small possessions that would fit into my backpack. I think that I had explained my plan to my folks earlier. I kissed them both, goodbye. I left the folded note on the ironing board and walked out, ready to leave Cleveland in two days–September 10th. My mother later reflected on the pain they'd felt while reading the note, realizing that they had no idea when they would see me again.

The Felton Bridge

On Tuesday, September 10, 1968, I loaded my guitar, sleeping bag, and full backpack into my friend's car. The passenger in the car was the fellow who had invited me to join his traveling party to California. We were driven to the freeway on-ramp, where we were to meet up with the other three people who would nearly complete our group. The principle driver had gone to pick up the You-Drive-It car. As we pulled up, there stood three fellow travelers–all strangers to me. Another guitar, duffels and sleeping bags, boxes of records and kitchen implements were strewn about, along with a very large dog, and a cat and her litter box full of fresh sand. The huge yellow dog–part Great Dane–wagged his massive tail and alertly watched his new pack form. The unwilling cat moaned unhappily, clamped securely in the arms of her girl owner. We added our gear to the rummage of belongings and introduced ourselves. It wasn't long before our car pulled up. We stared, with chagrin, at a Chevy Mazda–a compact car. The driver stared glumly back at the five people, pets, and possessions. He told us that the owner's stuff filled the trunk and that we would have to jam everyone and everything into the interior of the car. We all fell silent as we eyed our own and each other's possessions. It was agreed that none of the record collections or kitchen stuff could go. The second guitar was also offered up. Everything that didn't make the cut was to be reloaded into the car that had brought two of us.

What remained was non-negotiable. We creatively set to work configuring the space within the little Chevy that would be our contorted traveling home. We unrolled the three sleeping bags across the back seat and crammed duffle bags onto the back window deck, squeezing the remaining luggage onto the floor of the back seat, jamming the guitar between the driver and passenger's bucket seats, and putting the cat box on the floor of the front passenger seat. Then we squeezed ourselves into the car. Four new friends crowded into the back seat. The huge panting dog was called, and he scrambled in and spread his bulk across everyone's lap. Fortunately, four of the six of us were relatively small people; the dog was friendly and happy just to be on the road. As we finished settling into the crowded car, I took the first turn in the comparatively roomy front passenger seat–a coveted position that we would share throughout the days ahead. The cat was passed to me through the open window. She instantly used the cat box under my legs. The sudden rank odor made me feel a little less fortunate to be riding shotgun. But we launched–calling goodbyes–and were off.

It would be a 2,343 mile road trip, and we planned to drive straight through. We drove past the St. Louis Arch at dawn. In Oklahoma we stopped to sleep by the side of the road, for four hours, when the three rotating drivers were all too exhausted to drive. At a rest stop in Texas, the cat escaped and climbed high into a tree. During a wait that seemed to last for hours, she must have gotten a pretty good look at the flat, heat-baked terrain and changed her mind about escaping. She climbed back down, someone grabbed her, and we were off again. A State trooper in Nevada pulled us over and stared disbelieving into the impossibly overcrowded car. After checking driver's licenses, car registration, and the You-Drive-It agreement, and learning that we were headed for California, he overlooked the marijuana pipe and baggy sitting on the dashboard. Rather than issuing a ticket, the unsmiling trooper told us to just keep on driving and to leave Nevada.

We arrived in Los Angeles, blurry-eyed and unwashed, forty-nine long hours after we had begun our exhausting trek. We called a friend who was expecting some of us, from the first phone booth we could find. He gave us directions to the one bedroom apartment he shared with his girlfriend. So, complete with dog and cat, we were delivered by the You-Drive-It driver to Tony's apartment. Our driver said farewell and took off to deliver the car and begin his own adventure. Bedraggled, and carrying our clutter of possessions, we knocked on the apartment door. Our new friend eyed us with blank resignation. We shambled in and spread out our vagabond jumble in his living room, which we were to share with his brother, also a recent refugee. Maybe it was the big dog and unhappy cat, maybe it was just the overwhelming un-bathed mass of us, but I could tell that the apartment's occupants were not real happy about having this sudden influx of people and animals into their one bedroom apartment.

Fortunately, we didn't stay together for long. Within a few days, our little-bonded band began to break up. In ones and twos, we made contact with California friends who could take us in, and we set off in our differing directions. I had a name and address of a commune in Felton (but no phone number), given to me by a close Cleveland friend. I held onto that scrap of

150

paper with great hope, believing it would lead me to a hip refuge. There, in a town I had never heard of, I thought that I might start my new life in California. Felton was in the Santa Cruz Mountains, hundreds of miles to the north of Los Angeles. After several weeks of freeloading, hitchhiking, and camping, from Big Sur to Yosemite, I hitched a ride with a kind family to the address on my scrap of paper.

The house was at the end of a dirt road, in the majestic redwood forest of the California coastal mountain range. At dusk, I knocked on the door of the ranch house, whose address on Zyante Road had been my long-hoped-for destination. It was inhabited by a loose commune of six men and women. They had, by degrees, taken over the house and yard while the owner had been virtually pushed out of his small home. He now lived in his giant Winnebago, parked on the dirt road. One of the guys answered the door and listened to my story. He said that he remembered my friend. I stammered that I had arrived to...well...for a visit. I was unenthusiastically invited into the house, and I met the loose crew of friends that had moved from the Haight Ashbury section of San Francisco, earlier that year. Escaping the storied but increasingly crime-ridden district, they had gathered in this redwood forest retreat, during the summer that had now slipped into autumn.

The expanding influx of émigrés had begun with a couple who lived in a converted school bus in the back yard. A Native American woman, quite pregnant when she arrived, had given birth to beautiful twin girls who were six weeks old. She and her babies shared the master bedroom with her man. Two other single guys completed the complement of the Zyante Road house's occupants. The house was separated from the road by a rocky creek bed. The property was accessible only by a primitive log footbridge, without handrails, that spanned the gully, twenty feet below.

I nervously tried to act hip and at ease. I was told that I could crash in the living room already claimed by two other guys. As I answered the few questions asked of me by my new housemates, I avoided disclosing the fact that I had partial sight. The old familiar shame burned within me, and I didn't want to do or say anything that might open the feared chasm of rejection. This experience was uncharted territory, as had been the entire California adventure so far.

These new people were all six or seven years older than I and, I thought, very hip. They were cool in a style that I hadn't experienced before. Their conversation was minimalistic and laconic. About half of the exchanges involved the utterance of a few simple phrases. "Far out" and

151

"Really" seemed to be the most often spoken statements, but timing was everything, and I didn't seem to quite have the rhythm down. So I tried to say nothing that would make me seem like I wasn't one of them. Shortly after dark, it was announced that we were going to go into town to hear the guy who lived in the school bus with his girlfriend play guitar at a little bar called The Grass Cookie. Everyone but the new parents of the twins got their jackets and began to troop out of the house. I had to dig my wool shirt out of my backpack, and so was the last to leave.

As I walked outside, I could hear the voices of those ahead of me and their footfalls on the bridge. As I stared into the darkness, the path leading to the bridge was discernible only as a vague gray span. Decades later, Dr. Ian Baily, one of the great leaders in low vision clinical evaluation, was to develop a measurement system for what is called contrast sensitivity. My particular type of vision loss results in very poor contrast sensitivity, or the inability to see the difference between areas of low contrast or shades of gray. In the extremely low light of the forest that evening, poor contrast sensitivity presented a terrible problem. I picked my way along the gravel path, but as I approached the narrow ravine, I couldn't see any contrast difference between the dark log footbridge and the blackness beneath it. I had been able to see the bridge during daylight, but now, at night, I could not see it at all. My mind raced and my heart pounded with fear. I could hear the others climbing into the cars and closing doors. It seemed to me that I had no choice. I had to act; I had to walk across the unseen bridge.

Gathering my courage, I aimed toward the sound of the voices, held my breath and started slowly walking across the narrow bridge. The rough logs were there, underfoot, for the first few tentative steps, and then I stepped into blackness and felt myself falling forward–headfirst over the side. A scream of terror began at the back of my throat, but my shame was more powerful, and only a clipped yelp escaped before I was again silent. I tumbled headlong into the empty air and then, with a fierce impact, I struck a section of diagonal log bracing about six feet below.

The underpinning had supported the other half of the bridge, which had collapsed under the weight of the ill-fated school bus, foolishly driven over the log bridge some months before. I had been spared from a fall to serious injury or worse. But I had violently hit my midsection and forehead on the rough log structure. The force of the blow punched the wind out of me, and a fierce pain burst within my head. I was panicked. I was lying, head down, on a sharp incline and I had to figure out how to get back onto the footbridge to rejoin the group before they came looking for me.

I considered calling out for help, but I quickly dismissed the idea. I was embarrassed and ashamed. In the dark, I carefully felt the log structure that had saved me. I groped around, found the connecting bracing, and pulled myself into a precarious standing position. Then I felt for and found the footbridge above my head. With great exertion, I pulled myself back up onto the narrow logs of the footbridge above me. With roiling fear and a terrible pain in my head, I crawled on my hands and knees toward the road, gulping air and gasping for breath.

As I finally climbed into one of the waiting cars, I fought to breathe normally. Someone asked what had taken me so long. I answered that I had gone back inside to use the bathroom. I couldn't tell them the truth—I had fallen off of the bridge because I couldn't see. That would have admitted how limited and damaged I really was as a human being. I was too humiliated to have asked for help crossing the footbridge. I was too ashamed to have screamed as I fell, too disgraced to have cried out for help climbing back up and, now, too beaten down to tell the harrowing events of the last minutes to this community with which I was so tenuously connected.

Stepping Out

My life as a member of the Zyante Road commune was largely lived in a state of observation. I wanted to fit in. I wanted to feel, at a fundamental level, that I was a real member of the loosely connected community; but I didn't have a life outside of the house and my clumsy attempts to engage its inhabitants were often painful. I had moved to California, a month before, without any concrete plans, and I did not intend to return to Cleveland. I desperately wanted to make my circumstances work and to find my way amid these new people and their laid back, post "Summer of Love" ways.

All of them were doing something, mostly part-time. Among the seven of us who shared the house's one bathroom, everyone else had things to do, leaving me to my own devices nearly all of the time. Carrie took care of her newborn twins. Jim, her man, spent many hours in yoga poses within their room. He would appear in the afternoon, without his glasses and wearing a yellow sweatshirt and, sometimes, one black sock. That was his complete outfit. He would smile and say something pleasant, and then nearsightedly scope out the big brimming ashtrays to try to score a good butt. I liked Jim. Ed and Maggie had each other's private company in the wonderful confines of their purple, once a school bus home. Evenings, Maggie was a waitress at the hippest restaurant in Santa Cruz. Some months before, Paul, the homeowner, had invited Maggie for dinner. She arrived with Ed, driving his converted full sized school bus. He decided to drive the massive vehicle into Paul's backyard, across the rustic log bridge that spanned the steep gully adjacent to the dead-end dirt road. The weight of the bus broke through one half of the log deck, but not the underlying log supports. After the shattered portion was removed, the bridge was left as no more than a rough footbridge with Ed's and Maggie's school bus home parked, semi-permanently, behind Paul's house.

Ed spent his days working on further customizing the bus and talking about his scheme to drive it down into the creek bed and up the opposing steep slope, then back into the wide world. Buzz was gone a lot, sometimes overnight, doing what I didn't know. Allen was likewise gone much of the time and talked about his former life as a big-time TV producer. Paul came and went in his Winnebago. He came into the house to go through mail. At other times, he would engage in the house's social life, looking bemused at the congregation of people who had slowly taken over his residence. Finally, there was an unattached girl named Marla. She was often around, and I thought a great deal about her when she was not. Marla didn't live there and she was Paul's occasional girlfriend, but she was a free agent and was often alone. Ed, Allen and I all played guitar. Some evenings, we would all unpack our instruments and play together. On these rare and wonderful occasions, I would feel like I had a meaningful, respected role and a part in the rhythm of the house.

Marla would sit and listen to our songs. Sweet and outgoing, she was a few years older than I was. She had a pretty face, a friendly demeanor, and a beautiful figure. One afternoon I was sitting in the kitchen, reading the first of the three books in the *Lord of the Rings* trilogy. I had bought the dense tome in Cleveland and ambitiously planned to read it on the road. But reading was slow and difficult and I hadn't gotten very far. I was reading at my usual crawl, through my thick magnifying lens, absorbed in the mythical adventure. I was curled over the book, with my face pasted to the paperback page, when I heard Marla speak. She had quietly walked into the kitchen from the open backyard of the house, framed by the ancient giants of the redwood forest. I looked up and there she stood, smiling and saying what a beautiful afternoon it was. Marla had been sunbathing in the buff and she stood, wearing nothing but her friendly smile. At nineteen, I was an initiated young man of the sixties. I had been physically involved with young women for three years, but Marla's nudity was wonderfully unexpected. I stammered something in response, taken aback both by her unanticipated appearance and by my stalking shame, having been caught reading in the only way I could.

Marla didn't seem to care about my low vision or magnifying lens. Perhaps by then, she had gleaned through observation that I couldn't see well, although I had not spoken directly about it. She had certainly seen me struggling to read, and I knew that she seemed to accept me, lousy vision and all. After all, she had spoken to me! I didn't really expect to strike up a romantic or even a casual physical relationship with Marla. She seemed too far out of reach. But as I sat there, fully dressed, gazing at her beautiful nude feminine form, I wanted to jump up, rip off my clothes, and shout "I'm one of you! I like nudity too!" But I was locked in my awkwardness and I felt too un-hip, so I just let the moment pass. Marla got the glass of water she had come in for and then went back outside to enjoy the remainder of the warm, late summer afternoon.

After I had bunked on the living room floor of the Zyante Road house for about a week, my old friend Tony arrived. Tony had given me this house's address. My buddy had gone back to Cleveland that summer after his father's untimely death. Now he had returned to California and purchased a new Triumph motorcycle with money from his father's life insurance policy. Everyone was glad to see Tony, especially me. Now I had an inside friend and someone I could spend time with. Tony began sleeping in the living room with Buzz, Allen, and me. We didn't speak of it, but we both knew that the arrangement lacked a certain sophistication. Tony had a plan, and I was delighted to learn that it included me. He had planned to buy a used camper which he envisioned as a home for both of us. His generous offer was so appealing. Within his camper, we would have our own space and mobility. A life of travel and adventure was waiting.

The day after Marla had left me longing in the kitchen, I climbed onto the back of Tony's motorcycle to go look at a used truck camper at a gas station in Santa Cruz. Tony spoke with the owner, who unlocked the back door of an over-the-cab truck camper, mounted on a green 1953 Ford pickup truck. The camper had running water, a tiny sink, two propane burners and propane light. There was a kitchenette table and dinette booth that converted into a double bed, and another, permanent bed that was over the truck cab. It was cozy and compact, and Tony wrote him a check on the

155

spot for our new home on wheels. The seller said a wistful goodbye to his camper, and Tony and I drove away. The little mobile home was terrific; we soon were happily ensconced as one of the vehicles parked on the dirt road in front of the Zyante Road house. Tony and I took turns sleeping in the bed over the cab. It was a wonderfully private, somewhat cramped space with a wide window that gave a fine view of the towering redwoods.

Shortly after we began living in the truck, Tony suggested that we invite the house dwellers out for breakfast. The camper's kitchen table booth could seat six, and luckily only four of the house's inhabitants were able to come on the planned morning. Jim, Marla, Ed, and Maggie accepted our invitation for oatmeal and coffee. We were looking forward to the breakfast festivities.

The morning arrived and Tony got up early. He did all the cooking, and he had slept that night on the lower convertible bed. He lit the propane lamp and started cooking on the two propane burners. The little camper filled with the smell of brewing coffee and cooking oatmeal. The warmth of the space was delightful, and I lay in the upper bed gazing at the majesty of the redwoods. I decided that this would be a great chance for me to casually exhibit my own proclivities toward nudity, and I would just slip out of bed and into the assembly *au naturel*. No big deal; just a man in his element, greeting his friends with the same comfort and ease that Marla had shown as she glided into the kitchen days before. A perfect plan, for what was to be a perfect morning. I feigned sleep as the door opened and in climbed our guests. Tony offered them coffee and seats at the booth. I yawned a "Gosh, is it time to get up already?" I loudly stretched and sleepily announced that I would be right down.

With a song in my heart and a barefoot boy's step, I slid off of the rumpled bedding and onto the table that adjoined the wall leading to the overhead bed. I stepped onto the plastic covered bench seat and dropped next to Marla, across from Jim, Ed and Maggie. There were a few moments within which I hung in a sort of suspended animation. I didn't really want to process the reality that grabbed me with its cold hand. Steam rose from the cups of coffee. But warmth ended there. Marla was wearing a down vest over a wool sweater, and the hooded sweatshirts and heavy plaid wool of the others made me realize that I had made a rather serious miscalculation. As I stared at our guests' autumn attire, I considered my suddenly out-of-season tropical look. I realized that the rising heat from the propane light and burner had given me the false sense of a toasty morning. At the top of the tight little compartment, my cozy little space had been as warm as a summer's breeze. But down below, here in the unblinking light of early October, the temperature was a bracing fifty-five degrees. I suddenly felt quite underdressed for the occasion. Goosebumps crawled thick over my cooling legs, torso, and arms, and I shrunk with the shocking chill of the plastic bench; but I had no way out but up. Laughing nervously at my mistake, I stepped back onto the bench, back up onto the table and I pulled my shivering frame back upstairs to slip into something a little more comfortable. As the Psalmist wrote, "For everything there is a season."

Chapter 9: Bitter Truths

Mark's Birthday

In 1969, I moved from Felton, amid the redwood forest, to a commune in northern San Diego County. There I lived, in a converted, ancient, adobe stable, on open land, which stretched over sandy dunes to rugged sandstone cliffs, high above the Pacific Ocean. My life was simple and hard, working as a non-chainsaw wielding member of the commune's firewood cutting crew and eating carbohydrate-dense greasy food. The unending work was physically taxing. It tested and stretched me.

I was achieving one of the goals I had set for myself when I moved to California—I was discovering that I could "make it" on my own. I had access to the beautiful Pacific Ocean and slept in an ascetic room, not unlike what might have been found in Mexico for unbroken centuries. I had a narrow bed covered in a rough Mexican blanket, a simple desk, and a small bureau. A heavy, hinged, wooden shutter covered the small room's only windowless opening. When opened, I could see an expanse of sandy dunes and hear the crashing waves. I could also climb out and be on the footpath to the Pacific.

After my first nine and a half months in California, I went home for the summer in June. After my humble living conditions, I was glad to get back to my mother's cooking, my double bed with its clean sheets, and my Cleveland friends. That summer, frequent trips to visit my brother, permanently confined within The Columbus State Institution for the Mentally Retarded, were necessary and essential parts of my coming home. I had visited in June with my grandmother and in July with my parents. I offered to visit for Mark's birthday, in early August, giving my mother, father, and grandmother a month off. I did not go with any expectation of really celebrating his birthday, since all that we could do was to take Mark away for a short respite. The hideous conditions of his life were unchanging. Visits were always pure emotional torture.

I was able to visit Mark on his birthday, thanks to Jeanne and Lydia who volunteered to make the long trip to Columbus with me. Jeanne was a woman of my mother's age, who I had met when she worked at The Well. We had become good friends in the years before I went to California, and that summer her home in East Cleveland was a gathering place for my East

Cleveland friends. I had met Lydia that summer at The Outpost, the new coffeehouse sponsored by the same church that had run The Well. The visit was planned, giving both of my friends their first exposure to the institution.

On Saturday, August 9, 1969, Mark's fifteenth birthday, we made the long drive to the Columbus Institution. We drove into the parking lot shortly before noon. Jeanne had difficulty walking, so Lydia and I went to get Mark. We entered the administration building and walked down the sour smelling hallway leading to the reception office. After signing in, we walked through the dreary passageways and back behind the buildings to get Mark from his second-floor ward. We climbed the black fire escape stairs and knocked loudly on the locked white metal door. Our knocking caused the ward's fifty, attention-starved, residents to crowd the door. As the white-clad attendant shouted at his charges, we could hear him rattle his clattering ring of keys, unlocking the heavy door. We entered and were swarmed by the throng of young men as they pressed themselves against us–hugging, grasping and touching.

Lydia recoiled from the shocking press of male humanity, by gripping my arm and pressing against me, as I searched from face to face for my brother. Mark forced his way to the front of the madding crowd, and I hugged him amid the sweaty heat of the moving and reaching mass of unbathed adolescents and young adults.

As always, we had brought Mark's own clothes for him to wear during our outing. He sat on his bed and silently changed out of the anonymous rags that were his daily uniform. The ugly shoes he wore were far too long and scuffed dull gray. His faded and threadbare pants were too short and too large in the waist for him, and he had been holding them up with one hand. He took them off, still buttoned and zipped. The entire time, the other residents continued to push themselves against us, craving attention and human touch. Finally, the attendant let Lydia, Mark, and me out of the crowded unit. We walked back down the metal fire escape, and out of the institutional maze, to Jeanne who sat waiting in her car. Jeanne and Lydia were lovely to Mark from the start, as they asked animated questions and pretended that everything was happy and normal.

We drove to a shopping center nearby, where there was a Kresge's department store. I had about fifteen dollars that I could afford to spend, and I thought I might buy him some rugged toy that he could take back with him. Fifteen dollars seemed like a lot of money for the purpose, and I felt confident that we would find some treasure that would delight my younger brother. Once again, Jeanne stayed in the car as Lydia, Mark, and I entered the small department store. I told Mark that I would buy him any toy that he wanted. The toy department was right inside, close to the front door. Mark instantly picked up a large plastic Batmobile, complete with Batman and Robin figures and lots of moving and removable parts. Mark had always been a big Batman fan. Lydia read the price tag for me. I was stunned. It was $25. I told Mark I couldn't afford that, but I encouraged him to find something else. He quickly picked up a plastic gun set, which I had to veto as well since guns seemed like a bad idea. So it went. I vetoed toy after toy; they were too expensive, too complicated, or inappropriate for other reasons. As the process continued, Mark's pace was accelerating. His frustration grew. Mark frantically hurried around the toy displays in a frenzy of agitation and excitement. Then, across the aisle, he spotted something and took off in a run. I charged after him, darting around shocked customers, as Mark rushed toward a display at the front of the store. I called his name, to no avail. As I reached Mark, he was grasping at a gray, steel strong box, displayed on a head-high glass shelf, facing the main doors. Mark was so intense, and the situation was developing so quickly, that it seemed to me that he was out of control. I acted on raw instinct, and the high-speed happening quickly spiraled into catastrophe. I ordered him to let go of the metal box. He didn't respond, continuing to unevenly pull the box on the crowded display toward him. Things were going badly, and I feared that he would break something or bring down the whole display. Unwisely, I grabbed him from behind and locked my arms around his chest, pinning his arms at his side. But Mark freed his left arm, cocked his fist, and punched the gray steel box with a powerful and direct blow. With a great metallic crash, the lock box was propelled off of the shelf, rocketing into the aisle, and clattering loudly onto the floor. I managed to pin both arms again, and Mark began to thrash, whipping me off of my feet, fiercely trying to break my hold and free his arms.

His great strength was put fully to the task of gaining his freedom. I struggled, beginning to drag him the short distance to the store's front doors. Mark yelled loudly. We were in an adrenalin-fed battle that pitched my grim will against his fury. I was gaining ground as we slammed into the double doors. Our unbalanced weight pushed them open, and we careened onto the sidewalk. As we struggled, Mark twisted around within my locked arms. He forced his arms up, through my bear hug, and attacked. With his right hand's jagged fingernails, he slowly clawed at the skin of my neck. At the same time, he forced his head downward, bared his teeth and bit into my chest through my shirt. With a vice-like bite, he clamped the flesh of my chest between his violently clenched teeth. The bite cut deeply into the meat of my chest wall as his left hand ripped at my left shoulder, tearing my heavy sports jersey. He gouged my shoulder and neck with his uncut fingernails while his teeth remained locked in stark rage.

The shock of the alarming pain, and the completeness of his rage, shoved me into instinctual non-resistance. I went limp and pleaded with my brother in my most beseeching voice. I begged, "Please, Mark, stop biting me. Please. You're hurting me. Please Mark, stop. Please stop." All at once, his paroxysm of ferocity ended. Mark released his jaws and opened his hands. My encircling arms softened around him, and he fell into my embrace. I held him as he wailed, in gasps of bottomless grief. A gaping crowd had gathered and murmured as they witnessed the spectacle of our drama. Then, a concerned policeman, hand on his holstered revolver, pushed through the crowd. I had begun to cry as well. "Please," I choked, "just leave us alone. We're all right."

The policeman, still gripping the handle of his service revolver answered, "Do you know this man?"

"Yes, officer," I spoke through my sobs, "he's my brother."

"Is he from the institution?" he asked. "Do you want me to take him back? I can get back-up. We can take him back."

"No, no, please," I wept. "Just leave us alone and tell all of them to go away!"

The crowd continued to stare, as we cried helplessly in the wreck of that Saturday mid-day. My shirt was torn in a jagged right-angle, and my neck and shoulder were deeply scratched and bleeding. My chest was the most painful of my wounds. It stung, ached, burned, and bled. The wide bite formed the perfect image of Mark's upper and lower teeth on the skin of my chest. The injury had also started to swell and bruise.

When Mark had run across the store, Lydia had been separated from us. She witnessed the violent confrontation and, afraid and unsure, she had returned to the car. She and Jeanne sat in the car paralyzed with uncertainty and unable to see us. After the policeman had dispersed the crowd, I stood on the sidewalk with Mark, having no idea where they were. Hoping that they would see us, I slowly walked us back and forth on the sidewalk. Jeanne finally saw us and pulled her coupe to the curb. I opened the back door, and we collapsed into the car.

After being denied toy after toy, Mark had seen what he really desired. He had seen a locking strong box, unknown to me to be a much-coveted object, that a few of the higher functioning men on his ward were

161

allowed. In their lock boxes, these fortunate few would secure keepsake trinkets, photographs, or any small personal item–protected from the open thievery that otherwise made owning anything impossible. A strong box was exactly the gift that he most wanted, but all I could see was accelerating agitation. When I foolishly tried to restrain him, he reacted blindly, out of hard-wired conditioning. My mistake had led to disaster. Mark had reacted with the survival tactic required in the degraded jungle of the institution. Attendants and inmates alike were equally capable of unprovoked attacks. Through the years, Mark's body always carried the unending bruises, scratches, and scabs from those beatings and fights. But on that Saturday, I was the one who had grabbed him from behind.

The Columbus Concert

I spent the short remainder of the summer of 1969 in Cleveland and then returned to my life in California. I didn't return to Ohio again until August of 1970. Of course, I wanted to visit my parents, Grandma Jane, and my friends, but I had made a commitment to myself that I would return to the Columbus State Institution for the Mentally Retarded, to visit Mark, at least once every year. It was a far cry from my monthly visits before I had moved west, but that annual grim pilgrimage made me feel like I was not abandoning my poor brother, altogether. I didn't feel good about the yawning, year-long gaps between visits. My absence was the bitter cost of my independence.

Lydia and I shared the Cleveland summer of 1969. Her parents had both been killed in a car accident, when she had been in high school, and a Japanese family had taken her in. Their son had been an exchange student hosted, years earlier, by Lydia's family. We had gotten pretty serious that summer. She was very busy preparing both her late parents and her late grandparents' homes for sale. In September, she flew to Japan, I flew back to California. She joined me in California the following spring. During the winter quarter of 1971 I had become a college student, studying at Palomar College, a sprawling southern California junior college. I continued to work part-time, as a member of the commune's landscape work crew, and I had started to teach a few private guitar students from out of the communal house.

I did not attend classes during summer quarter. I never took summer classes. The rhythm of academics seemed to require summers off.

162

Coursework would begin again in September. Lydia had flown back to Boston to visit her brother and to buy a car that we were planning to drive back to California. In August, before I settled back into my student responsibilities, I flew back to Ohio with the ticket my parents had gladly provided. I would meet Lydia in Cleveland, visit, and then make the long trans-continental drive with her back to Southern California.

When I visited Mark alone, I had to take a city bus to the Greyhound station in Cleveland, ride the Greyhound to Columbus and, then again, catch a Columbus city bus for the sad trip to The Columbus State Institution. I could count on staying with friends in Columbus; this always provided a respite in the otherwise bleak journey. When I visited Mark by myself, on foot, I could not take him off grounds. I could either visit Mark on his locked unit ward or take him to the little commissary where I could buy him a hamburger and a cup of coffee or a Coke. Then I would hug him and Mark would cling to me and sob; my heart would break again with the bleak knowledge that Mark would remain there, facing an unchanged, wretched life sentence.

But in 1971, Lydia's involvement and car gave me the power to break the pattern. Having the flexibility of transportation, I phoned the institution administrative office and volunteered to put on a concert for the residents. After talking through the mechanics, with several levels of administrators, the plan was set. The concert would be held on a Friday evening. I was twenty-one, Mark was sixteen. The administrator told me that there was a gymnasium with a stage and a rudimentary public address sound system. On the appointed day, Lydia and I drove to Columbus on Friday afternoon. I put on my Sgt. Pepper-like, blue, satin tunic with its gold lame, Romanesque collar. A friend had purchased it for me when he returned to Cleveland, after living in New York City. The flashy shirt had gotten little wear. I wanted to give Mark and the other residents a bona fide show, and I also needed to fortify my self-image about being a real-life entertainer.

We got to the institution, and we were directed to the auditorium. We entered, about twenty minutes before the concert was to begin. The place was already packed with hundreds of people from the wards, and the din of yelling and excited vocalizations was jarring. I walked to the stage and unpacked my guitar. No sooner had I put the guitar strap around my shoulder than, surprisingly, Mark walked onto the stage as well. There were two live microphones on floor stands, on the empty stage, ready to use. Torn paper and cardboard sheets hung in tatters at the back of the stage–apparent

163

remnants from a previous event. After a brief but poignant hug hello, Mark stepped to one of the microphones as if we had done this very thing many times before. About ten feet apart, Mark stood at one microphone as I stood at the other. I greeted the crowd, and they hollered an enthusiastic response. I sang and played folk and rock standards. Mark sang every song with a generally wordless, but always melodic lyric. He played air guitar as he punched out the few words he knew. He sang right in pitch and in time, with high energy, real showmanship, and natural stage presence. I felt energized and boosted by Mark's help. He stood center stage. I was stage left. Between songs, he would get the crowd going by calling into the microphone, "What do you want?"

The audience would roar back, hundreds of voices shouting together, many of which could not form words. But amid the swelling vocal responses was the unmistakable word–"Peace!" The overall impact of Mark's and my interactions and Mark's rapport with the crowd was magical, and I found myself truly enjoying the entire evening. At the end of each song, Mark would turn and wait for me to tell him, off mic, what we would sing next. He would then announce it to the audience, which would, in turn, shout back their enthusiastic approval. We sang to irregularly clapping hands and the crowd's raucous voice, as we led them in spirituals, folk standards, and popular songs. By the end of the ninety-minute show, we were sitting on the stage; we ended the evening with some quieter songs.

Then the magic was over. The crowd began to be moved out under the direction of their ward attendants, and I packed my guitar back in its case. Mark stood on stage with me until everyone else had gone; then the remaining attendant quietly told him that it was time to get back to his unit. He seemed to recognize the poignancy of the moment. Mark and I hugged, and we both shook with emotion; sorrow overtook us as he was led away. Lydia stepped to my side as we stood in the now empty auditorium.

Lydia was a photographer, and she had a fine thirty-five-millimeter camera with which she had taken some black and white photographs during the concert. When we returned to California, she developed the roll, and there was the most wonderful picture of Mark that I had ever seen. In the foreground of the shot were the backs of the heads of the audience in the crowded gymnasium. Standing at the microphone, under the wash of stage lights, in front of the torn backdrop, stood Mark. His hand was in motion–a soft blur thrust over his head in an unmistakable peace sign. His face was animated, yet relaxed and very purposeful, caught in the moment of a call into the silver bullet microphone. I stood to the right in the frame, the lights casting a reflective sheen off of my tunic. The camera captured my broad smile as I looked happily at Mark pumping up the crowd. My guitar suggested that the shot was taken during a musical event, but Mark was the focus of the crisp image, and his energy, control of the stage, and dynamism, were palpable in that remarkable moment. As with all impermanent magic, the photograph and its negative were accidentally destroyed.

After the Music Ended

It was early September 1971, when the phone rang in my communal California home. My mother spoke in phrases broken by choking sobs of the deepest sorrow. Mark had tried to run away from the institution, and he had been apprehended and taken back by police. Mark was in a lock-down prison unit at the institution, and my mother needed me. Someone needed to go to Columbus, visit Mark, and find out what was happening. She choked and cried, as I overflowed with compassion for her and with dread about Mark's situation. Would I be able to come back? She said that she and Dad could not handle the trip. I told her that I would come right away. Eighteen hours later, I sat on an American Airlines flight from San Diego to Cleveland. My folks picked me up at the airport.

We had dinner and, after a night's sleep, I was on a bus to Columbus. From the Greyhound bus terminal, I walked to the familiar corner of Broad and High Streets, across from the state capitol. I boarded the Broad Street bus and got off across from the front gate of the hated institution. I made the long walk up the drive, through the vast lawns, to Administration, where I was given directions to the building that held my brother. A hard-faced, talkative attendant opened the series of locked doors leading to Mark's cell. He told me about what I had only feared. Police, using an attack dog, apprehended Mark on the sidewalk, down the street from the institution. He said that Mark was a tough customer and it hadn't been pretty. His reference implied the force that must have been required to subdue Mark.

Mark was in a locked, narrow cell with a heavy metal door. The attendant opened the final door. I entered, and he slammed it heavily behind me. It was 2:00 p.m., and Mark lay unconscious from a bludgeoning dose of Thorazine. Light, from the small, wire-embedded window in the cell door, shined down in a colorless square of pale daylight, onto Mark's shoulder. It was the only light in the small room; the darkness of the prison cell pressed

165

in, graduated in shades of shadowed gray. Mark was sixteen. He breathed heavily in his drug induced, mid-day sleep. I touched my brother's shoulder, in the gloom of the prison afternoon. Mark stirred and then snapped into a fear-filled reflex. He was coming up, in jerky spasms, out of the coma of beatings and drugging. He cried out, "Wha! Wha! Wha!"

"It's okay, Mark," I intoned gently. I held him, trying to ease his terror and my shock. It's me, Jeff," I said in a low voice. "You're all right. Everything's okay." Mark pulled back, and for the first time, I saw his face in the faded daylight. It was sickening. Purple-black bruises covered his eyes and his cheeks. Deep gouges striped his face, neck, and arms. The swelling of his beaten face was so extreme that I would not have recognized him. Mark's mask of injuries told the story of the repeated beatings that he had endured. My brother's eyes rolled in their sockets as he dragged himself into consciousness. Then he focused on me. He grabbed me, buried his head in my shoulder, and sobbed. He cried, deep and long, and as hard as a man cries when the floor of hope has been ripped away. I could do nothing but hold him and brace myself against the pull of the emotional undertow that sucked me toward its black hole—the bottomless swirl of pain, the familiar heartache of shirked responsibility, my long absences, and my inability to meet his needs, combined.

My own little brother suffered in the grim pathos of prison—for what crime? Mark cried for a long time. He had been sleeping in his clothes. He groggily sat on the side of the bed and put on his ill-fitting shoes. I wasn't sure what he wanted, but I thought that we might at least get outside. I yelled for the attendant. As his steps approached, Mark gripped me as fear tightened his muscles.

"Please," I asked, "is it all right if we take a little walk?"

"Where do you plan to go?" the attendant narrowed his eyes.

"Just outside," I responded.

He grunted his begrudging consent, and we followed him through the chicken wire webbed light of the hallway. He unlocked the third door, and we started walking through the complex of institutional buildings. Mark led the way as we moved wordlessly toward his intended goal.

Just a few weeks before, I had been there as a hero, a musical philanthropist, a welcomed, anonymous star. Mark led me into the newish building where the gymnasium was housed. He pushed the elevator button, and we wordlessly rode down to the lower level. The door opened and Mark led us through the empty darkened hallway, lit only by emergency exit signs. He shuffled into the auditorium, and I set up three metal folding chairs from a stack against the wall. We sat down in the quiet of the place where, just weeks before, we had held the stage and brought joy and music to so many. The only illumination was from the forty-watt ghost light that shone dimly from the stage. Mark was so drugged that he leaned immediately against my shoulder and slipped into unconsciousness. I pulled him gently down into my lap, and he lay across the folding chairs and slept. I stroked his hair lightly, avoiding his battered face. Time slowed to a crawl. I slept as well.

After some period of time, I awoke. I awakened Mark and told him that it was time for me to leave. He pulled himself to his feet, and we shuffled out of the gym. We retraced our steps, back down the hallway, to the elevator to another level, and made the long walk back through the maze of dreary buildings. We knocked on the lock-up's outside door and, after a minute, the attendant turned the key in the heavy door and we were ushered into the prison building. Doors were unlocked, and Mark and I moved down the long hallway, through gray daylight. We were escorted to the door of Mark's cell, and we entered as the attendant waited in the hall. I helped Mark take off his shoes and his pants. I turned back the rough bedding, and he lay down. I laid the covers over him, and he fell again into the dreamless sleep of drugged blackout. I tucked him in and whispered goodbye. I left my younger brother under the penitential supervision of the white uniformed attendant with the flat top, long side burns and mean eyes.

I could imagine how, after the concert, Mark had been flying high. For a while, he might have been pumped. Perhaps there were other teenagers and young adults in the institution who were jealous and angry about the special attention Mark had received. Maybe, to bring him back to reality, a few of them grabbed him and began to beat him up. It might have happened during one of the fifteen-minute breaks when they were allowed outside. I can imagine how Mark might have kicked and scratched and broken away from his tormentors. Running through the freshly mown lawn in the late summer, he made it to the main gate. He wasn't gone long. Minutes later, a policeman with a German Shepherd, cornered and grabbed Mark on the sidewalk, not far from the front gate. Mark's hysteria, at the sight of the snarling and snapping dog, likely brought on the club and the fist to subdue him. Mark was delivered back to the attendants, and it was then their turn. As was the practice when someone had run away, they really worked him over and then injected him with a chemical blackjack, repeated regularly, to ensure that he would be knocked out for days.

After finding the administration building, I told the receptionist that I was looking for the office of whoever was responsible for Mark's "care". I was directed to the psychiatrist's office on the second floor. The office was painted the uniform, institutional light green, with a layer of brown dirt, and the residue of years of cigarette smoke. The doctor's gray metal desk was piled high with file folders–several stacks over a foot high. A large metal ashtray overflowed on the middle of his desk. He sat, amid the low file folder towers, lethargically smoking an acrid cigarette that burned close to the filter. In a very tired voice, he told me that he was responsible for nine hundred individuals, and that he wasn't treating anybody; he was just providing crowd control.

He paused and stared dully out the window. He said that he remembered Mark because of his recent police involvement. Without checking any records, he reported that Mark was receiving 800 mgs. of Thorazine daily. He said that he might have recognized Mark by sight, regardless of his recent interaction with his case, but that generally, he saw each of his nine hundred patients only once a year. I was looking for someone who could change Mark's circumstances, but he seemed like just a terribly overworked guy without the resources to bring any quality of life to the miserable souls with whom he was charged. More than two thousand people were crowded together in the institution's wards. Three times a day, they shuffled through the regimented trip downstairs for meals and, when the weather was good, fifteen minutes in the yard. But now Mark was in the hole–locked in solitary confinement for an indefinite period. In just days, Mark's life had fallen from the joyful celebrity of our concert performance to confinement as the lowest among the low.

The psychiatrist did not apologize for his work but radiated a bone-deep weariness. He had no illusions about his purpose or capability. I thought about how different his work life was from what he might have imagined during his years of preparation to be a healer. I went back to Cleveland with a heavy heart. In the quiet of the finished basement of my parents' home, that had been my bedroom; I wrote the lyric to a song that captured my despair:

WHAT IS THERE FOR ME TO SAY?

What is there for me to say?
We both know where it stands:
I can't stay and you can't go—
There are shackles on our hands.
We're brothers close in spirit
And I hear your message clear,
I've come to say there is no way
To get you out of here.

Son of sorrow, naked rage
Frustration on the run
I know your aching as my own
But nothing can be done.

If I could break these shackles
That tie up time and space
I'd free us both from bondage
And find a quiet place,
Where we could live as family—
Whole and well and free.
If there is truth or a living God
This time will come to be.
You shall be free.

What is there for me to say?
We both know where it stands
I can't stay and you can't go
There are shackles on our hands.

Of all the aching family
Yours is the curse to bear.
I cannot bring you freedom
I've only love to share, love to share.

© Jeff Moyer 1970

Dad's Cancer

In 1971, I moved from southern to northern California to join a friend living in Palo Alto. As winter quarter of 1972 got underway, I was feeling a void in my life. I had a growing itch, a need to find a way to be of service to someone other than myself. Although my world was expanding, I wasn't at peace. I had become a successful member of the Foothill College community—in some remarkable new ways.

Beginning in grade school and continuing year by year, physical education classes had always been a source of humiliation, risk, exclusion, and emotional pain. Most of the classes involved playing team sports with fast moving balls that I couldn't see. Other classes required my demonstrating physical prowess, or learning new skills modeled beyond my ability to see. But at Foothill, for the first time, I was taking physical education classes that did not involve hand/eye coordination or normal visual acuity. I was finding, with my growing success, that I could even define myself as an athlete. I was swimming in a demanding snorkeling class that would include an icy Northern Pacific check out dive. A friend had given me a complete neoprene wet suit. I intended to become a fully certified scuba diver by taking the scuba course offered in fall quarter. I had also taken a cross-country running course, and I learned that I could run for over three miles and enjoy it. I was in great aerobic shape from biking sixteen miles every day, back and forth to school, plus my rigorous physical education courses.

The classroom was also opening new horizons for me. I was taking courses that excited and engaged me—poetry, psychology, American history, and anthropology. Overall, I was feeling the heady success of challenge, genuine effort, and good grades. In February, I attended a weekend poetry workshop at Asilomar, a wonderful retreat center on the Pacific. I received positive and supportive feedback on my writing—an altogether unexpected experience. But, in spite of this expansion in my sense of my own abilities, I felt empty. The center of that void was the constant, dull heartache of my little brother's institutionalization. But I was not willing to move back to Ohio; I loved California. So instead, I wanted to do something to help somebody— anybody—who was in real need. I had just begun to puzzle through the nature of my itch when my reverie was interrupted.

In April, I received a phone call from my parents that shook the foundation of my young world. My father had been diagnosed with cancer.

The epic journey, which he would live, began with a lesion under his tongue, on the floor of his mouth. At first, Dad said, it felt like a canker sore. He expected that, in a few days, it would run its course; but when it didn't, he asked for his brother's opinion. Chuck examined the lesion, in his dental office, and prescribed a round of antibiotics. But the sore didn't respond. Dad was then referred from dentistry to oncology. The diagnosis was grim. Dad had mouth cancer. No one imagined the dark nature of what was to come. An eight-year odyssey began. Everyone in the family had dealt with lots of adversity: my brother's disability and institutionalization, my low vision, and my Dad's job loss two years earlier. We would apply the same resilience and acceptance to this problem. There was no question in my mind; Dad would fight it and win.

The standard of care was to kill the cancer with a combination of toxic chemotherapy and radiation. Dad underwent a few weeks of intense chemotherapy, requiring hospitalization. Mom mailed me photos of my father in his pajamas, in the hospital, tethered to a chemo drip that intravenously delivered the chemical slurry to the tissue of his mouth. With a white tape headband, reminiscent of a Civil War head wound bandage, to stabilize the drip line that went under his skin and to the soft tissue under his jaw, Dad didn't look very happy in the photos. Following the hospitalization, Dad began radiation therapy. In preparation, Chuck pulled nine healthy bottom teeth. Dad took the loss of his teeth like a determined fighter absorbs a stiff blow. But, like a boxer in a title fight, Dad's punishment had just begun. Then there came six weeks of daily radiation. During the treatments, Dad instinctively lifted his tongue to the roof of his mouth, over the cone that targeted the radiation. His doctor was a slave to the limits of the day's technology, but something must have gone terribly wrong. Perhaps the prescription was too strong; perhaps there was an error in the way the lab executed the script, but the bludgeoning impact of those toxic rays, initially burned and blackened the skin on Dad's lower face. But, we still thought that we were dealing with a manageable, curable, medical problem. I had been deflecting my concern by using humor. I created and sent greeting cards that I hoped would convey my concern, buried under sardonic and bizarre wit. I cut out photos of my hairy head and pasted them onto preposterous magazine ads adding outrageous one-liners. I also began to write poetry to him that would ultimately be placed in a book full of my serious verse about his suffering.

As I became painfully accustomed to the idea that my father was fighting cancer, I began to again consider how I could find a way to be of service in the world. I harkened back to what my limited skills were and decided to look for a volunteer job as a guitar teacher for someone in need. In the fall of 1972, I spoke with the executive director of the newly opened Peninsula Center for the Blind and Visually Impaired and offered to teach guitar to anyone who wanted to learn. The word went out and a handful of students with visual disabilities, young and old, signed up. Soon lesson preparation and teaching began, and I found what I had been seeking. I taught guitar and continued college classes throughout that school year. In ongoing discussions with The Peninsula Center's director, we discussed the social and skill development needs of teenagers with vision loss, and I was given the chance to put together a comprehensive, six-week, summer project. I would have my first chance to shape and lead a program.

I was living in a rented house with a varietal fruit orchard, lots of fenced yard, four large dogs, a friend's army-helmet-size desert tortoise, and two men who had responded to my ad. When I first had moved in, I shared the house with Lydia, my former girlfriend, and her college roommate. The men individually responded to my ad in the newspaper, seeking roommates, after the women had moved out. That summer had a busy and purposeful rhythm, crowded by the background reality that my father had cancer and that my brother was languishing in hell.

After Project Self-Help (the six-week, summer youth program at the Peninsula Center) had ended, I was planning on my annual Ohio summer visit. I braced myself, not knowing quite what to expect concerning my Dad. When I arrived in Cleveland in August, I discovered that the onset of the health problem that had turned out to be cancer had had an unanticipated positive result. Dad's drinking had been heavy and non-stop for ten years or more, and his alcohol dependency had taken its toll on his body, his spirit, and every relationship in his life. In addition to the red blotches that covered his cheeks, Dad's hands shook much of the time. The shaking had become so extreme that he couldn't legibly sign his name. I can only imagine what Dad thought about his own drinking. Months before, his brother had advised Dad that he shouldn't consume any alcohol for the two weeks that he would be taking the prescribed antibiotic. So with that quiet proviso, and without any support, Dad had quit drinking—cold turkey.

When I had been with Dad for a few hours, I realized that his presence and interactions had changed dramatically. Dad's anger had disappeared. Gone were the bluster and sullen silences. Dad spoke humbly and sincerely. After 5:00 p.m., instead of the predictable drunkenness, Dad was now always sober and alert. The slurred speech and belligerence were gone, along with the cheerless, hung-over mornings, during which attempts at conversation would be answered with a terse word or silence. In their place were doughnut runs and talks over coffee. My father was back! Our communication became a joy. Although the ongoing news concerning his body's reaction to the toxic blast of cancer treatment was difficult, the father I remembered from my early life lived again. Dad showed real interest and response to my life in California. But true to his stoic nature, he didn't share his thoughts concerning his own health or his future.

Chapter 10: New Goals

Aim High

In early 1973, I was living alone, in a one-bedroom place, on the third floor of a California-style apartment building in Mountain View, California. A few months before, I had moved out of the crowded house in Palo Alto, with the guys, the tortoise, and the dogs. I'd moved into the sunbaked apartment with a new girlfriend. The relationship ended a few months after the move, but I kept the place and lived alone. The third-floor walk-up faced a center courtyard which contained the apartment's greatest asset, a modest swimming pool. I practiced yoga every day, using a book with large line drawings, to learn the poses and exercises. I had become a certified scuba diver through the Foothill College class, and I owned all of the necessary scuba gear except an air tank. As soon as the cool winter weather turned warm, I began to swim laps every day. I had swum in the unheated pool several times during the winter, wearing my ocean-going frog man outfit, but I felt a bit conspicuous as neighbors, with nothing else to look at, would gather on the balconies to watch me. It must have been comical to see me swim back and forth in the tiny pool, wearing a complete wetsuit, mask, snorkel, and large ocean flippers. I was biking daily to Foothill. I carried my bike and book backpack up and down the apartment's staircases. I was in the best shape of my life.

At Foothill, I was finishing the last courses I needed to complete two full years of college work. Soon, it would be time to get on to my upper division courses. I would have to leave my comfortable little life and move, to study at San Jose State, I thought. It had been six years since I had begun college at Cleveland State. My ever-present insecurities, about being able to succeed at full-time university work, and my vagabond ways, had led to my slowly developing college career. To compensate for my tentativeness, concerning my viability as a student, my nearly full time school life had always been pursued in tandem with various work roles. I had worked as a firewood cutter's helper, ditch digger, landscape laborer, guitar teacher, pizza joint guitar player, dishwasher, house painter, and as a youth program director. But, through it all, my role as a college student was at the center of my identity. Finishing my undergraduate work remained an unswerving, if slowly developing, life goal. I would finish all of my lower division courses

174

that winter quarter. In the spring, after classes were behind me, I had lined up full-time work as a tree trimmer's assistant.

During the summer, I would again return to my job directing Project Self-Help. My education plan was to apply to San Jose State University for the fall quarter. San Jose State was about thirty miles south of Mountain View. I thought that by staying in the area I could maintain my friendships, plus my Saturday and summer work with the young people with visual disabilities. Just before applications were due, I sat in The Foothill College counselor's office. He reviewed the results of my meandering college record, and the scores from a vocational interest inventory test that he had suggested I take. He hunched over his desk studying my folder. Without looking up, he asked me what I planned to do next. I told him that I was going to apply to San Jose State.

Then he looked up, "San Jose State? Why don't you apply to Berkeley? You're smart, you have the grades, and Berkeley is a better school. Aim high! You should apply to Berkeley."

I felt the unexpected swell of pride at his endorsement of my ability, but I also felt the weight of self-doubt. I admitted that I didn't think I could make it at Berkeley. I had always feared academic failure. School was extraordinarily demanding, struggling as I did with my optical aids and readers. I confessed that Berkeley seemed out of reach. He was firm. He simply re-stated that my grades demonstrated that I was Berkeley material. As I left his office, he called after me. "Aim high! Apply to Berkeley."

The next week, I sat at my second-hand-store, kitchen table working on my Berkeley application. I had received my transcripts from Cleveland State, Palomar College, and Foothill College. Now I wrestled with the required essay concerning why I wanted to go to the University of California at Berkeley. After putting as fine a point as I was going to on my drafted pleading, I rolled the application form into my portable manual typewriter. I laboriously typed, from my handwritten third draft–stopping every time I thought that I might have made a mistake. I would re-check my efforts by pressing my magnifier and eye to the letters that had just passed under the typewriter's strike zone. Painstakingly, I typed the essay and then slowly read it over. I sealed the envelope containing my completed application and check. I wondered what the likelihood was of my being accepted. I walked down the block, and I slipped my dreams for the future into the corner mailbox.

Six weeks later, I nervously opened the letter from The University of California at Berkeley. With bursting joy, I read my acceptance letter. I had done it! I'd applied to and had been accepted by one of the great universities. In a few months, I was going to throw myself into the feared crucible of really serious full-time university work. I was going to be a junior at Berkeley! The moment held the unfamiliar sweetness of new membership in an elite academic community. Never before had I felt such validation of my native ability. The future was daunting, but brighter than I could have imagined.

Over the Edge

I had been riding to Foothill, eight miles each way, since I started classes there. The bike was also my transportation for everything: taking my giant bundle of laundry to the laundromat, hauling bags of groceries, and carrying my precariously balanced guitar to the lessons I taught. My bicycle riding was required for the life I was leading, and an ongoing act of defiance and high-risk foolhardiness.

I was bucking the conclusion that Dr. Kazdan had come to when I was eleven, that I could no longer see well enough to ride a bicycle. I had actively and repeatedly rebelled against the impact that his proclamation had had on my two-wheeled locomotion. But in 1971, at age twenty-two, I declared the bike ban officially over. I bought my first ten-speed bicycle, and I took my place as a permanent member of the biking world. Only weeks later, on a stormy night, I ruined that well-balanced–albeit inexpensive– machine when I plowed into the back end of a parked car. When I struck I was launched over the handlebars, crashing into the car as I banged and tumbled over its entire length–landing in a heap on the wet asphalt in front of it. But I was undeterred by the collision. It could have happened to anybody, I rationalized. It was dark. It was pouring rain. My glasses were covered in vision smearing raindrops. The car was in the shadows under a tree. I had to ride home.

After riding the bent-framed wreck for a couple of months, I bought another, expensive English bicycle. My new bike was a Dawes, painted a fine British racing green. It had red taped, decoratively-tooled underslung handlebars, a narrow hard leather racing seat, and was built for speed. I really loved that machine. Bicycle riding was a high-risk activity for me, I knew, but it gave me independence and allowed me to pursue my life in the sprawling Bay Area. I was lean and physically fit, and loved the feeling of power that the bike provided. Living in California with its mild winters, also

176

allowed me twelve months a year of independent, leg-powered mobility. But, after my first accident, I prepared better for the rains of winter. I would don my surplus store, orange, hooded rainproof jacket and pants, waterproof work boots, and broad brimmed hat. I would feel almost invincible. I had a few upgrades added to the bike which were supposed to help it stop in the rain. Special brake pads added to stopping power, along with textured tire rims. The bike did brake better when wet, sort of. Of course, when I had slammed into the parked car, the brakes weren't a factor. I had never applied them; I hadn't seen the car at all.

When I started Foothill Junior College, even in pouring rain, I would ride in heavy rush hour traffic. I felt intrepid, resilient, and almost indomitable. I fundamentally knew, however, that I was vulnerable and was riding the frightening fence line of my vision's limits. I considered my situation one of rational risk. I rode, or rather drove, my bike as if I had the same rights and even the same power as anyone else on the road. At stoplights, I would follow the motion of traffic, since I couldn't see traffic lights. I would slow and stop when I saw or heard cars stopping. When the line of cars began moving, I would push off from the right side curb or the median strip, and then have to merge with left turning traffic, as I traversed the broad and busy intersections of six lane California highways. Yikes! My low vision, high-risk bicycle riding meant that I had to maintain a constant high state of vigilance, as I assessed the traffic around me and made the split-second decisions required to avoid collisions. But, in spite of my best efforts, my constant bike riding was rife with harrowing near misses and the occasional accident.

Once, while crossing the street slowly within a boulevard's pedestrian crosswalk, I was hit by a car going about forty miles per hour. I heard her horn and had begun to go back, so my back tire was hit at nearly a ninety degree angle rather than being struck broadside. It was really a miracle that, although I was thrown about twenty feet on my bicycle and the bike was twisted under me, I escaped without a bruise. Actually, I was delighted when the young woman driving the car that had struck me nervously offered to have my ruined bike repaired immediately, at her expense, in exchange for my not calling the police. An hour and a half later, I was back on the road, riding what felt like a new bicycle. Only the frame and handlebars had been salvageable; the rest of the bike had to be replaced. My life as a bicycle rider meant more to me than basic transportation. I admit that I was into the fantasy and mystique of bicycle chic. I cinched my running shoes tightly onto the bike's pedals using toe clips, and I wore a piece of rakish headgear–an Italian-made, black, leather bike-racing helmet. It wasn't a standard solid bike helmet, but a tightly fitting, padded series of leather straps. I wore leather, fingerless bicycle gloves and, when the weather became warm enough, cargo shorts. My biking costume made me feel very hip. But I was also deluding myself into believing the myth of my image.

After I had received my acceptance letter from Berkeley, and after all of my classes were over, I rode to Foothill one warm spring afternoon, feeling–well–overconfident. I went for a simple last errand. After I picked up my final term paper, I was nearly alone on campus. Without any other students to dodge, I decided to put my sleek ten-speed bike through its paces. The modern campus's broad sidewalks met in ninety-degree angles as they framed benches, gravel, and lawn. The sidewalks were about a foot higher than the rest of the campus's landscaping in some places, a curious hazard. But that afternoon, I wasn't thinking about hazards, I was thinking about speed. I took advantage of the campus's emptiness. For the first time, I powered along the smooth concrete, taking the corners at considerable speed, leaning the bike into exhilarating turns. I was really flying around two tightly spaced corners, when I struck disaster. I turned too soon while ripping around the second corner. My bike's front wheel left the sidewalk, dropped a foot, and slammed into the gravel and the adjoining sidewalk's concrete edge. I was hurled headfirst over the handlebars and onto the waiting concrete. I instinctively threw out my left arm and I crashed onto the sidewalk, hitting on my forehead and elbow. The racing helmet's padded straps provided a small bit of cushioning for my skull, but my head was violently snapped back and to the right, and my elbow was torn open in a jagged wound. For the first few moments, I lay motionless on the warm concrete; then I slowly began assessing my injuries. My elbow burned and bled profusely, and my head and neck felt like I had been hit with a sledgehammer. But with groggy relief, I realized that nothing was broken. I pulled myself to my feet. With blood running down my arm, soaking my bike glove, I was able to force the skewed handlebars back into their proper position. The front wheel's rim was bent. I pulled it back into very rough alignment, and then I discovered, with relief, that I was still able to slowly ride the bike. I wobbled to the house of a member of the sponsoring woman's club, which was throwing a pool party and cookout for my program's teenagers with blindness and low vision that afternoon. Fortunately, she lived nearby.

The hostess cleaned and bandaged my elbow. Later that evening, an emergency room doctor sewed up my elbow's jagged wound. An orthopedic surgeon said that I was fortunate that my neck injury wasn't more serious. I had torn muscles in my neck, and I had caused a disc to bulge. He gave me prescriptions and a neck brace–a stiff, white cervical collar. I was in pain and moved very slowly. The accident laid me up for six weeks.

I took advantage of my convalescence. Every morning, I would put my tie-dyed purple Speedo on and grease myself from forehead to toes with Johnson's Baby Oil. I would lie on a chaise lounge in front of my third-floor apartment, listen to books on tape, and bake in the unblinking sun all day. During those six weeks, I roasted myself to a cinnamon brown and let my shoulder length black hair and wooly beard continue to grow, ungroomed and unchallenged. My recovery eased from none, to a few, to all normal activities. After I could ride again, the bicycle was, once again, repaired.

Soft Pretzels

After I had healed from the injuries resulting from my self-inflicted bicycle accident, I made a date with Mariah. I had met her shortly before the mishap. We were introduced through a mutual friend from Cleveland. Mariah had grown up in Cleveland, gone to college, and was living in a rambling group house with a pool. We had planned a hike in the nearby redwood forest as our first date. Mariah phoned to say she didn't want to hike because she was hung over. She suggested instead that we help Sandy (one of her four housemates) with her little, soft pretzel business. Sandy was working at Stanford University's crafts fair, and she needed to have the freshly baked pretzels delivered to her busy stand. We would pick up the hot pretzels from Sandy's older sister, who was baking the frozen pretzels in an electric conveyor oven in her garage. Sandy was selling them from her mobile pretzel wagon. We picked up two large boxes of big soft salted pretzels and headed to Stanford.

Sandy was a strikingly attractive woman, in her halter top, short shorts, and with her street vendor style. Her red, wooden and glass pretzel cart stood on large wooden wheels. It was parked next to a stone bench which surrounded a splashing fountain. Sandy leaned against the cart and we fell into an instant ease. Her long thick brown hair fell past her breasts.

179

She was tall, relaxed, and appreciative of our delivery efforts. Her sister wasn't much of a pretzel baker; many of the large soft pretzels were quite doughy and undercooked. Sandy picked through the pretzels, putting the good ones in the glass enclosure of the cart. She was going to throw the under baked ones away. After she had sold out and was turning customers away, I asked if she minded if I sold the less than perfect pretzels at a discount. She laughingly gave me the go ahead; soon I had loaded the white, gummy, treats into the glass-sided, red cart and was happily-"Honestly, these are undercooked,"-hawking them for fifteen cents, a ten-cent discount. Sandy was impressed by my initiative; no one was impressed with the pretzels.

Mariah, Sandy, and I were pals together for a few weeks, hiking, doing the pretzel shuttle, and generally getting to know each other. Then, Mariah couldn't go with us for one of our outings. That afternoon, Sandy and I became a couple. In seventies California style, I moved into their group house in early June.

The house was surrounded by a high, board fence and an expanse of concrete, around the kidney shaped pool. Much to my delight, the norm of the house was swim-suits optional, and everyone chose to bask, in the sun in the pool area, *au naturale*. So I sunbathed and swam with my new friends, in the buff, allowing the only area of my lean body that had not been not deeply darkened by my weeks of sunny rehabilitation, to begin to bronze as well. We shared communal meals, and the house was a wonderful and easy place to live.

With real vigor, I threw myself into the work of planning and directing the second year's expanding Project Self-Help. But in August, after the program ended, it was again time to return to Cleveland to visit my family and to go and see Mark.

On a Saturday, my parents and I drove to Columbus to begin the grim ritual of signing in, and then walking up the black iron fire escape to Mark's floor of the ugly, dirty, brick building which contained his life. The August heat was oppressive; we handed Mark a striped tank top, as part of his usual, complete change of clothing, for our outing. He changed out of the stained and threadbare shirt and ill-fitting dungarees, and into his own, new clothes.

As always, the other fifty men who lived with Mark, in that one room, swarmed around us hungrily, pressing close for human touch. When Mark was dressed, we left the ward as always the heavy door slammed and was locked, with jangling keys, behind us. Mark looked awful. His hair was unwashed and greasy and stuck to his forehead in filthy strands. His face was peppered with pimples and scabs, and under his eye was an ugly green-yellow bruise. Mark's eyes were glazed and listless, and his face showed no emotion. He dragged along under the impact of the heavy sedation that, three years before, the psychiatrist had referred to as "crowd control". Mark wanted a cigarette. Before we got into the car, Mom gave him one of her L&M's. Mark stood and quickly smoked the cigarette right down to the filter.

Mark had begun smoking in 1963, the year he entered the institution, when he was only nine years old. Mark craved cigarettes all the time. I had quit smoking the year before and I despaired, thinking of how that tough choice would never be Mark's. He was a slave to the tobacco addiction with which he had been helplessly saddled.

At nearly nineteen, Mark's face was bloated and his stomach was extended in a sagging paunch. Whether a side effect of the medications that kept him in his sluggish stupor or the by-product of the institution's diet, the results were the same. Mark was listless, overweight, and dirty. We did our usual restaurant meal, snapshots, and back to the institution. The photos captured the strain and extreme tension of the day. No one smiled except for Mom, whose sorrowful eyes betrayed the joyless grin she forced for the camera. Back in the institution's parking lot, I told my folks that I would walk Mark back. Mom said let him have the clothes, rather than taking them back for next time. I walked with Mark from the parking lot, back into the back pathways of the institution, and up the fire escape staircase to his ward. He was so drugged and dull, that he did not hang onto me and cry as usual, but shuffled back inside the open door, unlocked by the grim faced attendant. He never looked back. I turned away from Mark's prison and walked to the car, feeling as beaten down as Mark did.

My visit ended and I returned to California. When I arrived, I shared with Sandy the sorrow of my visit, and I again told her about the constant pain that I lived with, knowing how desperate and depraved Mark's life was. But our life in California, that late summer, involved our developing plans to move sixty miles north to Berkeley. My heartache was, as always, put on hold.

Chapter 11: Becoming Berkeley

Physically Disabled Students Program

In August 1973, Sandy and I made plans to move from Palo Alto to Berkeley. One day while I was directing Project Self-Help, Sandy drove her Karmann Ghia to Berkeley and rented a wonderful little place–the second floor of a charming carriage house which stood behind what had been, in 1900, the Governor's summer mansion. Sandy had a keen eye for design; soon the place was freshly painted, bright newly sewn curtains were hung, and we set up housekeeping on our own. Our idyllic living space was complete with two towering redwood trees in our private yard, a wood burning stove, and a little roof deck for our small hibachi grill. Our new home had been the hayloft and upper areas of the little carriage house, and the peak roof, with exposed beams, made for an airy and light-filled space. It was a cozy nest for our new life which revolved around my role as a student at Berkeley.

A few days before classes started, I began to get oriented to the vast campus and surrounding area. Berkeley's catalog, which we pored over, included the services offered by the Physically Disabled Students Program. I had never heard of such an office, but the program offered reader referral. Finding a reader for college texts had always been a time-consuming, hit-and-miss problem. I typically would stand up in my classes, during the first session, and announce that I was looking for a reader. Some readers, so recruited, proved to be wonderful, talented, and committed. But others, well intended, weren't very good readers and didn't enjoy the work. Over time, some good readers tired of the long hours of reading aloud.

The idea that a program existed that would provide a referral list, was a huge improvement over what I had always done before. Sandy read me the number from the small print catalog, and I called the office. The phone was answered "PDSP", by a friendly woman named Zona. I introduced myself and Zona outlined PDSP services. A new world of access was opening before me. She suggested that I come down to the office, before classes started, to meet the staff and to pick up my key for the remarkable Blind Students' Study within the recently built Bancroft Undergraduate Library. During that first call, Zona also gave me the names and phone numbers of several readers. I decided to ride my bike over that afternoon.

My identity, concerning disability, had broadened a bit. For the second year running, I had directed Project Self-Help, geared for children and teenagers, all of whom had some degree of disabling vision loss ranging from low vision to blindness. Some of the young people had multiple disabilities. The connection with those children and young people was maintained during the GYST (Get Your Self Together) Project–a school-year Saturday recreation program which I also ran, sponsored by a women's club. Through the experience of knowing those kids, I had begun to realize that my identity was not limited to a kinship with others who, like me, had low vision. I now understood that I also had identity and shared community with people with more severe visual disabilities and blindness; and even multiple disabilities. That budding realization was a real change from my earlier, more limited sense of self. Prior to those programs, I had identified with people who had low vision or were fully sighted. I had felt somewhat ill at ease around people who were blind. That barrier had come down with first-hand experience. However, I wasn't certain about my comfort level concerning people with severe physical disabilities. But I was willing to deal with it and eager to develop my new Berkeley network. So I rode my bike the few blocks to the specified street near to the campus, chained my ten speed to a parking meter, and found the old apartment building which housed the PDSP office. I walked in and was greeted by Zona, the happy and outgoing woman with whom I had spoken. She welcomed me like an old friend and introduced me to her adult son, Ed Roberts, who lay in a semi-reclining posture, in a power wheelchair that he controlled with one finger.

Ed was nearly totally paralyzed from a teenage bout with polio, but his open smile, inquisitive and intelligent brown eyes, and engaging personality quickly put me at ease. Ed had been the founder and former director. He introduced me to the office's current director, who also used a power wheelchair, having been paralyzed from a spinal cord injury.

Then Ed introduced me to Dennis Fantin, who was both blind and the peer counselor for blind students. Dennis looked like a Nordic god. He had shoulder length blonde hair, a brown, neatly trimmed beard, and the muscular body of a weightlifting, serious athlete. Dennis was even happier and more outgoing than Zona and Ed. This office made me feel more comfortable than any new place I had ever entered.

Dennis gave me a key to the amazing Bancroft Library's Blind Students' Study, where I could set up an office for my tape recorder, meet readers, or take taped tests. Dennis also described the other resources available to me. While I was talking to Dennis, Ed came into the room, where we sat, and asked me to give him a hand, getting a file from the file cabinet next to me. I quickly excused myself from the offered responsibility, explaining that I couldn't see to read the file tabs. Ed said he didn't need me to read–he could do that–he just needed my hands. So Ed told me which file drawer to open, and then, giving voice commands, directed my hands slowly along the files until I touched the one he wanted. Through that simple method, the files were retrieved. I was quietly stunned. Here was a real, living example of strength through symbiosis. His eyes, my hands! I felt totally at ease with Ed. I felt exhilaration from the experience that I couldn't really get my head around, but I knew that I was somehow being changed and broadened.

When I went to the Blind Students' Study, I also met Bob Metts, a graduate student in economics, who had had polio like Ed. Bob, however, had lost only about sixty percent of his muscle function. Ed could only move his head, right forearm, and little finger. Bob could walk, with a severe gait, and he used his good arm to drive a golf cart. It was his means of easily moving around campus and the streets of Berkeley as well. Bob shared Zona's, Ed's and Dennis's optimism, wit, and high energy. We became fast friends. Bob had one of the other offices at The Blind Students' Study. The Cave, as we called it, was in the lower level of the Bancroft Library, at the center of campus. The Blind Students' Study was a locked suite of offices that were soundproofed and, within which, one could use a tape recorder or have a reader read without disturbing any other studying students. There were also typewriters, Braille writers, and a fantastic, wall-sized, tactile topographical map of campus–complete with every building, pathway, and campus contour–labelled in Braille. The remarkable map, a gift from the School of Architecture, was a real help. Bob told me to claim an empty office. By the next day, I had moved my reel-to-reel, adapted tape recorder, tapes, and coffee pot into my new study space. Bob had one of the offices because of his physical constraints. It gave him a place to study and rest, which was centrally located.

I phoned the first reader on Zona's list, and I hired her over the phone. We met before classes started. She was a graduate student who read for several students. We set up a system for her to reference my class syllabi and to record the needed reading on to a stack of reel-to-reel tapes which I provided. Pat began recording the articles and required books, as soon as classes began. She faithfully, with poise and understanding, read everything that I had to learn onto my used and reused reels. The ease and reliability of her flawless service allowed me to spend the forty to fifty hours per week, which became my standard weekly study schedule, listening and re-listening to the texts that I was required to master. I had never had such wonderful accommodations for school, at any educational level.

I was also benefiting from a new innovation in magnification technology. I had seen a new device, a closed circuit television video magnifier, or CCTV, during the summer of 1973, while working at the Peninsula Center for the Blind and Visually Impaired. The device was a powerful combination of off-the-shelf elements, video monitor and camera, with a high-powered close-up zoom lens mounted to a metal tubular frame. The CCTV allowed one to zoom in on print or handwriting and to magnify it to whatever size was needed. Its magnification power was far beyond the capability of optical magnifiers like the ones I had been using for twelve years. The CCTV provided a giant leap forward in my ability to read. I spoke with my rehab counselor, from the California Department of Rehabilitation, about purchasing one for my college work. He said that they had never bought a CCTV for a college student before, but I was not to be deterred. I wrote a simple cost/benefit analysis, estimating how I would use fewer hours of reader service with the machine, making it pay for itself in savings on otherwise needed reader services.

The Department of Rehabilitation must have been convinced. Soon the wonderful new electronic magnification device had been purchased for me. But the taxing reality of using the electronic system for extensive reading was slower and more visually tiring than I had imagined. I discovered, to my chagrin, that I still could not read long articles (and certainly not books) using my new CCTV. Readers were going to have to do all of the heavy lifting for my reading-intensive courses. But with the CCTV I could, for the first time, easily read my class notes. I kept the device on my desk, at home, and the ease of sitting in a comfortable posture to organize, review, and study my voluminous class notes, gave me the ability to really study like never before. Prior to the CCTV, my study sessions were limited by my endurance. I'd endured both ocular and muscular strain as my reading eye ached, and my neck cramped from postural strain. With the device, I could zoom in and study my notes for as long as I could focus–not as long as I could endure the pain.

During those first months, I met many other students with disabilities. This offered me an ever broadening exposure to a wide spectrum of visual and other disabilities. Some students were paralyzed from bouts of polio, some had cerebral palsy, some had central nervous system degenerative diseases, and others had experienced spinal cord injuries. All of us lived with severe disability and received a range of invaluable services from PDSP. We were all focused intently on our academic programs. I don't recall any student with a disability dropping out, or not finishing their degrees, for any reason. We were all full members of Berkeley's diverse, inclusive, and unique community.

A thread of common identity that knit us together was our membership in the burgeoning, socio-political Disability Rights community. We shared, although subconsciously a common disability identity. We all had made it into Berkeley to study and apply ourselves, to party and to celebrate, and to experience the exhilaration of youth and the wonder of that life stage's broadening horizon. I came to understand, in those first joyful months, that my identity did not stop at being visually disabled. I was a member in good standing of the community of people of all disabilities, and we shared common experiences of discrimination that reached across the divide of our differences. The identity of disability was political, interpersonal, and psychological. I felt the new sense of belonging growing within me.

Then the first quarter ended. I painstakingly had typed my term papers on the new, electric, portable typewriter that I had bought, to speed my typing. I prepared for final exams, reading and organizing my class notes, using my wonderful, new CCTV and re-listening to segments of texts that my reader had recorded. The finals were arranged, with willing professors, to be taken using a typewriter and a tape recorder. The PDSP office offered to facilitate such arrangements, but it was never necessary. I felt good about my preparation, and I waited anxiously for the results of my efforts to arrive by mail.

My grades arrived and I nervously opened the official University envelope. The thin yellow sheet inside listed the courses and my grades–all A's! I was overjoyed. Only at Berkeley did I finally experience what being tested on my knowledge–rather than my vision–felt like. I had really done well and I thought about my junior college counselor, whose belief in my ability had empowered me to apply to, and be accepted by Berkeley. There they were. My grades were in my hands. Simple accommodations and steadily applied, hard work was all that was needed.

Sandy and I married on December 1, 1973, shortly before the quarter had ended. I was beginning married life, applying myself to my studies, and feeling capable, successful, and focused. The shame that had plagued me all of my life, concerning my limited vision, had begun to recede as my identity as a competing, succeeding person with a disability blossomed.

The Power of Partnership

The gathering of young people with disabilities in Berkeley, in the seventies, was truly remarkable in many ways. The impact of our efforts is felt today. Organizations we founded and that had been run by people with disabilities and their supporters, forged many of the models from which today's Disability Rights Movement's programs have grown. Disabled student's programs and independent living centers began in Berkeley. Those grassroots organizations have had impact internationally. The movement began with Ed Roberts' acceptance as a student at Berkeley in 1962. Like me, but a decade before, Ed had first completed two years of work within junior college before applying to and being accepted by Berkeley. But the University of California didn't know about Ed's disability and was caught unaware. They were flummoxed with this fellow who slept in an iron lung, and who required attendant services for every functional activity of academic life and daily living. To address his needs, Ed was housed at the Cowell Hospital, on campus. He soon recruited other young people, with severe physical disabilities, to apply to Berkeley, join him, and to live there as well. Ed became aware of burgeoning Federal programs to support minority students in college. Perceiving the potential, Ed went to Washington and ultimately received federal funding for the first program in the nation to provide services for students with physical and visual disabilities, on a university campus. His program would enable students, with severe physical disabilities, to be academically integrated and to move out of the hospital and into the broader Berkeley community.

Berkeley's Physically Disabled Students Program began. The comprehensive program included peer counseling, assistance with navigating government services, wheelchair repair, personal attendant and reader referral, and assistance with the functional aspects of independent living. Eventually, it also was responsible for the design of the Blind

Students' Study on campus. The model applied the same paradigm, concerning the effectiveness of peer support, which had empowered other minority self-help efforts. Services were provided by young people, who shared the disability experience with those they counseled. Upon graduation, Ed (and others) needed similar services within the community.

Ed Roberts and his cadre of others with disabilities founded The Center for Independent Living, CIL, to provide that constellation of needed services. Legions of young people with disabilities flocked to Berkeley. They were drawn by CIL's services, California's generous benefit program, and Berkeley's quickly evolving, south campus area's architectural accessibility. Berkeley was quickly changed. Advocacy, by PDSP and CIL, affected brick and mortar realities. Curb cuts and ramps made the city surrounding the campus accessible to people in wheelchairs. Berkeley quickly became the most accessible university and community in the world, for people with severe physical disabilities. Due to inaccessible environments and lack of needed services, the same individuals who thrived in Berkeley would have been confined to their homes, or within nursing homes or institutions, in virtually every other city in the world.

The University of California at Berkeley had admitted blind students for many decades. Around the turn of the twentieth century, a few blind students had been accepted at Berkeley, like Dr. Jacobus tenBroek and Dr. Newel Perry. They became teachers and attorneys and established the first disability rights organization in the United States, the National Federation of the Blind. But, as in my own struggles, there had always been barriers. Inflexible teachers, the impossible mechanics of standard testing, barriers to materials and study areas, and general lack of accommodations meant a substantially more difficult academic experience. However, beginning at the dawn of the twentieth century, students with visual disabilities did attend and graduate from Berkeley with honors in spite of the barriers. PDSP opened its doors addressing the unmet needs of blind students, but most importantly the extensive, heretofore-never-met needs of students with severe physical disabilities.

Many of us formed friendships with people with disabilities different from our own. That exposure, in the setting of Berkeley's highly charged political backdrop, provided a context within which one could begin to think politically about disability as a broad Civil Rights issue, requiring coalition driven action.

I also saw the power of strength in partnership, through the example of friends. Bob and Dennis were housemates. Both were graduate students, and both lived with severe disability. Bob had been left with forty percent muscle function following childhood polio. Dennis was blinded at fourteen, after falling from a roof. Both Dennis and Bob were bright, funny, and creative. They both loved outdoor adventure. The housemates signed up, with a program called ETC, for a weekend river rafting trip down one of northern California's whitewater rivers. The program took people with disabilities on white water river trips, in sixteen-person, inflatable rafts. After one trip, Bob and Dennis were hooked.

But being participating passengers was not their real interest; they wanted to have their own raft and figure out how to run the river themselves. They bought a smaller raft that was powered by a single oarsman who sat on a centerboard. Their plan was daring. Dennis would be the oarsman, powerfully controlling the raft with his long-developed physical strength and stamina, and Bob would captain and navigate, calling out river conditions and their own oaring commands to Dennis. Together, they studied river navigation and techniques for handling the hazards of wild rivers. They developed the shorthand commands that Bob would call out for Dennis's execution. Here were two men with complete faith in each other's abilities, combining their passions for adventure with their complementary and symbiotic abilities. The raft could carry passengers as well, and soon Bob and Dennis were offering white water river trips to their friends.

In the late spring of 1975, Sandy and I were invited on one of their weekend white water adventures down the Stanislaus River. With the anticipation of high adventure, we headed off in sandals, shorts, and tank tops, armed with a fair quantity of beer and the kindly herb. After several hours of driving, we joined the others gathering at a rented A-frame house.

Bob and Dennis would take half of us down the river on Saturday and the other half on Sunday. On Saturday morning we launched the raft– three passengers in front of Dennis and Bob–and me behind. The river was high, fast, and cold, from the Sierra Nevada's snowmelt. Bob peered around Dennis and assessed the river's upcoming navigational challenges. Then, he called out their unique shorthand, and Dennis skillfully powered around hazards, boulders, and standing waves, rowing with careful strokes through rocky shallows. After a thrilling morning, we stopped for lunch.

Shortly after we re-entered the river, on the second leg of the trip, the river flexed its watery muscle. As the intrepid duo navigated to the left, around a great boulder in the middle of the river, the fierce current abruptly shoved the raft. The rubber craft was pushed sideways, forcing the front of the raft up the boulder's steep face. The back of the inflated raft was thrust sideways and down, into the raging river; churning, ice cold water rushed into the place where Bob and I sat. We were all wearing life vests. Bob was knocked onto his back and was suddenly being pulled out of the raft and into the wild river's surging current. I grabbed Bob and pulled him back into the raft. He grabbed the rope that ran around the raft, with his nondisabled hand, and held fast. I entered the frantic effort underway to force the raft off of the rock. The fearsome force of the river was keeping the raft pressed against the boulder's nearly vertical side and slowly moving it still further up the rock's face. Four of us were slipping and awkwardly reaching, as ideas about what to do were yelled back and forth. We eventually kicked and pushed the little boat free. The raft spun around, as Dennis strained at the oars to right our position. We bailed the frigid water from the raft's interior, using our hats and the coffee cans brought along for just that purpose. Quickly, we were out of danger and back on course.

River rafting involved risk, but both risk and complete faith were needed when Bob and Dennis strapped Ed Roberts, totally paralyzed, into the bottom of the raft, on a later trip. The partnership between those two young men was so complete–so natural–that they made their improbable white water symbiosis look easy. Bob's eyes were paired with Dennis's body, spurred by both of their wills, intelligence, skill, and competence. Their community river adventures were one of the sidebars of the dynamic Berkeley story in the seventies.

Another duo of men with disabilities was inspired to follow Bob and Dennis's pioneering lead. Michael and Mark also bought a raft, and Michael's eyes and Mark's brawn resulted in another powerful partnership that plied the waters of California's wild rivers. Michael and I were students at the same time at Berkeley, and Mark had been one of the young people I had worked with through my recreation projects. Mark attended Berkeley, a few years after I did, and added his intelligence and drive to the disabled community.

A few years later, Michael, Bob, Dennis, and others masterminded a courageous effort that led to Jimmy Carter's signing of The National Wild and Scenic Rivers Act–legislation that saved many of America's wild rivers from being dammed and lost. Michael and two other men spent ten days chained to a boulder at the site of a dam to be constructed on the beautiful Stanislaus River. Their hardy protest made national news as they hunkered down in their camouflaged rabbit warren, hidden from the view of searching law enforcement, to bring public attention to the threat of the loss of wild rivers planned for dam projects.

Center for Independent Living

My academic life at Berkeley had continued at the same steady, demanding pace that I had set for myself when I began. I studied forty to fifty hours a week, and as graduation approached I received my invitation to join Phi Beta Kappa. I was thrilled with that stamp of approval but felt a greater joy when I received a letter informing me that I was to receive the one Departmental Citation in recognition of outstanding undergraduate accomplishment in Social Welfare. It was explained to me that my academic prowess was a requirement, but that the citation honored me as the student who had accomplished the most outstanding work in the field of Social Welfare during my years at Berkeley. The award recognized the summer and Saturday programs for young people with visual disabilities which I created and directed.

As I prepared to graduate from The University of California at Berkeley in 1975, I mulled over my possibilities for potential employment. My degree in Social Welfare was a vocationally oriented undergraduate degree that prepared me for an entry-level, social work position. But my vision was so limited that I knew that I wouldn't be able to handle the forms, files, reports, and other print requirements of such a job. I also knew that I might still face the type of discrimination that I had, years before, when the personnel officer at G.E. told me that they didn't hire "the handicapped". In addition, working in what would likely be a governmental agency seemed as if it might be pretty dismal and dull.

I was thrilled to hear from the Social Work School secretary that a job announcement was posted for peer counselors at The Center for Independent Living. CIL was looking for people with disabilities, to do social work-type peer counseling through a federally funded demonstration project. CIL had been established in 1971 and was well known to all students with disabilities at Berkeley. My old friend, Ed Roberts, directed the independent living center. The Center was staffed primarily by people with disabilities, and its grass-roots personality and politics were familiar and appealing. The Federally funded project was researching the efficacy of the peer-counseling model. It seemed like it would be a great job within an organization that had energy and focus, and provided needed support services for community members.

During my interview, a soft spoken gentleman, with a spinal cord injury, studied my resume and application and asked if I would be interested in a job as coordinator of blind services instead. The job had come open when its coordinator had been promoted to head the federal project. The interviewer felt that my freshly earned degree in Social Welfare and my three years of administrative experience, managing programs for young people and teens with visual disabilities, made me a great candidate. I eagerly accepted his offer, and the week after I graduated, I began my new job.

CIL occupied the second floor of a shabby old office building near campus. My job involved providing both direct services to people with visual disabilities of all ages, and management of the other staff in the Blind Services Department. We offered a ragged range of services including peer counseling, orientation and mobility instruction, transportation and information, and referral. The program had been funded by Berkeley's Community Action Program, and had been titled: "Services to Berkeley's 'Out of Sight' Residents". I never used the project's silly name.

CIL was revolutionary in several ways. We served people with disabilities. Handicaps were understood to be the barriers, both environmental and attitudinal, that blocked people with disabilities from achieving their personal and political potential. We saw ourselves as system change agents, and we offered unique services that empowered individuals with disabilities, to live in the community. We defined our mandate as filling gaps in existing service systems and advocating to change public policy and public programs. There were gaping unmet needs and barriers resulting from public policies that blocked individuals from receiving education, employment, and community integration.

In 1975, CIL addressed the needs of people with physical and visual disabilities only. Deafness, cognitive, and emotional disabilities were not within the center's purview, but we tended to speak globally as if we were capable of meeting everyone's needs. We were not really inclusive, in that sense, despite our own press. But we did cast a broad net. For our diverse clients, we provided specific services enabling independence with support in the community, as compared to the ghastly and stultifying alternative of nursing homes or institutions.

Ed Roberts conducted the final interview with me. Ed offered me the job. I considered myself fortunate to be working under a man with such

192

socio-political vision and drive. Ed had charisma, a straightforward yet warm interpersonal style, and an impressive track record. I knew first-hand the real value of PDSP's services, and CIL was in every way a community-based expansive extension of that model. CIL was the beachhead of a new social movement, as much as a center delivering specific services.

It was with enthusiasm and a sense of revolutionary zeal that I set to work bringing order and accountability to my little department. There were only four other employees in my department. Within a matter of weeks, two of them had broken cardinal rules and were released. One didn't show up for work for two weeks, the other pressed sexual advances on an unwilling female client. I hired Jon, a licensed social worker with low vision, who began providing peer counseling groups, individual sessions, and information and referral for clients. Jon was skilled, laid back, and he and I became fast friends. For the first time, I had a friend who shared low vision and a common professional and political orientation. Carol was our orientation and mobility instructor. Her work involved teaching independent travel skills to people who had no other means of obtaining them. She taught the art of independent mobility through white cane use, and orientation to specific places or travel routes. Many of our clients were seniors who lost vision in later life. Carol delivered training that kept them happily living in their own homes and communities. Without such independent travel skills, their continued independence would have been in real jeopardy. Bobbie was hired to drive the Dodge Dart that I selected for our transportation program. CIL already had accessible vans. Any client who needed transportation for some serious purpose, and who was unable to take a bus, was eligible for her driver services. I did intake, referring clients to my little band, while also providing information and referral, peer counseling, and interfacing with our funding agency and the center's administration. But CIL was also involved in regional training programs, and I was quickly drawn into roles within those landmark efforts.

Peter, in his forties—one of the older members of our CIL community was a master social worker and counselor. Peter had been partially paralyzed since his early twenties and had used his personal experience and his professional training, to develop a powerful and innovative way of acknowledging and processing the psychosocial and emotional aspects of loss and grieving. His classes provided us with tools that could readily be applied in our peer counseling. Peter wrote a grant and was funded by the Federal Regional Rehabilitation Services Administration, to conduct week-long in-service training programs for state rehabilitation counselors in our federal region. I joined Peter to design and help conduct training, within that program. I directed the training for counselors providing service to consumers with visual disabilities. Counselors from California, Nevada, Arizona, and Hawaii, came to us for their week of learning first-hand about the experience of living with loss. Counselors who worked with clients, who had physical disabilities, were asked to use wheelchairs for mobility, for the entire week. Counselors, who served clients with visual disabilities, were required to wear wrap-around sunglasses, which I had modified by placing nearly black photographic negatives behind the lenses, allowing no useful vision. With those limitations, they sat in classes, ate their meals, and lived with CIL staff members throughout that week. Participants who were required to use wheelchairs found the experience eye-opening, but were not as psychologically challenged as the rehabilitation counselors under my charge who underwent powerful emotional demands that seemed to altered their personalities and thrust them into life experiences that gave them great empathy with individuals who lived day to day with profound vision loss. The program worked, and we gained in reputation within the Federal Regional office in San Francisco.

One afternoon, Carol, the mobility instructor, brought Mary Jane by the office. Mary Jane was a statuesque blind woman who had been a professor at San Francisco State University prior to the onset of her blindness. She and I instantly hit it off and began collaborating on the design of a college course we would teach through Antioch College West. Antioch College was beginning a degree program through CIL's federally funded Peer Counseling program, and we became adjunct faculty, teaching a course we entitled "The Blind Experience". Professionals from agencies around the Bay Area, and CIL staff and consumers became our students.

But my duties primarily concerned the day-to-day mechanics of my department. I needed to find a larger office space, since the cramped single office we occupied didn't have adequate desk space or phone lines for all of us. On the building's next floor was a corner office for rent. It was a single large room, three times the size of the narrow office that we occupied. It had windows on both outside walls. After the building manager had shown me the space, I decided to rent it. I could picture my little crew happily settled in the new, relatively spacious office. But, because of the many windows, the room was so bright that my highly light-sensitive eyes hurt from the sunshine reflecting off of the white walls. There was only one solution–paint the room a darker color. Sandy looked at the space and helped me pick out a nice, dark, blue-green paint. I bought several gallons of the paint, which looked better on the little color square than it did when rolled onto the walls and ceiling. But I had committed myself to the aquarium-scum paint hue. I invested hours during several painting sessions, including an entire Saturday spent with a visiting friend assisting me with the paint job's trim. I felt great about my preparations for our new digs. I let myself into the office by opening a window off the fire escape. I didn't want to be delayed by something as petty and procedural as signing a lease and getting a key. I apparently hadn't been perfectly clear with the landlord about committing to rent the space, but I had told him that I was pretty sure. Considering the number of empty suites in the old building, that seemed quite adequate. After the work was done, the room was an unusual, murky color that I had never seen on office walls or on anything else before. But my primary goal was achieved; the light reflectivity was subdued and manageable, and my eyes didn't ache from the brilliance of the white walls and reflected sunlight.

All I had to do was sign a lease and move in. I became distracted, and a week or two went by before I again took action on the new office space. I took the elevator up to the new office's floor, to inspect my painting again before I would phone the landlord to close the deal. To my shock, the nameplate of a new occupant hung on the door. I pictured the scene of the landlord, opening the door of his sunny corner office to show to his perspective tenant, only to find the room painted that dreary dark blue-green. Guerilla painting crew at your service! A new tenant had signed a lease, and I had lost my quiet, corner office. I never told that landlord, that it had been I who had turned his bright office into a study in gloom.

Meanwhile, ours was not the only department within CIL that was feeling growing pains. CIL was gathering new grants and quickly expanding programs. The entire organization had outgrown its quarters. It was announced one afternoon, shortly after the painting caper, that we were all going to move cross-town, to the south side of campus. Ed Roberts explained that we were moving to a new location–a former auto dealer's showroom and garage on Telegraph Avenue. The showroom was quickly subdivided into open, wheelchair-accessible aisles for desks, and a few closed accessible rooms for administration. But there was still not enough room for everybody, so Blind Services, staffed entirely by people who could walk, was moved into the dingy second floor, parts storage area. Up a flight of stairs, Blind Services became known as occupying the bat cave.

After we moved, my responsibilities expanded with two promotions, in quick succession, that soon had me directing all of CIL's direct services. I liked the increased administrative responsibilities as Deputy Director of

195

Services, but the job took me entirely away from satisfying direct client contact and left me deep in the dense world of grants, paperwork, and staff supervision. That juncture marked the split in the road, when I took the path of administration rather than counseling.

Shortly after I had graduated, I had applied to the Masters of Social Work (MSW), program at Berkeley and was accepted for the fall quarter. There were two tracks in the MSW program, and I had chosen Organization, Planning, and Administration rather than counseling. I hoped that my career would have impact and create change, for the better, in society. I felt that I could achieve more, through planning and developing programs, than I could by counseling one on one. Berkeley's MSW program was structured as four quarters of full time class work, then two quarters of full-time internship field placement. But I had fallen in love with the mission and energy of CIL, and I did not want to quit work to go back to school. I petitioned Berkeley's program to allow my full-time work responsibilities to serve as my administrative internship, while carrying a modified, reduced class schedule to be spread over the two years of the program. The School of Social Work refused. So, with a heavy heart, I withdrew my application.

Ed Roberts to the rescue! Ed was on the advisory committee for The University of San Francisco, (USF)'s new Masters of Rehabilitation Administration (MRA) program. The MRA program was to begin in January of 1976. Ed told me that he was too busy to serve on the committee and asked me to participate in his place. I was honored by his trust. Although feeling totally unqualified, I agreed to replace him and serve on the advisory committee. USF's Rehabilitation Administration Program was revolutionary in every way. Housed in a Jesuit university, it was run by a radical, Jewish guy named Isadore Salkind, who was bringing accountability and leadership to the bay area's vocational programs for people like my brother Mark. I sat at the advisory committee with the graybeards of radical, and traditional, disability program development. The committee included one of the gentlemen from the regional, federal Rehabilitation Administration Office in San Francisco, who I had known through my work at CIL. I liked the highly professional and yet highly progressive master's program they were designing. The MRA program was designed for full-time administrators, and it seemed like a perfect match for my graduate education. I applied and was accepted as a graduate student in the first class. In 1976 I began my life once again as a student, as well as a full-time employee of CIL. The graduate program was structured to serve working administrators, and its format was nine straight days of intense seminars,

196

from Saturday through the following Sunday, every three months. It was while I was a graduate student at USF that Mary Jane and I spoke one day.

She asked me what I intended to do when I graduated with a master's degree in Rehabilitation Administration. I didn't even stop to consider. I told her that I planned to administer a really good institution and to move my brother Mark there. Mary Jane, incredulous, asked me why in the world I would want Mark in an institution rather than in the community. Her perspective stopped me dead in my tracks. After thirteen years of enduring Mark's placement in the dreadful confinement of The Columbus State Institution for the Mentally Retarded, I had been indoctrinated with the idea that Mark had to live in a colony of others with severe cognitive disabilities. Forced by Mary Jane's questions, I had to unravel my own beliefs and thoughts, and recognize that I had accepted an unthinkable assumption, unchallenged. Mary Jane was suggesting that a different model could come into existence, wherein Mark could be supported in the community, and I began to ponder how such a societal sea change might be wrought.

Through my work in our cutting edge field, I had learned that in a very few innovative, small-model programs, people like Mark were living outside institutions. These demonstration projects were being proposed, as new societal models for community integration. One place in Texas paired adults with severe physical disabilities with adults with cognitive disabilities, allowing each to provide needed services for the other. I turned such an arrangement over in my mind, but Mark didn't seem like a good candidate. There was another place, where a sort of commune farm had been established for adults with cognitive disabilities. Maybe Mark could live happily on a farm, doing simple chores. But these were tiny demonstration programs. Could I get something like that started from scratch?

Life Changes

On September 26th, 1976, my life was dramatically changed by the universal experience of becoming a parent. My son, John Kyle Moyer, burst into the world on Sunday evening after Sandy labored for forty brutal hours. We were members of Kaiser, where rotating shifts of doctors observed Sandy's protracted labor, but no one took overall responsibility. Our son was born dazed but alert. John Kyle arrived and I returned to work a week later, quite ready and willing to pull the full weight of active fathering.

However, my work at CIL was not a typical job that one leaves at the end of the workday, to move back into the sanctity of private life. Rather, the work was on the forefront of the Disability Rights Movement. The operative word is movement. We were quite aware of the importance of what we were about and how many eyes were upon us. Anyone engaged in a leadership position was expected to make the same commitment articulated by Thomas Jefferson and agreed to by the signers of The Declaration of Independence: "...we mutually pledge to each other our lives, our fortunes, and our sacred honor".

Chapter 12: Change Agent

504 Demonstration

At CIL, we were expected to pledge, virtually, all of our time. I was the only director who was married and the only one who had a child. I took both of my responsibilities seriously. I was a fully engaged father and husband. But I also was the Center's first Deputy Director of Services, during a time when we were growing as an organization and as the independent living movement was coming into being. CIL was the movement's flagship and first center. As such, impromptu evening meetings with drop-in visitors and dignitaries from around the country and the world–hungry for details rich with content–were commonplace. At five o'clock, I knew that a diaper needed to be changed and a mother needed relief and adult company. But often, this family consciousness clashed with an entourage of visitors arriving for their evening's tutorial on independent living. From time to time I would delay my return to home, as I took my place among CIL's leaders, explaining what we did and how we worked. But I guarded my home life jealously, and generally excused myself, heading for my home commute.

On April 4, 1977, CIL was abuzz with plans for the political demonstration that was to be held the next day on United Nations Plaza, in front of the San Francisco Federal building. The issue at hand was the Federal government's four-year delay in promulgating or releasing regulations for Section 504 of the Rehabilitation Act of 1973. Section 504 simply stated that any organization, system, or bureaucracy that receives Federal funds, couldn't discriminate against people with disabilities in education, employment, or services. It was sweeping Civil Rights legislation. Under the auspices of the American Coalition of Citizens with Disabilities (ACCD), our demonstration was to occur in conjunction with other protests at Federal regional offices. We would ask regional Health Education and Welfare (HEW), and Office of Civil Rights (OCR), regional directors to call the Secretary of HEW, requesting the promised signing of the unacceptably, long-delayed regulations. ACCD was the first coalition based advocacy organization that brought people of all disabilities together for common cause.

Recently inaugurated President Jimmy Carter had run on a platform that included the promise to sign the regulations that had been drafted by the Ford administration. Nixon vetoed the Rehabilitation Act of 1973, the law that contained the Section that needed the regulations at hand. Public outrage resulted in a Congressional override of his veto. Section 504 was controversial because it promised that no otherwise qualified person with a disability could be denied education, services or employment by any organization using Federal money. School districts, hospitals, and universities were afraid of the cost of compliance with such regulations, and their powerful lobbies kept the regulations spinning in perpetual bureaucratic limbo. Drafts had been released for public comment and then taken back for administrative review in an interminable cycle of delay. ACCD had friends, inside the young Carter administration's HEW staff, who leaked to us their freshly drafted regulations–an internal document not meant for public scrutiny. Jimmy Carter had gained the wholehearted support of the disability rights community with his promise to sign the drafted 504 regulations. But the difference between those regulations and the Carter Administration version was dramatic and disheartening. The new regulations basically offered no better than "separate but equal", a posture that would have ensured ongoing segregation and isolation of people with disabilities.

The day before the demonstration, CIL's leadership team gathered for a teach-in and brain storming session concerning the next day. Halfway through the meeting, it occurred to me that we would need a bullhorn. Having participated in Civil Rights and anti-war demonstrations in the sixties and early seventies, I knew the importance of being heard; I knew a bullhorn was essential. When I learned that detail had not been covered, I said it was necessary and I left the meeting to locate one for rental, and to arrange to pick it up. The details that were discussed after I left the meeting included the fact that the organizers were planning a sit-in that would go on as long as necessary. Back in my office, I got on the phone and soon located a store that had a bullhorn and I set off by bus to rent it.

On the way, I reflected that rally music would also be very helpful. When I got home, I pulled out Pete Seeger's album, *We Shall Overcome*, and listened to the familiar, stirring anthems of the Civil Rights movement– drawn from hymns and spirituals. I thought about our issues and began to write new lyrics for the familiar old melodies. Those songs had

200

communicated the faith and passions of the Civil Rights movement, and now they would carry our story. I wanted the songs to convey, in simple terms, why the arcane matter of federal regulations was of such importance to us.

On April 5, 1977, I kissed Sandy and John Kyle goodbye. Armed with the bullhorn and my guitar, I walked to the BART (Bay Area Rapid Transit) station for my trip to the United Nations Plaza in San Francisco and the demonstration. On the BART train from Berkeley to San Francisco, I finished the lyrics for the songs, squinting at the pocket notebook as I wrote.

When I arrived, scores of people were already chanting and walking in a protest circle. There were many folks in wheelchairs, that had come from nursing homes or their own homes supported through our few new independent living centers. But there were also people with blindness, deafness, cognitive and emotional disabilities, and parents of children with disabilities, and friends–all there to send the message forth: "Sign 504". We had been given large campaign buttons to wear during the demonstration. I had pinned mine to my denim jacket. It read "HANDICAPPED HUMAN RIGHTS–SIGN 504–ACCD". The use of the word "handicapped" suggested the cusp of language usage that was being straddled at that time. The buttons were produced by the national office of the American Coalition of Citizens with Disabilities in Washington, DC. In Berkeley, we would never have used the word "handicapped" in that way. We referred to "people with disabilities" and "handicapping environments and attitudes". The use of language was of powerful importance to us. However, at the ACCD office the traditional language was still in use. Demonstrations were slated for the ten federal regional headquarters–for the offices of HEW and OCR.

I set down my guitar and assessed the situation. Many of the demonstrators carried signs, and a weak chant had begun. I put the bullhorn to good use as I led the chants while others gave instructions concerning the organization of the hundreds of demonstrators, with and without disabilities, who began to circle in the large walking and rolling demonstration. By late morning, a microphone and PA had been set up, and speakers were educating and motivating, as the media and general public took note.

The program included stirring oratory by San Francisco's state assemblyman, Willie Brown, the Reverend Cecil Williams, activist minister of Glide Memorial United Methodist Church, and Ed Roberts, the newly appointed director of the California Department of Vocational Rehabilitation. I was taken back to the 1960s when the power of the civil rights movement was carried by the passion of black ministers and organizers. I swelled with pride realizing that we were being joined by that same powerful community that had kept the dream alive, and now were adding their voices and their commitment to our struggle. Ed Roberts rolled up the ramp to the low wooden stage, and spoke into a microphone held by an aide. Ed had recently become Director of the massive California bureaucracy critical to people with disabilities, and as the titular head of the disability rights movement, his impassioned speech held a silent and rapt audience. Others had spoken including Judy Heumann, who had been the demonstration's chief organizer, along with other women from CIL. Ed finished and I ended the rally by leading the singing of a song that would become the anthem of the demonstration–a re-write of a spiritual and moving Civil Rights song, "Keep Your Eyes on the Prize". The last chord of the song rang out. Judy Heumann was handed the microphone, and from her wheelchair instructed the demonstrators to enter the Federal building and to head to the sixth floor, where we would divide into two groups to visit the regional offices of HEW and OCR.

It took a long time for the hundreds of demonstrators, many in wheelchairs, to take the building's several elevators to the sixth floor. Once there, however, our task had just begun. We were to move into the designated offices and request that the regional directors call Washington to ask for Joseph Califano, President Carter's Secretary of HEW, to sign the promised regulations, drafted by the Ford administration. Over two hundred people crowded into the two outer offices, alarming the receptionists as the wall to wall gathering of wheelchair, crutch and cane users, people with dog guides, people with white canes, those using sign language, and others politely pressed into the confined space. Early in the afternoon, the Directors had agreed to meet with us. They did not call Washington and a standoff developed. Joseph Maldonado, the Regional Director of HEW, was unable to move from behind his desk, being blocked by the solid mass of demonstrators. When he asked for a path to be opened, so that he could use the rest room, he was told no. Judy Heumann told him that since people with severe physical disabilities couldn't use the inaccessible public restrooms, neither could he. The regional directors, although willing to talk to us, were not willing to comply with our polite but firm demands, and after the afternoon's stalemate, the office's staff prepared to leave the building, having been unable to convince us to do the same. Shortly after five o'clock, the Federal building's legions of employees were streaming around and through us, down the crowded elevators, out and away from the noisy rabble who were making themselves at home in the marble corridors and the offices of HEW and OCR.

I had been in the OCR office, and Judy had been in HEW. As we conferred in the hallway, Judy asked me with an insider's smile if I had brought my toothbrush, and I stared at her blankly. Recognizing my confusion, she asked if I hadn't been told that we were planning to stay there overnight and for an indefinite period. The radical plan came to me as a complete surprise. I told Judy that I had responsibilities at home, and that I would come back in the morning, but that I had to leave. It was quickly negotiated with Federal building representatives that if an individual with a disability left the building, they could not come back in. But if a demonstrator was an attendant, serving the needs of demonstrators with disabilities, he or she could come and go. My name was placed on the attendants list, developed that first day, giving me *carte blanche* to come and go from the demonstration.

Because my vision loss was not obvious to observers, my role as an attendant was established. I continued to work at the Center for Independent Living, was able to attend my graduate school classes, and see to my responsibilities to my wife and infant son. I commuted to the demonstration frequently, and I always took my guitar. I was one of the informal morale officers and part of the communications team. Acting as the demonstration's troubadour, I told our story with song. I played and sang, outside of the main doors of the massive Federal building, as employees came to and left from work, and I would walk slowly through the vast halls of the building, singing at the top of my lungs, to the office staff that I passed. Other demonstrators would join me, and we would create quite a bit of music in the vast circular, reverberating marble hallways or open stairwells that acted like natural echo chambers. The passport of being on the attendants list gave me freedom of movement not enjoyed by the protest's rank and file. Most had significant disabilities. Others were able-bodied people who were serious supporters of the Disability Rights cause and brought needed skills and commitment.

Federal building administrators tried to drive out the sit-in. They cut off telephones very soon after the demonstration began, then hot water as well. Power wheelchairs that required overnight charges would find wall outlets without power. The little community organized into teams to provide for food procurement, communications, security, and other matters great and small. Safeway, The Black Panthers, McDonalds, and other groups provided food. While I was there I saw the elevator doors open and several very respectful, well-dressed, black men came up, carrying garbage-can-size containers of well prepared and much-appreciated food. Everyone became beleaguered as the demonstration dragged on, and some folks were really battered by the punishing circumstances.

Steven had multiple sclerosis. When the demonstration began, Steven entered the building using a support cane for mobility. But the stress and attendant fatigue took a devastating toll on his body. Steven's health deteriorated quickly and he experienced a significant loss of functional ability. He spent most of the demonstration unable to move from his mattress in a back room of one of the office suites that we occupied. Sensing the historic nature of what was developing; Steven diligently, day after day, recorded news reports and the sounds of the demonstration around him on his cassette tape recorder, capturing a unique historic audio record.

My friend, Mary Jane, was one of the demonstrations true political and spiritual leaders– an active, energetic, ambulatory, blind woman at the beginning. Despite ongoing attempts to establish and maintain order, individual possessions and demonstration materials would clog the sides of the hallways. The flotsam and jetsam were always changing; Mary Jane tripped on some clutter, badly spraining her knee. Mary Jane also led a hunger strike until the demonstration's nurse urged her to stop, for health reasons, after eleven days.

Dirty hair, body odor, rumpled clothes, and sleep-starved eyes were universal. Despite all that, the human spirit that drove everyone on was strong, and the bond that formed between those who lived so heroically on the sixth floor of the San Francisco Federal building, was palpable to any of us who observed it. Although I considered myself a genuine ally and a member of the protest, I was not paying the ongoing price.

As the demonstration dragged on, I thought about how Section 504 provided for Civil Rights for education and employment. If its protections had been in place when Mark and I were kids, perhaps Mark would have been provided the support he needed, and he would have been able to stay in our local school. If he had been integrated into the neighborhood school and if proper educational and social supports had been provided, he would not have been institutionalized. I would have been given extra time on tests so that my knowledge might have been tested instead of my sight. General Electric would not have been able to tell me that they didn't hire "the handicapped". Section 504 was vital and far-reaching. Great legal protections were embodied in the law's simple language.

Twice, Judy asked me if I could arrange to spend the night at the demonstration, so that I could play at early morning rallies. Hence, I awoke early on the morning of April 15, after spending the night tossing and turning on a marble staircase landing, with a coarse army blanket as a cover. After a welcome cup of coffee, I decided to wander outside to play at the front doors to be heard by the Federal employees as they arrived at work. When I walked onto United Nations Plaza, in front of the Federal Building, I stumbled upon a microphone and public address system, set up for the morning's rally. I tested the system and the microphone was live, so I decided to take advantage of the amplification. I began playing the demonstration's songs. A television camera crew started filming me, and I figured that a local television station was gathering footage on the demonstration. The unfolding story was generally part of the regular nightly news in the Bay Area. A blonde woman, who I didn't know, walked up next to me and began singing a harmony on my melody–keeping time with the tambourine that I carried for just such purposes. I thought that we sounded great together and the cameraman kept filming throughout the performance. I played at the rally, along with the speakers from the demonstration and the public figures who added their voices of support. Throughout the afternoon, I sang inside the building.

I left at five o'clock to get home for the celebration of my wife's birthday. I took the BART train and then walked the several blocks home thinking about the day's activities. The phone was ringing as I walked in. It was my sister Bonnie in Bowling Green, Ohio. She excitedly told me to turn on the CBS Evening News to catch the beginning of the program, as she had happened to do three hours before, in the Eastern Time Zone.

A minute later, the program began. My early morning performance was the lead-in, before the show's title and introductory announcement. There I was, filmed at the microphone. The lyrics of the song I was singing told our story. Walter Cronkite read the day's news, beginning with the unfolding story of the demonstration. We were the top of the newscast and the footage, of me at the microphone, was the video image that played as he read. I realized that the film crew had shot the footage in the morning, in order to have the video tape flown to New York, for its incorporation in the CBS Evening News. Everything that I knew about the power of music was reinforced by my songs' use, to communicate to the world what we were doing.

After twenty-six days and a highly visible trip to Washington by a Judy-led demonstration team, the effort was successful. At the conclusion of the sit-in, Mary Jane left the demonstration, using a wheelchair for mobility–required after her fall. Ironically, Mary Jane was unable to get up the stairs of her own Berkeley home. She spent a week sharing Judy's accessible apartment after the exhaustion and inconvenience of the political action. The demonstration drew to a close when, as Jimmy Carter had promised as a candidate, Joseph Califano Jr., Secretary of HEW, signed the regulations for Section 504 as drafted by the Ford Administration. He also signed the regulations for Public Law 94-142, passed in 1975, The Education for All Handicapped Children Act, (renamed IDEA, Individuals with Disabilities Education Act). Like 504, PL94-142 had languished, without regulations, due to the lobbying resistance of school districts.

But now, the two cornerstones of America's Disability Rights protections were in place, and advocacy toward enforcement could begin. We felt a thrilling sense of power and accomplishment. One hundred and twenty-five people had stayed on the sixth floor of the Federal building, for a record setting twenty-six days–the longest occupation of a Federal building in United States history. It was accomplished by people, many of whose disabilities were so severe that in most communities in the United States they would have been forced to live in nursing homes, institutions, or the confinement of inaccessible places of residence.

Introduction

The San Francisco 504 Demonstration had changed Federal law, changed me, and caused a rumble that quaked within every institution addressing education, employment, and service to the community. That was true for The University of San Francisco's MRA program, newly established and busy shaping its first class, of which I was a part.

The USF program had been developed by Isadore Salkind, a wise and effective grassroots leader who expanded the scope of real change within community programs that served individuals with severe disabilities. Iz and his staff were receptive to all new ideas and progressive practice. Hence, my involvement with the independent living movement and certainly

206

the 504 Demonstration was of keen interest. A quarterly nine-day seminar met during the 504 Demonstration's twenty-six-day sit-in.

I led a sort of field trip, to the demonstration and rally, at which I would be playing. I came and went. For those who could not leave, those of us who carried on our normal lives and who slept in our own comfy beds must have seemed a bit callow. Fellow demonstrators, dirty, tired, and care worn from the weeks of harsh living conditions must have wondered at my new role as tour guide. Before I played at a morning rally, I led my fifteen respectful, graduate student MRA classmates and our faculty, through the marble hallways, crowded with demonstration signs, wheelchairs, sleeping bags and makeshift accommodations of all kinds. I remember a glaring, silent woman who communicated such resentment as I introduced her to the clean and rested administrators with whom I shared identity. But I clung to my role as demonstration member and musician and received some guilty pleasure from the esteem with which my fellows at USF saw my advocacy. In some ways, I felt that my identity as a demonstrator was unwarranted.

Gratefully, I accepted the request to arrange for Judy Heumann to speak to the next MRA graduate school session, after the demonstration had ended. This would be an opportunity to give credit where credit was due. Judy had been one of the demonstration's chief organizers and was also the most articulate and forceful advocate, amid that cadre of effective and unrelenting radicals.

Judy and I worked together at CIL; she was Director of Advocacy, and I was Director of Services. She agreed to come across the San Francisco Bay from Berkeley, to USF, and I was pleased to have arranged for what promised to be a spirited and intelligent talk and exchange of ideas.

Introductions matter. Judy's pedigree in Disability Rights was impressive. She had been turned away from New York City schools because of her post-polio wheelchair use, but her mother's tutoring and advocacy became her source of education. Judy had gone on to work as a staffer for a United States senator, had been appointed executive of a New York City based Disability Rights organization, and had been recruited by Ed Roberts to head CIL's advocacy efforts. She had led the 504 Demonstration, and her standing as spokesperson gave her genuine gravitas. I had a range of factoids from which to draw, for my introduction. Judy was to meet me in the hallway outside of the lecture room at the appointed hour.

A few days prior to Judy's talk, I heard a little story that I thought would both place Judy in the proper light as a woman fully committed to the movement and suggest that my own level of engagement was not as great.

So rather than drone on with details of Judy's background, I decided to use the metaphor as an opportunity to acknowledge that during the 504 sit-in, I had come and gone rather than staying full time as Judy and the other champions of that difficult sojourn had.

Beginning in high school speech class, I had recognized that public speaking came naturally to me. I could extemporaneously pontificate, glibly draw on a few ideas in order to speak at great length and generally use my natural gift to considerable advantage. So I didn't feel the need to prepare, at any length, for the short preface I had been asked to provide to Judy's presentation. I would set the stage and accomplish a piece of unfinished business. The day arrived.

I was waiting for Judy as she powered up in her electric wheelchair, along with her personal care assistant who had driven her van and now was going to enjoy Judy's lecture to these interested and involved Rehabilitation Administration graduate students and executives. We greeted each other warmly and entered the room crowded with my classmates, the entire staff of the Rehabilitation Administration office, and University of San Francisco faculty and dignitaries who had come to hear this impressive woman's thoughts. We settled into the front of the room, and I began. All eyes were on me, and the assembly listened with alert interest to my opening remarks.

"I have known Judy for several years," I began, "and have worked for her, and now with her, at The Center for Independent Living. Judy heads Advocacy. I head Services. Judy has been a leader in the Disability Rights Movement for her entire career, and her recent organization and direction of the 504 Demonstration has surely changed the national landscape for all of us who live with disabilities." I was on a roll, and I was gaining oratorical momentum, as I began the nut of the introduction.

"I know that you heard from me last session about the importance of the 504 sit-in, and I did play a minor role in the undertaking. But Judy's role, and in fact her entire life, has been given over to societal change for people with disabilities. In thinking about the difference between Judy and me, I am reminded of a story about a chicken and a pig, standing together, looking at a billboard advertising an eggs and ham breakfast at a local restaurant. The billboard was a close-up of the breakfast offering, and both animals stared at the fried eggs and slice of ham on the giant billboard. The pig turned to the chicken and said, 'For you it's just involvement. For me, it's total commitment!' And then, with slow and deliberate timing, I turned to Judy.

"So," I intoned, "if I am the chicken, I would like to introduce..." My mind suddenly felt the sharp teeth of the ghastly trap, which I had so

208

carefully set for myself, closing mercilessly. Time stopped. Judy's expression soured, and the sudden smell of fear–my own–filled my nostrils. Every face that stared in disbelief at the staggering gaff that was developing before them, as I was frozen in a combination of embarrassment for me, and for Judy, mixed with the thin hope that I might rescue myself from this verbal cliff's edge over which I now teetered.

"If I am the chicken," I repeated, "I would like to introduce the most powerful and committed advocate I have ever met–the Queen of Disability Rights–Ms. Judy Heumann!" The wreckage was undeniable, but having put lipstick on that metaphoric train-wreck, I hoped that no one would notice the sudden transformation from disaster to shaky dignity.

Ever since that day I have prepared more fully, thought through every metaphor, and been a far better public speaker. I think that Judy has forgiven me and, hopefully, long forgotten that moment in our shared experience.

Bidding Berkeley Goodbye

1978 held a profound turning point in my life. The bottom fell away when California's angry voters passed Proposition 13, sending a shock wave through local governments and community agencies. The mandated rollback in property taxes, demanded by Proposition 13, triggered a sudden, terrible shrinking of local government's resources. Many programs, from libraries and swimming pools to services for people in various forms of genuine need, were cut back or discontinued. When Prop 13's slashing impact hit, I was CIL's deputy director for services. I was writing grants and managing a range of independent living services. The locally directed Federal and State funds that flowed into Berkeley were the lifeblood for CIL and for other organizations serving previously disenfranchised groups. Independent living services and California's generous support and attendant care benefits were making living outside of nursing homes and institutions possible, and people with severe disabilities flocked to Berkeley from across the United States.

CIL was a blur of activity with services that included advocacy for environmental modification, attendant referral, advocacy with governmental agencies, accessible housing identification and modification, wheelchair repair, van modification, accessible van transportation, counseling, mobility instruction, and interpreter and reader referral. All of the services that we provided were essential and innovative; CIL provided services to nine hundred people monthly.

Clients drove vans that we had modified, had their wheelchairs repaired in our shop, lived in places they had found through our housing office, hired attendants from our pool, and ate in accessible local restaurants because South Berkeley's flat terrain and mild weather led to a community wherein accessibility was expected and made good business sense. We had grant funds from twenty-four sources, and we needed money to keep the great airship aloft.

Required writing did not allow for much creativity. As deputy director, every month I would have to sign off on the well over nine hundred triplicate forms for Alameda County's Title XIX Services. The teetering stack of invoices typed by a secretary were impossible for me to read without the video magnifier that sat on my desk, not that I would have wanted to read them anyway. I signed the stack on a worktable, in the clerical department where they had been generated. The clerk would orient me to the signing task, since my signature alone as director of the center's services was required. I would begin, signing my name mechanically–over and over– somewhere near the line on the forms. As I signed my unseen and increasingly unrecognizable signature, a vague sense of meaninglessness concerning my job would creep under my skin. I was not developing new or more effective programs. I was truly a mid-manager, blindly signing off on bureaucratic forms.

My job had changed. It was in stark contrast to the excitement and sense of accomplishment that was more representative of my years in Berkeley. The years I had spent at the University, and then working for CIL, had been a heady time. I had been part of a historical sea-change, concerning people with disabilities. At The University of California at Berkeley, I had benefited immeasurably from the revolutionary Physically Disabled Students Program that had offered me simple accommodations that gave me equal access to education. As a result, I graduated with highest honors. I soared, the evening of graduation, when I received my department's singular citation.

At CIL I was part of the national buzz, and I palled around with Ed Roberts himself, both in Berkeley and at national meetings. I was in his office on the day he got the call inviting him to become California's Director of the Department of Rehabilitation, the nation's largest State rehab agency. We went back to his house, where he was settled into his iron lung, for some serious creative work. I began dictating a possible first statement to his new employees, within the California Department of Rehab. Ed told his secretary to take down my dictation. My ghostwritten words became the first communication that the twenty-five hundred employees of the vast State agency would read, from their revolutionary leader. Ed was going to Sacramento, but I was stuck in CIL's thickening bureaucracy.

When Proposition 13 hit, the CIL program was broad and shallow, and only a few part time employees staffed most departments. Apart from the Research & Development grants which funded some programs, CIL's lifeline services were all billed to the County. The day after the election, I was given the grim charge of cutting $100,000 out of my $300,000 departmental budgets. The already low-fat budgets needed to be rapidly pressure-cooked and become starvation leaner and certainly meaner. Without a doubt, CIL was about to become far less effective. I hated budgets–the administrator's daily fare in the best of times–but this horrible task would be changing people's lives. With jumbo magnification from my video magnifier, I studied the numerous columns of figures for the cost centers within my division, on the wide spreadsheets. CIL's policy was to employ a majority of people with severe disabilities.

Due to the income restrictions of Supplemental Security Income, employees with disabilities were limited to part time work in order not to jeopardize their financial benefits, including critical medical insurance and support for personal care attendant services. Mine was one of the few full-time jobs in my division. As I struggled to achieve the necessary budget cutbacks, I drew a line through my salary and fringe benefits and, thereby, met one fifth of my mandated, depressing goal. My job responsibilities would have to be divided among the remaining overworked administrators. Late that evening, I finished my bloody work. The following morning, I met with Phil, CIL's exhausted executive director. Phil was a large man with a bushy mustache and tinted glasses. Phil sat in a power wheelchair, paralyzed, years before, from the neck down by an auto accident. I gave him the worksheets containing my recommended budget cuts. I also, sadly, tendered my resignation. Phil accepted the news numbly–one more woe from Prop 13. A dark quiet settled over the bedraggled center.

I had loved my three years of work at CIL but, before Proposition 13, I had been thinking about my career's development–beyond the grassroots independent living movement. I had a freshly minted graduate degree in rehabilitation administration, from the University of San Francisco, and an ultimate goal of landing a job as an executive director or State rehabilitation administrator, where I thought I might really make a difference. I had a wife and young child, and I wanted a job that could pay the bills, provide some security–a job that that ended at five, and that gave weekends off.

At CIL, I had always felt that I was vaguely disloyal to the cause when I left at five, which is when the extra work concerning CIL's mission often began. This I felt, although I was one of the few employees who had a family and who began the work day early. But it was late in the day when the place was jumping. I knew that I wanted–needed–to shift gears and to find another job, that would advance my career and allow for family life.

Berkeley had been a state of mind–an identity like nothing I had ever known–a badge of honor, activism, and gold-standard, leftist hip. It came to pass that I would be going from The People's Republic of Berkeley to Old Moneyed Palo Alto, to work for a company in the rehabilitation engineering, assistive technology field, staffed by intelligentsia from Stanford. I received some derision about selling out, from the more vocal of the CIL young lions and lionesses, but my intuition said that this was the change that my growing family and I needed.

Berkeley had taught me that I could succeed academically, with a few simple accommodations. Berkeley had taught me that disability was a universal construct and that all of us, with disabilities, were united by common experience. It had shown me the power of human cooperation and symbiosis. Berkeley taught that the power of civil disobedience is real, and it demonstrated the American ability to create change in our government's actions. And Berkeley had taught me about the normalcy of disabilities–all of them. I reflected on the many lessons I had learned from studying, working, and living in Berkeley. Being empowered and self-directed, I bid my years in the trenches of Berkeley a fond and wistful farewell, and I turned my face to empowerment through assistive technology.

Chapter 13: Transitions

Telesensory Communication

Michael Williams, a writer with severe cerebral palsy, was the president of the CIL board while I worked there. Michael's speaking voice was hard for most people, including me, to understand. I would often have to ask him to repeat his utterances several times, without my discernment catching hold. In those days, Michael used a simple letter board when his voice could not be understood. Michael would painstakingly point to letters, and his interlocutor would watch and slowly assemble words and sentences. Since I could not see his letter board, the attempted conversation would end in awkward silence. Out of my embarrassment, I found myself avoiding contact with him. Mary Jane, also blind, would sit and talk to Michael, asking him to repeat, as frequently as necessary. She would laugh uproariously at his wit, once the communication was understood. I envied their easy style. By their example, I began to see that my fear of asking Michael to repeat himself and my dread that I might not understand, kept me from becoming Michael's friend.

I came to perceive that my failure to connect with those, whom I couldn't understand, was due to the fact that the situation pricked my fear of not understanding them. I had been ruled by trepidation. But with stiffened courage, I began to seek out Michael. He was patient and, a time or two, we both laughed as communication stalled. My anxiety dissolved. Additionally, I knew that I was uncomfortable with not being able to communicate with deaf people, so I studied sign language for two years, through a little class for those of us with vision loss, at CIL. It was run by Joanne, the coordinator of our new Deaf Services department. I got to know Joanne and her husband, both of whom were deaf. I went to their home and felt very welcomed. My job required communication with staff and clients from CIL's new Deaf Services department, and daily practice quickly developed my signing skills. But although I could sign with increasing fluency, my limited vision made reading other's signs very difficult. Signs had to be formed very slowly, and sometimes I would need to augment my vision with touch. Communication was a big part of my work.

Shortly before my job at CIL ended, I was invited to be a guest on *Just Like Everybody Else*, a public television interview program on

213

disability. Dick, a fellow with multiple sclerosis who used a wheelchair and who was the communications manager for Telesensory Systems, Inc. (TSI) hosted the series. The cameras rolled as he interviewed me on the brightly lit television stage set. The experience was stimulating as I comfortably conversed with Dick. After the first interview on the topic of low vision, Dick invited me back to record a second program, on self-esteem. Off camera, Dick talked about his communications job for the prestigious rehabilitation engineering company. Born within Stanford in 1971, the same year as CIL, TSI was on the cutting edge of the burgeoning electronics revolution.

The company grew out of the Stanford Electrical Engineering department, with the development of the Optacon–a portable print reading device for people who were blind. The Optacon, (Optical to Tactile Converter) used a hand-scanned, miniature video camera that was rolled over print. The Optacon converted the optical image into a vibrating, tactile form, felt on the finger pad, through an array of one hundred forty-four blunt vibrating pins. John Linvil, chair of Stanford's Electrical Engineering department had a daughter, Candy, who was blind. The Optacon was his invention to enable her to read print. I had met his pretty daughter in 1974, at the Peninsula Center, as she sat and read with her Optacon, as I prepared for my summer youth project. In 1976, TSI had also developed the world's first talking calculator, then available in four languages. I wistfully imagined what managing TSI Communications must be like.

Dick phoned the day Proposition 13 passed, to tell me that he was leaving TSI and asked if I would be interested in applying for his job. Here was a stable, creative job for a great company in young Silicon Valley. After Prop 13's firestorm, I needed a job. I thought that working for an assistive technology corporation would strengthen my resume. In addition, the position required a great deal of writing. I was uncertain whether or not I had what it took, concerning that skill. But I knew that I needed its proficiency to continue to grow professionally. I wanted to believe that I could become a journeyman, wrangler of words. This would give me the push I needed and would force me to face the beast and write every day. I could not have foreseen how profound the lessons in communication would really be. This job and the arc of my life were to intertwine with great poignancy.

TSI would give Sandy and me a chance to move back to sunny Palo Alto, the city from which we had moved to overcast Berkeley, five years earlier. Palo Alto was in a nearly perfect weather pattern–very different

214

from chilly, foggy Berkeley. Sandy jumped at the chance to get back to warm Palo Alto.

I submitted my resume as a candidate to replace Dick. I added a voluntary writing sample, a marketing piece based on my research concerning the company. Then came some serious interview vetting and, joyfully, I was hired.

As we prepared to move in July of 1978, I was twenty-nine years old. I was happily married, with a beautiful son, and I had been thoroughly politicized by the Disability Rights Movement. I was offered a job where preppy-hip and clean-cut was the look, and shirt and tie was the dress code. That was a far cry from CIL and Berkeley, where beards, long hair, tee shirts, and jeans were the norm. However, I always dressed a cut above, given my administrative roll. We moved from the shaggy cool of Berkeley to the smart chic of Palo Alto. I began to run a communications department, supporting marketing, and providing public relations for the successful young company. The communications department staff consisted of two graphic artists, a secretary, and me. I wrote all of the copy for marketing materials, including our newsletter that reached twenty-five thousand readers, worldwide. Occasionally, I would be interviewed by national publications or broadcast media. I took a course on Public Relations, planned and managed a press conference at The National Press Club in Washington D.C., and was expected to be the accurate and persuasive voice for the company. I also managed communications about the Talking Optacon, a monumental research and development effort that had been underway since 1976. That required balancing the impressive engineering team's capabilities, and the marketing folks' best-case optimism. Engineers and programmers were patient interview subjects.

As part of the marketing department, we were sculpting expectations about our development efforts for the company's customers and the world of blindness at large. My writing was edited and critically sliced and diced, by senior marketing administrators. Then, I would re-write and re-submit, until we all agreed on the content. The marketing department was promoting the development of the Talking Optacon, a revolutionary, hand-scanned reading machine. Through digital magic, print—as seen by the chewing-gum-package size, hand-scanned Optacon camera, was to be announced in synthetic speech output. Marketing had claimed that the device would be easy to use, portable, and affordable. The marketing dream machine description was the hopeful face for a really stunning research and development undertaking.

My job was to thoroughly understand what was going on in Engineering R&D and to paint a word picture about our future product. I came to know the teams of software and hardware engineers that were working on Optical Character Recognition (OCR) and Text To Speech (TTS).

The marriage of the efforts of the OCR and TTS teams was required to take the hand-scanned electronic image, as seen by one line of the Optacon array, and then, to generate synthetic speech. The software had to identify the letters and punctuation, interpret the string of characters as written words and sentences, and announce them through what was being developed–the world's best speech synthesizer. TSI had a committed and highly talented engineering staff; many had graduate degrees from Stanford and The Massachusetts Institute of Technology (MIT). The gender-neutral engineering team worked with a focused intensity, applying the cutting edge of technology to the needs of people with disabilities.

To understand the colossal nature of the Talking Optacon project, (one of several TSI had underway), consider that the work began with a seven-year development effort by an earlier team at MIT, directed by Dr. Dennis Klatt. Dr. Klatt was the leader at MIT, on speech recognition and speech synthesis. He laid the foundation for the entire field of speech synthesis. Ironically, Dr. Klatt had been diagnosed with cancer of the larynx, as he was creating the world's first, highly intelligible, computer-generated, synthetic speech. But the computer's talking was not "real time" nor was it instantaneous. The speech was produced by a PDP-11/70 refrigerator-sized development computer, which took six minutes of number crunching to produce one second of synthetic speech that was recorded on tape for later playback. When the computer's work was done, the tape could play the connected seconds of recorded speech, creating a very human-like, naturally inflected voice. The result of the MIT work was transferred, and TSI's team of twenty programmers and engineers began a four-year nonstop effort that had two interlocking goals. TSI's challenge was to transform the program into one that could run in real time, in microprocessors that would generate the reading machine's speech output. Simultaneously, the other team of programmers and engineers worked on the dense alchemy of OCR development. A total of over eighty person-years of work, between MIT and TSI, were brought to bear on the multiple development tasks required to create the Talking Optacon. This made the project, I believe, the most extensive and intensive engineering development effort on any assistive technology concept to that time, or perhaps ever.

Speech and understandable communication was important to me, both professionally and personally. In 1976, two years before I joined TSI, my father's cancer had spread to his throat. Surgery had taken extensive tissue, including most of his larynx. As a result, Dad lost his ability to speak and swallow. He would be nourished, from then on, through a thin flexible tube that went into his stomach.

Without a lower jaw or larynx, his speech was reduced to a difficult to understand, thin whisper. If only technology had been able to offer a portable typewriter that talked, Dad would have been able to communicate with everyone. In 1979, TSI's years of concentrated effort resulted in the completion of the engineering prototype of the long awaited Talking Optacon.

Eight prototype Talking Optacons were hand-built by members of the engineering team. Each elegant box held five microcomputers that ran in a complex electronic dance–taking the data stream from its attached Optacon docking port and resulting in wonderfully clear, synthetic speech. The Talking Optacon, or HS-1, was the most sophisticated electronic device for consumer use that had ever been developed. This was before the advent of personal computers. Five microcomputers crunched furiously away at a staggering rate of fifty thousand calculations per second. TSI used the full power of the day's technology and pioneered many firsts. The prototypes were truly engineering marvels. But, however effective the systems were in the engineering lab, extensive user experience with the systems was needed. An in-depth user evaluation of the complex machine was required as a shake-down cruise.

At that time, corporate austerity measures reduced my beloved marketing communications department to a one person, graphics-oriented department. Again, I was to be out of a job. Scrambling, I convinced the head of Engineering R&D to let me create a job within engineering, to develop and manage field-based trials for the Talking Optacon. The job would be funded through subsidized field evaluations which I was responsible for developing. When a sighted engineer, using a visual display, hand-tracked printed text with exacting Optacon technique, the beautiful machine read aloud in a rich baritone voice with emphasis and what sounded like understanding. Comparably, the blind user had to roll the Optacon's miniature video camera in a very straight line, keeping the image in the center of the vibrating lines of blunt pins felt by the index finger. That array produced the tactile images through which thousands of blind, Optacon users had read text for years. But the camera had to be hand-tracked very accurately, across the line of text, keeping the letters in the middle of the array for the HS1 to read properly. The print had to be high quality in order for the OCR to accurately identify the passing letters. When the tracking was poor, or print wasn't clear enough, the sophisticated system would read what we simply called garbage. But the blindness field's expectations of the system were very high. After all, TSI had been producing a steady stream of marketing materials beginning before I got there, promoting how good the system would be, based on the long-held marketing projections.

One Saturday, I received a call from J.J. Jackson, a friend who was very close to Stevie Wonder. Stevie was in San Francisco and wanted to buy one of the Talking Optacons for a blind school in Africa. After a series of hurried arrangements, I was picked up in Stevie's stretch limo, followed by a BBC van filming a day in his life, to go to TSI's engineering lab. That afternoon, Stevie Wonder was instructed by the president of the company, in how to use the finicky device, and he attempted to scan a paperback edition of *The Elephant Man*. The president and I looked on helplessly as the machine's OCR stumbled along, as it attempted to recognize letters in the paperback's denigrated type. Stevie and all of us struggled to understand the error-strewn voice output. It was hopeless, and I explained to Stevie that, in any case, we couldn't support one of the prototypes being shipped overseas. The transatlantic cable (the only means of trans-oceanic telephone connection in 1980), did not provide the clarity needed for remote computer diagnosis–a forward-leaning attribute of the system's design and planned support.

But out of that experience, I established a friendship with Stevie. I later taught him to use The Versa Braille, our new electronic Braille, portable computer. Stevie used it to give a speech in Washington, D.C., in support of the Martin Luther King Holiday. The Versa Braille was the world's first personal computer.

Quite apart from the shaky demonstration for Stevie Wonder, I had the task of finding field research homes for the eight Talking Optacon prototypes. I wrote proposals to The Veteran's Administration and private blindness agencies all over the country, to fund the prototypes' evaluation. One agency that agreed to participate was the Cleveland Society for the Blind. I wanted to move back to Cleveland, to be able to help my parents and to give my son the experience of having an extended family. I also sorely needed, for his sake and my own, to become my brother Mark's, advocate.

Beginning in 1980, I traveled regularly to Los Angeles, San Francisco, Chicago, Cleveland, Washington D.C., St. Louis, and Atlanta to install the HS-1 devices, train the evaluation site coordinators, and then, over time, to evaluate users' responses to the device when applied to the full life spectrum's reading needs. The consumer evaluation was conducted within Schools, a Federally-funded Rehabilitation Research and Training Center on Blindness, Veterans Administration blind technology research and evaluation centers, many individuals' homes and workplaces, consumer organizations of people with visual disabilities, and private agencies serving people with visual disabilities. After a year and a half of serious evaluation, composite feedback demonstrated that the system's hand-tracking requirements were too stringent, making the HS-1 Talking Optacon too difficult to use. It was insufficient in its scope of real world applications, to which it could be applied. The marvelous magic boxes were not going to be effective reading machines.

It was the end of the line for the Talking Optacon. However, everybody loved the clear, synthetic speech with its natural inflection. The voice was light years ahead of the other synthesizers of the day. The speech was so superior that the device became a product–The Prose 20/20. In 1986, Dr. Steven Hawking, the world-famous physicist, selected the synthesizer to serve as his own voice. The device can be heard in the movie, *A Brief History of Time*, as Dr. Hawking narrates the film.

But before the synthesizer was manufactured in 1980, we at Telesensory Systems had the state of the art, speech synthesizer prototype, field ready. Looking for other uses for the speech synthesizer in assistive technology applications, we wrote a proposal to the National Science Foundation. The grant was to explore the synthesizer's use as a speech output device for people who could not speak, or whose speech was not understandable, due to the severity of their physical disabilities. After the proposal was granted and the engineering development system was fabricated, I was assigned the field-testing of the one-of-a-kind, engineering-created, demonstration augmentative, communications system. Dr. John Eulenberg, a visiting scholar at Stanford, joined the effort. John was loaned part-time to TSI. John's artificial language lab, at Michigan State University was, perhaps, the day's finest custom augmentative communication center. TSI's engineering department's NSF-funded team built a device with multiple types of possible input devices. It required a van to move it, in seven large wooden crates. We installed the wonderfully functional, engineering conceptual device at a school in Los Angeles, under the direction of a skilled and technically gifted teacher, and within the home of my old friend from CIL, Michael Williams.

Michael's six weeks with the system proved to be a very fruitful period for us and for the writer and humorist. When we came to pick up the system, Michael entertained us with his creative and eloquently written segments, spoken by the device. His hilarious imitation of the periods' fast talking, car lot huckster commercials was very funny. Michael's beautifully crafted reflections on communication, announced by the system's deep resonant voice, were truly moving, and we hated to disassemble the prototype to take it away. Michael nearly cried as we packed up the microcomputers, keyboard, and components. He jokingly called us bastards and told us that we were taking away his voice. We were. Thanks to the assistive technology we developed, Michael Williams and I had explored an entirely new landscape in communication. The augmentative communication, engineering prototype gave me a new appreciation for the depth and texture of Michael Williams' mind. But the lessons of alternative communication were also closer to home.

On December 31, 1979, my father called at 11:15 p.m.–2:15 a.m., Dad's time in Cleveland. His voice was a forced thin whisper. He spoke slowly and I listened carefully, asking him to repeat, when I didn't understand. That conversation with my father lasted over an hour and spanned the turning of the decade. It was one of the sweetest, most poignant conversations that my father and I ever shared. We both recognized that his days were numbered.

John Eulenberg had told me about his own father's death and how at the end, their communication was reduced to hand squeezes. One squeeze meant "Are you awake"? One squeeze in return signaled "Yes". Two squeezes meant "I love you".

In May 1980, in conjunction with an evaluation run by an assistive technology evaluator from CIL, we hosted an international symposium on the state-of-the-art of voice output communication aids. As the conclusion of the NSF Project, we used the event to craft an acronym that we hoped would stick as the field moved into the future of this exciting aspect of rehabilitation engineering. The VOCA (Voice Output Communication Aid) Conference, was held in Berkeley, gathering the chief inventors of such technology, manufacturers, and for the first time–consumers. Their own voices and thoughts were in the hands of the professionals who had come together to listen to our findings, and to severely disabled individuals dependent on their VOCA's. I was going to be the moderator for the two-day gathering. But it was not to be. Instead, I sat at my father's bedside in Cleveland as he approached death.

Dad couldn't whisper due to the oxygen mist flowing into his tracheotomy opening. The last exchanges we had were the simplest and most profound. Using John Eulenberg's terribly simple lexicon, I asked if dad was conscious, and then we both signaled with double squeezes. My father passed away on the Friday afternoon while, in Berkeley, the conference that had focused so eloquently on the future of human communication was ending.

The Viking's Journal

When he was in high school, my father was nicknamed "Smiling Jack", and with his lantern jaw his handsome face would open easily with his winning grin. Dad was referred to as "the handsomest man I ever saw" by more than one person—both male and female. His easy baritone voice often blended into barbershop quartets and song sessions, to his ukulele's accompaniment. In short, my dad was a popular, friendly, and good-looking man. People thought that he was Greek, Spanish, Mexican, or Hawaiian. Dad's complexion, his black hair, and deep-set dark brown eyes, were, (we thought), vestiges of a long-ago Native American ancestor. But Dad's appearance changed in middle age.

When Mark was born with obvious cognitive disabilities in 1954, Dad's moderate drinking became more of a daily habit. Dad began a life on the road in 1957, when he was 36 years old. He worked as a traveling salesman, with a hard drinking boss who would often travel with him. Dad's heartache and work patterns led to many years of alcohol abuse. Dad's handsome face became blotched with the stain of broken capillaries, and a jagged scar below his eye gave testament to his having fallen down in the midst of one evening's stupor. In 1970, Dad lost the job working for the little company owned by his drinking buddy. Together, he and the owner had represented and sold the industrial machines of Cleveland's steel equipment manufacturing companies. Dad was a good salesman and his efforts helped the owner mightily. Thirteen years of my father's life were dedicated to building the company's reach and income, permitting the owner to move his family into a gracious home, and the company to a custom-built office and warehouse. But the years of drinking had taken their toll on Dad, and although he did not drink before 5:00 p.m., his morning breath could smell of last night's liquor. One morning in 1970, Dad had arrived at a factory to install a machine, with breath that suggested a late night drunk. His hands had begun to tremble, in response to the copious quantities of vodka he consumed daily. The plant foreman thought that he was drunk. Dad was reported to the company's owner.

Not long before, the owner had laid off the one other salesman, who had worked for him for many years less than my dad. The steel industry was beginning its implosion in Cleveland, due to owners skimming profits rather than reinvesting in modern, steel forging plants. The little company that employed Dad had been feeling the effects of that decline. Between the accusation and Cleveland's steel empire collapse, Dad was canned. After thirteen hard years of faithful service to the little, family-owned company, he was ignominiously turned out. In recognition of his years of service he was given his road-worn company car, a three-year-old Pontiac that he had driven one hundred fifty thousand miles, throughout Ohio and contiguous states, building the company that now had no use for him.

Numb, Dad drove home in the middle of the day with a cardboard box containing his desk accessories, photos, and coffee cup. Life yawned before him with no place to go during the day, no job title, and no identity as a working man.

Mom typed up Dad's resume and he interviewed unsuccessfully for the meager job openings that presented themselves. Dad continued to drink hard, for another two years, as he floundered in the unemployment backwater of Cleveland's depressed steel industry. Mom's job as an executive secretary at General Electric paid the bills and provided health insurance, but Dad had lost a lot more than a paycheck. Dad was without purpose, adrift, and alone. I was living in California then. Mark was institutionalized, and Bonnie lived one hundred fifty miles away with her young family. However, destiny was about to present Dad with his truly epic struggle in a woebegone life, already filled with pathos.

In 1972, when Dad was fifty-one years old, cancer was discovered under his tongue. Before the diagnosis, his brother Chuck, a dentist, had prescribed an antibiotic, hoping the lesion was an infection. Chuck advised Dad not to drink while he was taking the antibiotic. Remarkably, after years of unchecked alcohol abuse, Dad quit drinking. He quit cold turkey, without the benefit of counseling or a support group. Stone sober, he entered his dark labyrinth. The sore did not improve. An oncologist performed a painful biopsy and diagnosed mouth cancer, an aggressive form requiring aggressive treatment. Dad was hospitalized, and for two weeks an arterial tube of toxic chemicals was inserted at his temple, snaked down his face, and then to the floor of his mouth, to the area of the cancer. Nine of Dad's bottom teeth had to be extracted to prepare for the x-ray, radiation treatments. Dad took the loss of his teeth like a determined fighter absorbs a stiff blow to the midsection. But like a boxer in a title fight, Dad's punishment had just begun. Following the extractions came six weeks of daily radiation. The bludgeoning impact of those toxic rays blackened the skin on Dad's face, but much worse killed Dad's jaw bone and much of the mouth and facial tissue. The decay process dragged horribly on, lasting for years.

My father was not a writer. But encouraged by many to tell his powerful story, he began to dictate his battle record to Mom. Dad's physician told him that radiation reacts differently with different people. Dad wrote, "Well, personally speaking, my reaction has been absolutely disastrous."

With stoic steadiness, Dad's oncologist watched the ruin that began to claim Dad's face. Operation after operation, he applied his most creative solutions and the most advanced medical science known. The terrible toll from the over-radiation crept on. Dad lived through protracted decay, skin grafts, and bone grafts. Ultimately, every scheduled reconstruction was undermined by the lifeless radiated tissue. Every failed plan demanded new intervention. Operations were every six weeks–sixty-three of them. During the construction of transferred flaps of skin, experimental attempts were made to build blood pathways through the wasteland of irradiated facial tissue. But the flesh was beyond repair. Dad's face developed a hole that opened through his cheek, and food and saliva would pour out. After more than two years, the hole was healed after multiple surgeries. Dad wrote in his journal that the healing was monumental, calling the incision line "a beautiful sight", and adding, "Look Ma, no holes". The slow decay of his jawbone and facial tissue was battled by the grim imagination, perseverance, and skill of the surgeon who had ordered the radiation that caused the ruin. The march of inevitable decline was not to be denied. Twice Dad had external plastic braces screwed into his jawbone with four silver bolts, as bone grafts were attempted, using windows of bone cut out of his hips. As a result, Dad's hips collapsed and limitations in walking ensued. But Dad was a courageous fighter, unwilling to succumb to deterioration's ceaseless pummeling.

Throughout the ordeal, Dad kept his running journal documenting the procedures, the frequent frustrations, and the inner thoughts of his private suffering. Dad's memoir was dictated in installments that Mom would transcribe in shorthand and then type on the IBM Selectric that stood in the basement family room. Mom would faithfully copy the segments' pages and send Bonnie and me chapters, in Dad's evolving opus. The writing detailed the bad news, hospital incompetence, the hopeful medical plans, the procedures, their failures, and Dad's resignation and re-birth of newer, smaller hopes.

"My aspirations are not as great as they used to be," Dad wrote. "My driving desire now is to be fitted with teeth and have my upper teeth either realigned or replaced, and be able to bite a sandwich and chew like normal people. I am a dreamer, but I am also a realist. This may never happen. If it doesn't, so what? I am still able to breathe in and out, and that simple function is a tremendous function." Dad's gratitude was reduced to appreciating his ability to breathe. The tenacity and strength of his will and spirit shines throughout the written odyssey, and Dad's appreciation for small acts of thoughtfulness and care from his family are mentioned repeatedly, particularly as the situation worsened.

In 1976, four years after the cancer was discovered, Dad was having trouble swallowing and a persistent pain had developed in his throat. He twice asked his weary doctor to explore the matter, without the physician providing a serious examination. After the third request, the doctor stuck a rubber-gloved finger down Dad's throat. The gloved finger he pulled out was bloody. His doctor understood that the cancer had returned and that the soft tissue of his neck had been invaded by a tumor of unknown size. An exploratory operation was scheduled. Although the extent of the operation was unknown, its gravity was not. It was made clear that the surgery could be life-threatening, since it involved tissue adjacent to the jugular vein. Surgery exposed a large tumor, on the right side of his neck that extended from below his hear to his collarbone. The tumor was removed, taking with it muscles required for swallowing and most of Dad's larynx. Dad was also provided with a required tracheotomy and a feeding tube that was inserted into his neck. The small latex tube that terminated in his stomach, was to deliver the thin liquids that could pass through the narrow opening, providing life-giving fluid and nourishment. Dad's diet was thereby reduced to thin, watery liquids.

I had returned to Cleveland from Palo Alto for the extensive, life-threatening surgery. When Dad returned to his room from post-op, after seven hours of surgery, his neck was thickly bandaged and his head was wrapped in tape that extended to his chest in multiple adhesive tape ropes to stabilize the position of his neck. He looked like a pharaoh in his headdress of bandages, and a silver tracheotomy ring showed below the thick white wrappings. For the first few days, Dad wrote short notes on a yellow pad, communicating his need for pain medication, wry observations, and inquiries about the family. Then one morning, immediately upon my arrival, he motioned for me to come close to him. He put his finger over the trachea opening and whispered, "I can talk!"

He said that he had discovered that he could still speak by experimentally closing off the tracheotomy and forcing air into whispered words. We were both elated, and the morning was spent in joyful short spoken exchanges. Thereafter, communication was either written, or it demanded a patient, conversational partner, as Dad would cover his tracheotomy opening and force a thin whisper, impaired in its clarity by his lack of a lower jaw.

On the liquid diet Dad's weight plummeted, but his growing thinness was never an issue. However, he felt that his facial appearance was freakish. He wrote about his disfigurement in his journal, noting that he now had the type of face that people in a crowd look at twice, "to make sure what they saw the first time is actually there." Yet he also wrote that he was surprised that he didn't look worse because of all the surgeries he'd endured.

"I look like a freak to me, but not in the eyes of those who love me, and surely that has to be the most important thing. Love is still very dear, and each day I'm alive, I thank God for that gift." His face was clearly disfigured. His lower jaw had the shriveled, sunken appearance that reminded me of E.T., the alien movie character with no chin, yet searching, hopeful eyes.

Dad's staggering sojourn included an unsuccessful, experimental transplantation of pig skin onto his shoulder when he had run out of available tissue of his own. He also was the patient who underwent Cleveland's first surgery using a surgical microscope, attempting to join small blood vessels in the doomed skin grafts. Dad would have to go to Chuck's office regularly to have beard hair plucked from inside his mouth. Beard-growing neck skin had been grafted through a complex series of operations to rebuild the floor of his mouth, following the devastation of the over-radiation. During one of his visits to his brother's office, Dad recognized an old friend in the waiting room. He didn't feel that he could speak to his friend and be understood. Dad attempted to make eye contact with him, but his old friend just glanced at him and then quickly looked away.

Chuck entered the waiting room and saw that the two old school mates were not speaking. He said, "Ed, you remember my brother Jack." They had been close friends in high school. Dad had even served as Ed's best man.

"No," Ed said, "I'm afraid we've never met."

My father felt invisible–trapped in a strange and unrecognizable form. Through it all, he had struggled and suffered against the enemies of cancer, over-radiation, and physical devastation, with heroic courage and humor. Near the end of his brutal odyssey, my father and I stood in the garage of my parents' suburban home. I had rushed to Cleveland, that mid-May in 1980 when my father had been told that he had about one week to live. The unrelenting cancer had advanced to his lungs. Every few weeks, Dad would be aspirated, a thick hypodermic needle pierced through his un-anesthetized side into his lung cavities, and the liquid that was filling them drawn off. After eight grueling years, the time was cloaked in a chilling finality as we felt the long-denied specter of death approach. The curtain was lowering on the last act of Dad's life's epic drama. Dad and I stood in my parents' garage and watched the evening's light fade from the blue purple sky.

Dad wondered aloud about why he had been left by God to suffer so, why he hadn't been taken years before. In his aching reverie, he said that he didn't know what his purpose was. Like everyone, he wondered what the meaning of his life had been. What was his legacy beyond his own time on Earth?

Dad died in my arms, a few days later. From his hospital bed, in a startled reflex, Dad had pushed himself up onto his elbows. I gathered him in my arms and was lowering him to the reclining hospital bed. I was gazing into his wide-open eyes as he passed from his body. Had I never believed in God, or in an afterlife, I would have started to right then. His eyes were full of awe, surrender, and complete wonder. I watched as my father saw eternity.

In 2003, twenty-three years later, I received a phone call from Betsy Wilson, an old friend and the founder of Let's Face It, a national resource organization for people living with facial differences. Betsy informed me that she had given my name to Laura Greenwald, a writer with the Cleveland Clinic, who was planning a book on cranial and facial differences. She asked me if I would be willing to speak with Laura. Betsy thought that Laura, a neophyte concerning the disability experience and the Disability Rights Movement, would gain a grounded perspective through a conversation with me. Laura called, and on a wintry afternoon we spoke in my home's country kitchen, where a warming fire burned brightly. I skimmed over the surface of the psychosocial aspects of disability: disability and loss, the disability policy model, and the evolution of Disability Civil Rights. In the course of the afternoon, I introduced her to my father's history, and I played her a recently discovered recording of my parents, my grandmother, and I, all singing during a family visit, shortly before Dad lost his voice. In the recording, my father's articulation had been obviously impaired by the loss of his lower jaw. But the warmth of his, and my mother's, singing was magnetic. Laura listened intently and with growing understanding. Later, at her request, I faxed her Dad's seventy-five-page memoir.

On the basis of those exchanges, as my father became a real person to her, she decided to focus her book on the stories of individuals with facial disfigurement. My father's heroic struggle became one of her book's stories– the only one that did not involve successful medical intervention to rebuild and alter facial anomalies. In the book, *Heroes with a Thousand Faces,* renamed *Eye of the Beholder: True Stories of People with Facial Differences,* Laura penned a fine chapter about Dad called, "The Viking". The title came from my referring to my father as a Viking. It was a perfect metaphor for the way my father faced his battle. I mentioned to Laura that according to legend, when a Viking warrior was to be put to death, he was required to jump into a pit of starving wolves. While death was inevitable, the condemned was permitted his sword, allowing him to battle until the end. That was the nature of my father's courage and strength. Dad's own words, drawn from his memoir, are interwoven with Laura's word-smithed narrative and my reflections. Dad's story will, undoubtedly, touch many lives, and perhaps through this, his purpose will be realized. I think that Dad's final reverie about his life's meaning, is answered in full measure by Laura's beautiful depiction of his courageous odyssey.

After Dad stopped drinking, at the beginning of his eight-year ordeal, his hands became rock steady once again, and he began the focused work of building ship models between surgeries. Six weeks after my father's death, I was in Louisville, Kentucky for a conference. I walked down to the Ohio River to see where The Robert E. Lee, the restored, historic side-wheeler was docked. Dad had crafted a model of that very riverboat. As I took in the splendid craft, I thought of my father's models. On the plane home I wrote this:

MY FATHER'S SHIPS

My father crafted ships that sail imaginary waters
Perfect scale replicas, so wonderful to see
With patience and with skill, he set each sail and strung each rigging
And set the planks in place on many ships of history

And its wave to the people as the big side-wheeler steams
Up that mighty, broad Ohio rolling river of my dreams
And its "Land ho! Captain Drake," we sail this unknown ocean
From the crow's nest of the Golden Hind, the joyous cries of land

The big, square-riggers sails fill in the homes of family now
And the sleek Blue Sloop cuts through the foam of
landlocked fantasies
He left these treasures with us, living crafts of grace and beauty
And his memory sails on with us, up the river, through the seas

And its wave to the people as the big side-wheeler steams
Up that muddy, broad Ohio raging river of my dreams
And the sails snap above us as the whales sing below
It's homeward bound with silk and spice on the west wind's
steady blow

The craftsman's tools lie still now and we chart our course
without him
Though the Cutty Sark and the Constitution ply on powerfully
I hear the boatswain's whistle and the creaking of the timbers
And I feel the salt spray stinging on this wide, uncharted sea

And its wave to the people as the big side-wheeler steams
Up that mighty, broad Ohio, mighty river of my dreams
And its "Land ho! Captain Drake", we sail this unknown ocean
From the crow's nest of the Golden Hind, the joyous cries of land
© Jeff Moyer 1980

Bicycle Accident

Small changes in severely diminished vision are hard to measure. Since age eleven, my best vision had been 20/200 in my left eye. During those years, I could see most of the eye chart's big E's heavy black lines. In my twenties and thirties, based on functional tasks, I feared that my vision had further deteriorated. I found that I could no longer read my college class notes, written with a felt tip pen on standard yellow pads. In graduate school, I began to write on special wide-lined paper with a heavier felt pen. Even with those adaptations, without electronic magnification, I still struggled to read my handwritten notes from classes and meetings. I also noted, with a depressing and fear-filled honesty, that I was not able to see as much of another's face. Growing blots of blindness were crowding out facial features. These and other disturbing changes to my vision had twice prompted me to seek both an ophthalmologist's and optometrist's opinion about what seemed to be ongoing vision loss. Both times, I was advised that my vision had not changed. The opinion was offered that perhaps my perception was the result of my imagination or concern-driven hyper-vigilance.

I knew very well that I was riding the margin of visual functionality and that the subtle changes I noticed were pushing me to the tipping point. Bicycle riding presented the most difficult and dangerous example. Ever since I had first defied my doctor and parents by renting a bicycle, during my summer away in 1966, I had chalked up numerous little accidents caused by my not having seen something critical in time. During that summer, I rode my bicycle between two steel posts blocking cars on a footpath at Ohio State. I hit the unseen industrial wire strung between them. The bicycle flipped and I landed abruptly on my back, with a blood blister straight across my chest and biceps from the taught, heavy wire. A few years later, while peddling down a quiet side street, I came within inches of riding face first into the rough metal edge of a yellow 'Men Working' sign. I jerked my head and felt the sharp edge of the metal graze against my ear as I sped past the danger.

When bike riding, I had to keep moving my eyes, compensating for the holes in my field of vision. Every time I had a near miss, I convinced myself that the problem was a lapse in attention, rather than a lack of vision so severe that I really couldn't ride a bicycle safely anymore. In 1980, my bicycle was a fully integrated (and I thought, essential), part of my life. I rode the five miles to work at Telesensory Systems, every day, wearing my bike helmet and business clothes. When I arrived, I slipped off my running shoes and put on polished loafers, closed the top button of my dress shirt, cinched up my tie, and tried to ruffle my hair free from the helmet's inner shape.

However, a cluster of repeated, near-accidents began to rattle my confidence. Palo Alto had many curbed-off or painted bike lanes. I relished the false sense of safety I felt, biking along, not competing with motorized traffic. My final week of bipedal locomotion began as I rode to work one clear morning. Out of nowhere, I saw a runner as he jogged passed me, running toward me in the bike lane. I was shocked, rattled, and relieved. I had not seen him coming at all, only seeing him as he suddenly appeared next to me. I had been paying full attention. I shuddered when I thought about what might have happened if I had hit the man. It was very disconcerting. Just a few days later, directly in my path, I had seen within a very few feet, another cyclist kneeling beside his bike, attending to something near ground level. Veering frantically around him, I just missed another horrible collision. I recognized that there was a tightening frequency to my near misses. I worriedly continued to ride what I thought was my indispensable bicycle, although I could no longer deny that I had become a danger to others and myself. The cold certainty that I had lost more vision morphed my last independent finger-hold into a choke-hold on myself, cutting off my way of life. To stop bike riding seemed unthinkable. It would mean complete mobility dependence. I certainly did not want to become any more dependent than I already was. So with growing dread, I rode on. Then, there came the final sickening demonstration of my inability to ride safely. That cataclysmic mishap made the decision for me.

The April morning was clear and warm. I was riding down a crowded, divided boulevard approaching El Camino Real, which meant preparing to cross a six-lane intersection. The highway was congested with morning rush hour traffic. Following the movement of traffic, (always my cue about the traffic light status), I put my foot down on the curb, as the line of cars stopped for the red light. Then, the idling vehicles powered forward. I slipped my curb foot back into my pedal's toe clip and began pedaling furiously to achieve the speed needed to join the advancing column of cars. The median strip, dividing El Camino, was a raised island of concrete that crossed the perpendicular pedestrian crosswalk and jutted past it. As I surged forward, I was looking behind and beside me as I squeezed next to the line of cars. I was riding close to the flow of traffic streaming around the concrete median. At the same time, a young woman had been riding her bike across the street, toward me, in the crosswalk. When she came to the center barrier, she was forced to go around the protruding concrete median. Facing the wall of oncoming traffic, she had stopped, feet on the ground. She waited for an opening in the line of vehicles, to allow her to slip back around the island and into the other half of the boulevard's crosswalk. I looked forward, just as I approached the end of the concrete median strip. She was standing in my thin outer edge of the traffic lane, now filled with cars rushing toward her. Strictly speaking, she should not have been where she was. As I sped across the intersection, although I turned around and must have looked right at her, my blind spots prevailed and I never saw her.

I crashed into her head on, the full force of my forward thrust driving my ribs into my bike's upright handlebar post. Our bicycle helmets made a loud cracking sound as they hit, as my bike's front wheel slammed behind her pedals, chain drive, and derailleur. The pain in my chest was immediate and intense. But before my feet hit the ground, my torrent of concern, apology, explanation, promise, and pleading filled the air.

"Are you all right? I'm so sorry–are you okay? I never saw you–I have lost some vision recently–are you okay? I promise–I promise–I'll never ride a bicycle again–I'll pay for the damage to your bicycle–of course–are you hurt?"

She stood in silent shock, looking down at her damaged bicycle. I was shocked and sorrowful–both for the possible harm that I might have just caused this bewildered, young woman, as well as for the loss that now had me trapped in its inescapable box canyon. As she pulled her thoughts together, in that moment following the accident's headlong violence, she said, in a shaky voice, that she seemed to be all right. Our hard-shelled helmets and my forward motion's cessation, as I struck my handlebar post, had protected our skulls for certain. She continued to look down, and she absently noted that her ruined bike probably couldn't be ridden. We pulled our bicycles to the far sidewalk from which she had just come. We exchanged contact information, and the woman numbly turned to walk her damaged bicycle toward her nearby home. Remarkably, a co-worker of mine had witnessed the accident and had stopped his Volkswagen bus just past the intersection. As I dully began to walk my bicycle toward work, I heard him call out to me. He lifted my bike into his microbus, and he drove us to work. He asked me how I felt and what had happened. As I answered, speaking was excruciating, and every breath burned. I later learned that I had broken two ribs. But in the hours after the collision, I was handling a far greater torment.

With a fierce finality, I was forever grounded. My beautiful, green, British racing bicycle, with its freshly yellow taped, under slung handlebars, and hard leather racing seat was no longer mine to ride. The concentrated tightrope act, taut with vulnerability, and balanced above danger had failed. My risk-rich defiance was history. I would never again power onto the roadway, grabbing the full freedom of leg-powered mobility. The consequences of my recklessness were irrefutable–a head-on collision. In the jumble of my emotions, I also felt relief and gratitude that the other cyclist had not been hurt.

The miles had fallen beneath my wheels, for some sweet years, because I had stolen freedom from the clamp of prudence. The end of that era brought a stab of loss–sharp, painful, and final. Fresh grief squeezed me and I felt the cloying constraints of my vision loss. My chains had caught up with me, and my membership in the club of the freewheeling had been canceled. In the sphere of mobility, I had become a dependent. I would be entirely beholden now to those who drove and to public transit. Palo Alto buses did not go where I needed to travel. The break with biking was abrupt and brutal. I felt numb, sorrow-filled, and defeated.

That afternoon, another coworker had heard about my fix. He lived roughly in my section of town. He called and offered daily roundtrip transportation to and from work. For a couple of weeks, he provided door-to-door service. Our schedules varied, but I stayed late when necessary and came in early quite often. I arranged my life according to his time schedule. Then a woman engineer working on the Talking Optacon project offered to start riding a clunky, old, borrowed tandem girls' bicycle with me. She suggested that we could ride the one-speed junker, providing her some needed exercise. I would walk the two blocks to her home every morning, and we would ride the rattletrap, old Schwinn, through the streets and up the hills to work in the sunny digital industrial park. It was fun to be back on two wheels as the stoker on the ill-fitting fifties Buick of a tandem. The bicyclist in the front of a tandem is called the captain. The seat behind is occupied by the stoker. A one speed bike of yesteryear, the tandem was limited and certainly did not have the elegant snap of my beloved Dawes English bicycle. The borrowed bike belonged to a young woman at TSI who was blind. It was a blue, rounded tank of a bicycle, but it was biking, and I still loved it.

Cleveland Again

Mom began dating Dick six months after Dad's passing. They married in 1981. One of the best things that came from that marriage was Dick's fresh perspective concerning Mark. Dick had not been beaten down by years of heartache and hopelessness, nor had he been convinced by decades of despair that nothing in Mark's circumstance could change. Dick joined Mom as she made the long painful drive to Columbus. He met Mark and saw his hideous living conditions. Dick was outraged at the appalling depravation and also felt that Mark was misplaced, with individuals with considerably lower cognitive ability. He was a command and control kind of guy, so he picked up the phone and contacted his State Senator's office, concerning Mark's situation. Dick's call came just at the time that a limited number of individuals, housed in the distant institution in Columbus were being selected to be moved back to smaller facilities in Cleveland's Cuyahoga County. The senator took action. After an evaluation of some sort, Mark was selected as one of the lucky ones to be moved back to his home county. After eighteen, spirit-crushing years, my brother was transferred from that ghastly prison and was moving up.

All of the personal effects and clothing that we had ever provided had been efficiently and systematically stolen. Mark and the others were handed a plastic trash bag containing stained, threadbare, ill-fitting clothes from the institution's common clothing stock. He climbed into a van, with several other fortunate residents, to be driven one hundred fifty miles to the grounds of another State institution. The North Eastern Ohio Developmental Center (recently renamed), was one of Ohio's large institutions like Columbus. It occupied a sprawling, wooded site in Broadview Heights, a distant Cleveland suburb forty-five minutes away from Mom. When Ohio's massive state institutions were built in the late nineteenth and early twentieth century, like prisons, staff housing was also built on the grounds. In 1981, a for-profit, residential service provider renovated the moribund enclave of staff dormitories and superintendent housing, and offered a place to live for fifty-six Clevelanders returning from distant institutions. Mark moved into a room, with just one roommate, in a sixteen bed, stark brick building within the little neighborhood, beneath the shadow of imposing institutional buildings–virtually identical to the ones he had lived in for so long. At twenty-seven, for the first time since he was eight years old, Mark had a bedroom shared with only one roommate, a closet, a dresser, a twin bed, and a modicum of privacy. I still lived in California, but I was traveling a great deal, and I was able to visit, en route, several times that first year.

The first time that I walked up the long concrete sidewalk to the shabby brick building, with Mom and Dick, we were greeted by several residents who sat and smoked on the cramped front porch. Mark was called and he greeted us excitedly. He led the way, bounding up the stairs to the second floor, to show me his room. Like the whole place, it was stark and drab. Mark shared his bedroom with a passive, quiet man. House Five was co-ed–eight women and eight men.

When we first walked in, staff members were unpacking bags of weekly groceries in the kitchen, and the place seemed almost homey. The other residents gathered around us as they had in Columbus, where fifty affection-starved ward residents would swarm, crowding in for a hug or human touch. Here there was a cluster, but just the occasional exuberant hug. The place had the acrid smell of strong disinfectant. A slight, talkative, muscular young man demonstrated how he could stand on his hands.

A large woman spoke aggressively to me, standing too close for my comfort. I had always played music in Columbus, and I had brought my guitar here as well. I cleared the idea with a staff member, unpacked my guitar, and began to play for the several residents who gathered around. Singing along lustily, Mark was having a great time. Suddenly, the same large woman stormed into the room and shoved me in the chest, knocking me backward. Gripping my guitar, I staggered and stumbled, barely avoiding falling. The altercation ended when a staff member pulled the still-storming woman away, complaining loudly as she went. I continued to sing and play halfheartedly, but soon stopped. The place wasn't wonderful, but House Five was a vast improvement over Columbus. Mark was forced to live with fifteen people, not of his choosing, in a segregated colony of fifty-four other recently-freed souls who, like Mark, had had their fortunes improved. Some residents had difficult behaviors and Mark, like everyone else, had no place to get away from them. And for some residents, Mark's constant talking could also be experienced as difficult behavior. This was still a whole lot better than living in the fifty-bed wards he had endured for nearly two decades. I returned to California after that first visit and focused on what was next for my family.

In August 1982, my work at TSI would be coming to a close, when two grant funded projects would end–both the V.A.'s grant supporting the Talking Optacon evaluation, and the National Science Foundation's Voice Output Communication Aid research and demonstration project. Sandy and I were looking at other job possibilities to which I might apply, and cities to which we might move. I considered jobs in Palo Alto, Washington D.C., Chicago, and Cleveland; but there really was no contest in my mind.

Cleveland was a powerful magnet since Mark had been moved there, and my mother and grandmother also were there. I really wanted my son to know his family. If I was in Cleveland, for the first time I could exercise some real advocacy and be of help to my dear younger brother. But Sandy needed some convincing. She had never lived in the frozen North, coming from the steaming South, before moving to the balmy West.

My heart's desire was to return to my graduate degree's field, and fortunately, I got an offer from The Cleveland Society for the Blind to become their new rehabilitation director. I had cultivated that blindness agency when I was looking for Talking Optacon evaluation sites, and they had become one of the locations for the field-based research. As such, I had created a circumstance that took me inside the place. I had worked with administration and funders, staff and clients, periodically, for eighteen months. Now I was going to be the rehabilitation director, responsible for a large and diverse multiple program staff. I looked forward to the new job, and despite her reservations, Sandy recognized the necessity of moving to a more affordable area than overpriced Palo Alto.

According to an article in The San Francisco Chronicle, Palo Alto had the highest housing cost in the country, while Greater Cleveland had the lowest. My hire date was set. I was to begin on Wednesday, August 18, 1982. Sandy flew back and rented a fine old house in hip Cleveland Heights. We planned a going away party for early August; several luncheons were scheduled at work, as I wound down a four year run at TSI. But two weeks before the carefully planned move, I was hit with a full-blown case of strep throat and all farewell events were scotched. I dragged myself out of bed after ten days and began serious packing. We had convinced an unemployed friend to drive the largest truck that U-Haul rented, while Sandy would drive our car. He had arrived the day we were packing the truck, blinking in a blur of vision needing serious correction. He had decided to train his eyes to see without glasses, according to a book entitled: The Art of Seeing, a 1942 publication by Aldous Huxley. It promoted the Bates Method for better eyesight, and Gary was convinced he could learn to see without the corrective lenses he had worn since he was a child. Huxley was a strong denier of the state of his own severely impaired vision. It is widely agreed that he lived with severe, low vision for most of his life. Trusting the method completely, Gary had not even brought his glasses. He had been doing the Bates' eye exercises, for four days, without any visual improvement. Gary joined the packing crew. With a lot of help from some stalwart friends, we filled the big U-Haul box truck, cramming it from floor to ceiling. We spent the last night in our home, turned in our keys to the landlord and, then, set off for our new life in Cleveland.

Without his needed spectacles, seeing no better than legally blind– with me as his useless navigator–my friend gamely drove the heavily-loaded truck east, carefully following Sandy and John who led in our little Toyota wagon. Late the first evening, we pulled into Reno. The bright lights that lit up the Nevada night made seeing the road and other vehicles very hard for him. He had to back into highway traffic from a crowded hotel driveway, after discovering that the portico lacked adequate clearance for the truck's height. It was slow going, with some real white-knuckle moments, but he managed to finally park the truck, avoiding all mishaps. The next morning over breakfast, we swore a blood oath to only drive during daylight, since his vision seemed to be hopeless after dark. In Iowa he mistook Sandy's wild waving, trying to signal to get off the highway to get gas, as friendly exuberance. Laughing, he waved back. As a result, he missed the single opportunity for miles, to fuel up. Sandy had been right, anticipating the truck's need for fuel, but my squinting friend couldn't see the fuel gauge slide below E. Ten miles later, the truck sputtered to a gasless stop. I stayed with the truck as he drove off in the station wagon, with a miffed Sandy and little John, to find a gas can and gas.

On August 12, 1982–Friday afternoon at rush hour–our little caravan drove through the western suburbs of Cleveland, through the factory smog and urban cityscape of downtown, toward our new home in Cleveland Heights. Thirteen years and eleven months before, I had left Cleveland as part of the great youth migration of the sixties, seeking my own identity within the magical lure of California. While there I had come to terms with my disability, earned two degrees, gotten married and started a family. I had administrative and University teaching experience and was about to start work at the helm of the extensive rehabilitation division of The Cleveland Sight Center. The Sight Center had deep roots in my long-ago past, and I was proud of the job that awaited me. I had years of experience working in the blindness field–a career area that I had once sworn I'd never pursue–but here I was. I would finally be able to salve the open wound on my heart; I was going to help Mark. The wandering son was moving back home, with his budding family. Complicated life chapters were ending and beginning. But, on that late summer's afternoon, it was good to be coming home, good to be back in Cleveland.

Chapter 14: Feeling My Way

The Confrontation

When we moved from California to Ohio in 1982, I wanted to create interactivity for my family with my extended roots, and I looked for opportunities to get people together. John was six and had been raised with scant contact with my extended family. Living in Cleveland, I was going to see that changed! One of the matriarchs of the family, my maternal grandmother, Mama Smith, was visiting from Florida. I invited her to spend the afternoon with my family and Mark, who had returned to Cleveland the previous year.

The mall was relatively close to Mark's sixteen bed dwelling, House Five, and I decided that it would be a fruitful outing for the entire family. That Sunday afternoon, it was particularly crowded and noisy. John had very high energy and pulled us into every toy store to check out the newest action figures or anything else that caught his eye, with the single-mindedness that only a six-year-old can muster. Mark was happy to be with everyone and away from the confinement of the depressing, large residential facility. He wanted to talk, drink coffee, and smoke, and he wanted some cool sunglasses. I needed a watch battery and shoe laces. Our grandmother probably wanted to just sit down and visit, and not do the mall crawl, as we plodded on, attempting to meet all of our divergent needs. Sandy stoically endured, as she kept our human caravan together amid the crowds. But I was in charge. The mall excursion had been my idea. I thought it would give all of us some quality time together. But the only quality that we all seemed to share was that our nerves had begun to be a bit frayed by the strain and tedium of the overall experience.

As we ended the long afternoon and headed for the exit, my son burst between two adults who were lost in talk, causing them to stop and stare at the little person who had interrupted their conversation. The tension I had been carrying was quickly intensified and found a righteous focus. I didn't snap–I boiled over. As a conscientious father, I chose to stop, confront John, and demand that he return and apologize to the strangers for his rudeness. I spoke to him in a stern, judgmental tone. Frozen, he gazed at me unblinking, in embarrassed silence. I could feel my intensity ratchet, as I insisted that he make amends at once, to the two people who now stood in mute witness to our confrontation. Sandy quietly suggested that we take up the matter later. I flatly stated that this was the time and mine was the way. I went back to insisting that John say he was sorry to the strangers. I bore down heavily as his gaze dropped to the floor. Mama Smith made a small worried sound as she frowned and twisted her purse strap nervously. She anxiously witnessed her grandson's wrath and her great grandson's humiliation.

One of the strangers stepped forward, offering that it was okay and that no apology was needed. I refused his offer and tersely stated the obvious. For his own good, I needed to have my son, now shamed in freeze-frame, do the right thing, my way. Scorched by my fiery intensity, the gentle stranger pulled back and helplessly watched the stalemate deepen. A silent gathering of passersby had formed, watching my unbending demand go unheeded. No one spoke but me. I was vaguely aware of the spectacle that I was creating and the real discomfort and strain that I was causing everyone, particularly my own dear son.

My brother, whose intellectual ability is measured in the early pre-school range, stepped silently to my side and spoke three words. He gently put his hand on my back and said to me in a low voice, "Peace brother, peace." The dark spell was shattered. I reached out and touched John's shoulder. I looked down and read the emotional wreckage from my anger storm on my child's upturned face. In a trembling voice, I told him that what he had done was wrong, but that what I was doing was worse. I apologized to the strangers, to my family and, most earnestly, to my son. I took my boy by the hand and we all left the mall.

Going Blind

One Saturday afternoon, in January 1984, I was playing with John on his bed. At seven, he was intelligent, wildly creative and very active. At thirty-four, I was a fully engaged dad, relishing this playtime with John. We were using a beanbag-weighted, Masonite-topped, lap-tray writing table as a platform for our play, with John's Star War action figures. My menacing Darth Vader was confronting John's truculent Luke Skywalker. I was lying down, with my face very close to the lap-tray stage, for our epic drama in miniature. Without warning, John puffed out his cheeks and made a guttural explosion sound as he unexpectedly jerked the lap-tray back and forth to create the special effect to match this downturn in little Darth's fortune. The

240

blunt corner of the board struck me directly in the eye. I was in serious pain and John was very concerned, in spite of my assurances that everything would be fine. My normally low vision was now also blurry in the better, left eye. I worried when it didn't return to lousy normal after a few days. Through our Kaiser network, I made an appointment for an eye exam with a general ophthalmologist. He took a long and thorough history and then conducted his examination. During the recitation of my woebegone ocular and visual past, I shared the standing diagnosis that I had optic and retinal atrophy.

Early in the exam, he noted that I had sustained no lasting injury from the accident. Then he spent some long, silent minutes, carefully studying the interior of my eyes, using the always-painful ophthalmoscope with its brutally bright light. He clicked off the examination tool and pushed the rolling stool away from the exam chair. He quietly stated that my diagnosis was in error and that my retinas showed every indication of retinitis pigmentosa (RP), not optic and retinal atrophy, as I had been told over twenty years before. He solemnly reported that he was certain that I had a form of the progressive retinal disease. He studied me. "Mr. Moyer, I can't tell you how long it will take, but you are going to lose the remainder of your vision. You are going to go blind."

His words were frozen like a telegraph reporting death, to be read slowly several times. My heart raced. My chest pounded. My breathing grew rapid and shallow. His voice seemed very far away as he detailed the heavily pigmented appearance of my retina and made a referral to The Cleveland Clinic's Specialty Retina Clinic. Then, he went over the information again. He added that I had certainly been misdiagnosed and, while there was no fixing RP, I should be under the care of a retinal specialist. I assured him that I would make the referred appointment. In shock, I gathered my briefcase and coat and left the office, taking the elevator to the ground floor. It was the dead of winter. My daily commute required walking over two miles, and I had dressed for Cleveland's arctic weather. I had come from work, wearing my warm dress coat with a thick fur collar and down lining, fur-lined gloves and waterproof insulated boots. In the lobby, I buttoned my coat to the neck, put on my stocking cap and gloves, extended my telescopic white cane, and picked up my brief case. I numbly walked out of the medical building into the late afternoon's winter dark. The building was on the perimeter of a large shopping center complex, although it was relatively close to the sidewalk. I had hiked to the medical building by crossing the long parking lot from the driveway, after slogging

241

through the slush-covered sidewalk from the bus stop. It had been a long way. But I didn't want to miss the next bus, so using dead reckoning, with my white cane as a stabilizing staff; I stepped into the deep snow covering the broad lawn. I started in the direction of the bus shelter. I struggled through wet, knee-deep snow, soaking my wool trousers. Cutting through my emotional stupor, I felt the misery of cold and wet wool around my stinging legs. I recall dimly observing that I hadn't made a very good decision about taking the overland route to the bus stop. My mind felt thick and slow.

I was nearly thirty-five years old. For thirty years I had lived with unwanted, severe vision loss. During childhood, my eyesight had deteriorated rapidly and then, after I had become legally blind, it had stabilized. Three times, when I was twenty-three, twenty-seven, and twenty-nine, I had gone to low vision specialists, concerned that I was losing more vision. After both optometric and ophthalmological clinical visits, I had been told that my damaged vision had not changed. My visual acuity, such as it was, remained the same at 20/200 in my left eye, and 20/400 in my right. My specific, very rare type of retinal deterioration results from the unperceivable blinking out of individual pixels within the densely detailed field of vision. Such subtle changes are impossible to measure accurately. But there had been undeniable, functional loss that had developed over years. I had been forced to stop riding my bicycle in 1980 when I knew for certain that I had lost the final, critical fragment of vision essential for fragile, fear-filled safety. That truth was unavoidable. My very limited, reading vision had deteriorated as well. But these changes caused me sadness, not panic. I knew that I saw a little less for some reason, but it was inconceivable that I would lose all of my vision. Low vision specialists had not advised me that it would happen. After successfully struggling against reduced vision for thirty years, blindness seemed like the worst eventuality that I could face.

I was snapped from my dismal reverie by the rumbling bus as it slowed toward the corrugated metal shelter, and I boarded with the other waiting passengers. Explaining that I was partially blind, I asked the driver to tell me when we were approaching my stop. I collapsed my white cane and I sat down in one of the front seats. I glanced at the unspeaking strangers who were crowded, each in their own solitude, on either side of me. I needed to share this shocking news that had me so far at sea. I wanted an anchor of empathy, of compassion. I rode the bus in silence for the thirty minutes it took to get to my stop. I turned this medical judge's decree over and over in my spasming mind–slow, but certain blindness. There was a terrible irony to my plight. I was a rehabilitation administrator, planning and developing innovative training programs demonstrating that sight loss did not end one's ability to work, or one's life choices. But although I had many blind friends and felt comfortable in the presence of all sorts and degrees of blindness, this was my own precious sight–not an abstract principle. I was nauseous with stalking fear, a smoldering dread. I got off at the usual bus stop, a mile from our home, and began to walk down and on the dark, quiet, plowed suburban streets. I couldn't walk on the unshoveled sidewalks.

Now I was alone. In my quiet routine, without any other demand, I looked–really looked–at everything I could see, noting the painful glare of oncoming headlights, the shape of parked cars, the vague outline of piles of plowed snow, the sharp contrast of black, bare trees against yards full of snow, the overlapping lines of tire tracks on the road. How wistfully sweet was the ability to see, even these ordinary, mundane things. Saturated with the dead weight of excruciating sadness, I recognized the familiar approach to our driveway, which I had snow blown that morning. Before I entered the house, I turned back and gazed into the darkness from the little porch. The snow and shadows of our trees now became artistry–a beautiful, sacred visual image.

I unlocked the front door and stepped into the warmth of my family's home and called out, "I'm home!" I took off my coat and boots in the little foyer. The television droned. I walked through the living room, bent over to greet and kiss John. In response, he mumbled an acknowledgment from within his television trance. I moved into the kitchen and kissed Sandy, who was very pregnant with our second child. Moving into our bedroom, I took off my tie and white shirt, hung up my sodden slacks, and put on a warm, faded Berkeley sweat-shirt, jeans, and walking shoes. Comfortable in my dry, at-home uniform, I went back into the kitchen. I poured myself a stiff Scotch on the rocks and sat down at the kitchen table, as Sandy continued to make our dinner. I pondered how to relay my heart-heavy, life-changing news.

Sandy moved around our large, country kitchen, and I sat watching her, attempting to organize my glacially slow thoughts. After a long silence, I said, "I saw the ophthalmologist. He said that I have been misdiagnosed all my life. I am going to go blind." It was the first time I had repeated the dark judgment. Throughout our married life I had cut the grass, raked leaves, shoveled snow, taken long walks with John followed by our cat, fixed and tended to the outside work of the places that we had lived. I had been largely independent, done the laundry, bought and wrapped presents–taken care of business. Sandy said nothing.

As I pondered her lack of response, a fact appeared in the desolation of my mental tundra. With sickening alarm, I remembered something. I had been in the blindness business for years and I well understood RP. It was hereditary. John Kyle, my wonderful son, and the baby now growing strong in my beautiful wife could inherit this curse. I could be passing along this slow road into blindness. Although I saw disability as normal, and blindness a way of being that was as acceptable as being sighted, possibly passing on blindness was not something I would choose to do. I did a quick review of what I knew. Unlike my own early history, John currently had no signs of diminished vision. In any case, I could do nothing about it. But a chilled concern settled over my hopes for my children's future. I decided to have a vasectomy, immediately after the birth, when all was well with Sandy and the baby. Whatever the chances, I would have no more children and tempt the capricious fates of inherited genetic abnormality. The murk of my mental misery spread. I felt very alone. I wanted Sandy to say something, but she did not. Her silence was likely a sign of her processing what this would possibly mean to our already strained relationship's balance and to her and our family's future. I said very little during dinner.

After I washed the dishes, I called a longtime friend and relayed the crushing news. He said, "That's a drag." That was his total reflection on the subject. His laconic reaction offered no emotional support. I ached. I wanted someone to recognize my plight.

Although I didn't want to cause her worry, I phoned Grandma Jane and told her that I was going to go blind. Grandma Jane began to speak but her voice cracked and she cried, broken hearted. Her grief gave me the human support I craved. My grandmother's sorrow was for the suffering yet to unfold. She wept for how hard she knew it was going to be.

Adapting

After being told that I was going to lose all my vision, undeniable, creeping minions of blindness advanced, as if on cue. I had begun to do a lot of public speaking. Previously, I would reference four by six file cards with heavy felt tip pen lettering, limiting each card to four or five lines of text. Although I struggled, my vision slipped and I could no longer read the cards. I could recognize that words were written on them, but I was unable to see their details. When my file card technique failed, I began to write in magic marker on yellow legal pads, a few words per page. But the march of retinal decline was relentless and, within a year, the safe haven of magic marker on legal pad also floundered.

I was born at just the right time to benefit from many offerings of new assistive technologies. As had happened earlier, with both telescope design and light-filtering eyeglass lenses, a breakthrough technological innovation saved the day. In 1982 I had begun wearing wonderful new glare-filtering prescriptive lenses, from Corning Medical Optics, that gave me visual comfort in sunlight and indoor fluorescent-lit settings. In 1986, the late Russell Smith, a brilliant rehabilitation engineer from New Zealand, introduced a new electronic magnification device called the View Scan. The View Scan included both a miniature camera for hand-scanning text and computer keyboard text entry. The device's visual display was a wonderful, orange and black, five by fifteen-inch screen. The display was high contrast and very low glare–perfect for me. The system, like the Versa Braille before it, was an early personal computer and had only a tiny 3K memory when the machine was turned on and used micro cassette tapes for document storage. Now, for the first time in my life, I could relatively easily write and edit. I could type and see the enlarged orange letters with far greater visual comfort than through any other technology or method. The system was like a heavy briefcase that could open on a podium, and I could give speeches and have my own accessible teleprompter. Rather than just replacing paper and magic marker, I had greatly expanded communication power with this new tool. Once again I felt more capable than ever, thanks to assistive technology.

I was the proud and triumphant reader of my own writing, presented in great scrolling text, as I confidently extolled the power of assistive technology. It took concentration and visual effort, but it worked. During those years, I was engaged in program development and administration at the Cleveland Society for the Blind's Sight Center. I had created The STORER Computer Access Center (Specialized Training Orientation and Rehabilitation utilizing Electronic Resources). The STORER Center was a new program that offered the full continuum of assistive technology services. We provided low vision and blindness services, and we helped many individuals become oriented to available technology: evaluation of alternatives, training, application engineering, and system rental for a wide range of adaptive computer devices. The innovative program focused on education, employment, and personal use. It opened wide the doors to all clients in our basic blindness and low vision rehab programs. The STORER

Center was regarded as the best program anywhere. Ultimately, we had clients from ten other nations and from thirty-five of the fifty United States. We helped many people get jobs and to keep jobs they already had, as their vision changed or their employer's technology advanced. I certainly was a great example of the employment success enabled by assistive technology. The tools I was using were wonderful and provided not only substitution for lost visual capability, but expanded functional reach.

But, although it seemed impossible, the slow acid of deterioration again rotted more of the delicate lace of my vision and I couldn't read the beautiful orange letters on the View Scan. The power of mega-enlarged, high-contrast letters was no longer enough. Nothing was. I was reaching the end of the road for visual reading and writing. I felt a sinkhole of despair opening under me and a cloying ineptness press in.

But, just as I was failing to be able to see the View Scan, Russell Smith's Sensory Aids Corporation introduced the Keynote. It was a lightweight, speech output computer that used the same Epson portable keyboard/computer as the View Scan. With the Keynote, I was immediately able to write, edit, read, and prompt myself through synthetic speech. What a revelation I experienced, moving from seeing to listening! I had not been able to read books since sixth-grade, relying entirely on readers or recordings instead. But I had struggled all those long years with reading my own writing. Listening to the Keynote's synthetic speech was far easier than reading, even the View Scan's wonder text. I had to admit that, even initially, the View Scan had been visually taxing. Now, as computer speech output replaced visual reading, a new and better alternative was at hand. In 1986, I was invited to British Columbia to provide the keynote speech at a Canadian government sponsored, disability consumer conference on assistive technology. For the first time in a public presentation, I plugged an ear bud into my ear, from the Keynote, and prompted myself as I delivered a ninety-minute address. I spoke on the United States' new Technology-Related Assistance for Individuals with Disabilities Act of 1988, using synthetic speech notes that spoke directly into my ear, unnoticed to the audience. Blindness was gaining on me, but, thanks to technology, I wasn't losing my functional ability to write and read, work and teach. I was typing, not handwriting, and I was reading through listening. My technological metamorphosis had given me ease, expanded capability and, for the first time in my life, reading and writing without strain. I had leaped the visual divide and found firm footing in an entirely new way of literate power.

Clearing the Path

Although today, my vision has been reduced to unreliable light perception, I know that unbelievably, my stubborn and resistant brain isn't quite convinced that I am blind. The visual cortex is the largest and most powerful processing center in the brain, and it seems to be rather bossy. Human beings are visual creatures to a fault. I am not alone in my unsupportable visual center of gravity. Low vision is as complex and individual as can be imagined. Having traveled down the long and varied road of slowly progressive vision loss, I have experienced low vision across a broad spectrum of effectiveness. There was a time when my vision was stable and reliable, within rather severe limits. During those decades, my visual capabilities were boosted dramatically, thanks to optical and electronic magnification aids. I have also struggled, unsuccessfully, to rely on my vision as my eyesight deteriorated. After crossing critical thresholds, when the battered retinal tissue had lost just too many pixels, sweet vision began to fail as my primary sense.

Beginning in 1971, I began to work with people with visual disabilities. I peaked in that career area, in my role as director of rehabilitative and educational services at The Cleveland Sight Center from 1982 until 1992. Throughout those two decades, I observed scores of people struggle with severe low vision. Sometimes they attempted to rely on their profoundly reduced vision when it was not reliable. But the mule-stubborn brain wants us to see, wants to rely on that most complex and dominant of the senses. Low vision rehabilitation involves optical aids, applied with the comprehension of when we can rely on our vision and when we cannot and must rely on our other senses. It takes training, patient reflection, and time.

I began to think more clearly about the continuum of vision after I heard a wonderfully cogent lecture by Dr. August Colenbrander, an ophthalmologist specializing in low vision. In 1975 he was the principle architect of the World Health Organization's (WHO) nomenclature on visual disability. WHO's definition of visual disability includes the following designations: a. normal, b. near normal, c. moderate, severe, and profound low vision, d. and moderate, severe, and profound blindness. To those not deeply involved with individuals who have experienced a range of vision

247

loss, the idea of low vision or blindness being subdivided into these narrower definitions may be hard to comprehend. I will not elucidate these categories. Suffice to say that Colenbrander's explanation made perfect sense, and it was instructive as I struggled to understand my own complex sensory world. Another useful paradigm of the lecture was how, at varying degrees of vision loss, our senses must be attended to as dominant or auxiliary. When vision is reliable, vision is dominant and our other senses act in auxiliary ways. But when one has low vision, one must understand the flex that may occur in sensory dominance. For example, we may be able to see well enough in daylight to navigate without a cane. Then, our hearing and touch are auxiliary to our dominant visual sense. But if our vision fails us, touch must become dominant. When we walk into the shade of buildings or trees, we had better have a cane handy to gather the ordinarily auxiliary, but now dominant information provided by touch, as touch becomes dominant and vision auxiliary. Alternatively, if we live with more severe levels of permanent sight loss, our sense of hearing and touch must become dominant as remaining vision slips into the auxiliary role. This reversal in dominance of sensory reliance is not a simple matter.

As far as I can remember, I had normal vision until I was five when my vision mysteriously began to wither. I can remember seeing "the man in the moon" and my mother's expression from twenty feet away. It cascaded downwards until I was eleven, reaching a plateau, at about ten percent of normal vision, in my better eye. I lost more vision during my twenties. At thirty-one, unavoidable functional evidence had made me give up bike riding. That was truly a wrenching dislocation from a freedom I had loved and upon which I had depended. The next year, frequent falls had forced me to stop long distance running. In 1983, at thirty-four, I was finally, accurately diagnosed with the rare blinding condition, cone-rod retinal dystrophy, an orphan form of retinitis pigmentosa. By 1989, steadily encroaching sight loss had me struggling with new and vexing limitations.

My office was long and narrow, with my desk at one end facing the door. One afternoon, I was sitting behind my desk, lost in thought about a thorny problem, when I suddenly heard the rehabilitation teacher-coordinator speak to me from beside my desk. I was startled. I had not seen her come in, and as I looked in her direction, I could still not see her. I tried to hide my shock as I answered her, but I was flooded with cold panic. My peripheral vision had always been better, so I shifted my eye gaze far to the side and I could make out her form. But when I relaxed my gaze and looked back in her direction, she was swallowed by the expanding inky swirl that was inexorably overcoming my visual field. The stealthy thief of blindness had claimed another vital threshold. In that moment, I lost my balance. My temporary toehold had crumbled and I felt myself tumble–grasping at air. Anyone who has experienced loss, and needed to continue functioning, knows how quickly we must regain our footing.

That evening, as I left work, I took new precautions. Beginning in 1975, I had used a telescopic long white cane, universally known as a symbol of blindness, to let others know when I might need assistance with some visual aspect of the world–like which bus had arrived. But I had not used my white cane seriously, as a necessity for detecting objects in my path of travel. That afternoon, however, as I left The Sight Center for the bus stop, I swept the path in front of me with the long fiberglass cane, in time to my step, wanting to ensure that I did not run into any unseen thing or person. It was not long before I recognized the necessity of always relying on my cane's extension of my sense of touch. The following week, as I walked from the bus stop to The Sight Center, my precautions proved prescient. That morning, I was unsettled by the sudden appearance of a pedestrian walking toward me. She seemed to jump into my visual field as she passed me. I had chalked up many near misses and one sure hit as a bike rider while speeding on two wheels, but this time I was just walking! I was just walking, and I hadn't seen this woman approaching. Then out of nowhere, she was there. I shuddered to think how easily I could have slammed directly into her if I hadn't had my cane in my hand. My cane provided early warning, telegraphing ahead that I could not see. Get out of my way! I expected a wide berth, helping to avoid a collision. From that day forward, the cane became my constant companion.

What had been a helpful symbol had become a critical tool. I had accepted the cane's use as a requirement with some resignation, but I began to walk with a bit of relief, appreciating the new information transferred through the cane's vibrations and its symbol as the sign of lost vision. The cane began to feel comfortable in my hand as I focused on the information I perceived. I could tell the characteristics of the ground's surface before me, detect curbs and barriers, and recognize an open path. As a traveler, I was slowing down and releasing my frantic struggle to see. The cane, once a symbol of weakness, had become a tool of strength. People do generally recognize its meaning. With it, I walk confidently, if a bit slower than I had. In fact, I had gone from the fastest pedestrian on the block to one of the slowest and most cautious. The old brain can be trusted, after all, to make prudent choices.

Save the Date

Vision enables us to do many things spontaneously, without planning or concentration. We glance at a calendar, walk independently through the world while we daydream, and we read others' faces. The latter is our primary means of recognizing each other, reading emotions, and measuring the impact of our words and actions.

One evening in 1989, I was punched in the emotional gut as I realized the isolating loss of one of my islands of central vision. At our family dinner, I sat between my daughter Laura and my son Kyle at our round antique table. Laura chatted happily about her day in kindergarten. As I looked at her, I became suddenly aware that I could no longer see her mouth move. From this distance, I had been able to see both her right eye and mouth at the same time. The rest of her face was blocked by the growing blindness that was gradually overtaking my ruined retinas. Try as I might, to shift my gaze and find that other visual keyhole, my central vision had been reduced to one little island. It was either look at one of my daughter's dark brown eyes or her pretty little mouth.

My ability to see faces was slipping away. It made me sadder than any of the other functional losses I had experienced involved with going blind. I considered, with a heavy heart, the coming time when I would not be able to see my daughter's or my son's face at all. I knew that I was not going to watch my children's countenances change as they grew up. I mourned this most personal loss.

During the same period, there were other waning vision casualties that were both more mundane and more essential to daily functioning. Keeping my calendar was one such task area. In 1989, my work week as a rehabilitation administrator was an ever-changing dance of meetings. For fifteen years, I had kept my schedule in a trim, spiral-bound calendar that offered one month, displayed on two opposite pages. Each day was represented by a square, about two by two inches, giving me room to print with a felt-tip pen, noting the time and one-word nature of scheduled meetings. It slipped conveniently into a folder with its waiting pad of wide-lined paper for notes. But that method failed when one dark day, try as I might, I could no longer read my block printing on the month's pages. After some research by The Sight Center's purchasing agent, a smaller, and much thicker calendar book was located that presented two days per page, with significantly more room for larger printing. While the space for writing was great, I noted with chagrin that I couldn't read the months that were written at the top of each page. So my secretary printed the month's first letter, on the corner of the book's pages, in two-inch magic marker block letters.

I also began printing with a magic marker. The crumbling erosion of vision loss decayed steadily and, by the next year, I could no longer read the days' numbers either. My patient secretary marked the required giant numerals on each day's half page, in her practiced magic marker hand. She also drew a thick line between the two days on each page. My own block printing grew to mega-font and soon, inch and a half high shorthand filled my calendar book. One afternoon, I sat gripped again in the vice of unwanted change as I stared hard at hieroglyphic, nonsense marks that filled my custom calendar. I knew that there were numbers and words on the calendar's pages–critical markers in future time that I needed. But that very day, a few more badly needed points of vision blinked out. Those essential fragments joined the ever growing, jangling, electric visual static that was my blindness. The web of my vision was being eaten away by a spreading interference–like television snow. The print calendar became as useless to me as a print newspaper. I could see marks, pieces, and parts of characters, but nothing from which I could derive meaning. Dismay marbled with horror. A creeping fear stalked me. Proud as I was of my resilient nature and unsinkable flexibility, this situation had me cornered. I had hit an impasse. Crawling along, reading a letter or two at a time of my printing–magnified tens of times under my video magnifier–was still possible. But without magical electronic assistance, my handwriting was of no use to me.

I had struggled with print from the beginning. In sixth-grade, mighty Braille was unable to overcome my obstructionist mind. I resisted it with all my force, although it was gamely taught by my special education teacher. I was a frightened and sad eleven-year-old, who was going to give blindness and all of its trappings the stiff arm. I would, through prayer and sheer will, stop the downward visual slide and not go blind. My Braille teacher's individual tutoring also taught me to type on a mechanical, large print typewriter. I learned quickly to love my new ability to type in a size that I could read with my magnifier.

My love of typing was matched by my loathing of dreaded Braille and what it meant. Because of my steadfast resistance, after only one year, I was returned to my neighborhood public school system. But now in 1989, at forty years old, I had lost the battle against encroaching blindness. In 1990, as I considered my circumstances, Braille–that once-despised tactile medium–seemed to be a real alternative. I dusted off that dormant section of my brain, and I discovered, much to my amazement and delight, that I remembered the alphabet so patiently pounded through my stubborn skull. I found that I enjoyed learning to read with my fingers, ending the painful ordeal of trying to read visually. My teacher had taught me to write Braille backward, using the slate and stylus–the mechanical clamped form that is used to emboss Braille in reverse–onto heavy Braille paper. I practiced and began using Braille daily. After a little brushing off, my Braille abilities were coming along. I would punch out short cryptic notes for my own use during meetings. I have always been blessed with an excellent memory, so a single Braille word could jog my recall. I also bought a Braille Dymo tape embosser and began to mark cassettes, prescriptions, and spices with the wonderful little bumps. But I had to keep my print calendar, since my only way to maintain my schedule was to rely on my secretary or other sighted colleagues to tell me what the calendar held. My Braille was basic, and a Braille calendar–wickedly difficult, at best–was out of the question. With gradual steady progress, I was becoming a functioning blind person. Relying on the cane and Braille, I was finding myself feeling good about the needed changes that I had finally been able to make in my daily style.

By 1991, I was beginning to really chunk-a-chunk along with the slate and stylus, and my Braille notes were personally functional. I was hired to do an eleven-hour seminar in Oregon, for which I relied entirely on a very cryptic, eleven-word, Braille outline. I happily relied on the use of my Keynote talking computer for document preparation. My sixth-grade teacher's typing lessons had led to a lifetime of typing and computer use, and at forty-two, I had clattered along at some well-greased typing speeds for years. My spelling and typing accuracy were poor, and my work had always required editing, but my fingers would blur over the keyboard, and my accessible voice output word processor was freedom itself. As the rehabilitation program developer, I wrote for hours every day. I detailed grant proposals, reports, and articles for professional publication–on programs particularly the innovative STORER Computer Access Center. As always, I was also writing songs, letters, poems, and other creative short pieces.

That winter, my hands had begun to frequently hurt. For my forty-second birthday, Sandy gave me a guitar lesson with Chris Proctor, national finger picking champion, and he was asking my middle-aged fingers to stretch and reach, at some supernatural lengths. I used my portable talking computer on the bus ride to and from work, and all the workday long. Constant typing began on the bus into work and often ended late in the evening. I was using my cane with a heavy tip as I walked to and from the bus stop on my daily commute. Heavy snows and unshoveled sidewalks had made for a difficult, very hand-intensive method of orientation. I punched my cane through the crusted snow, seeking the tactile signature of the frozen sidewalk beneath.

The combination of extensive typing, pounding white cane use, heavy briefcase carrying, and extreme guitar playing built the critical mass. Repetitive strain injury found the perfect stormy behavior. Such injuries occur from long-standing repetitive hand use, and in my case, from a tipping point event that overwhelmed my tendons and soft tissue—already under assault. In early March of 1991, I had agreed to serve as a peer reader, citizen participant on a Federally-convened panel of rehab professionals that were to read proposals, judge them against a strict series of criterion, and recommend recipients for available National Institute on Disability and Rehabilitative Research grants. The process involved reading a fifteen inch-thick stack of dense proposals over a weekend. Then, I had to rank them on a complex series of criterion. Monday morning I was to fly to Washington D.C., to spend three days working on a panel evaluating all of the proposals that had been dispersed through the group. I was expected to arrive for the marathon process, armed with all proposals read, judged on the thirty-nine point, detailed profile, using a numeric scale, and to be prepared to argue my perspective with the other panelists based on my notes and memory. The proposals arrived Thursday. I had scheduled twenty hours of readers, beginning on Friday evening and ending late Sunday. The tag team readers read the volumes of required materials aloud. I listened, typed, asked for re-reads of specific sections, and plowed doggedly on. My aching hands hurt, going into the weekend, and the burning ache intensified as the focused hours wore on. The adage, "no pain, no gain", was popular then, and it rang in my ears. I tried to ignore the growing, stinging discomfort in my fingers, hands, and forearms, during the long hours of relentless work. Quite by accident, I discovered that I could find some pain relief by pushing the keyboard forward, extending my arms as I typed. But pain would return, and I would push the keyboard yet further away, providing temporary relief. By Sunday, I was typing with my shrieking arms fully extended. On Monday morning when I awoke, my hands were curled into fists of contracted, spasiming pain. I flew to Washington in agony. Using my computer to reference my prepared notes during the work sessions was brutally painful. Returning to Cleveland, I began the protracted process of seeking medical counsel concerning my ongoing misery. Seven head-scratching doctors later, I understood that I had developed repetitive strain injury, the most common work related injury in these computer-driven times. Custom, plastic resting braces, anti-inflammatory drugs, and forced inactivity was instituted as I attempted to allow the inflamed tendons to heal. As an active blind person, it is impossible not to use your hands for essential functional activities.

But I tried. I couldn't use the cane. It hurt. I began to pay a co-worker gas money to provide transportation to work. I was forced to give up typing and began to dictate my writing. My Braille–writing slate and stylus were impossible to use, and reading Braille itself was now painful, due to the required extended hand position. Guitar playing had to be suspended. Many of my life's familiar avenues for independence, creativity, and productivity were blocked.

Then a great development! At a conference, Deane Blazie, an old friend and technology genius, showed me a new product he had invented called the Braille'n Speak. I experimented with Deane's prototype. Since Braille is written with a seven–key keyboard, requiring much less stretching and torque on the fingers, it was doable rather than the impossible pain of the standard computer keyboard. The little machine, about the size of a VHS cassette, had large relatively light touch keys. The Braille'n Speak was a multi-function personal computer with a word processor, calculator, and joy of joys–a calendar! Suddenly, a solution for many of my problems had been found. Practicing the desired songs gingerly, I played guitar for Deane's son's wedding, and I earned my Braille'n Speak in return. A technician in Deane's company customized my machine by cutting the key springs in half, and my hands were spared more strain through the resulting super-light touch. Now, over twenty-five years later, I use a Braille Touch tablet, evolved from Russell Smith's last technological marvel, the Braille Note. It is a supercharged, multi-function Braille input, speech output computer. It is quite like the wonderful Braille'n Speak, but with vastly expanded capabilities–Braille input, and voice and electronic Braille output–a perfect, elegant, and powerful solution.

Chapter 15: "My Voice Has Wings"

Music is the Message

When I was a teenager, my guitar was a vehicle for romantic and political expression. Being able to play guitar opened a circle of friends, particularly through The Well coffeehouse. It was a wonderful center of earthy, high-minded idealism and social action in East Cleveland that was at the center of my social world from 1965 until 1968. Girls loved the guitar, and I loved their dreamy attention and my status as an activist guitar player. The Well was forced to close in 1968 and with it went the performances at community, action-oriented churches, rallies and demonstrations. When I left Cleveland, in September of that year, the guitar became an instrument experienced in isolation or within very small groups. I would carry the guitar to parties, unpack it when other musicians were around, and always look for opportunities to play. The irresolvable pathos of unending grief about Mark's suffering in The Columbus State Institution led to my writing deeply personal songs, expressing my anguish and my promise to somehow get him out. But I had no real audience for my compositions, or for the songs I learned from albums by blues, folk, and rock artists. Like many other musicians, I was always hungry to play, to be heard, to express myself through song. More than once my friends were the audience for my guitar playing, at parties and every social occasion, and I suspect that I often played too long.

Beginning in the mid-seventies, I also started writing disability-related parodies that could always gather a crowd at a conference hospitality room. Favorites like: "There Are No People like Blind People", "We All Work in a Sheltered Industry", and "Guiding Teeth–Attack Dogs for the Blind", were my stock in trade. But I would have to sing over the boisterous noise of the room, and I found myself often hoarse from prolonged singing at full volume.

Both at CIL and TSI, my professional life offered some unique and wonderful experiences that opened different perspectives on singing. In 1977, when I was CIL's deputy director for services, I played at a fundraiser for our new Deaf Services department. I split the bill with the headliner, a band comprised of a drummer and guitar player, both of whom were deaf. They had amped their instruments to such an extreme that the music could be physically felt, as the force of sound waves created a remarkable visceral experience. The instruments, pumped through powerful amplifiers, created music experienced as rhythmic blasts of energy. However, as a hearing person in the audience, the only way to be heard over the fantastic volume was to scream into another's ear. The entire audience was deaf, apart from a few of us who worked at CIL and could sign. The musical genre was literally called "deaf rock". The deaf rock music experience was immediately understandable to the newcomer, as the music strikes, driving sound waves with such force that the music can be felt. However, those of us who could hear were exposing ourselves to sound at such levels that temporary hearing loss resulted.

My musical contribution was at the other end of the sensory spectrum. My songs were to be appreciated as lyric statements about the Disability Rights movement. I opened the musical evening and played during the band's breaks. The audience was comprised of hundreds of folks for whom my singing could not be heard. A talented and artistic interpreter signed the songs as I sang, and the room became fully engaged.

Over a decade later, my application of assistive technology helped others, whose voices were not useable, to sing. I was applying the lessons learned from a decidedly non-musical technological undertaking. TSI had received funding from the National Science Foundation to explore new technological vistas in voice output communication aids, or VOCA's. I involved CIL to assist with the consumer evaluation of the day's VOCA technology. CIL's consumer evaluation proved that none of the day's VOCA technology was acceptable. Part of the evaluation process included the gathering of a user wish list for the future's synthetic speech output devices. The professional community would soon rename VOCA's AAC, Augmentative and Alternative Communication systems. Users wanted voices that were gender and age specific, and that could express other types of human communication beyond declarative speech. People, who were unable to speak, wanted to sing with their VOCA's. My job included summarizing the VOCA evaluations for the NSF final report. The idea that people who were unable to speak, still wanted to sing, moved me deeply.

Music had always been a keen part of my life, and I pondered the yearning for that flight of expression. In a few years, that understanding would be joined by advances in technology and professional partnerships. During the nineteen-eighties, my songwriting expanded exponentially. The feedback, concerning my disability-related political and personal songs, made me begin to believe that I might have something to say as a songwriter. In 1985, I started to really apply myself to songwriting. Songs began to pour out of me in amazing numbers. Part of the change was due to my new functional ability–being able to compose and edit my written work–thanks to the View Scan, the massively enlarged visual display-based computer. For the first time in my life, I could comfortably read and, through the magic of word processing, edit, correct, polish, and refine lyrics.

My biggest fan, Grandma Jane, (my father's mother) died in 1985. With some of the inheritance that she left me, I bought a used, four–track, cassette recorder and a couple of second–hand microphones. It was a sophisticated recording unit with the capacity to do multitrack recording. I began to record songs, adding multiple vocal and instrument tracks. The results were encouraging. I was going to pursue music seriously. I decided on my company's name: Music from the Heart. A logo, letterhead, business cards, and mailing labels followed. Music from the Heart was born and I was in business. Simultaneously, Stan Rolf, a willing friend began to convert our large, open basement into a finished family room with adjoining sound studio–all for the love of music. Stan, my buddy was a talented guitarist and bass player. He and I had begun practicing my songs every Friday evening. His belief in the quality of my writing was a great boost. Stan, my musical partner was truly an anchor in the early movement toward taking my songs onto a larger stage. In the new basement studio, with my basic gear, we had a place to record, practice, and focus. We began to create a separate little life around my original music. And best of all–it was working! I was finding opportunities to perform and gather positive feedback. We played on a local, live, folk radio show several times. Stan, his brother–in–law, and I also played several early and affirming gigs. Our threesome shared a bill with several Cleveland major–acts at a fundraiser which I organized for a Sight Center co–worker who had brain cancer. We headlined the Ohio's Statue of Liberty's Centennial event. We were playing, on the statehouse plaza, just across the street from the bus stop where I had so often waited for the bus that would take me to the Columbus State Institution for the Mentally Retarded. Despite the excitement of the day, I could not shake the sadness from those decades of memory.

But all musicians need ongoing, affinity audiences, and I realized that mine was the community that cared about Disability Rights. I began to promote my unique musical offering, focused on themes related to disability. I had a body of work, drive, and ambition. Making numerous cold calls, I eventually spoke with the conference planner at the ARC state office (formerly Association for Retarded Citizens). She was planning a conference for spring 1988 and was willing to hire me as the luncheon keynote. I will forever be in the debt of that trusting woman. My first solo, professional engagement was booked–the luncheon keynote for ARCs big, live audience. I planned to record the performance and to produce a live album to sell and market my work. The day arrived and I packed my studio tape recorder, guitars, and microphones. With Sandy and my four–year–old daughter, Laura, we drove to Akron for the show. One of the hotel's AV guys had considerable experience recording, and he jumped in to change cassettes and set and monitor recording levels. Overall, the performance was pretty good. Back in my studio, and in a small studio in Cleveland Heights, I added upright bass throughout and lead guitar to a couple of tracks. The concert recording was going to be produced as an album.

Prentke Romich Co. (PRC) was and is a Wooster, Ohio-based assistive technology company that developed and marketed sophisticated AAC devices. Barry Romich, PRC'S president, was an old friend, and I asked him if he would consider helping to get the word out about my upcoming release. Barry asked me to perform a lunchtime concert for the PRC workforce, to test my mettle. After the audition, Barry made an offer. If I would write a song on behalf of those who could not speak, and who used AAC devices, PRC would market the cassette. I penned "My Voice Has Wings", an anthem for people who spoke with the day's quickly evolving AAC, speech synthesis systems. Cliff Kushler, a fine musician and brilliant programmer, was in charge of PRC's research and development group. Studying PRC's baritone synthesizer's control protocol, he proffered, that the voice of PRC's technology could be programmed to sing. It was decided that we would have PRC's speech synthesizer sing the opening track, "My Voice Has Wings". I recorded the song's instrumental tracks at the same little Cleveland Heights studio at which I had recorded the upright bass. The pianist added a lush chord bed and, back in my studio, I hired a jazz guitar player to fill out the instrumentation. Then, I sang my cameo part of the duet. I had the background ready for Cliff, the PRC engineer. Timing the synthesizer's singing to the background accompaniment, he set to work and, some weeks later, arrived at my home for the weekend, ready to work in my little recording studio. It took eleven hours for Cliff and me to record the communication system's custom singing on the four-minute song. The process required "punching in", phrase by phrase. Cliff's programming and exact timing were great. He hovered over the communicator, controlling the synthesizer's vocalization of sung phrases built using phonemes (individual elements of spoken speech), pitch, and duration. Often, it took several takes to get every measure's worth of singing recorded exactly in time with the backing tracks. The synthesizer did sing every phrase in a perfectly timed, charming clarity and with fully accurate pitch. This synthetic singer sounded warm–a kind of spooky auditory experience–and we reveled as Cliff, my collaborator gave the communication aid's voice a real jazz–stylist personality and attitude, as the coda's ending phrase repeated over and over. In October 1988, with the power of PRC's mailing list, hundreds of press releases were mailed and were picked up by publications across North America, Europe, and the English-speaking assistive technology world.

The cassette album was launched. With PRC's reach, the release of the album, *Do You See Me As An Equal?* hit a broad distribution in the disability world, resulting in numerous newsletter postings and an article in a British publication. I had my first recorded beach head as a Disability Rights performer. AAC singing had begun. The next month, I was invited to attend a national conference on consumer involvement in federally funded rehabilitation programs. Robert Williams, the newly appointed head of the new Developmental Disabilities Administration created by President Reagan, gave the keynote. Robert, who has severe cerebral palsy, wrote a stirring speech, intending to deliver it using his PRC, AAC device. Unfortunately, the communicator was back at PRC for servicing. Instead, a colleague sat with him on the stage and read Mr. Williams' speech. To conclude his remarks, Mr. Williams' introduced a song that he said expressed his thoughts about the power of the day's assistive technology. It was recorded, using the voice of his own AAC system. Then, "My Voice Has Wings" was played through the auditorium's sound system.

I had never met Mr. Williams. A song becomes ours when we love the idea it conveys, and when we decide to sing the song with our own voice. I had recorded the song with Mr. William's synthetic voice. Then, my song had become Mr. Williams' song, and he had shared it with the hundreds of people–with and without disabilities–who attended that landmark gathering. I sat in the audience, holding my breath, as our song filled the auditorium. Mr. Williams received a standing ovation. Following his speech and the song, I introduced myself to him and we had a heartfelt and wonderful exchange. Thank you, Mr. Williams, for giving wings to my song.

MY VOICE HAS WINGS

There are walls of solid granite
There are walls of brick and steel
There are walls that people build inside
That hide the way they feel.
But of all the walls among us
There is none so hard and cold
As the one that locks a voice inside
Silent thoughts are never told.

My thoughts can soar my voice has wings
For years my voice was locked away,
Now I can sing
Hear me now, hear me now,
Hear it ring!

Locked behind the walls of silence
Feeling helpless and alone
We have known the yearning hunger
For a voice to call our own.
Now we have that key to freedom
Now the gate is open wide
No more captive in the silence
Free now from the bonds inside.

My thoughts can soar my voice has wings
For years my voice was locked away,
Now I can sing
Hear me now, hear me now,
Hear it ring!

Now birds are meant to take to wing
For birds are meant for flight
And we are meant to join our thoughts
For language is our right
This age has given us the skies
Our tools have let us soar
And now the age has given speech
Together we explore!

Take this tool this bridge to freedom
Help me build my way along
Every voice deserves a channel
Every voice deserves a song.
Through its power we touch each other
Thoughts and questions, stories, songs.
Hear the walls of silence crumble.
Through our language we belong.

My thoughts can soar my voice has wings
For years my voice was locked away,
Now I can sing
Hear me now, hear me now,
Hear it ring!

© Jeff Moyer May 1988

They're Singing My Song

My father shaped my ethos about music, as a gentle background and loving bond that drew people together through community singing. Twenty-one years after his death, I sat in the lobby of a Pittsburgh hotel and listened to a few dozen people sing various songs that I had written, using the wonderful array of voices that were selected through their twenty–first century AACs (augmentative and alternative communication systems).The song files were downloaded into their devices from the laptop of an engineer from PRC, the world leader in AAC devices. This was not the first time I had heard such singing, but it was the first time I had been so anonymously present and heard so many AAC users singing my songs. Several different system users were singing "My Voice Has Wings". There were thirteen songs available, in total, and lyric sheets enabled participants at the Pittsburgh Employment Conference to decide if they wanted to sing one of these songs. Those interested, lined up in their wheelchairs, to have the songs they had chosen downloaded into their communicators. My interest and involvement with AAC singing has had many other fine moments along the way. I have performed duets with AAC singers, since 1990, before many audiences. After our first AAC recording, Cliff Kushler, the PRC programmer, with whom I worked, subsequently programmed many songs I had written for PRC's systems. I had been joined on stage by AAC singers who were singing songs I had written for PRC company events. Several of my songs were burned onto computer chips to be installed for recording and performances by Third Street Kids, a performing arts group in Tucson, Arizona, for which I was music director. By 1991, AAC users could select a voice from a catalog of eight, which allowed them to have a voice that matched their gender, age, and personality. A song I wrote for PRC, "We Are Growing", was programmed into all their new AAC devices. A few of those songs, sung by AAC systems, can be heard on several of my later albums.

They were followed in 1997 by the release of a project that really gave wings to many voices. Kevin Thomas is the father of Angie, a very musical AAC user in Indiana. Kevin programmed all of the songs from *We're People First*, my album published in 1995, with a print activity guide. One track from *We're People First* is a recording of Third Street Kids, an inclusive chorus of kids, one of whom sang at several shows with me using his AAC system which can be heard on the album thanks to Cliff's programming efforts. Kevin wrote the song code for all the songs, plus "My

Voice Has Wings", in both male and female pitch ranges. We released a computer disc of those files in 1997. Then, in 2000, we burned the AAC song files directly onto the *We're People First* enhanced product CD. It was those files, converted by PRC engineers to drive the new software-based synthesizers, which, today, power the voices of current AAC users.

But that day in Pittsburgh, I sat thinking of my father and how his sweet love of community music inspired and shaped my approach to singing. Thank you, Dad. Without you, I doubt that I would have understood the importance of giving wings to voice. I have been fortunate to team up with some great technical geniuses. But it was you, Dad, who laid the foundation for my understanding of the meaning and value of singing. Your voice is silent, but for many, many others, wings of song now lift–beyond the barriers of limitation.

The Americans with Disabilities Act

In 1988, I received an announcement about an organizing meeting in Columbus, Ohio, where Justin Dart Jr. would speak concerning the proposed Americans with Disabilities Act. Mr. Dart had a well-deserved reputation as a recognized leader, furthering the Disability Rights Movement. I made arrangements to attend the meeting, one hundred fifty miles away. The ADA was a proposed, sweeping Civil Rights law that would further the inclusion of people with disabilities, in every aspect of American life. I knew about the proposed law and I had followed Mr. Dart's career. One of his defining moments came after President Reagan had appointed Mr. Dart as Director of RSA–the Rehabilitation Services Administration–the federal bureau that oversees the vast national vocational rehabilitation bureaucracy. RSA helped countless Americans with disabilities to work and live independently in the community by providing funds for state voc rehab services. I had personally benefited from voc rehab's funding throughout my college career. My job at The Cleveland Sight Center involved providing services purchased by Ohio's and many other states' voc rehab agencies. Those services were eighty to ninety percent funded by RSA. As a cost-savings measure, President Reagan cut the budget of RSA, along with all other federal agencies. But RSA was a tax-generating agency, returning people with disabilities to gainful employment. Unable to change the President's mind about the cuts, Mr. Dart gave his office's annual address to Congress and, in a politically suicidal action, blasted the Reagan Administration for its fiscal foolishness and disregard of the needs of America's disabled citizens. Following his address, he immediately tendered his resignation.

When Mr. Dart gave a speech, he didn't just read prepared remarks. He delivered powerful and beautifully timed, spellbinding oratory. That day in Columbus, I heard his lofty words ring out. I thought of a time when such highly developed speech was not uncommon. But such polished rhetoric is not often heard in the television age. Here was a truly gifted and inspirational gentleman speaking of coalitions to create change, unity of purpose, political action toward Disability Rights, and of the community organizing required to make it happen. To hear him was stirring and uplifting. Mr. Dart used a wheelchair for mobility and spoke with the deep and resonant tambour of a robust and potent visionary.

After the presentation, I approached Mr. Dart and introduced myself. That month, I had produced my first album of Disability Rights music: *Do You See Me As An Equal?* I asked Mr. Dart if he would consider allowing me to record his oratory for some future musical project. He considered my offer and agreed, and we exchanged cards. I went back to Cleveland, very excited to have made such a wonderful contact with a man who certainly would have historic impact.

Mr. Dart and Yoshiko, his wife, spent years of truly tireless advocacy developing both political and grassroots support for the passage of the ADA. Through his leadership, the country's Disability Rights community had awakened to the possibility of the envisioned Civil Rights law. The Darts had visited each state five to ten times, speaking and organizing support for the ADA. Cleveland's Disability Rights community staged a rally, and I was asked to play at the event within the city hall rotunda. I wrote the "ADA Anthem", and first sang that song at that rally and then others. I wrote letters, sent faxes, and sent a telegram to the White House, encouraging support. The ADA was passed in May 1990, following extensive negotiation and compromise with numerous constituencies. The ADA passed following a three-year effort, bringing a great sense of accomplishment. The presidential signing date was to be announced.

I returned to work, from my family vacation, a day early. There on my desk, atop the week's unopened mail, was a crisp linen envelope with the simple return address, The White House, Washington D.C. After days of wondering what it contained, my secretary was eager to know its contents. It was an invitation to the signing ceremony for The Americans with Disabilities Act, to be held the following morning at 9:30 a.m. on the South

Lawn of The White House. Had I not come back a day early, I would have been reading the invitation as the historic event was happening. I telephoned Mr. Dart and reminded him of our meeting two years before. I told him about my song, "The ADA Anthem" and how I had played it at rallies. I asked if I might play it the next day, during a time when a solemn song commemorating the moment might be appropriate. Mr. Dart considered my request. Within a few hours, a call came inviting me to perform, at the reception at the U.S. Senate the following evening. I was elated. I booked a seat on the next day's first flight to Washington and on the last flight home.

Early on the morning of July 26, 1990, I dressed in a light gray, wool suit, grabbed my guitar and backpack then hiked to the bus stop for an early bus to the Rapid Transit train and the airport. On the flight, I rewrote a few lines of the "ADA Anthem" to match the historic day. I took a taxi to The White House's southern entrance. With my invitation and identification I was guided through the gates of that hallowed American home. I was more than an hour early. The lawn had been turned into a vast seating area which was about to accommodate the largest gathering ever to witness the signing of a bill into law. A Marine, in full dress uniform, escorted me to a seat in the front row of the public section, right behind the section reserved for Representatives and Senators who had yet to arrive. The lawn soon swelled with the two thousand and five hundred advocates from the Disability Rights community, government workers, and Congressional members from both sides of the aisle, whose votes had made the law a reality. Senator Ted Kennedy took a seat directly in front of me. The Marine Band played stirring patriotic tunes, and I sat gazing at the beautiful portico of the home of Lincoln and Roosevelt. I realized that I was not invited to play at that event because the Marine Band had already been slated to fill the time. I remembered the civil disobedience, the grueling ordeal for the advocates with disabilities who lived through the twenty-six-day sit-in at the San Francisco Federal Building, which had provided a foundation stone for this historic and moving day. Our non-violent civil disobedience, the longest occupation of a federal building in history, had resulted in the signing of the regulations for Section 504 of the Rehabilitation Act of 1973. 504 was the foundation upon which the ADA was built. I reflected on the great difference that thirteen years had made. In 1977, we were the radicals and malcontents–the rowdy hoard of people with disabilities pressing for the signing of the long overdue regulations for Section 504, and The Public Education for All Handicapped Children Act of 1975. Today, we were in league with a broad coalition of Congress, the administration, business, and a host of professional and consumer organizations. Together, we were about to witness the signing into law of the most sweeping Civil Rights law in a quarter century. We were welcomed with ceremony and pomp onto the White House lawn, in sharp contrast to the civil disobedience required thirteen years earlier to press for change. What a remarkable and swift evolution of events!

The President and Justin Dart, Jr. came out from The White House, onto the raised platform that stood above the seated invitees. As the President walked out, the Congressional delegation stood as one, in applause, totally blocking the view for those in our section who used wheelchairs and could not stand. There was a loud chorus from the wheelchair seated–yelling repeatedly, "Sit down! We can't see!" The elected dignitaries looked around to see what rabble was speaking so forthrightly. Upon seeing the scores of wheelchair using individuals, the standing throng did promptly sit down, with more than a few expressions of apology. Such fine and ironic theater! President Bush spoke about tearing down the shameful wall of discrimination and signed the Bill, handing the historic pen to Mr. Dart. It was a symbolic and fitting tribute to a great patriot and American hero.

Following the signing ceremony, we all filled Lafayette Park, across from the White House, and heard stirring speeches by Senator Ted Kennedy, Senator John McCain, Congressman Tony Coelho, Congressman Steny Hoyer, Senator Tom Harkin, and others who had led the legislative process of getting the ADA passed. Nearly all of them had disability in their families and were motivated by the same passion that drove all of the advocates that were there. Food was served, and a real festival energy took hold. That evening, a reception in a large hearing room at the U.S. Senate, capped the day. More short speeches were delivered by the same leaders. Senator John McCain had been responsible for the establishment of the telecommunications section that would allow Americans who cannot hear or speak, to use the telephone through a relay system. Then it was time for me to play the "ADA anthem". I sang the verses and taught the short chorus, which many sang with me. The music filled the room, mingled with the murmur of ongoing conversations. I felt a sense of pride and unity with this collection of advocates and leaders who had each heard the call and done their part, to see this wonderful new law enacted. I reconnected with many old friends, as we all celebrated together. Like Cinderella, my evening was cut short by the ticking clock. Soon I was rushing from the reception and climbing into a cab, to return to the National Airport and the last flight home.

Shortly after the ADA was signed, I learned of a training program sponsored by the United States Department of Justice and DREDEF–The Disability Rights and Education Defense Fund. DREDEF is a national advocacy organization that was an outgrowth of Berkeley's Center for Independent Living. In partnership with the U.S. Department of Justice, DREDEF was offering intensive training for people with disabilities, to support the long road toward the ADA's implementation. I applied, was accepted, and attended a weeklong intensive training program on all aspects of the broad and complex ADA. After a year of pro bono and fee-generating advocacy, I applied for and was selected to attend advanced training. That ongoing experience further opened my eyes concerning discrimination, exclusion, and the power of advocacy and law.

In 1992, following unresolvable differences with the fourth executive director for whom I had worked, I left The Cleveland Sight Center and hung my shingle as a consultant and advocate. I was hired to provide ADA training to governmental agencies and businesses. I served as an expert witness on several court cases and provided free advocacy and counsel to scores of desperate people from across the country. The ADA was now sewn into the fabric of our lives–with imperfect, random, and sluggish change resulting. In 1996, after my speaking career had taken off, I was invited by an old friend to give a keynote presentation at the annual meeting of the Georgia's Governor's Council on Disability. He picked me up at the Atlanta airport, and we drove through the city and countryside toward his gracious home. On the way, he intoned in a low voice that we were passing a state institution where people with differing disabilities lived in a huge complex. His voice was heavy with incredulity and disgust, as he said that thirty thousand people were confined there. I was stunned and silent. The visceral clench of heartache and pain, from the nineteen years of my own brother's institutionalization, flooded back. In the face of this institutional monstrosity, the ADA's elevated language and promise seemed hollow and mocking. Thirty thousand souls pressed together for the crime of being different. How could such a place exist in these enlightened times?

In 1999, the landmark ADA Supreme Court case, Olmstead vs. Georgia, upended the status quo. Georgia's and all states' institutions were deemed to be in violation of the ADA's pledge for integrated settings. The Olmstead decision lifted high the ADA's majestic promise and set a new benchmark, that state institutions violated the Civil Rights of their inmate-

267

residents. A new day was surely dawning, and the ADA was the source of the new light.

THE ADA ANTHEM

In the Disability Rights Movement
Are the streams of constant change.
For the worse and for the better,
In flux it had remained.
But to move it with decision
Toward human dignity,
We gathered as one,
There was work to be done
For we held only part of the key.

ADA, we stand as one to see it through.
ADA, Civil Rights, overdue.

But to shape new legislation,
Based on laws as then in place,
Bringing power to the people
Whose lives these things embrace.
We formed a coalition–
And the system surely moved.
We gather today,
Now with ADA,
The balance has improved.

ADA, we stand as one to see it through.
ADA, Civil Rights, overdue.

And for those labeled, "disabled,"
The change will be perceived–
A freer step across this land
On the road to liberty.
So we'll celebrate this action,
The law that's ours today.
A journey we share,
As together we care,
As we work for The ADA.

ADA, we stand as one to see it through.
ADA, Civil Rights, overdue.
Civil Rights so very long overdue

For Purple Mountain Majesties

By 1991, the digital revolution had brought personal computers into the workplace and to many homes and classrooms. The assistive technology world had made considerable inroads concerning computer access for people with visual disabilities. There were–and are–software programs and speech synthesizers that could direct computers to speak the words on the screen. Braille was being generated on one line, mechanical arrays that presented computer displays in that touch format, and Braille embossers were generating paper Braille as computer output. Custom programs and hardware were enlarging computer displays–making them readable for users with partial sight. Although these adaptations to computers were available, specialized technical services such as orientation, evaluation of alternatives, training, engineering support, and accessible computer rental were very few and far between. In 1991, at forty-two, I had been working as director of rehabilitative and educational services for The Cleveland Sight Center, for nine years. Prior to The Sight Center, I had worked at TSI, the gold standard for blindness assistive technology companies, providing comprehensive training and customer support services for their innovative technology. Jim Bliss, TSI's president, served on an advisory committee for The Braille Institute, a Los Angeles-based private blindness social service agency. During my tenure as TSI's communications manager, Jim had been asked to provide The Braille Institute with a comprehensive list of yet-to-exist assistive technology-related services. Jim asked me to do his homework and to draft a list for such a complete services program. That exercise gave me the opportunity to really focus on what a full services program would include.

When I interviewed at The Cleveland Sight Center in 1982, I spoke about that vision, for an inclusive service program, on computer access. I was hired and, in addition to managing the Center's ongoing rehab programs, was given a free hand to develop that innovative computer access service.

Jim Storer was an avid assistive technology user, an active board member, and head of the Rehabilitation Advisory Committee. Jim had been blinded at age six and all his life had used contemporary assistive technology–eagerly and thoroughly. Through Jim's direction, The George B. Storer Foundation provided grant funding, which served as the match, required to draw down grants from The Ohio Rehabilitation Services Commission. Together we had created The STORER Computer Access Center.

I hired and developed a staff of dedicated assistive technology specialists. We gave the Center its rightful name, and STORER became an acronym for Specialized Training, Orientation, and Rehabilitation utilizing Electronic Resources. In 1983, we served our first consumers. The Center's computer-oriented services proved to be greatly needed by individuals far and wide. The STORER Center also served as a training ground for those interested in establishing similar programs. We were unique, and we soon developed a national and international reputation. We served clients from thirty-five other states and from ten other countries. It was a heady time, as I presented at national meetings, and my articles became the lead in numerous journals.

In 1991, the telephone rang, and a gentleman named Mike Long introduced himself. Mike was a senior writer for National Geographic, and he was writing an article on the sense of sight. Blindness and low vision would be included in what would be the main article in an upcoming issue. Mike told me that three people he had interviewed suggested that he talk to me about computer access. After we spoke at length, Mike decided that a three-day trip to Cleveland would be in order. An itinerary was put together providing ample time for observing The STORER Center, visits with Jim Storer, and a chance to speak with the people whose expertise made the STORER Center hum.

The day Mike arrived from Washington, I met him at The Cleveland Clinic Inn, his hotel, and we went to the four-star restaurant contained therein. As we settled into a most gracious evening, Mike began to talk about what had brought us to this moment. Mike shared that, as part of his initial research, he underwent a state-of-the-art eye exam at the Wilmer Eye Institute in Philadelphia. He was given the shocking revelation that he had the early stages of macular degeneration and would, over time, lose his central, detail vision. What had started as a focused writing assignment, on

271

the broad topic of the sense of sight, had suddenly become a deeply personal inquiry that resonated for Mike concerning his impending loss. Mike was pursuing an extremely broad range of topics and themes concerning vision and vision loss in his research. Among them, he was focusing on the profound experience of losing vision and how people dealt with that reality. Over dinner, we skated over many topics; Mike's pen scratched a steady stream of notes in a trim spiral notebook, pulled from an inside jacket pocket. Mike showed genuine interest in my psychosocial insights and my personal stories. All the while, he knowledgeably ordered a gourmet meal, from aperitif and appetizers, through dessert and cognac. It was a truly wonderful, memorable meal and evening. The next day, Mike was in and out of my office as he observed The STORER Center in full operation. Clients were learning computer skills in the cubicles that held the array of synthetic speech, electronic Braille, and large character output systems. We had state-of-the-art computers interconnected through a new innovation–a local area network–and servers that tied our system to the larger world of research through the internet's predecessor, the Arpanet. At the STORER Center, our clients were studying computer access for educational and wide-ranging work-related applications.

That evening, Sandy drove Mike and me to Jim Storer's home for dinner. Jim and his wife, Deedee, lived in a gracious rustic home at Walden II, a nature preserve that Jim had established, conserving extensive virgin Ohio woodland above the towering banks of the Grand River. On the way to the Storer's home, Mike shared an ironic story. In 1969, when the Cuyahoga River burned, Mike was the photojournalist who, through a National Geographic photo spread, brought world attention to the scourge of environmental pollution for which the Cuyahoga River became emblematic. Now, we were going to dine in the midst of a wonderful natural treasure, in a pristine forest on uplands, above another Northeastern Ohio River. Mike had been the photo editor who had documented the Cuyahoga's degradation and immolation. His fold out, photographic image of the burning river was seen by National Geographic readers and became one of the Environmental Movement's iconic images. However, Mike mused that the disaster led to the formulation of The Environmental Protection Agency and the beginning of the environmental movement. Mike had also been a Navy pilot, and his keen sense of sight and his career as a photo journalist made his looming loss of sight all the more poignant. The Storers offered a gracious, gourmet dinner followed by time in Jim's study where he demonstrated the interfaced array of devices which he used for his personal research. A STORER Center applications engineer, who was also blind, had devised a one-of-a-kind system. Jim could search articles in encyclopedias stored within CD libraries and then convert the articles to Braille and print them on his Braille embosser. He could also scan print documents, comparably convert them to Braille, and emboss them–resulting in custom Braille books that gave Jim the ability to read in his preferred format–paper Braille. A few years before the internet's primacy, Jim Storer could satisfy his love of history through personal access technology. His access came through The STORER Center's cutting-edge services. When Jim planned a trip to Greece, he would arrive having digested volumes of information about the ancient civilization. He was ready to explore its sights, with knowledge drawn from his reading of Braille books extracted from his wonderful information access and management system. Mike was both genuinely interested and quite impressed with Jim's command of the integrated array of equipment.

On the third day, Mike returned to my office and summarized his findings. He thought that The STORER Center was an interesting and important resource. But Mike honestly concluded that it looked like any other computer lab. Since photographs told the stories in the National Geographic, he wasn't going to focus on the access program. My mouth went dry. But Mike added that on the other hand, my office was visually interesting with its custom amber lighting, enlarged computer and video magnifier displays, and my small Braille and speech computer. Further, he said that he was intrigued by the way that I was handling progressive blindness. He would write about that. Mike would send out the photographer working on the story. Joe McNally became my next contact from within this National Geographic team. Joe arrived weeks later, and we spent a day and a half together. Joe shot many photos of me within my office and using my portable computer around Cleveland in other locales. Joe and I hit it off, just as I had with Mike. We talked about his adventures, working as a photographer for the magazine. I marveled at the amount of time that went into the preparation for this–a major article–eighteen months for the writing, with the photography following close behind.

About a year after Mike had come to Cleveland, he telephoned me and asked if I would be willing to read the article and make any corrections I felt should be made, based on my background as a blindness rehabilitation professional and a man who cared about accurate word usage. I would have an important part in the refinement of this National Geographic, front cover piece. I was being asked to be a guest editor. The draft arrived in print, and with a sighted assistant's help, I reviewed Mike's writing and made some changes. Whenever the continuum of vision loss was being referenced, I used "visual disability" to include all degrees of blindness and partial sight. I applied people first language principles, replacing "the blind", with "people with visual disabilities". But when I read the paragraphs that Mike had written, drawn from his time with me, I was thunderstruck. Mike hadn't used any of the pearls of wisdom, which had flowed out of me as the wine had flowed in. Mike had referred to me as a man "who doesn't take himself too seriously." He wrote that I said that there was a certain peace in giving up trying to see. Mike quoted me: "I've been intellectualizing the hell out of the fact that I've been losing my vision, but I'm still grieving." That quote served as a counterpoint, I thought, to the thrust of his reflection on my response to loss–gentle acceptance. I believe that a measure of our mental health is how long it takes us to transform heartache, anger, embarrassment, and other difficult feelings into humor. I always try to make it a fast turnaround. When my daughter, Laura, was a little girl, she would ask me, when I returned from work, what funny thing had happened to me that day. She was really asking me what difficult thing happened to me that I could relay as a funny story.

Mike recounted several stories that gave a wry slant to my coming to terms with declining vision. Of course I recalled telling the stories, but I did not expect that these cast-offs would become the centerpiece of my contribution. One of the offhand remarks that made it into print was my comment that I can gaze at a streetlight with real appreciation, thinking it is the moon. A longer anecdote was a tale from my time in Berkeley. Sandy and I were walking down Telegraph Avenue, on our first evening there, and I remarked that I understood for the first time, the line from "America the Beautiful"–"for purple mountain majesties". Sandy asked what I was talking about. I replied that I was taken by the beauty of the Berkeley Hills in the distance. She asked where I was looking. I pointed. Sandy replied that I was looking at the roof of the International House of Pancakes.

Mike Long was facing the gripping knowledge of the certain deterioration of vision that would lead to his loss of the ability to take a photograph, drive a car, read a computer screen, or recognize people. He fed back, that I had demonstrated to him that there could be humor and peace of mind after the loss of normal sight.

The article appeared as promised, as the cover story in the November 1992 National Geographic. My half page photograph was embedded within the dozens of other photo images captured by Joe McNally, who has been recognized as one of the greatest one-hundred photographers in the twentieth-century. Following the magazine's publication, I was in Washington D.C. for advanced ADA implementation training. Mike invited me to The National Geographic Society to attend a luncheon in my honor and to meet the staff that had worked on the article and, later that day, to dinner at his home. In the lobby of The National Geographic Society, there is a dome that depicts the night sky on January 27, 1888, the day the venerable institution was founded. I could see those bright electric stars–the first stars that I had seen for years–a real thrill. The luncheon was an elegant meal of soft–shelled crab, enjoyed with more than a dozen staff members who had worked under Mike on the article's photo editing, caption writing, layout, and final preparation. We dined in a private room, surrounded by ceiling to floor photographs of African animals–photos so large that even I could see and appreciate them. But it was Mike's home that was most meaningful to me. There, in Mike and his wife's living room, stood two Steinway grand pianos upon which they performed piano duets. I thought about the loss that would ensue when Mike would no longer be able to read sheet music. I hoped that he would develop the ability to play by ear–the intuitive feeling for his instrument that could transcend not being able to see the written score.

Joe McNally selected two photographs which he had taken in Cleveland for the publication. One shows Jim Storer at his desk, holding up a computer CD containing five encyclopedias and other reference texts. Jim, surrounded by his extensive computer access workstation, holds the disc toward the camera. Although Joe (and I) loved that photo of Jim, it didn't make the final cut for use in the article. The other photograph which was printed is a remarkable demonstration of a tightly staged photo essay. I am talking on the phone while gazing, within inches, at a video screen upon which is being displayed part of a name, and a three digit telephone extension. Beside me is a computer screen with comparably enlarged text. Both screens display white on black images. The room is awash in soft amber light, and one can see on my desk, an open notebook with enlarged felt tipped pen notes on heavy lined paper. Next to that notebook is a small, seven key, Braille computer with speech output. I am wearing Corning Medical Optics Protective Lens Series, dark red, wrap-around glasses. Although the average reader would have no specific knowledge of the devices involved, it is clear from the photo that a man with severely reduced vision is engaged in productive work. The caption identifies me, gives an overview of my work, and quotes my attitude about loss of vision. Not a bad image and reflection, I suppose, to be seen by generations of future children who will sit in grandma's attic and flip through bygone issues of National Geographic. That is, if kids in the future will have attics to explore and, if grandmas will still keep copies of National Geographic. Ah, well–they can always read them online.

Hitting the Road

In 1992, unwanted and jarring changes crashed into my life. After a decade, my job as rehab director at The Cleveland Sight Center ended. I was fired. Conflict with the executive director led to abrupt termination. I tumbled backward and down into freefall. The loss of my job had seemed impossible. I was forty-three; I had plotted my blind proof employment arc for twenty years, sketching out my systematic advance. I had loved the aspects of administration that involved creating new programs and improving old ones. However, the last four years of the job had demanded dismantling programs, not building them, and I resisted the required budget cuts. That had been at the heart of my conflict with my boss. I was an advocate with a laser focus on programs that would give independence to Sight Center clients, and he was first and foremost concerned with budgets and redirecting money into the Sight Center's considerable endowment. But none of that mattered now. More significant than this termination was the loss of my career. I couldn't leave Cleveland. I was essential to Mark's quality of life; my brother could not be moved out of Cuyahoga County. Services could not be transferred from the Cuyahoga County Board of Mental Retardation and Developmental Disabilities to any other Ohio county, let alone any other state. I would not leave him again. There were no other jobs in town in blind rehab, my carefully hewn specialization. So, it was with a high degree of uncertainty, but with required bravado, that I entered the world of consultants. I began to promote a career drawn from my wits, propelled by my need to feed my family and my drive to not fail.

Stresses, like job loss, can rattle loose windows and widen hairline foundation cracks in relationships. After nineteen years, multiple strains on Sandy's and my marriage caused it to crumble. As the collapse began, we sought marriage counseling. We were at a toxic impasse. The therapist proposed a trial separation–six months apart–after which we would decide one way or the other. Following half an anguished year, in isolated corners, we decided to call it quits. The extreme stresses of those days tipped the balance away from retrieval. I was angry and tight as a drum. Sandy was cool and distant as the moon. Neither of us could imagine any hope for a different life together, than what we had known. We had become irrelevant to each other's lives. Self-examination, from a distance, can be useful. Although I said so at the time, I now, regretfully, can truly acknowledge my major share of responsibility for the demise of the marriage.

The pressure cooker of that intensity had other results. My ophthalmologist had said that stress could exacerbate my unavoidable vision loss. During those high-pressure months, my limited vision quickly grew much worse. Midlife crisis does not begin to describe the disorienting, unnerving, and bruising changes that buffeted me during that period. But necessity required that, amid the rubble, I find the foundation stones upon which to rebuild.

The separation began a month and a half after my job ended. I moved into a two-bedroom apartment where I set up my life and my new office as a consultant. The apartment was a mile walk from my family's house. The proximity allowed me to independently pick up Laura, then eight, on Wednesday afternoons, and every other weekend. Kyle, then fifteen, dropped in for dinner once a week, or whenever he could fit me into his full schedule of school, play rehearsals, and his band practices. My relationship with my kids was paramount. Laura and I applied ourselves to cooking, doing simple box science experiments, and crafts. Beginning after Thanksgiving, we baked numerous kinds of family recipe Christmas cookies. Just before Christmas, Laura would carry six weeks' worth of our bounty home, packed in Christmas tin containers, carefully layered with waxed paper.

I loved those homey accomplishments of ours. When Kyle visited, we would listen to cassettes of his and my recent musical productions. We would share observations on each other's artistry. He would also teach me about contemporary music, making keen observations on bass lines borrowed from The Beatles and other cogent musical insights. I had left my recording studio intact within the family's home for Kyle, who had been using the gear effectively for years. At fourteen, he had produced *United Snails*, his first album of original songs, which had gotten airplay on local, college radio stations.

I was writing and recording in my new home studio, purchased for me by Ohio's Blind Services Rehabilitation Bureau. I was visioning my future, both as an ADA consultant and as a musician. My assumption was that I would be primarily earning my living by offering training on The Americans with Disabilities Act and serving as a consultant wherever I could find opportunities. I paid for professional photos–playing guitar and the standard suit and tie, head shot. I wrote a one-page flier and worked with a graphics artist on a logo, material, cards, and letterhead. Ready for customers, I hung out my shingle as "Consultant on Access". I mailed my new materials to the broad network of professional associates and colleagues I had gathered in my Rolodex, then I waited for the phone to ring. It didn't ring much. Undaunted, I went down my list and made cold call after cold call, adding new names to my growing spider web of network connections. It wasn't easy; enough work to support my family and to keep the apartment going was hard to come by.

The ADA's first deadlines for compliance occurred within the first years after its signing in 1990. As those milestones came and went, it seemed that the only consultants getting work were attorneys and architects whose clients were taking a "cover your assets" approach to the law. So, reading the signs, I set about looking for another career. I decided to cast my net into an entirely different pond.

Over the years, I had increasingly performed at schools and for youth programs. It was time to alert Cleveland area schools that I was available for assemblies and residencies. I designed a brochure mailer, concerning that work. I had promoted an invitation to The Clinton White House into a front page story in *The Cleveland Plain Dealer*. I stamped each brochure with a bold stamp reading "As featured on page One, *The Cleveland Plain Dealer*". Then came the tedious secretarial task of entering mail label information for the twelve hundred schools in our sprawling four county area. The cost of secretarial time, postage and printing, was a considerable burden for my meager finances, but I felt sure that the phone would soon be ringing off the wall. The response was, well, underwhelming. One school responded, a resounding return rate of .08%. But I prepared thoroughly for the assembly and was very well received by students, administration, and teachers. I played instruments from my world instrument collection, demonstrating how our commonality can be seen through families of instruments, invented across the globe. I put together a playlist of original songs that thematically encouraged hope, peaceful conflict resolution, and acceptance of difference and disability. My life as a school performer was launched.

Gradually jobs in other states began to happen. During the nineties, my road often led to Tucson, Arizona, where I served as music director for Third Street Kids, 3SK, an inclusive arts program for kids with and without disabilities. I was first invited to conduct a musical workshop with 3SK

278

shortly after the director was given a copy of my first album, *Do You See Me As An Equal?* In 1989, she had begun to integrate one of my songs in her company's performances. Eventually, 3SK got a contract from the Tucson Unified School District to perform in every one of the district's seventy-three elementary schools. My responsibilities and projects were ongoing with 3SK. Seven individual weeks per year; I would work in Tucson, conducting workshops and rehearsals with the inclusive troupe of performers. I provided school assemblies with the director, and with a very talented young keyboard player and vocalist who was born blind in Mexico. His family had moved to Tucson to give him the advantages of the Arizona School for the Blind. Three times a day we would set up, perform, tear down, and pack the van with the instruments and sound system. Marcia Berger, the executive director, provided sign language interpretation for the interactive assemblies. Frank Hernandez, the other blind musician, and I shared the musical program. We sang in English and in Spanish, and Frank translated everything spoken into Spanish. Our program, in three tongues, was always fun and well received. In addition to Tucson's elementary schools, we did our program on the Tohono O'odham reservation and at events on both sides of the Mexican border. After school, we were off to the Third Street Kids' classrooms for workshops, and for the creation of new songs for musicals and performances. I played and sang with the troupe at festivals and 3SK events. Out of the 3SK experience, I wrote an activity guide with accompanying CD, and called the family of materials: *We're People First.*

In 1995 we put together a cross-disability, cross-artistic form presentation and submitted the concept to an international disability forum: The Fourth International Abilympics, to be held in Perth, Australia. The theme of the conference was "A World Working Together". Our presentation was to incorporate that concept. We were accepted, and we began rehearsing for the international event. Our program was based around four of my songs which I sang solo, and as duets with a wonderful young vocalist who had a form of progressive, joint hardening arthritis. While I sang and played, five of the troupe danced behind me. They used a type of cross-ability dance which included a young man with cerebral palsy, in a sports wheelchair. All the songs were signed, and our troupe included a young woman who was deaf. In total, four disabilities were represented. I wrote a song for the event entitled, "A World Working Together". It included verses in English and Spanish and one verse without language, entirely sung using la la la.

The time came and we flew to Australia. The artistic event included artists from twenty-six countries. Performances ranged from a solo musician who was blind, on a traditional Chinese bowed instrument, a troupe of Pakistani gymnasts (all land mine survivors), all of whom were double amputees, a group of Chinese synchronized wheelchair dancers who were paraplegic, Japanese actors who were deaf using giant fingerspelling hands, and an Indonesian rock and roll band comprised entirely of musicians who were blind. We were the only participants who included more than one type of disability. It was truly an American demonstration of diversity and creativity. The conference organizers decided to close the conference with my song: "A World Working Together". There we were, on stage, with all of the artists from around the world–150 in all–all playing and dancing, and signing my song. Gold lamé capes flew behind the Chinese wheelchair dancers as the Pakistani gymnasts tumbled across the stage. It was signed in six different languages, and the Indonesian rock and roll band backed me up. Not everyone spoke English or Spanish, but everyone sang la la la. We brought the house down. It was truly a moment of terrific power, joy, and international collaboration.

Back in Cleveland, I eagerly accepted every offer to speak, play, teach, and advocate. I never paid a dime for advertising. The requests came from individuals who had seen me perform or found my website, established in 1996. I was asked to provide a keynote concert for a special education administrators' conference, held on the banks of Lake of the Ozarks in Missouri. Following the concert, a gentle and effective special ed administrator from North Dakota asked me if I would come to his state the following February.

He was a natural leader and was well regarded by his peers across North Dakota. His initial request was for a concert at a teacher recognition event. I suggested that I could work in schools as well, and we quickly developed an expanded vision for the scope of my visit's work. After brainstorming, he networked with all of the other regional special ed directors, and they each reached out to their schools. He arranged a remarkable two-week tour. The regional special ed administrators themselves would, after my work in their region, drive me the great distances to the planned transfer points. There I would load into another administrator's car to repeat the cycle. Driving across the entire state, from Bismarck to Jamestown, I was aided by those committed professionals. The trip was also, for me, a genuine education in the collapse of rural America under the onslaught of corporate agriculture. One of the special ed directors gave the history of a ghost town that we were passing. He said that over very few years, the town's high school, cooperative grain silo, post office, general store, grocery, gas station, hardware store, drug store, convenience mart and, finally, the elementary school, were all closed and shuttered. The town had one open business–the bar. The town's lonely, sole resident was the bartender. Farmers would drive to the bar from the surrounding region. I performed for one percent of the State's population. During two solid weeks, I put on fifty shows in Head Start classrooms, elementary, middle, and high schools, colleges, nursing homes, and churches. The experience was exhausting but wonderful.

One morning, I was taken to a middle/high-school for a performance that wasn't scheduled until two hours after my arrival. I sat in the teachers' lounge waiting and enjoying a cup of coffee. The school counselor brought a teenage girl in to talk to me. She had low-vision which was at about the same level that I had had when I was in school. However, this girl had never been to a low-vision clinic; she had no magnifier to aid her reading. My heart went out to her. She told me that she lived in a little town of six houses. Six houses! The thought of being so isolated, so alone, made me think about the advantages I had enjoyed, living in the places that I had, with their specialized services and resources.

When I got home from that trip, I carefully wrapped my beloved magnifier, which had served me so well for so long. I could no longer see print with its magical enlargement, but I thought my new protégé would be able to use it to good effect. Two years later, I was again performing in North Dakota and the young girl, now a high school senior, came up to me– stronger and far more confident than I had remembered. We had corresponded a few times during the intervening years. She gratefully thanked me for the magnifier and told me how much it had aided her. Better than that, she had been inspired to advocate for herself. She had been to a low-vision clinic and had received the specific examination and optical aids from which she could best benefit. It was a real thrill to catch a snapshot of her growth.

Thanks to the advocacy of the special ed director and a mother-advocate who was also a special education teacher and mother of an adoptive son with Down syndrome, I toured North Dakota for a total of five weeks, over a three-year period. Several experiences during those road trips were truly unique.

It was a cold winter afternoon as I set up in the gymnasium of a state psychiatric hospital. The resident-patients slowly shuffled in and sat on the bleachers facing the gym floor on which I stood. Like many folk singers, my musical program combines performance with participatory singing, involving short songs, choruses, or the ancient African technique of call and response singing. When an audience is enthusiastic and engaged, like all performers, I find myself energized. But when the audience does not respond, my energy and the music can fall flat. Gray late winter light dully lit the gym. The lethargy and dreary pall that hung over that audience in the psychiatric facility was as thick as a Berkeley fog and twice as chilly. After two songs without response, I stopped singing and addressed the people sitting passively in the bleachers. I told them that they weren't taking any responsibility for the experience that they were having. I spoke about healing from disability's losses and putting energy and direction into every action, every word, and every exchange with others.

The audience began to stir, respond, and become awake and alive. I could hear the bleachers creak as everyone sat up straighter, and cleared their throats. Man, did they sing out! During a break between songs, a nervous, gentle fellow from the audience approached me and asked if my throat was dry. I said that it was, and he hurried off and came back with an ice-cold can of Pepsi, purchased from a vending machine, at his expense. He presented to me with a stammering humility. He said it was his gift to me, stating that he wanted to help. I accepted his gift gratefully but was so choked up that I had trouble introducing the next song. After the concert, the audience mobbed me and many hands were shaken and hugs were exchanged. The activities director said that she had never seen such an energetic and positive response from the residents. Normal expectations can lead to normal behavior. Music is the universal language–touching both thought and feeling–capable of binding communities together.

Another experience is worth recounting. Jamestown is a college town, with a broad range of schools, offering widely differing degrees of inclusive education. The Catholic school has virtually no children with disabilities. The public school has a wide sweep of disabilities, mild to severe. In that community a long-standing, special, residential school provides education for kids with severe and multiple disabilities. Thanks to a concentrated organizing effort by the mother-advocate, I worked in all of them. My written and recorded materials, *We're People First*, went into the

282

schools in advance of my visit, and the same selected songs were introduced to the children in all of the schools. The culminating event of my week's work in Jamestown, as had happened elsewhere, was a community concert. I performed with an ad hoc chorus of kids, singing as a backup choir with me. In Jamestown, selected kids from thirteen schools sang. Six hundred and fifty children–with and without disabilities–sat behind me in the Civic Center arena. They each wore differently colored school tee shirts, providing a bright patchwork of color-coded school pride. Thousands of their parents, families, and supporters filled the amphitheater's seats. The kids who used wheelchairs sat on the basketball court's floor around me; the others filled the section that rose behind us. What a thrilling community-binding experience! Happiness and good will emanated and the kids all sang with one, unified intent. I had taught the schools the closing song in both sign language and English. The ad hoc choral director stood watching me, while directing the combined choir in both languages. I wore a ponytail in those years. At one point, I reached up and swept my hands back over my hair, attempting to tidy the loose hairs that tickled my face. The teacher repeated my hands through the hair as did the six hundred and fifty kids, wondering, no doubt, what that new sign meant.

Road Notes

When I first began establishing myself as a Disability Rights musician, I had some lucky breaks. I knew a very talented young blind man who was then working for Ohio's Governor's Office on Advocacy for People with Disabilities. I mentioned to him that I had a body of songs that motivated, educated, entertained, and spurred advocacy. He told me that he would suggest my name to the planning committee for an upcoming statewide conference on disability and advocacy. I received an invitation to perform, and I began to plan the set of songs that I would play, following the governor's speech at the final evening's program, ending the three-day conference.

I communicated with the sign language interpreters who would be signing my lyrics, practiced and rehearsed the short, spoken segments introducing songs. I generally felt ready. The day came and I went to Kent State University for the event. Three hundred and fifty attendees filed and rolled into the large banquet room for the evening's dinner and program, which featured an address by Ohio's governor. A problem for the conference planners developed. The Fairmont Theater of the Deaf, which was to share the evening's bill with the Governor Dick Celeste and me, had canceled at the last minute. I was approached by a worried member of the planning team who asked if I could expand my performance to fill in the time now empty in the after-dinner program. I was elated and quickly began adding songs to my playlist. The governor was delayed, and time wore on as we waited for him. After nearly an hour wait, Governor Dick Celeste arrived with his aides and bounded onto the stage. He was beginning late, and he spoke longer than scheduled. Then, it was time for me.

The summer's evening had faded into night as a powerful thunderstorm arrived in Northeastern Ohio. Lightning flashed, thunder cracked, and rain drummed hard against the windows. I played song after song. I could hear chairs moving in the large room. I thought people are going to the restrooms or maybe going into the lobby to phone their friends to tell them to hurry over to the university to catch the rest of my performance. Two flagging sign language interpreters spelled each other as my expanded set rolled on. I noticed that applause seemed to diminish with each song. I figured that maybe my lyrics were so poignant, humorous, or stirring, that reflection was the reaction of a growing number of listeners. Besides, I knew they were tired after the three-day conference. I played for well over an hour, finally striking the last chord. The interpreter dropped her weary hands. Silence filled the air as the lights were brought up. The interpreter turned to me and said, "They're applauding."

"Who?" I asked.

"The people at the front table. They're deaf. They applaud in sign."

She showed me the sign for applause. I acknowledged their affirmation in sign. Then I realized that the only people left in the great room were those at that one table–they couldn't leave. They had come together in a van driven by the interpreter. The rest of the room was empty. An old aphorism came to mind: be sure you quit playing before they quit listening.

Performing for school audiences is not for the faint of heart. High schools can be particularly formidable. I was singing the concluding song of my assembly for a rural high school in Texas when the bell signaling the end of the school day rang. As I belted out my passionate closing verse, the students, as one, heavily clomped down the bleacher stairs and headed for the exits, streaming around my position on the gym floor with the microphone stand, instrument tables, and me–still singing. Sometimes it was the school's expectations that caused me to work all the harder to make my point. In a school in North Carolina I was asked to do a short program for the special ed classroom, following the assembly for the general population of students. That special ed. classroom was filled with gentle, attentive, and well-behaved kids. My assembly was about acceptance of difference, creating a kind and respectful school, and including everyone. Apparently everyone in that school did not include the kids down the hall.

My life on the road has given me a rich and diverse range of experiences. I have eaten in school cafeterias and greasy spoons, stayed in threadbare motels, and flown in single engine airplanes. I have supped at family tables, slept in spare bedrooms, and been driven by scores of volunteers. I have also stayed on the concierge floor of skyscraper hotels, eaten in fine restaurants and, occasionally, even flown first class and in private planes. But the quality of any trip is always reflected through my interactions with the local people.

Mountain Home, Arkansas was the site of a nerve-jangling moment and the receipt of some remarkable customer service. One late summer evening in 1992, I was taking a small airplane from St. Louis to Hot Springs, Arkansas for a keynote the following day. We first hopped from St. Louis, Missouri into Harrison, Arkansas and then flew the short distance into Mountain Home. The final leg of the flight was Mountain Home to Hot Springs. In Mountain Home the remaining passengers de-planed, leaving me and the two pilots to finish their milk run.

Darkness enveloped everything except for the brightly lit little airport terminal building. The pilots powered the seventeen seat aircraft down the single runway toward take-off. Just before the plane's wheels would have lifted off the tarmac, the little plane violently shuddered to a sudden stop. Both pilots leaped out of the darkened cockpit. The captain threw open the door and hurled the attached ladder to the ground, as his co-pilot snapped open my seat belt and pulled me suddenly to my feet.

"Can you run?" he asked me with great urgency.

"Yes," I responded. He spun me around and grasped my shoulders from behind.

"Ready?" he shouted into the night.

"Ready!" came the rapid reply from the tarmac. Without another word, he shoved me out of the open door. I didn't even touch the stairs. I was thrust out of the airplane's door, fell several feet, and was caught by the upper arms by the other pilot. Instantly, the co-pilot jumped to the ground and they each grasped one of my arms and we all ran hard away from the plane.

As we ran, I gasped out the question "What's going on?"

The pilot said, "The plane is on fire. It might explode." Once inside the little airport, they told me that an emergency light had flashed, indicating a fire and that then they saw the left engine flaming and streaming smoke into the night. They pulled the panic cord and we evacuated the plane. The emergency cord cuts all systems including fuel, electricity, and hydraulic and it is for just such emergencies.

The airport's lone attendant offered coffee and acted like this was an everyday occurrence. Her name was Sunday Papa. As the pilots nervously stared at the abandoned plane, through the window of the waiting area, Sunday chatted easily. The men carried on an intermittent cell phone conversation with a mechanic at their regional hub–Little Rock Airport. After several minutes, when the pilots were convinced that the emergency was passed, they walked to the aircraft and climbed onto the plane's wing to repair the problem. They took off the cowling that shrouded the engine and stepped through the mechanic's long distance directions. The repair took two hours. Close to midnight, they walked back into the waiting area. The pilot quietly explained that they had pulled what they called the panic cord, cutting all of the plane's fuel and power systems. They had found and repaired the problem that had caused the fire, but only a certified mechanic was allowed to re-attach the panic cord, a requirement to carry passengers. The pilots apologized, re-boarded the aircraft and took off for Little Rock. Sunday Papa turned off the coffee pot and the lights, locked the door and drove me to a motel. The young desk clerk knew nothing of the open requisition that the airport had for crew layovers and just this sort of emergency. But Sunday convinced her to give me a room, while she drove to an ATM to get cash from her own account. She said that she would pick me up at 6:00 a.m., in about five hours. She had booked me on the first flight into Hot Springs. Chipper and pleasant, Sunday Papa arrived at six and drove us to the empty airport. She had already opened the one room building, and freshly brewed coffee was waiting. Sunday Papa should be a corporate consultant, providing training on outstanding customer service.

One of the most remarkable individuals I met during my travels was the late Kim Peek. When preparing to play the role of Raymond for the movie Rain Man, Dustin Hoffman spent time with several individuals who were autistic savant. But Hoffman's primary study was Kim Peek of Salt Lake City, who sadly died in 2009. Kim was unique among those with savant genius. In most cases, three or four areas of extraordinary ability are present within those who are autistic savant. Kim had fourteen jaw-dropping abilities, including American and world history, historic calendric knowledge, sports history, music, general encyclopedic knowledge, and mathematics.

His father had worked for the Bell Telephone system and would bring home Yellow Pages from around the country. Kim enjoyed the phone books in several ways. Kim's eyes worked independent of each other. He could rapidly and simultaneously add the numerals in the list of phone numbers on opposite phone book pages resulting in two accurate gigantic sums. Kim also read and absorbed facts from those directories and from complete encyclopedias.

I met Kim when we were both working within the Tucson school district, for Disabilities Awareness Week. Kim's dad was traveling with him, acting as his interlocutor and moderator during presentations and conversations with others. During high school assemblies, students submitted sealed questions in Kim's areas of expertise, and Kim flawlessly answered them. When we met, his father asked me for my birth date. I responded: February 20, 1949. Kim stated, "You were born on Sunday and you will retire on Thursday," (assuming I retired on my sixty-fifth birthday.) His father asked me where I lived. He told me the area codes, zip codes, major highways, and radio and television stations from Cleveland. Kim's brain itself was studied at UCLA, where he was nicknamed "Kimputer". At dinner, his father asked me to direct questions to Kim within his areas of expertise. I asked him questions about Cleveland Indians players nicknamed Lefty and he told me the three men's years of play, batting averages, and other specific statistics. Concerning American history, I asked him what presidents had hailed from Ohio and he then asked if I meant what presidents were born in Ohio, had lived in Ohio when they ran for office, or retired to Ohio after the presidency. I asked about the Galilean telescope, a telescope design I was familiar with because I used one. The use of Galileo's design had resulted in a powerful hand-held telescope that could focus from within eighteen inches to an infinite depth-a tremendous functional improvement. Kim responded with a short synopsis of Galileo's life, then the year of the telescope's development, other facts about it, and then a short statement about the optics of the telescope.

Mr. Peek spoke about his disappointment concerning the film Rain Man and its ending, wherein Hoffman's character is re-institutionalized. He said that he had written a sequel that followed the brothers into a new life chapter. In his screenplay, Hoffman's Raymond was empowered by his brother to use newly discovered talents. It was learned that Raymond had savant abilities in botany and they were used to great effect. Raymond's brother establishes a commercial nursery wherein Raymond provides scientific leadership, and employment is provided for many individuals with disabilities. Raymond lives successfully and productively outside of the institution. But Mr. Peek said the studio wasn't interested. Apparently, Hoffman had so closely empathized with the character Raymond that it took him a long time to return to his own personality and clear his "empathetic, inner autistic savant". According to Mr. Peek, when Hoffman received the Oscar for his performance, he snapped into Raymond's persona and had a hard time shaking it. Hoffman was afraid to again play Raymond. It is a tragedy that the sequel will not be produced because Rain Man's plot reinforces negative stereotypes about the ability of people with such disabilities to successfully live outside institutions. Further, in the movie the only use to which Raymond's savant abilities were applied was toward his brother's gambling at the tables in Las Vegas. Movies can, and often do, great harm to the public's perception of people with disabilities. Rarely are they used to the great effect to which they could be put to shatter stereotypes and reshape public attitudes.

One of the advantages of blindness has been being freed of the distraction of the physical world. Since I can't see historic buildings, majestic scenery, dazzling sunsets, or anything else, my experience of locales has become reduced to and focused on my experience with people. I have found people everywhere willing to go out of their way for this stranger. Countless individuals have guided me across crowded hotel lobbies, through airports, and have offered needed information.

I learned through a folk music store that centuries ago, in the British Isles, a blind middle-class child would be given harp lessons and, as a young adult, would be provided with a harp, a driver and cart, with which to hit the road to earn a living. Thus, the harpist could make a social contribution as an itinerant musician singing the news from town to town–a troubadour. Many musicians with visual disabilities have found the music trade blind-proof, and I am very grateful that I have been able to follow in the cart tracks of those who rolled on before, sharing their music with the wider world.

Chapter 16: The Rocky Road Back

West Fourteenth Street

I believe in networking and the power of personal relationships. During my years working in rehabilitation, I had opportunities to meet and work with other professionals, across that broad field. I volunteered on a committee to study and make recommendations concerning needed community services for consumers with cognitive disabilities. The head of that working group was the residential director for the Cuyahoga County Board of Mental Retardation and Developmental Disabilities, CCBMRDD. Her job involved the complex process of moving the Board's clients onto the emerging, three-dimensional, residential chessboard, scattered across sprawling Greater Cleveland. The variety of housing options ranged from state institutions to quiet group homes in suburban neighborhoods. The different options were an uneven matrix of assigned settings, based on family involvement, degree of need, functioning level, selective assignment, history, timing, and luck. Overall, there were about one thousand "beds" in the system, but there were more than two thousand people in our county waiting to receive residential services. Typically, the only people who moved off of the waiting list and into a facility were those in emergency need, such as individuals whose parents had died. Mark had been a ward of the state from the time he had been remanded to a state institution in 1963. Although Mom had recently regained guardianship, thanks to advocacy-driven changes in state law, Ohio was still fully responsible for his care. Mark had been moved, in 1981, from the Columbus State Institution for the Mentally Retarded, back to Cuyahoga County and into a sixteen-bed Intermediate Care Facility for the Mentally Retarded (ICFMR). And although woeful, Mark's situation had been upgraded and was fixed. Within Cuyahoga County's crowded system, people did not move "up" into better housing circumstances. Anyone receiving residential services was considered lucky, compared to those languishing on the long waiting list.

The committee on which I served with the residential director, met intermittently for a year and a half. We developed a professional regard for each other through those meetings. Over time, I relentlessly informed her about the abuse that Mark was enduring. I periodically, gently beseeched her to consider getting Mark into more favorable circumstances. At such times, she would remind me that individuals were not upgraded.

I felt fortunate when Mark had first moved into the ICFMR "House Five". Phoenix Residential Services, a for-profit organization, leased the house and the enclave of the other numbered houses that made up their little neighborhood. It had once housed the employees and superintendent of the massive state institution on whose grounds the houses had been built, perhaps a century earlier. The owner drove a Rolls Royce, the executive director drove a Mercedes, and the staff was paid minimum wage. Mark's life within House Five was fraught with dysfunction. During one of our first winters in Cleveland, the temperature plummeted to thirty degrees below zero. It was on one such bitterly cold winter day that I arrived to get Mark for his three day Christmas vacation. Sandy and I were told to wait while staff helped Mark get his overnight things together. Mark came downstairs carrying the odd yellow suitcase Mom had given him, and we headed toward the door and the unforgiving December weather. Sandy stopped and told me to look at what Mark was wearing. My younger brother was wearing rubber thong sandals over thin socks, and a summer nylon golf jacket. Incredulous, I protested loudly to the lethargic staff. I was told that those were Mark's only clothes. Mom always had provided Mark with proper clothing including a warm winter coat, leather running shoes, and winter boots. But like Columbus, in the ICFMR Mark's personal possessions were regularly stolen. With no recourse we walked the short distance to the warmth of the car, for the fifty-minute drive home. When Mark returned after Christmas, he had been again temporarily outfitted with proper clothing, coat, and footwear for the fierce winter weather. The residents had a continuum of abilities. Institutions have hierarchies, and Mark was among the lower functioning members of his sixteen-person, aggregate-living setting. Clothing retention demonstrated the disparities between the residents. Some were always dressed to the nines, while others wore threadbare, second-hand rags and flip flops. After several more pairs of new shoes had disappeared, Mom, in exasperation, bought Mark a new pair of white running shoes. To protect his ownership, she wrote MARK in huge upper case letters, with indelible marker, along the entire side of each shoe.

On my next visit, after he had been given his "name brand" shoes, Mark again was wearing cheap rubber sandals.

I asked, "Mark, what happened to your shoes?"

"David took them," Mark complained.

I walked up to a member of the staff and asked them to look in David's closet for Mark's shoes. Initially, the staff was not willing to invade David's space to search for Mark's shoes. They explained that David had the right of privacy for his possessions. I argued that Mark claimed that David had taken his shoes and that Mark's emblazoned name would identify the purloined footwear. I insisted, and the staff relented. There, in David's closet, in plain sight, were Mark's new shoes. They were returned to Mark. But Mark's difficulties were not limited to his inability to maintain his possessions. The men and women in the ICFMR had all lived in institutions for years. They had been conditioned by the violent environments from which they had come. Fights resulted. Generally, though, when Mark was upset, he would act in ways that were self-injurious. Twice, unbelievably, he had punched out the small glass windows in the house's steel fire doors. The sheer force of his blows broke the inch thick protective glass embedded with chicken wire. Mark severely lacerated his left hand driving it through the window's glass. One of those injuries led to emergency surgery and a cast on his badly injured hand.

In early December 1992, I went into Mark's room to do an inventory, to figure out what he needed for Christmas. All that his closet held was one completely threadbare flannel shirt and two pairs of worn out trousers. None of the clothes had been Mark's, and Mark's clothes were not there. Next, I went to Mark's dresser. Mark's dresser had previously been adjacent to Mark's twin bed. But unknown to me, the position of the dressers had been changed. There were two identical dressers in Mark's room, which he shared with Tommy. I pulled open the top drawer of Tommy's bureau thinking it was Mark's. There, were numerous hip packs, baseball hats, and other gifts given to Mark that had gone missing. Other drawers were crammed with Mark's socks, underwear, and polo shirts. I reported the obvious misappropriation to the staff. Mark's dresser was nearly empty– a scant few pair of underwear and socks. After eleven years in House Five, Mark owned nothing. Gone were birthday gifts and other purchases made within the previous four months, Mom and I had bought Mark five outfits, shoes, underwear, and a coat–all taken. I decided to visit with other residents and their rooms were full of personal possessions and their closets were chocked full of clothes. But Mark was at the bottom of the food chain, and he had no defense against the ongoing theft that robbed him of everything provided for him.

I called my acquaintance, the residential director, the next day and reported the fresh details to her. I begged her to explore other alternatives and to see if there wasn't some other place she could find for Mark. She wasn't happy about it, but she offered that a "bed" had just become available in an eight-bed group home on West Fourteenth Street, on Cleveland's near West Side. She reminded me that she didn't move people within the system, once they had a placement, but she would do me the favor of providing Mark's profile to the house for consideration. I was Mark's advocate, but Mom was his guardian and had the authority that legal designation confers. Overjoyed, I phoned Mom and told her about my foot in the door. I hadn't anticipated her resistance. Mom wasn't certain the change would be a good idea. She was wary of the uncertainty and dangers of a community placement. I pulled out the stops and tried to dispel her worry. I emphasized the quality of life improvements resulting from Mark living with only seven others and the closer proximity to our homes. The conversation ended with Mom still unsettled and undecided.

Meanwhile, Mark had been invited to the West Fourteenth Street House for an introductory dinner. The residents all seemed to like him. A week later, Mom phoned and reported that she and Dick had driven passed the potential group home and that they had been shocked to see its inner city neighborhood. The old Victorian house sat between an auto body shop and a church with a hunger center. Mom had phoned Mark's county worker and asked to discontinue the application process. I learned of her action from the residential director. Desperate, I phoned Mom and asked her to consider what a miracle it was that my contact had arranged Mark's upgrade. This was a singular opportunity. I beseeched my mother to reconsider. Half-heartedly, Mom agreed to call and withdraw her objection.

Mark's second dinner at the West Fourteenth Street House closed the deal. He liked the other residents, and they liked him. He particularly hit it off with Vicky, a small woman with whom Mark happily smoked after dinner. The house members voted Mark in. I was overjoyed. On a cold Tuesday morning, in February 1993, I waited inside Mark's new dwelling. Along with house staff, we were about to welcome Mark to his new home. The formerly grand, old four-bedroom Victorian house had been rehabbed into a functional, although cramped, home for four men and four women. Mark finally arrived, driven by an employee from House Five. Just like his move from The Columbus Institution, a plastic trash bag contained the assortment of rags that had been collected as Mark's wardrobe. My reputation as Mark's advocate was well known as I was about to learn. As the House Five driver opened the door and did not see me waiting inside, he, in a tentative voice asked, "Is his brother here?" I took his nervousness as a compliment. I was a constant and unrelenting advocate.

I got Mark settled, took him to lunch at a nearby restaurant, and said goodbye. For the first time, Mark did not plead for me to stay or to take him with me as I left. Instead, he was busy chatting with his new staff and obviously feeling quite at home at West Fourteenth. The following Sunday evening, I took Mark out to dinner with the same friend who had assisted me the day he moved in. We returned to his new home for a little concert. The eight residents all gathered in the living room and I began to play. I had only begun, when Vicky stood up growling a string of invectives against me. Without warning, she grabbed the end of the heavy coffee table in the center of the gathering and upended it, sending it crashing to the floor. A staff member guided a still loudly cussing Vicky into the kitchen. The jarring disruption made it difficult for me to continue to play. With the concert cut short, I hugged Mark goodnight and left the West Fourteenth Street House. That dark foreshadowing suggested bitter fruit to come. Mark's relationship with Vicky proved to be a blessing and a curse. I think that they enjoyed an intimate relationship and always smoked together on the old house's porch. But Vicky also shared her seething and poisonous rage. Vicky came from a toxic family and had an actively abusive sister. Weekend visits with her sister always ended badly. In contrast, Mark had my friendly support and frequent visits. My caring presence was an instant source of jealousy. Resentment simmered, and Vicky began repeating negative statements about me to Mark.

I was enjoying a new relationship as well. Maggie and I had met when the apartment pool opened in June 1993. Our friendship slowly bloomed into romance. Her warm and genuine nature shone in the way that she interacted with Mark. Maggie treated Mark like a real person–like a friend. She joked with Mark and although she didn't smoke, she would even light his cigarettes. I had kept to a schedule of seeing Mark once a month, relying on friends to provide transportation. We were just twenty-five minutes away, but not driving limited me from more frequent visits. I mentioned my discontent and Maggie offered to help. She asked how frequently I wanted to visit and I replied that I would like to see Mark weekly. Maggie thought about it briefly and then said that she would make the commitment to drive. Thanks to Maggie's selflessness, my visits to see

Mark became weekly, beginning in 1993. After three decades, thanks to Maggie's selflessness, I finally was able to provide Mark with ongoing family contact. I began to really support him as he made his way in his world of strangers and less than desirable living conditions.

Patience

When we moved back to Cleveland in 1982, I began sharing the responsibility for Mark's visits and overnight stays with my mother. For example, Mom and Dick would pick up Mark on Christmas Eve. He would spend the night and Christmas morning with them. Mark would then be shuttled to my family's home on Christmas Day for a two-night stay with us. I extended Mark's visits as long as possible, believing that everyone benefited from his time with us. Mark got the pleasure and renewal of time with his family, and my kids, Kyle and Laura, had a chance to get outside of themselves and relate to a family member who needed their love and patience. Patience was the most important attribute anyone could bring to his or her interactions with Mark. Impatience and a short temper could quickly make interactions difficult. Our family's holiday support for Mark rolled on, unchanged, for a decade.

Mom's health had slowly deteriorated, although at sixty she quit smoking, began to exercise, and to eat more carefully. But at seventy-one, she had advanced coronary artery disease, had endured extensive, vascular surgery, and had, fearfully, suffered several mini strokes, cardiac fibrillation, and a seizure. Mom's energy faded. She was not the same perky, buoyant woman who had endured so much and gamely pressed on, bearing her life's difficulties with élan and resilience. When Christmas 1994 arrived, Mom was weak and frail. I was chagrined when she phoned to ask, with a quaking voice, if I could handle Mark for the entire visit. It concerned me primarily because of what it said about her health and also because of the additional responsibility it placed on me. I was living in an apartment during my separation from Sandy. The day before Christmas Eve, Mom unexpectedly stopped by. At the door of my apartment, trembling, she handed me some party food and wrapped presents. I walked her down to her car. I waited for a farewell hug. With difficulty, she unlocked her car door, turned and dropped exhausted into the driver's seat. She was too tired to stand. After expressing my concern, I leaned over and kissed her goodbye. Mom drove away and I turned my attention to Mark's upcoming visit. Mom was hospitalized with virulent pneumonia two days later. When Mark visited, he took over my bedroom. I slept on the futon in the living room. During his overnight visits on his birthday, Thanksgiving, Easter, and Christmas, Mark's holiday stays had been a family affair. But now, I was to handle Mark's visit solo.

On Christmas Eve afternoon, my buddy arrived. We drove to West Fourteenth Street to get Mark. Our three-day visit would be the first ever without any other family support. In Mark's personal heaven, his perpetually lit cigarette would be complemented by a bottomless cup of coffee. Oh yes, and add a pile of Christmas or birthday gifts. I had hidden the gifts, but on Christmas Eve the little, decorated tree and unavoidable media ramp up to the big day gave him the bubbling anticipation of soon-to-be-fulfilled, present-lust.

He knew that the presents would appear. My activity options for his visit were limited, and the plan for the three days was threadbare. On Christmas Eve, we watched television and had dinner. On Christmas Day, Laura, then ten, and Kyle, eighteen, were to arrive in the afternoon for our family gift exchange. My son John Kyle had asked to be called Kyle when he was thirteen. I wanted to hold Mark off for as long as possible, in order to make his present opening an integrated part of the family experience. Mark always received more gifts than anyone else, partly because he always needed clothes and personal effects, and partly because he was so easily pleased by inexpensive gift items. Gift giving had also become more gratifying, because after the three decades during which everything given to him was immediately stolen, now only expensive things like leather jackets disappeared.

My sleep, the night before Christmas, was disturbed several times by Mark's frequent awakening. Two or three times, he shuffled out of the bedroom seeking cigarettes and presents. I would explain that it wasn't time to get up. I would sit with him while he smoked his allotted cigarette. Then, without complaint, he would quietly go back to bed. Christmas Sunday came earlier than I would have wished. It began for us at 5:30 a.m. I groggily knew that further resistance to the beginning of the big day would be futile. After the obligatory smoke, breakfast was the next order of business. Once Mark was awake though, the desire to open his gifts became obsessive. My plan was to dole out a few presents before the kids arrived– one present every two hours. The kids were due at 1:00 that afternoon. But their Christmas schedule lagged. The kids' morning ran long and they arrived at my place in the middle of the afternoon. Both Mark and I were

295

very glad to see them, and we had a pleasant, abbreviated visit. We slowly exchanged gifts and then Mark happily opened the remainder of his pile. A plate of Christmas cookies, baked with Laura during previous weeks' visits, was enjoyed. All too soon, the little family get-together ended. Kyle and Laura were gone, as was the greatly anticipated peak experience of the visit.

I faced the two days stretching before us knowing that time would languish without much structure or variation. Christmas Day wound down; I played Christmas carols and we sang. We watched a little television, I cooked dinner, Mark smoked as allowed, and time dragged. That night's sleep was again interrupted by Mark's several forays wanting a smoke. Then, it was Monday. I was bone-tired and crabby as I made coffee. Despite my entreaties to make it last, as he always did, Mark quickly drank his cherished cup of joe and hot milk. After breakfast, Mark became bored. His requests for cigarettes and more coffee were incessant, and I began to answer him with curt, clipped responses. My irritation was on a slow boil. Rather than suggesting that we sing together, an activity that we had repeated and that I knew Mark enjoyed, I had settled into a tight silence and allowed the mindless drone of the television to take the place of meaningful interaction.

With a day and a half to go, Mark wandered into the kitchen. It was too quiet. I was sleep-deprived and feeling quite put upon and put out, but I forced myself to get up to see what Mark was up to. I walked around the corner into the small kitchen. There was my brother, bent directly over the front burner of the gas stove, lighting a cigarette from the blue flame that blazed at full force. I had previously been a smoker and when I had found myself without matches or a lighter, I had used the same dangerous technique. But I would carefully approach the flame from the side. Mark was leaning face down directly over and into the high, dangerous flame. I snapped as my fear flashed, and my fatigue and frustration exploded.

I bellowed, "What are you doing? Mark, don't do that!" Then I angrily clicked off the burner's flame. Facing Mark, with his unlit cigarette, I declared how dangerous it was, and then, realizing that he had also sneaked the smoke, I added his helping himself to the cigarettes to my loud rebuke. Mark had seen where I had placed the pack. I made no real attempt to hide it and, as always, Mark generally had honored the boundary and would only smoke when I gave him a cigarette.

My heart was hammering with the fear of what might have happened. I was angry and frightened. I made no attempt to be sensitive or kind. Mark's eyes dropped in shame, as his head bent and his shoulders slumped.

He softly and meekly said, "I'm sorry Jeff. I'm sorry, brother."

His humility was a stark contrast to my volatile reprimand. In stop action, I saw the impact of my selfishness. I was being unkind, although I was alarmed and concerned. However, my rough treatment was undeniable and unnecessary. The problem was not Mark. My lack of patience was the problem. I was impatient because I lacked the willingness to exert patience. My point of view and emotional laxity was the cause of the difficulty. Mark required that I develop the capacity to express my humanity in a consistent, giving, open-handed, and gentle way. Mark taught me that the only limitations that are worth my recognizing are my own. Those, I have a chance of changing.

Edgewood

Mark's group home on West Fourteenth proved to be a place of great heartache. Mark had lived in brutal and crowded places for thirty years. That endemic violence had poisoned him, when pressed, with a hair-trigger temper and explosive anger. Mark and Vicky remained a constant duo. She grumbled a steady murmur of repeated invectives against me. After a lifetime of yearning for contact, Mark began to refuse to see me. Once, Mark and Vicky were sitting on the front porch when we pulled up to take him for our Sunday evening dinner at a quiet tavern that had become our haunt. Mark took one look at me and spun on his heel. He went back into the house, slamming the door loudly and yelling his opposition to going with me in a furious burst of obscenity. During that period he would angrily object to going to our restaurant outings, often en route or even after we had been seated or served. At such times, Mark would become louder and more wound up until his goal of going back to his urban group home had been realized. Then he would storm into the house without as much as a hug. It was misery making. Mark had always longed for my visits, loved our time together, and hated to see me leave. Suddenly he was rejecting me–angrily repeating Vicky's blood oaths. His bombastic disruptions were full throttled, and my attempts to ease things back onto emotional solid ground generally failed. All I could do was to follow his wishes as quickly as possible. It was baffling, but still harder changes were to follow.

Mom was hospitalized the day after Christmas, 1994, with pneumonia. Two weeks later, she had rallied. In late January 1995, aggressive pneumonia pounced again, and this time, she couldn't fight back. Mom died on January 29, 1995, after a decade of deterioration. I had watched her fire, her spark, and her fierce light blink off in the several weeks prior to her passing. A communication, by Mark's county social worker, began her final decline.

Mark had attended a co-ed county workshop every weekday since he returned to Cleveland in 1981. One day Mark gestured to a woman he liked, inviting her to join him in the men's room. Bathrooms were the only place in the facility where there was anything like privacy. Once inside, Mark and the woman quickly engaged in standing intercourse. They were discovered by a staff member who reported that Mark's partner was smiling as she leaned over the sink counter. Although there was no sign of coercion, Mark was taken into police custody as the potential perpetrator of what was deemed as rape. Legal action on the accusation was held in abeyance while the woman's family was asked if they wanted to press charges. Mark's case manager was given the grim task of communicating the situation to our family. Mom, as Mark's guardian, was contacted first. He reported that Mark was in police custody, facing potential rape charges. I was on the road in Arizona when I got his next call. The suggestion that Mark had been responsible for rape pushed Mom into a fall of bottomless despair. Since Mark's birth, such stereotyped aggression had been Mom's worst fear. I returned to Cleveland and began handling the somber matter. The young woman's family did not press charges. Mark's friend was non-verbal and incapable of spoken consent, but her behavior and affect communicated enthusiastic participation and pleasure. But the damage was done. The lack of formal charges did not lighten Mom's bleak heartache as she staggered under the weight of the initial communiqué's crushing language.

I asked to have a meeting on the matter, resulting in a gathering with nine of the county's professional and administrative staff. The county's sexuality counselor reported that Mark's partner was unable to comment on her willingness but had chosen to enter the rest room, was smiling, and appeared to thoroughly enjoy the act. Circumstances suggested that the sex was completely consensual. I reminded them that the workshop had called the police and Mark's social worker had framed the situation as rape. After squirming through some initial posturing responding to my questions, the

Social Worker eventually did admit that his terminology had been inflammatory. I communicated that our mother had been emotionally devastated by his language's implications. I asked him to contact Mom to revisit and correct the facts of the matter and apologize for his use of the word rape. Although he agreed to contact her by phone and letter, he initiated no communication at all. Following the meeting, despite my repeating the case worker's apology, nothing I could say to Mom could soften the brutal impact the suggestion of rape had dealt her. Always tenacious, this was the final straw and she lost the will to live. Mom passed away six weeks after the incident.

Although I offered to pick Mark up, a compassionate staff member from the West Fourteenth Street House brought him to her memorial service. Mark was dressed in better clothing than at any previous time, wearing a new, cable-knit, white sweater and new slacks. After the service, during the reception, Mark sat, head on his chest, heartbroken. Even the rare appearance of out-of-town relatives did not bring him the usual pleasure.

At my eager initiation, I was made Mark's guardian by the probate court. With that designation, in addition to my ongoing advocacy, I now had the control to serve Mark's best interest.

His life on West Fourteenth had continued to take a decidedly dark turn. Four men and four women shared the four-bedroom house, with its two common rooms and kitchen. There was no place to get away from other residents' difficult, repetitive behavior. The house members' rough edges cut into each other, creating unending friction and raw wounds. Vicky, although of small stature, carried oversized, smoldering grudges toward a few others. She learned to wield Mark's steel, forged in the blast furnace of institutions. Mark was armed with a street-fighting savagery, hardened by three decades in prison-like institutions, and he could be triggered. Mary was a big, angry woman with a very difficult set of behaviors. I had witnessed her particular brand of dysfunction first hand. On a Sunday, Maggie and I were silently standing in the front room of the West Fourteenth Street house waiting for Mark. He was upstairs preparing to go out with us. Mary wordlessly walked up to us and slapped Maggie hard across the face. Mary didn't just slap strangers; she would hit Mark and other housemates on a daily basis. Vicky couldn't take on Mary, but she could urge Mark into action. Mark would usually listen to the counsel of his higher angels, but his inner mainspring could become completely overwound and twice he exploded and delivered punishing beatings to Mary. Staff would intercede, and Mark's pounding rage would be subdued. At such moments, Vicky was nowhere to be found while Mark would be left holding the bag, unable to understand or to describe Vicky's role in the mayhem. In short, Vicky was the brains and Mark was the muscle and fall guy. I learned all this from communication with a sympathetic staff member.

Vicky had also modeled the heaving of furniture as a form of acting out. At best, she could only upend a coffee table or tip over a chair. Mark, under pressure, when provoked, had always had a superhuman strength. After living on West Fourteenth for a few months, Mark too began to hurl furniture–an entirely new behavior. During one outburst, he upended a four-drawer file cabinet, knocked over a desk, and threw a wingback chair across the room. Staff had their procedures down for such emergencies. They would quickly clear the other residents out of the house and phone for back up.

One morning, Mark was about to sit down for breakfast at the large communal dining table. Another resident made a remark at which Mark took umbrage. He hurled the plastic pitcher of milk he was carrying, against the wall, showering the room with its contents. As staff quickly moved everyone out of the room, Mark pushed the heavy wooden table over and was lifting it over his head. But before Mark could heave the massive thing, he slipped in the spilled milk and the table crashed down upon him. It opened a deep gash in his face, requiring stitches.

The county called a meeting to discuss programming options. The choices were few and I felt helpless. At its conclusion, I was driven to the bus stop by the same social worker who had told our late mother that Mark was being held by the police concerning rape. Now, deadly serious, he said that if Mark's behavior could not be brought under control, he would be sent back into an institution. There, he stated, control would be possible. I remembered the beatings, the heavy sedation, the chemical castration, and the lock-down prison unit. I remembered the sadistic attendants behind always-locked doors. I was told by one that he punished Mark, then sixteen, by making him lay face down under his iron cot for two hours and that he would be kicked back under if he tried to crawl out. It was an unthinkable threat, the return to hell.

Not long after that meeting, Mark acted out the worst mayhem against his physical surroundings yet. He knocked over or threw every piece of furniture in his path and then body-slammed himself against a large bay window. The windows' glass and frame shattered, and my brother jumped out of the jagged opening onto the house's front porch. Then, he was off the porch and running down the busy city street. Like his frantic escape attempt from the Columbus State Institution, twenty-five years earlier, police apprehended him. This time he was taken to the nearby Cleveland Psychiatric Institute for a ten-day evaluation. I was called. I wondered at the incongruous fate that had opened the door of seeming opportunity for Mark with the West Fourteenth Street house, only to shove him headlong into this sickening spiral of unintended consequences. He was held in Cleveland's dismal, public psychiatric hospital.

While at Berkeley decades before, I had read an article about the backgrounds of people who found themselves in psychiatric institutions. The one factor that they all had in common was that they had come from living circumstances within which they were never alone, and they could not get away from other people. Mark had lived in crowded, dysfunctional settings for thirty-two years and, in the professional jargon of the day, I was told that Mark had developed institutionalized mental illness. He was locked in a bleak, crowded, sterile ward in the large psychiatric institution. No one else on the ward seemed to have a cognitive disability whatsoever. Mark was adrift and quite out of place.

Maggie and I visited every afternoon. We would take giant bags of popcorn and my guitar. Everyone would gather around us in the one common room with its prison screen on the windows and its metal chairs bolted to the floor. I would start playing and we would have a spontaneous party. The residents and staff gathered around and even danced. I recall a white-coated psychiatric nurse dancing with several of the men under her care. The nightly popcorn was a hit, and the place took on an air of near-normalcy with music and laughter. After four evenings of our popcorn parties, on the fifth evening, the front desk guard told us that he had been told that the popcorn was banned. The bag of popcorn went back into the car; with its absence, the parties lost their appeal. Again the white-coated woman was back in her office with the door closed, and most of the patients wandered the blank hallways mumbling to themselves.

Mark was held at The Cleveland Psychiatric Institute, twice, following violent outbursts. Both times, he was contrite and confused. Mark knew that he had done something wrong and would apologize and repeat what he was told to say about how to behave. After the observation periods, he would be sent back into the toxic confines of the West Fourteenth Street house where Vicky would again begin dropping her poison pellets into Mark's dormant acid. The explosive reaction would be tripped, and he would again act out violently. The staff members had been confiding their perception of the Vicky-Mark problem with me but were unable to find a solution.

In February 1995, I was in Alaska working for a week at a statewide, multiple disability conference. The phone rang in my hotel room early one morning, and Maggie told me that Mark had badly beaten Mary, his aggressive female housemate. Mark had been permanently removed from the West Fourteenth Street House and was within the custody of a secure, emergency housing provider while decisions were made about his fate. Maggie went to see him. I was thousands of miles, and several time zones away. Given the terribly disturbing circumstance, I wanted to be by myself but, instead, I had to prepare to perform my keynote concert. Over the next days, I could only offer concerned support and appreciation for those managing the spirit-crushing, complex reality. Mark was without a home, without any mooring. My dark imaginings crowded in–could he be sent back into the bowels of a state institution as threatened? Would his passport to the community be revoked and would a dead-end institutional prison be his lot?

A few days later, I arrived back in Cleveland late in the evening. The following day, Maggie and I drove to the place where Mark was being held under triple guard. In the secure apartment, there were three curt staff women and Mark. Although it was within an old house, the place had a detention center air about it. My brother heard me enter and sheepishly came out of his bedroom and greeted me with deep remorse. I was vetted by the staff, questioned about where I would be taking Mark, how long I would be gone, and given a cell phone in case of emergency. It was a stunning level of control. Mark was clearly in serious trouble, and he knew it. He had beaten Mary, causing severe injuries requiring hospitalization. Mary's constant hitting, Vicky's voodoo, and Mark's stored fury had created the perfect storm. His future hung under uncertain judgement, and I waited.

After several days, I was informed that Mark was stepping down from locked-down custody to temporary community housing, while a long-term placement was sought. I had to scramble to immediately provide bedroom furniture for Mark's new residence. The house was a dilapidated duplex in an inner city, rough and run down slum. One side of the two family dwelling held four men–three with whom Mark had previously lived. Mark and one other man, and their staff, were alone on the other side of the double house. When we picked up Mark for an outing, we were vigilant and would carefully observe the characters on the street before we left the car. During the following months, one by one, the other men were all moved into the community. Then, Mark lived alone in the run down empty house, supported by ever-changing staff. The aging rental was owned by a nearby order of Catholic brothers who planned to tear it down, once emptied of its lone occupant. As a result, the house crumbled in moribund disrepair. Rain dripped through the ceiling, rodents ran up and down the staircase, and the toilet backed up. Problems were ignored. One evening, the electricity was turned off. Mark was afraid to go upstairs in the dark to go to bed. I suggested to the nearly hysterical staff woman that he sleep on the sofa in the candle-lit living room. Mark's housing there was supposed to be temporary, no longer than ninety days, but he lived in that slum dwelling for a full year. His terrible living conditions dragged on. I felt gratitude that he had not been moved back into an institution, but his circumstances were ghastly. My brother was unhappy, lonely, and confined in disgusting living conditions.

Since Mark's occupancy there began, the plan had been to establish a supported living home for him and a couple of other guys. Several meetings in the intervening months, with county personnel and the service provider, had presented scant housing options. Two of the rental houses offered to me for consideration, were located in the other side of Cleveland's sprawling megalopolis. Two others that I actively pursued were blocked, by the prejudice of landlords, in acts of blatant housing discrimination. When they learned of our intention, one property was suddenly already rented and the other was taken off the market. After months of delay, I expressed my frustration to the non-profit's exasperated executive director.

She said that her agency wasn't solely responsible for finding Mark a new place to live. With that comment, I questioned if the authority for finding Mark a rental was being shared with me? It was! I jumped at the chance and approached a friend in the real estate business, who also had a brother who lived with disability. We discussed my need to have Mark live nearby and, within a day, he found a small, three-bedroom rental on Edgewood Drive, two blocks away from my home. It was a cozy ranch house on a quiet street. The deeply wooded backyard opened onto the blacktop of a mall's parking lot.

The owner lived in New York City; he had been a high school chum. In fact, I remembered the house from visits when we were classmates at Brush High. Somehow, our past didn't matter. When he learned of our intent he changed the lease, demanding a full year's rent in advance. It was the ugly scourge of housing discrimination all over again—and from a fellow I had once called a friend! No matter, I was not going to be denied this perfect solution. I contacted an attorney specializing in disability law. He contacted the rental agency and received notification that indeed, one year's rent as security deposit was required. Hitting the brick wall of blatant housing discrimination, he put the landlord on notice that we were going to take him to federal court under the Fair Housing Act Amendments. After $1,500 in legal fees (the best money I ever spent), my old "friend" relented and returned the rental contract to its original first and last month's standard deposit. I signed the lease and scrambled to furnish Mark's new home. A generous friend offered to sell me a truckload of good, used furniture from his late parents' home. Thanks to his largesse, I was able to furnish Mark's house for a song. Moving day arrived, and a very jubilant Mark moved in–a glorious, happy day! He selected the master bedroom with windows looking onto the wooded backyard–his own personal, quiet forest. After 33 bitter years, Mark was moving into a serene, wonderfully normal house in my neighborhood. I could easily walk to see him. I delighted in dropping by and savoring the privacy and dignity that Mark had in the little house; the impossible had come true.

On Edgewood, Mark finally had a home of his own, a place where he could enjoy the simple gifts of a calm and normal community life. Mark thrived and blossomed as never before. Gone were the explosive acts toward people and property; gone were the yelling and cussing. Mark could be by himself, close his bedroom door, turn on his television or radio, or both, or sit in the living room with his staff person and watch TV or videos. For the very first time, he was able to keep whatever we gave him. Soon Mark had a leather jacket, a warm coat, boots, and gloves–items that lasted from year to year. His growing wardrobe was always laundered. Mark's room was orderly and kept neat by his own hand. At 41, he was at home for the first time since he had been a child. Mark had lived for nineteen years on a foul, fifty-bed ward, amid two thousand imprisoned souls, and in a chain of miserable places for another fourteen years. The house's staff became a sort of extended family for us, and Mark became part of a few of their own family circles. A lovely and maternal, African American woman slowly became his primary caregiver. Mark began attending her church's potlucks and her extended family's gatherings. Daryl, a gentle, painfully shy man, joined Mark at Edgewood. He became Mark's enduring housemate and friend.

Monticello House

In Cleveland and Northeastern Ohio, a nonprofit corporation, North Coast Homes, buys, rehabs, rents, and manages regular residential dwellings for supported and independent living by adults with cognitive disabilities. North Coast Homes is nothing short of a dream come true, for those of us long on the road toward community reintegration. I expressed interest, and a meeting was held with a North Coast Homes representative. Daryl's father and I explained our needs and desires in a meeting at Daryl and Mark's house on Edgewood. I specified that I wanted Mark to live within walking distance of my home in case of emergency. I also wanted a house with enough room that Mark could get off by himself to blow off steam as needed. I pictured a place with a dormer on the second floor where Mark could be alone. The North Coast rep stated that the house would have three residents, with a third to be added after the move. Three guys? Then, I really wanted to ensure that there would be "getting away" room for my brother.

No promises were made about time. The next year, we were told funding cutbacks had made waiting lists even longer. The house they were living in was fine, but I had signed the lease, and I was also responsible for maintenance, yard care, and snow removal. One late Sunday evening I was called by a frantic staff person to tell me the toilet was overflowing. Plunger in hand, we drove to the house, and I plunged out wads of paper towel that had clogged the toilet pipes. Problem fixed, and a good thing because it was the only trick I had in my plumber's bag. I paid for ongoing maintenance issues, to have a window air conditioner installed, and to have the back stairs rebuilt. I certainly was looking forward to my being freed of that load. After many months, our names advanced to the top of the waiting list. The process was in motion and I felt hope rising like a freed bird. One rainy November night, we drove to a potential house, recently on the market. The prospective house was on Monticello Boulevard, a busy residential and commercial street. A penetrating rain fell in sheets, that bitterly cold November evening, as we scurried into the side door of the brick bungalow. The place was homey and had a good sized front room, den, large kitchen, two bedrooms, and a bath on the first floor. There was a finished basement with laundry, plus a second floor with two bedrooms, a sitting room, and a full bath. It was perfect–lots of room for three guys–lots of separate spaces. I didn't need to poke around every room; I liked it on the spot. Darryl's father agreed, and we said yes. The paperwork took a month and the refurbishment took several more. What a wonderful job North Coast Homes did. New windows, furnace and air conditioner, new bathroom appliances, new kitchen appliances, new driveway and garage doors, fresh paint and carpets were all installed. They turned the place into a really problem-free, welcoming home. Darryl's father tagged a downstairs bedroom for Darryl, and I happily claimed the upstairs for Mark. It was exactly what I had wanted. I saw to the purchasing and installation of window treatments and the needed appointments for Mark's new bathroom. North Coast put in handrails on all the stairs per my request. The move was scheduled for June 2002.

But, the first time I went over to survey the house before Mark moved in, my heart sank. I had only seen the house on that one stormy night in November. But now, on a warm June afternoon, I discovered a previously unknown, very unwanted and quite upsetting neighborhood feature. As I walked down the driveway, toward the side door of the brick house, unseen, behind a high stockade fence, a large and ferocious-sounding dog began barking threateningly from the next-door neighbor's yard. The dog snarled and growled a deep roar; he threw himself against the board fence with his considerable weight, sounding as if he just might break through. This was a very bad thing.

In 1970, after running away from The Columbus State Institution for the Mentally Retarded, the Columbus Ohio Police, with the use of a fierce German shepherd police dog, had apprehended Mark. Ever since that horrific experience, Mark has known terror–an unreasoning visceral fear of dogs. When Mark sees or hears a dog of any size, from any distance or under any circumstance, he is thrown into a terrible hysterical wild-eyed paroxysm of panic. It doesn't matter if the dog is a yipping toy poodle behind a closed garage door, or a snarling Doberman within biting range. Mark's panic is the same whether a dog is barking or in visual proximity. To my great chagrin, Mark was moving into a house with an aggressive and ferocious dog next door, providing an ongoing trigger for his abject fear.

My joy was dashed. Thinking we might appeal to their compassion, I asked Mark's staff if they would speak to the neighbors. Not only unsympathetic, they were hostile to the gentle request for cooperation. However, after observing Mark's obvious fear as he ran from car to house as their dog menacingly barked, eventually they began to take the dog inside when they anticipated Mark's comings and goings. Their compassion had been awakened but the dog's panic-creating effect never softened. When I would go to the door to get Mark to go out for dinner or come to my house, his reactions varied–from sheer terror, as he ran to the car–to a paralyzing fear so severe that he would refuse to leave his home at all. My heart would sink in helpless, compassionate witness. I once heard horror and terror defined: terror is being afraid of one's own death; horror is the state of having witnessed the terrible death of another. Mark's fear can only be described as terror–wordless, and gut-wrenching to behold. Although the problem wasn't solved until the neighbors moved away, I did appreciate their belated efforts to help assuage Mark's severely frightened reaction.

Matthew moved in, completing the house's complement of three roommates, and the three men settled into a generally peaceful life together. The place was staffed and managed by Jewish Family Services Association, considered the best residential services providers in Cleveland's Cuyahoga County. One holiday season, not long after the Monticello house became a thriving center of community integration, I received an invitation to attend a family get-together at Mark's house. All of the families of the house's residents were being invited to a holiday open house, a chance for the little house to become an even more welcoming and inclusive community for those of us within its circle of love and connection.

We arrived. There, gathered for the event, was a little picture of America with rich diversity, engagement, and interdependence. The place was decorated with both Christmas and Hanukkah decorations. Darryl and his father Harold were there–the only Jewish members of the gathering. Harold, a widower and retired businessman, was his usual gregarious and garrulous self. His voice boomed out above the chatter of the gathering, and he and Mark had a spirited and happy exchange. Harold had always been very good to Mark, and their friendship brought me particular comfort. Harold had found a radio that was easy to operate, and he purchased one for Mark, in addition to the one that he bought for his son. Daryl was increasingly at ease in such social situations and made short forays into the festive gathering. Previously he had spent nearly all of his time in his bedroom, watching television. He greeted me, and I was delighted at his growing trust and his obvious pleasure with his new home. Matthew, the third member of the house, an African American man, spoke with his sister who, like me, provided much direct support for her sibling. They visited, and the warmth of their love was palpable. Maggie and I spoke with Ellie, the motherly woman staffing the house, a recent immigrant from Eastern

Europe. Her unflagging attention to the spread of food and drinks, and her genuine hospitality, gave the party a real family feeling. The house was, as always, immaculate. A boom box played music in the background, and I said a quiet prayer of thanks.

The years leading up to this moment of summary celebration had been long and difficult. This was the first time I had ever been invited to any event at Mark's home. There was no question that Mark was at home. He spoke to everyone as a proper host should–happy and relaxed. He was a social being, a man with a warm and generous nature, thriving on companionship and the pleasures of mundane life–taking out the trash, mopping the floors, and doing the dishes. Here, at last, Mark had a home of his own, interconnected with the lives of his housemates, and a stable group of care providers.

Over the years, Matthew moved out, and Kyle moved in. The three men of the Monticello Boulevard home were living lives not unlike those of any other lucky human beings. They all went to work at sheltered workshops, enjoyed their leisure, made choices about attendance at faith communities, and enjoyed eating out. Mark and Daryl appreciated the time and attention of loved ones and we had reached out to Kyle who had no family support. I think we were fortunate to be part of their open circle. Each of the three guys added to the others and enriched the lives of all of those who came into contact with them. Ours was a world that had not yet been completely accepted–the notion of community inclusion of all members.

Yes, stares, scowls, and sneers still happened at restaurants and at the mall. But, so also did moments of kindness and compassion. At a Starbuck's, two young men were seated at a table next to us. Mark always talks to strangers and draws them into his stream of consciousness, concerning whatever is currently moving through his mind. On that particular occasion, Mark was pumped about new tennis shoes that our sister Bonnie had just purchased for his birthday. He pointed out his shoes to the men. They could have ignored him; they could have smiled and returned to their conversation. But instead, they really engaged Mark, telling him that they thought his shoes were cool. Mark was very pleased. Such friendly, voluntary participation in Mark's world was not uncommon, but always touching. Every similar act of kindness was one more thread that tied Mark to the community and wove interest and color into the fabric of his life.

Every law in the quilt of Disability Rights legislation includes the overarching principle of inclusive settings. But, community inclusion is not a matter of legislation. It is a matter of the human heart. Every word and every interaction matters and can either aid or injure. Tolerance should not be the goal of how we treat each other. Rather, acceptance is a more elevated and more suitable target for social evolution.

Mark's move to the Monticello house represented the end point in an odyssey of twenty years of advocacy, five moves, and the gradual, but inexorable, progress toward community integration for one man and one family. The following poem, "Just A Home of My Own" summarizes Mark's life, up to the point of community reintegration, ending with the penultimate move to the Edgewood house. All of the elements of community integration were reached by the end of the time frame, about which this was written.

JUST A HOME OF MY OWN

Well my name doesn't matter–This is not about me
For my story is like many millions you see,
It's a story that needs to be told right away
Cause it's not in the past. No, still goes on today.
Like a knife it can cut to the heart–to the bone.
What I want isn't much, just a home of my own.

Now when I was a child, now when I was just small
I lived with my family though not long at all.
The doctor said they ought to put me away
For the family he said it'd be better that way.

So my clothes were all packed and we drove far away
To a big crowded place where five thousand did stay
With no family or love, crowded rooms with locked doors
Fifty beds fifty chairs, dirty cold cement floors.

First they stole all my things and I had to wear rags
And my shoes weren't my own just a pair from a bag.
And they hit me and hurt me, tried to make me behave.
How I hated each day and inside I just craved.

Like a knife it can cut to the heart–to the bone.
What I want isn't much, just a home of my own.

All the things that did happen, I never could tell.
I guess you could say I was living in hell.
And they gave us all drugs so we wouldn't get mad.
Some just slept or just stared, it was real, real bad.

Once they threw me down stairs, down a black fire escape.
And my leg bled and bled, they said it was a mistake.
Then the sore got real dirty and I got real sick

310

And even today it still hurts and I limp.

And I got a disease just like everyone there
Called hepatitis, though I don't really care.
But each year things got worse and the beatings worse too.
Once I tried to run away but the cops beat me too.

Like a knife it can cut to the heart–to the bone.
What I want isn't much, just a home of my own.

For nineteen long years I had to live there
Then I moved to a place they said had better care.
There were sixteen of us and my things still got taken.
It was crowded and dirty and I hated to wake in
That place every day but no one heard my voice,
'Cause they never asked me and it wasn't my choice.

So for eleven more years I remained in that place.
I was never alone in a nice quiet space.
Not a room of my own, not a place I could hide.
It was kind of like jail and with me locked inside.

Like a knife it can cut to the heart–to the bone.
What I want isn't much, just a home of my own.

Then I moved to a place that they called a group home.
There were eight of us there but no one had I known,
It was in a bad place, some folks called it a slum
And I talked to the folks on the street they called bums.
But my things still got taken and I never could get
Away from the people, you'd hate it I'll bet.
A woman kept hitting me, then my anger was shown.
Not a nice place to live, and it wasn't my home.

Like a knife it can cut to the heart–to the bone
What I want isn't much, just a home of my own.

All the places I've lived from the first to the last
Every staff, on each shift, the routines as years passed,

Every staff person's part now like dust 'neath my feet.
One by one they get pulled, now I'm losing my teeth.
They said in three years I will have lost them all,
'Cause I didn't brush right, was it really my fault?
No more teeth, no more food that you bite and you chew,
Teaching–nobody's job–not important to do.

Now these things that have passed, were they out of my reach?
Or were things that I missed lost, cause no one did teach?
Maybe past now for me but for those who can learn,
Will you fill their life's need or like me will they yearn?

Like a knife it can cut to the heart–to the bone.
What I want isn't much, just a home of my own.

Now they tell me I might get a place that is mine.
Maybe even a pet, that would really be fine.
A place that is clean, where I could always stay.
But there are other people don't want it that way,
Someone said I would cause lots of trouble and such
And they don't really want to live near me that much.
They don't even know me but they act real scared
Like I'll hurt them or maybe I'd break what is theirs,
That's not true, that's not fair, in the past I got mad.
'Cause of things I have told–I was angry and sad.
Places crowded and awful, places dirty and old.
And now I'm past forty, soon I'll be old.

Just pretend for a minute that my life is you,
And imagine that there was nothing you could do.
If you never had any place where you could go
Where you lived with your family or friends you did know.
If you lived in a place where some folks weren't so nice,
'Cause they were upset, 'cause they paid the same price.
If you lived with so many not related to you.
Tell me how would you feel; tell me what would you do?

Like a knife it can cut to the heart–to the bone.
What I want isn't much, just a home of my own.

Now my life will get better with new neighbors and friends.
And I thank my brother–on him I depend.
I know with his help this long struggle will end.
He knows what I want he's my guardian and friend.
What I want is a space I can call just my own,
What I want isn't much, just a home of my own.

© Jeff Moyer November 1996

Bonnie's Birthday Bash

Bonnie and I both supported Mark. During the fourteen years that I lived in California, Bonnie and her family visited Mark regularly and buoyed our parents through their mounting ordeals. Bonnie moved away from Cleveland in 1965. But despite considerable distances, she had been there for the long haul. I recall my guilt knowing that my sister was buttressing the family's fragile structure, while I watched from afar in California. When I moved back to Cleveland, I assumed the lead role as Mark's advocate. My proximity to Mark was a requirement, but not a sacrifice. I was glad to finally be substantially helping, and I felt very gratified to become the wheel horse in our team effort. Mark settled quickly into Edgewood House and thereafter his life became structured around weekly and yearly routines. Mark's weekdays were spent at the county-run sheltered workshop. Weekends he attended Sunday school at a special program for adults with cognitive disabilities and enjoyed our weekly meals out. Holidays were spent with my family. But hands down, the annual peak experience became Bonnie's birthday visit. Bonnie took on throwing Mark's birthday party, every year, beginning in the early nineties. Bonnie and her husband Dan would bring every element of the cookout and birthday bash, from burgers and briquettes to balloons. Dan would fire up the grill Bonnie had purchased, and her homemade party spread would be laid out in the kitchen and on patio furniture that she also had bought. Her creative, themed homemade cakes were always delightful and delicious. When she wasn't managing the festivity's food, Bonnie would snap smiling photos of Mark, with family members and housemates, for later framing and her birthday party memory books. My son Kyle was always there, as was my daughter Laura when, after she moved to California, her vacation in Cleveland coincided with Mark's big day. Dad's brother, Uncle Chuck, and Aunt Simi–

our family elders–always came, and their presence made the party a three generational celebration.

Mark would happily open his presents, but Bonnie herself was Mark's greatest and most anticipated joy. The required, six hundred mile, round-trip drive from Cincinnati was the price Bonnie paid to add her never-failing support. Abundant Christmas gifts and weekly phone contact gave Mark the sure knowledge of her constant love. Bonnie also served as my sounding board, as I have wrestled with problems and managed Mark's affairs. Our roles have differed; our love for Mark did not. In 2008, Bonnie and Dan moved to Texas. But year in, year out, Bonnie's stalwart attention to Mark's birthday did not waver. Family membership comes with birth, but the belonging and connection that make family members more than blood relatives can only be gained through the investment of time, attention, and treasure. Bonnie recognized her importance in Mark's world and, annually, made whatever sacrifice was required to serve Mark as his sister supreme.

Chapter 17: Beyond the Barrier

Talking Signs

In 1981, while still living in the San Francisco Bay Area, I visited Smith-Kettlewell Eye Research Institute's Rehabilitation Engineering Research and Training Center. San Francisco's Smith-Kettlewell incorporates one of two dozen such federally funded centers. The RER&T Center's mandate is to create engineering solutions that can assist people with disabilities in becoming employed. The Smith-Kettlewell Center applies technology to the needs of people with blindness and low vision. One small example of their work is a wonderful chromatic tuning machine that sits in my recording studio and can generate pure tones from across a three-octave range, allowing me to quickly tune any of my many stringed instruments to exact pitch.

That day, decades ago, I was visiting the Center, concerning a reading machine–the Talking Optacon engineering prototype. Smith Kettlewell was one of the field evaluation sites for the experimental system. I was managing the human factors research, under a grant from the Veteran's Administration. The Center's several knowledgeable, blind employees were giving me expert feedback, on the print to speech system's laudable attributes and considerable limitations. After lunch, we focused on Smith-Kettlewell's current technology innovations. Bill Gerrey, a brilliant engineer who is blind, demonstrated a new orientation access system that he and other inventors there had recently developed. The system, known as remote infrared audible signage, or RIAS, consisted of two new elements– infrared voice transmitters and receivers. Transmitters, positioned above the doors in the Center, broadcast repeating human voice messages over silent and invisible infrared light. The transmitters identified the room and gave directional, wayfinding location information. Bill showed me how to use the system. I pushed the only button on the TV remote-sized receiver and swept it in front of me, from side to side, as if I was using a flashlight to find a sign in darkness. As I pointed at Bill's lab door, "Engineering Lab, Engineering Lab, Engineering Lab," was announced in Bill's recorded voice through the receiver in my hand. The repeating loop continued, clearly announcing the room's identification and precise location, as I pointed at the lab's door. When I swept the receiver increasingly away from the sign, Bill's voice faded as static grew until the signal was lost. Then, with a movement back, I was again pointing directly at the sign and the door. The system was absolutely intuitive and easy to use. At Bill's urging, I borrowed the receiver and headed down the hall, effortlessly scanning and looking for the needed men's room. As I pointed at each sign, in turn, I learned the identification of each room and exactly where they were. Voila! Here was the men's room. I located it easily and independently. That was an entirely new experience! My standard method of finding restrooms was hit and miss. I would evaluate likely locations by the clues of other people's entering and exiting. If a door seemed promising, I would then look for the visual sign and get within a few inches of it to try and read it with my extremely low vision. More times than I wish to count, I have made the critical mistake of walking into the wrong restroom. For years, my large blind spot could blot out the WO in WOMEN and I would read MEN. Once, after walking into an empty women's room, I quickly stepped back into the restaurant with an authoritative posture, planted my feet and took out a note pad and pen from my sport coat pocket. I purposefully scribbled some gibberish on the open notebook. Then, I looked up with a stern expression and swept the tables with a look that welcomed a challenge. I said, to no one in particular but to everyone who saw me enter and exit, "City inspector."

I returned to the lab at Smith-Kettlewell by following the RIAS signs. I reflected on the time, six years before, when I was working as head of blind services for Berkeley's Center for Independent Living. Hale Zukas, CIL's powerfully effective accessibility advocate, took me to a corner in Berkeley to show me an intersection with Berkeley's revolutionary curb cuts. Hale wanted me to evaluate them from the viewpoint of a person with vision loss. The city's newly installed, model curb cuts were the first in the nation. CIL was a coalition organization, considering and balancing the needs of people with both physical and visual disabilities. As a result, the curb cuts were slightly offset from the straight line of sidewalk travel. This design allowed for preservation of the critically important curb for blind pedestrians, signaling the sidewalk's end and the street and crosswalk beginning. As I considered the uses for RIAS technology, I imagined how curb cuts and RIAS could both be implemented at intersections and throughout public transportation systems.

Although not ubiquitous, curb cuts were being installed in many public places in the San Francisco Bay Area of 1981. The developmental epic of RIAS has taken many turns as the technology has moved from the Smith-Kettlewell lab to the real world.

In 1993, I was consulting on disability access for a Cleveland museum's gallery redesign. I phoned Bill Gerrey to learn about RIAS technology availability. He directed me to Ward Bond, a technology developer who had taken over the product development process. Ward had established Talking Signs, Inc. to move the system into broad application. Smith-Kettlewell's location and early advocacy efforts ultimately resulted in many Talking Sign installations throughout her home city. San Francisco installations included City Hall, Main Public Library, a multi-level park, and shopping plaza, Moscone Convention Center, Caltrain Station intersections and BART stations–one thousand RIAS signs installed. The San Francisco supervisors had recommended RIAS on all public buildings. I offered my assistance and spoke to Ward at length about my belief in the importance of the system. Ward and I struck up an ongoing relationship. The next year, Ward had a heart attack and I was asked to volunteer to staff a Talking Signs exhibit booth at a national graphic sign conference in Chicago. That experience welded my conviction, and I recognized the difference my involvement could make in the progress of the access technology's implementation.

In 1995, I was performing at the American Council of the Blind's national conference in San Francisco. The conference hotel had been made a research lab as competing electronic orientation systems were being evaluated by conferees. The concentrated RIAS installation demonstrated the great utility of the technology. During the brief period when I was given the receiver to experiment with, I easily navigated the hotel's unfamiliar corridors and found the needed rest room, gift shop and Public Relations office quite by accident. A Smith-Kettlewell scientist was conducting the human factors research. I became more deeply committed, to see that the technology would be implemented on a wide basis. In 1997, I was invited to perform at the San Francisco Civic Auditorium for the twentieth-anniversary celebration of the historic 504 Demonstration and sit-in. I had traveled to San Francisco without a sighted guide and I arrived at the unfamiliar Civic Auditorium well in advance of my musical performance, in order to become oriented to the building and the stage.

Upon entering the Civic Auditorium, an employee recognized that I was blind and I was offered a Talking Signs receiver. This was my first experience in a public building with a comprehensive permanent Talking Signs installation. Learning orientation to a new building is an exhausting undertaking for me. I usually allow a full hour to learn a new building's layout so that I can independently navigate. But rather than having to concentrate on developing a mental map, memorizing specific right and left turns, counting steps and so forth, I simply used the RIAS system and was able to move easily and stay oriented without advanced planning.

I was in the Civic Auditorium for approximately five hours and had a truly liberating experience. In addition to locating restrooms, the auditorium and backstage entrances, water fountains, and other functional locations, I came across several event stations such as an oral history recording room and information booth. I took full advantage of all of the opportunities, thanks to my discovering them with RIAS. I found my travel ability and feeling of well-being instantly amplified. The effectiveness of the system and the freedom it provides cannot be overstated. Other users, like me, who are not especially good travelers, as well as real pros, have experienced and demonstrated a level of confidence and self-reliance never before possible.

Blindness isn't bad, I've been told, if you don't mind ambiguity. Not seeing faces, money, or beautiful sights must become acceptable losses. But not being able to find the restroom, the right bus, or not knowing the status of the 'Walk/Don't Walk' sign is not acceptable. I want to know exactly where those things are and have my direction precise before I begin crossing a busy street. That is what these accessible signs do. In a hotel in Chicago, I walked directly to the men's room and put my hand on the door's push plate, having been guided exactly by a RIAS transmitter–accurate to within one inch. In East Lansing Michigan, I scanned five buses in a transfer plaza. Hearing my bus's announced destination, I walked directly and confidently to the door of the waiting coach. In San Francisco, I monitored the 'Walk/Don't Walk' sign and stepped off the curb at the exact moment when the signal changed. In Cincinnati, I surveyed a new RIAS installation I had designed within a museum, and moved purposefully through the crowded exhibits following RIAS beacons. As always, I also used my white cane to find drop-offs or curbs and to avoid other pedestrians and obstacles.

In 2003, Ward Bond telephoned. By that time I was the Ohio Representative for Talking Signs and Ward told me that my congressman, Steven LaTourette, was on the House Transportation and Infrastructure Committee, soon to be writing the renewal of the Highway Bill. Our plan was for me to ask the congressman to have RIAS included in all Highway Bill projects. I put a folder together, including the impressive list of projects we had installed under various agencies of the Department of

Transportation. I included a letter of support from The Secretary of Transportation, Norman Mineta, and a full color spread on our technology from *The Cleveland Plain Dealer*. I was met by Congressman LaTourette and ushered into his inner office. Congressman LaTourette had studied the materials which I had sent in advance of my visit. He asked how he could help. I asked whether the Highway Bill could require RIAS in all public transit projects that it funded. He said no, that was regulatory in nature. Then he asked if I had a specific project in mind. I held my breath and then plunged in with a needed, on-the-spot, big idea. Nowhere was there an intermodal, regional demonstration of the technology–just isolated islands of RIAS access. I proposed a regional demonstration project involving intermodal access with RIAS transmitters on all buses and trains, at intersections, and within transit stations. We had the technology, the history of successful projects, and the research to support such a demonstration build-out. The congressman agreed to co-sponsor an amendment authorizing such a regional project if we could get two co-sponsors. Ward and I went to Washington for a week-long, intensive lobbying effort. We developed co-sponsoring support from Washington D.C.'s Congresswoman Eleanor Holmes Norton, a Democrat, and Republican Congressman Richard Baker, representing Ward's home district–Baton Rouge, Louisiana. We made friends with critical staff of the all-important Senate Banking Committee. Ward arranged speaking opportunities for me at national conferences of the Blinded Veterans of America and the American Council of the Blind. I spoke to those conventions, and both organizations passed resolutions supporting the RIAS MAP (Remote Infrared Audible Signage Model Accessibility Project) and RIAS overall. At those national conferences, over two years, we sat at a booth and asked people to sign individual letters of support for the drafted amendment to the Highway Bill. Folks lined up and waited patiently to add their names to the growing swell of support. Back in my office, my secretary laboriously typed their home and congressional representative's addresses on each original signed letter. We prepared to fax the 800 plus endorsements our advocacy had collected, when the time was right. We did it! RIAS MAP became SECTION 3046 of the 2006 Transportation Act and after bids from numerous cities Seattle was selected to receive the Federal funding for the project. Seattle Sound Transit installed RIAS transmitters in six of their regional, light rail, Amtrak, and bus transit stations.

Talking Signs technology provides information and orientation access–a civil right. There is no other means that offers directional, pointable, audible signs. Dogged progress has been made in establishing one RIAS international standard. RIAS transmits on a fixed infrared frequency. As a result, any receiver can be used to read the oldest RIAS transmitter, broadcasting the name of San Francisco's Cafe Mediterranean, installed in 1983. The Japanese National Railway has installed RIAS transmitters throughout the national train system and within one thousand crosswalks. In Norway, Italy, Canada, and in cities within the United States, islands of RIAS access exist.

Extensive research over two decades has demonstrated many aspects of the technology's effectiveness, including increasing safety and accuracy of crosswalk use. It has demonstrated that blind subjects develop mental mapping of large public places and ease of destination location when Talking Signs are installed. Wherever RIAS has been installed, people who have visual disabilities have become enthusiastic supporters.

In Colorado Springs and Lansing Michigan, home of Michigan State University, all city buses are signed with RIAS transmitters announcing the number and destination of each bus. There are always twenty-five or more students with severe visual disabilities attending MSU. Incoming classes of students are oriented to the system by the campus disability office, and they immediately start using their RIAS receivers. Some students, who had previously relied on door-to-door paratransit service, have begun to ride the buses and to enjoy their expanded freedom. When we have RIAS orientation access, we move, without advanced training or familiarity, within all public transit environments. Accessible signs for pedestrian crossings, buses and trains, station locations, and dynamic signs are all needed and provide seamless, intermodal access. It is time that signage and orientation access be seen on par with the physical access, now widely enjoyed by our friends who use wheelchairs, and the communication access available to our friends who are deaf. It is our vision to have a complete regional installation RIAS MAP project, to result in orientation access being mandated under the Americans with Disabilities Act Access Guidelines. As Congressman LaTourette told me, the matter is regulatory and we will have regulations!

The difficulty in making RIAS as ubiquitous as curb cuts is that blindness, as a specific disability, was not included within the Americans with Disabilities Act. The Senate leadership, through the office of Senator Tom Harken, felt that blindness would be too expensive and would hence kill the law's possibilities of passing. We were told blindness would be covered when the law was re-authorized. However, when the ADA Amendments Act of 2008 was passed, blindness was still not specifically addressed. Hard to believe, but true indeed. Hence curb cuts are required by ADA regulations, but accessible signals for pedestrians with visual disabilities at intersections are a matter of local discretion. The regulatory process–that is, forging new regulations–moves exceedingly slowly.

Following the Seattle demonstration project, Ward and I realized that we had to be far more specific in our next legislative goal. A few transit stations was just creating more islands of accessibility, not the regional demonstration inclusive of intersections, buses and trains, transit stations, and changing signs that we had envisioned and needed to gain regulatory inclusion. As a true demonstration, we needed to provide seamless accessibility in a region for those who can't see or read signs. So we began to plan for a regional build-out of the technology within a target city–our national city, Washington D.C. We conceptualized NEWMAP National Empowerment for Wayfinding Model Accessibility Project. As part of the 2010 Highway Bill re-authorization, we would develop support for the funds to put RIAS transmitters on all buses and trains, stations and intersections throughout the Capital City. We went to Washington for a solid week of lobbying every month from September 2009 through June 2010. We developed support from different disability national advocacy organizations and then bipartisan support from Congressional Representatives and Senators with lead sponsorship from Congresswoman Eleanor Holmes Norton. NEWMAP was scheduled as a high priority amendment for the Highway Bill of 2010. NEWMAP would have made Washington the first truly accessible city in the world. Our personal and legislative plan was closely timed.

We went to Washington for our final week, working with corporate and advocacy partners in early June. I would donate my kidney to save Ward's daughter's life on June 24. According to what I had been told, I would, be healed and strong enough in three months, to be able to go back to Washington with Ward in September, 2010, to finalize our efforts towards the amendment's inclusion in the planned bill. We hoped that NEWMAP would provide the demonstration needed to require that information and RIAS wayfinding access would be covered by ADA regulation. Were it not for the Republicans Congressional pledge to deny President Obama any legislative victory, the Highway Bill scheduled for 2010 and NEWMAP would have become a reality.

Talking Signs Inc. was a little business with no income at the end. Without NEWMAP, we were forced out of business in 2011. For the tens of millions of Americans with disabilities that block seeing or reading signs, this access is still denied. President of the company, Ward Bond exhausted his personal resources and died in poverty in 2015. I paid for our last year of travel to Washington through a second mortgage on my home. Our Smith-Kettlewell scientist, Bill Crandall underwrote hundreds of thousands of dollars of Talking Sign expense from his personal wealth. Bill died in 2018. We each lived by Jefferson's entreaty to pledge our lives, our fortunes and our sacred honor to this great cause. While access to information and orientation through signage, is still a civil right, it remains a right denied.

Justin Dart Oratory

There have been many figures that have moved through history, creating both political and interpersonal impact. Their role in directing monumental change has given them a type of immortality. On a personal level, their magnetism and charisma have made them beloved by many. Such celebrity draws the focus of frequent perspectives, reflections, and biographies in their wake. That was the remarkable significance of the late Justin Dart, Jr. The first time, and every time, that I heard Mr. Dart speak; I was transfixed by his unifying message and the power and eloquence of his oratory. Mr. Dart's strength came from first-hand experience, beginning with a devastating bout with polio at age 18. After a successful business career establishing Tupperware Japan, he met and married his wife Yoshiko at age 38. His passion for disability and human rights was developed in partnership with Yoshiko. Mr. Dart told me that living with paralysis from polio; he realized that he was shielded from the real limitations of disability by his wealth and his ability to hire support staff to compensate for his functional losses. The Darts were living in Japan when their mutual quest began. Justin and Yoshiko moved to a simple farmhouse in rural Japan without the supports, or basic conveniences, which he had previously enjoyed. During the period of contemplation in that simple Japanese farmhouse, they forged their commitment to disability and human rights. Justin Dart's powerful career as a disability rights leader was always imbued with his unifying message of the right to life, liberty, health care, education, and employment for all citizens within the inclusive American experience. Mr. Dart taught and urged collective action.

After I first heard him speak, I asked if he would consider allowing me to record his oratory for use in a future disability rights recording, integrating his oratory and my music. He graciously agreed to that request for future collaboration. But it would be eleven years before the opportunity would present itself, for me to follow up with Mr. Dart. During early 1999, I began planning a recording project requested by TASH, a leading disability rights organization of the day. The project would produce an album in recognition of their twenty-fifth anniversary. I inquired of TASH's executive director whether the organization had a relationship with Justin Dart, Jr. The director said that they did and that Mr. Dart had delivered the keynote address at their 1996 international conference. I filled her in on my decade-old agreement with Mr. Dart and I asked if she would contact him, concerning recording a few paragraphs of the 1996 TASH keynote for the album project. Mr. Dart agreed to the request.

In September 1999, I set up my recording equipment to capture and preserve Mr. Dart reading four paragraphs of double spaced text excerpted from his address from a few years earlier. A wheelchair user since his bout with polio in 1948, Mr. Dart lay in a hospital bed on the day of the recording, weakened by two heart attacks, twenty months before. We were recording in his home office in Washington, D.C. Mr. Dart, Yoshiko, and several of their foster daughters from Japan greeted me warmly. The Darts maintained a demanding schedule of advocacy and meetings, in spite of his diminished strength following his heart attacks. That September day was no exception. The recording task was taking valuable time and making real demands on his diminished physical strength. That beautiful afternoon, Mr. Dart was wearing a crisp white shirt, red, power tie, and dress slacks. He was breathing oxygen powered by a humming machine that was highly audible in my microphones. I reluctantly asked if the machine could be turned off–a clearly audacious request. Mr. Dart gently consented without comment and asked Mrs. Dart to please turn the powered oxygen system off. The recording began and he quietly read the text. I asked him to read it again. I think that we both knew that the recordings were lacking the verve and energy of his famously powerful eloquence. I stopped the recording and suggested that his words would be heard by people years later, and I asked if he could imagine six thousand people listening to him for the first time.

Mr. and Mrs. Dart exchanged a few quiet words about the situation and I was deeply touched by the obvious love and regard that the couple held for each other. Upon his request, Mrs. Dart raised his hospital bed so that he was sitting more fully upright. Mr. Dart asked her if she would please bring him some orange sections. As he ate the orange, he told how

324

his father, once a professional football player, would eat oranges at the half to gain strength for the conclusion of the game. Mr. Dart cleared his throat and began to read. He spoke with full, majestic, electric power. The recording was perfect and needed no re-takes whatsoever. Mr. Dart's speeches were famous for stirring phrases that made every audience feel like he was acknowledging and lifting them up as great contributors to the cause of disability and human rights, while challenging them to dig deeper; to motivate and educate others and continue to strive toward the goal of a fully inclusive society.

As I was packing up my recording gear, I asked Mr. Dart about his wonderful speaking style. Mr. Dart reflected that when he decided to enter public political life, he knew that he would need to be a powerful public speaker. He had worked over several years to master oration, by repeatedly listening to the recorded speeches of Franklin D. Roosevelt and Teddy Roosevelt– two historic figures whose majestic speaking styles had been recorded and whom Mr. Dart greatly admired. By repeatedly listening to the pacing, inflection, emphasis, and articulation of two of the twentieth century's finest orators, Mr. Dart began to build a foundation for his own powerful and towering public speaking.

During the years leading to the signing of the Americans with Disabilities Act, Mr. and Mrs. Dart traveled to every state five to ten times for Justin to speak and uplift audiences toward political action in support of the developing ADA. His oratory expressed an inclusive and sweeping vista of challenge and opportunity, a call to action and an elevated and patriotic statement of hope. His speeches rang out with unforgettable phrases and themes, and with memorable intonements, articulating the Disability Rights perspective. Justin Dart expressed the singular and overarching principles that would be embodied in the ADA, as well as affirming the other broad brush ideas of right to life, inclusive education, the arts, assistive technology, universal health care, employment, supported living, and community integration.

I took my recordings into Metrosync Studios–where I had recorded twelve albums with Frank Vale, my talented producer, collaborating musician and arranger–where the TASH album was being produced. Frank filtered out the noise of city buses and airplanes. I wanted the recording to sound as if Mr. Dart was speaking in a great hall. Frank added several digital effects to create the audio illusion that Mr. Dart was speaking in an arena or vast public place, as he often had. Mr. Dart's phrasing and pauses gave the perfect sound tableau within which his echoed words gave the desired effect. I have played segments of the four-part recording at numerous presentations across the country, sharing the inspiring sound of this historic man's great voice. Justin Dart, Jr. died in his home on June 21, 2002. All movements need leaders–spokespersons and standard bearers whose speeches direct, educate and motivate. His voice still rings out, years after his death. In 2008, I gained the support of The Smithsonian Institution's National Museum of American History to include Mr. Dart's oratory in their planned traveling exhibit of disability history and to be held in their permanent collection. The National Constitution Center in Philadelphia dedicated Mr. Dart's battered wheelchair as a permanent exhibit on July 28, 2012. At the press conference for that day dedicated to disability rights, I played the "ADA Anthem" and a segment of Mr. Dart's recorded oratory. They now use those captured recordings, in their ongoing educational programming on disability rights. The following are Mr. Dart's keynote excerpts which he read on that warm September afternoon in 1999. Sadly, my stirring, but brief recording seems to be the only good quality voice archive of this singular figure of America's disability history:

You have provided cutting edge leadership, initiatives that have given millions of Americans with disabilities the potential to move out of institutions, out of poverty, and off of welfare to productivity and community. From independent living, IDEA, and deinstitutionalization, to supported employment, supported living, assistive technology, self-advocacy, and the historic ADA; you have led the way. Your passionate principles and creativity have enlarged the lives of millions of people like me. I thank you, I congratulate you on your courageous leadership–you are the real patriots of today!

Americans hunger for a positive agenda; a vision based on shared values, common sense, and a record of practical solutions. You have created the foundations of that agenda. Let us refine it and communicate it to America.

I propose a revolution of empowerment. A revolution that will empower all twenty-first century Americans to live their God-given potential for self-determination, productivity, and quality of life.

Our vision, America's task now, is to go forward–to keep the promise of justice for all. Envision an America for all! Envision education for all! Envision health care, jobs and communities for all! We are not going to be second-class citizens anymore. We will live free and equal in our communities. We envision freedom, dignity, and life for all! We will fight to the end of time for equal access to the American dream.

Absolutely. Don't wait for anyone. You don't need a title or an invitation to make history. You can be a revolution of one. Today–Speak out! Reach out! Mobilize! If you can motivate; if you can activate; if you can educate just a handful of those beautiful Americans who are now spectators in the struggle–we can win! Unity is power. Let us overwhelm fear and fallacy with our vision of an America that empowers all. Solidarity–forever!

The Late Justin Dart, Jr. Recorded Saturday, September 18, 1999
Field engineering: Jeff Moyer and Dan Dotson

Contract for Social Support

Growing up, I was always moved by family and community singing of everyday songs. It brought us together. Then in the sixties, songs sang out about Civil Rights, peace, a clean environment, and the end of inequality. Such songs were life's soundtrack for many of us. Beginning in my teens, I sang anywhere I could–in coffeehouses, in my brother's institution, during Saturday tutoring programs, in churches, on urban porches. When I began working with kids, I led singing and taught guitar. Then as an adult, I began to sing in arts programs, at camps, in schools, and for children's programs of many sorts. Diversity programs were popular, but disability wasn't included. There just weren't any songs that addressed disability. At forty-three, I began to earn my living through music. I sang traditional and my own songs, that carried many messages, including the normalcy of disability and broader themes of forgiveness, love, service, and personal responsibility.

Somehow, though, audiences' passive listening to my solo singing didn't seem to have much impact. Remembering my own experiences with group singing, I recognized that my captive audiences needed to be more involved. They needed to sing the songs themselves. Perhaps, then, they might internalize the messages of the songs. I began writing new songs that were easy to learn. I used the traditional style of call and response, simple choruses, and big "hooks", typically repeating the name of the song. It wasn't difficult to get my youthful audiences to sing. But from my informal observation, their attitudes didn't seem to change. Singing by itself didn't do it. The big ideas weren't getting through. Perhaps, young people needed

327

discussion to drive the concepts deep into their growing understanding. I wrote an activity and discussion guide called *We're People First*–A Celebration of Diversity. Each lesson was tied to a song. The companion recording included twelve songs plus karaoke-style accompaniment tracks. I believed that they would think, they would sing, and they would come to own the ideas as the lyrics were internalized. Adults loved the materials, but I still wasn't certain I was getting through to many kids.

In 1997, I was in Indiana speaking to a middle school audience. *We're People First* had been published, and was being used within the school's classrooms. My road show taught or reinforced songs from the collection and urged students to stand up for each other. I wanted to educate school communities about the need to stop the ridicule of kids being devalued because of their differences, including disability. The thought came to me on stage that a contract–a commitment–was needed for them to make a personal pledge to stop the pervasive problem of exclusion, ridicule, and violence against devalued students. On the spot, I challenged the students to make an inner commitment not to ridicule anyone else for any reason and to ask others to stop if bullying, put downs, and name-calling persisted around them. I spoke about Mark and the suffering he had endured. I specifically referenced the epithet "retard", since it was in such common use as hate speech. The students and their teachers were silent as I asked them each to privately consider making the courageous commitment to end such hurtful language. After the assembly, I was taking my two-wheel cart full of gear and instruments out of the school, requiring the slow and careful easing of the heavy cart down the school's main staircase. The wide stairs led to the school's front doors. Seventh and eighth-graders, laden with backpacks over their parkas, rushed noisily toward the glass doors, streaming around my sighted guide and me. Four teacher monitors flanked the staircase and watched and listened to the children as they hurried toward the doors.

Amid the end-of-the-day hubbub, one voice shouted above the tumult. "Out of my way, retard!" The vulgarity seemed to hang in the air. Four teachers and scores of kids heard the insult. They had all been in the assembly minutes before, but no one said a thing. If the term, "nigger", "bitch", "kike", "prairie nigger", or any other expression of hateful language had been used, the child would have been grabbed, sent to the principal's office, given consequences and perhaps counseling. But "retard" did not register in the same way, although it carried the same razor-edge viciousness and intent to hurt.

I went home and began work on a musical play with counseling guide named, *How Big* Is *Your Circle?* The play portrays the experiences of victims, bi-standers, and bullies. The story follows seven students as they learn courage, unity, and bind their wounds. Each of them recognizes their common experience of exclusion and ridicule due to a diverse range of factors. They realize that, together, they can protect themselves and change the school culture by challenging put-downs and bullying through united action. They develop a supportive school community. For students, it addresses their current life circumstances; for adults, reading the play does help connect us to those monumental moments in our childhood that shape or twist us into the people we become.

The play's premiere was scheduled as a grand event at the School of Fine Arts, in Willoughby, Ohio, where sixty-five young musicians and actors prepared for the opening performance. I had spent time with the students, and their directors had focused their attention for months, on the play and its content. But even after the serious work of memorizing their parts and going over and over the play before its premiere production, I still heard young actors refer to each other as retards.

After puzzling over how to break through the numb social skin of students, I had an inspiration. Maybe what was needed was a process to focus individual commitment. So I developed such a written personal commitment–a one page "Contract for Social Justice". The group-process-oriented document sets out basic points of understanding and agreement. Groups of students around the country have signed and committed to these simple guidelines for more inclusive living. Perhaps, this will assist some in developing new awareness and new behaviors.

CONTRACT FOR SOCIAL JUSTICE

Purpose: This personal contract has been developed for the purpose of bringing focus to a number of values and standards that require personal commitment and action to help realize. Agreement to sign this contract does not mean that an individual can automatically live according to these standards. Rather, this agreement is a set of principles that can serve to guide one's thinking, decision-making, and actions, and can serve as high-minded goals for effective living.

Points of understanding:

1. I understand that any social group behaves according to the actions of individuals in the group.

2. I understand that social groups are both formal and informal. Formal groups may be organized or exist because of circumstance–such as members of a class. Informal groups exist whenever people share common space–such as students sitting together on a school bus.

3. I understand that I am responsible for the actions of groups with which I take part whether my actions are active or passive.

4. I understand that actions of social groups can result in injury to others by their exclusion from the group, by ridicule, and by speech and physical action that is intended to harm or embarrass.

5. I understand that one individual, taking courageous action, can protect another who is being targeted by a social group through speaking up and protecting the right of all people to be safe from exclusion, ridicule, and violence.

Points of agreement:

1. I agree to interrupt the use of put-downs, and ridicule of any individual or group for any reason including but not limited to: Race, religion, age, gender, country of origin, physical appearance, academic or skill ability, economic status, disability, or sexual orientation.

2. I agree to protect the rights and dignity of all others by speaking out when I hear put-downs, ridicule, or other negative speech toward another in my presence.

3. I agree to open myself socially to all individuals and to be willing to take action that includes protecting individuals that may have experienced exclusions or put-downs previously.

4. I agree to work to develop patience, understanding, and kindness toward others and to be guided by the simple and powerful Golden Rule.

5. I agree to promote social groups that include anyone interested in joining and that promote a positive and healthy regard for all people.

6. I agree to support others who have also committed to these principles and to take individual responsibility for the creation of a safe and inclusive school, community, and world.

Signature   Witness   Date

At a concluding workshop in Coeur d'Alene, Idaho, following a week during which I had worked with every fifth-grade classroom in the sprawling district, every one of the fifth-grade students had signed the contract and promised to attend to its precepts. There, twelve hundred fifth-graders read the document aloud, and the unity of the students was palpable.

At a Starbuck's recently, I waited with Mark at the counter for our order. Mark was speaking to a stranger and I was attempting to re-direct Mark's attention to me instead. Two young men also stood at the pick-up counter. One of them said with a sneer in his voice, "Retard!"

I focused my attention like a laser on the young speaker. "That's hate speech. My brother has a cognitive disability which he can't help. But, your insult is pure and simple hate speech. Mark does not deserve your contempt, he deserves your kindness." The young man did not respond. I wonder how he might have behaved if he had been asked to consider the Contract for Social Justice when he was in school.

Chapter 18: Rooted In Strength

Upper One Percentile

In 1979, my son, John Kyle, was three years old. We had been rather undecided about what to call him. At first, it was John, then John Kyle, then J.K. That morphed into Jake. Then, we went back to just John. I can't recall what the name was that we were using in 1979, but whatever it was, we lovingly referred to our son with the fatigue that parents can lapse into when talking about a child who runs them ragged. John was high energy, bright, and nearly exhausting to live with. Compared to other kids, he was a real handful. Sandy was a wonderful mother, very much cut from the holistic cloth of the seventies California counterculture, and she sought and applied her best efforts toward natural solutions to the situation of our son's whirligig energy. Sandy tried diets that eliminated normal foods that might cause hyperactivity. Books like *The Feingold Diet* filled our bookshelves. John had scant access to junk food. To illustrate how pristine his diet had been, on Halloween as he sat on the floor examining the contents of his trick or treat bag that had been scattered around him, he picked out the little box of Sun Maid Raisins–the only thing he recognized among the treats that had been dropped into his Halloween bag.

My proclivities in seeking a solution to the stressful situation were different. My collegiate training in Psychology and Social Work made me focus on a psychosocial cause for John's highly energetic and very demanding interactive style. I found a family psychology clinic that offered a diagnostic service for young children. We answered questions concerning John's mental flexibility, his ability to shift from one mindset to another, problem-solving, planning, organizing his thoughts, and controlling his impulses. We were told that these skills were critical to anyone's capacity for flexibility and frustration tolerance. After the clinician had seen John for six sessions, we were called in for the definitive answer concerning John's circumstances. The clinician shared that John was not hyperactive, but that he had a low threshold for frustration. The psychologist suggested that we should be more patient with him and that he would develop a higher threshold for frustration over time. I puzzled over the meaning of what I was hearing. I knew that I had really tried to be a patient, good parent. I felt like I was being told that it was me who had a low tolerance for frustration and that if I developed patience, things would get better. So I went home, attempting to become yet more patient.

When John was four, he participated in a preschool, run by a Quaker church–a group highly patient by reputation. One morning, I went to John's little preschool to play and sing with the children. While the other little ones sat politely and sang along, John was on his feet, exploring things outside the circle of my musical activity. Sandy and I were taken aside, and the teachers speculated that John might be hyperactive. I explained to them the reassuring professional opinion that he had a lower threshold for frustration than other children. Their blank expressions suggested that this hypothesis about child behavior had not been part of their training.

A similar dilemma developed in kindergarten. John's difficulty in staying focused and participating in the quiet group learning activities continued to present problems. During a school-requested meeting, John's earnest kindergarten teacher reviewed the now-familiar problems with us. We patiently explained that John had a low threshold for frustration and that he would outgrow this behavior as he matured. She did not agree with us and reiterated her functional assessment that our son had hyperactivity. We left the school unconvinced and not understanding how such a gulf between perspectives could exist. We had put John through a rigorous evaluation. A specialist had given us a diagnosis that was not widely understood, but that we believed.

In August 1982, we moved from Palo Alto to Cleveland, and John started first-grade at Coventry Elementary School in Cleveland Heights. Coventry School had been built on the open school model, wherein low walls separated classes, but not noise. The place was a little disorienting for me with the sounds of other classrooms fully audible and attention-grabbing. The first-grade teacher reported early in the year that John was bright, restless, and had a hard time attending to the instruction she was providing. The teacher suggested medication. She said that children with hyperactivity were being genuinely helped through pharmaceutical solutions. We patiently explained that John was not hyperactive, but had a lower than normal tolerance for frustration. I silently thought that some ceiling to floor walls might help all of the children's ability to concentrate. Medication had been proposed before; however, we were opposed to the approach for several reasons. On the other hand, we were seeing such a consistent problem that there was no question that John had a real behavioral pattern that was getting in the way of his learning. The ongoing, discouraging feedback from teachers continued. We moved in 1983 to

Highland Heights and a new school system. John was always well-liked by his teachers, but the drumbeat persisted that he was the class clown, that he distracted other kids, and that he often had trouble concentrating. The report card comments were unchanging, and his procrastination and avoidance of his little homework assignments proved to be an increasing problem throughout the first three years of elementary school.

We decided to explore chemical imbalance or some organic brain issue that might be vexing his scholarship. At the end of third-grade, I heard about a promising evaluative program at Cleveland's University Hospital. Run by their child psychiatry clinic, it promised an inter-disciplinary, thorough assessment of causality for behavioral and learning difficulties. That summer, John spent many afternoons being evaluated, tested, probed and analyzed by the interdisciplinary team. But it didn't come without a cost to John, who was troubled by the experience. After one of the first sessions, he asked me why he was there. John shared, that while in the waiting area; another child asked him why he was seeing the doctor. John said he didn't know. The boy shared that he had tried to kill himself. In spite of my non-judgmental and careful explanations, John was developing a negative attitude about being evaluated again. At the end of the assessment, we were given the team's conclusions. The verdict: John had both visual and auditory processing deficits (learning disabilities) and was gifted. At last! With great relief, I read and re-read the summary that shed welcomed, clarifying light on our son's reality. The letter went on to recommend John's enrollment in a Montessori School that had a class for kids who were gifted and had learning disabilities. We visited with the principal one evening after work and heard about the fantastic results they had in turning kids' academic and social lives around. Things were looking up–this was manageable. The principal promised that John could learn to self-direct his learning needs and would, in time, grow out of the dysfunction of his current pattern with school life. We were sold. The school was private and its tuition wasn't cheap, but what could be more important?

We signed up and for three years John attended the school with his classroom of nine teachers and thirty kids. We were enlisted as partners in this new confederation of adults addressing John's educational growth and behavior change. Meetings with his teachers developed a familiar pattern. Sandy and I would first meet with the phalanx of educators who would somberly review John's behavior and classroom performance, and then poor John would be summoned. With the stern jury of his teachers looking on, I would then become the spokesperson and enforcer for the assembly and I would tighten the thumbscrews of their judgment. John would listen, tight lipped, and I would feel that I was participating in the inexorably slow attempt to turn the stubborn rudder of his will. After the second year, the Montessori School, vexed, suggested that John should undergo a comprehensive psychological evaluation with a child psychologist who specialized in learning disabilities. This time, a twelve-session evaluation was undertaken. My poor son! The therapist, week by week, would apply his best clinical skills as he attempted to develop John's psychological profile. After the last session, we expected gems of insight. For John's ordeal and our time and money, the therapist instead offered that he had never met a child so unwilling to open up. He said John would not talk, so there was nothing to report. Twelve hours of one-on-one and nothing to say? John's behavior made sense to me. He had been put through many batteries of tests and I suspect that he just decided to shut down.

Overall, though, John did have academic successes within the Montessori program and developed some genuine friendships among his classmates. The three years were well spent, although the constant inconsistencies between the school's predictions and pronouncements, and my dear son's experience were disquieting. He didn't seem to quite fit their model, but I was heartened by the idea that they were preparing him for a return to regular education and success in the classroom. Although the school did offer classes through eighth-grade, we decided to return John to middle school in seventh-grade, when everyone else would be starting the new school as well. The blending of all the district's elementary schools into the combined seventh-grade, would make John just one more student in the churning pubescent tide. We hoped his three-year hiatus from his local elementary school would not stand out. The teacher corps from Montessori halfheartedly agreed that John was ready to return to public school and with a final serious entreaty to him about applying all of his adaptive skills, they bid him a fond farewell.

Middle school began, but midway through the first semester, John was in deep academic trouble; we were summoned for the all too familiar parent conference. Each, in turn, the unsmiling instructors reported the familiar litany; failed tests, incomplete assignments, distracting behavior. I explained that John had learning disabilities and that he would benefit from some special consideration—perhaps tutoring or a coach to help him get and stay organized. I shared the reports from his previous school and the earlier evaluation. The school district had its own tests. So Nola, the district's psychologist conducted yet another maddening series of tests for John. She phoned about the test results. Nola evenly stated that John had no learning disabilities whatsoever. According to Ohio special education regulations, John had no disability and was entitled to no services. I was dumbfounded. How could it be that University Hospital's team had found very specific learning disabilities, and that three years of expensive and tailored education had focused on them–and now they did not exist? Nola was quite clear that she was correct and that the behaviors we were seeing had nothing to do with a disabling condition. She stated that John was intentionally being difficult, hyperactive, impulsive, and inattentive. We were told that we needed to get with the program and let him grow out of this "stage". He needed more structured help at home and consequences to assist him with the development of self-discipline. Sandy began spending every evening sitting with John, as he suffered through his homework and attempted to work through the math that he had not learned during classroom instruction. It was an ordeal for everyone. Just before his first semester ended, he applied a sudden burst of focus and effort, and he completed his term papers and did well enough on his finals to pass every course. With that demonstration, Nola was fully vindicated. But the pattern continued of his semester-ending, heart-stopping flirtations with failure. Nola crowed that his gallows conversion demonstrated his true abilities. He could do the work, he could focus, and he could succeed if he wanted to.

For six years, Nola and I had regular conversations, meetings, and even lunch. I repeatedly asked for the kind of assistance John needed. But Nola said that John was not eligible. Her messages to me varied, from predictions about at what year marker John would reverse his course as her own sons had, to exasperated declarations that I was a nervous father and should back off. And always there was the underlying accusation that John just wasn't doing his part, wasn't concentrating, and wasn't succeeding because of his own failings. His last minute efforts saved him repeatedly from failing and summer school. Sometime during middle school, John decided that he preferred his middle name, so John became Kyle. Kyle and I did the uneasy dance that changed in form, but never in its basic dynamic. I was the stern, but supportive father; he was the creative, difficult, and sometimes recalcitrant son.

Soon Kyle's school life blossomed outside of the classroom. He discovered drama, music, leadership, and his own personal style. He was well-liked by students, teachers, and counselors. Kyle always organized and led a band that was a hit during the annual battle of the bands competition. Kyle was a real offbeat original, and during his band's shows, he integrated his considerable stage presence, sense of humor, musical talent as songwriter, guitarist, performer and band leader, into real entertainment. One band was called Pre-Atomic Plaid and they all wore mismatched plaid shirts, vests, pants, and hats. Giant plaid underwear was strung on a clothesline above the band and across the stage. Some of his songs were gentle and some dripped with edgy teenage angst. Kyle acted in every play, taking the lead, in his senior year, in two productions including *Les Misérables*. He also acted, every summer, in a youth theater program. Kyle ran for and was elected Vice President of Student Council, just as I had. In general, Kyle's school life was a terrific success, while his academic performance was nothing short of heartbreaking.

Kyle graduated young at seventeen. After a year delivering pizzas he and I packed up his Volkswagen Fox and he beeped goodbye and drove to Florida to enroll in Full Sail University, the best recording engineering program in the country. Full Sail, although oddly named for an accredited collegiate program, was a two-year, hands-on undertaking. Kyle applied himself. Quarter by quarter, he passed his coursework in sound engineering, reinforcement, and recording. The last quarter of his program, he called me and wrestled with the dilemma of not having learned the difficult math (always his worst subject), required for competence in the studio. Kyle decided to repeat the last quarter, which included the math course, delaying his graduation. Kyle learned what he needed to know, graduated, and proudly accepted his degree in recording engineering. He drove home, arriving Christmas Eve after his twentieth birthday. He began to look for the needed internship, the hazing that recording engineering demands of its would-be apprentices who are seeking to become sound engineers and producers, at the helm of the mixing board for performances and recording sessions. Internships were not paid and were indefinite in their duration. A source of free labor for studios, they promised the intern only the scant potential of crawling into one of the scarce, minimum wage jobs, without benefits, that might open some fine day. With Kyle's newly minted degree, he soon found an internship.

The work was with a company that provides live performance sound amplification or reinforcement. Kyle's job was to manage the monitor mixing board during performances and give the various band members individualized, custom mixes through their stage monitors of the blended sound the band was creating. While on stage, the monitor is the speaker that delivers the mixed band's sound to the musicians, with different sound alloys required by different members. The demands of the job required multi-tasking of real-time attention to numerous details. For anyone, it would be nerve-racking and stressful. But Kyle's lifelong difficulties with attention to multiple tasks and maintaining focus made it impossible. After several months of hard-wrought effort, Kyle realized that he was not being successful. He resigned with a heavy heart and a spirit battered by the experience.

A friend's teenage daughter had been diagnosed with attention deficit disorder by a specializing psychiatrist. I wondered if Kyle might agree to be evaluated by the psychiatrist, whose specialized techniques had assisted in diagnosing my friend's daughter. Kyle concurred and he made an appointment. Following the tests, the specialist told Kyle that he had attention deficit, hyperactivity disorder, in the upper one percentile of severity. After eighteen years of flawed diagnoses, and the refractive blur each created, the answer was finally at hand. Each wrong, labeling pronouncement had projected its limiting overlay onto Kyle's life and education. Finally, there was a clear, definitive, and logical explanation of what had been true from the beginning. It was a relief and a terribly frustrating moment. I had been unsuccessful in helping my son gain the handle he needed to grapple with his own disability, his own style, and his own unique life's demands. Then I found a great book that detailed what ADHD is and how it works. Kyle's life was described in spades. The inability to concentrate until disaster looms–the disorder and disorganization–it was all written large in Kyle's life story. When Kyle was twenty-one, the truth was revealed. But Kyle's self-esteem, education, and schooling had been spent in the search.

ADHD involves superior intelligence along with the incomplete connections between the left and right hemispheres of the brain. Without full engagement of the left hemisphere, the "executive" functions of planning, anticipating consequences, delayed gratification, and attention to mundane details go wanting. Creativity is no problem and spontaneous, intuitive, and artistic expression blossom in full measure. I learned, and I talked to Kyle at length about the condition. After Sandy and I divorced, she became an acupuncturist and Chinese medical practitioner. Kyle had tried several prescription pharmaceuticals that promised help, but none proved successful. However, a Chinese herbal formula that his mother prescribed proved to be of immediate benefit.

I was struck with the parallels between our lives. We had both experienced real disabilities that had been denied by experts, misdiagnosed, and our parents had wholeheartedly committed to the judgments of professionals concerning our children's circumstances and needs. We had both suffered from the resulting disconnection, as we struggled with tasks beyond our abilities. When we learned the true nature of Kyle's disability, I apologized to him for the years during which I hadn't understood what he was living with and for not finding the needed path through the diagnostic labyrinth. ADHD is still poorly understood by most of us, and I know that every teacher, counselor, and therapist that Kyle worked with did his or her level best to help him. Kyle's answer to my apology tells a great deal about the wisdom and compassion of my son. He said that it was okay and that he was glad that he grew up as he had. I asked what he meant. He said that he always knew he was different, but never knew why. Kyle told me that his life experience had taught him not to judge others and to have compassion for those who are different. His life had taught him that differences are normal, to be expected, and generally, can't be understood or explained. I am still working on absorbing that wisdom. As William Wordsworth wrote in 1807, "The child is father of the man".

Comedy Club

Since childhood, Kyle had watched me rail against the ridicule of people with disabilities–especially cognitive disabilities. During a sketch on *Prairie Home Companion*, Garrison Keeler spoke about how depressing it was that his daughter had a retarded cat. I turned off the program and wrote a letter of protest to the show. In response, I received a non-committal letter from the producer. For many years on "Car Talk", Tom and Ray Magliozzi regularly lowered themselves to cheap one-liners concerning having to "retard" a spark plug. I raised my voice in protest (along with others, I expect) and the insult stopped. On "This American Life", one of the stories dealt with the speaker being seen as a "retard" when she was participating as a helper on a museum tour with a group of adults with cognitive disabilities. I engaged with Ira Glass, the producer, and he agreed to change the show's policy about the use of that word. It seems that even on NPR, "retard" jokes are the last bastion of allowable, edgy ridicule of "the other". After the election of George W. Bush, the late Robin Williams joked about "retarded Texans". Crude and cruel ridicule of people with cognitive disabilities is, sadly, the rule, not the exception. Such vicious word assaults have always brought my blood to a boil. Kyle was born of that cloth and has joined me in my opposition to such exclusionary intellectual elitism.

In 1997, Kyle was twenty-one when he returned to Cleveland from Florida with a hard-won degree as a sound engineer. He had been dislocated by time and distance from his high school friends who had remained in Cleveland. That winter, Kyle re-connected with his circle of male friends from high school. One Friday evening, they met for drinks at a comedy club. The young men sat around the cocktail table and sparred in that posturing, jocular way, that testosterone-driven males have of pushing each other against the edges of propriety and comfort. Then the lights dimmed and the comic began. His first offering was a retard joke. So were the second and the third. Kyle's internal pressure built beyond the point of giving the guy a pass.

"Hey!" Kyle stood and called out to the comic at the microphone. "That's not funny. You're ridiculing people for something they can't help."

"Hey man," the comic rejoined, "get a life. These are jokes."

"No, they're not," Kyle responded tightly. Jokes are funny. You're mocking people because of their disability!" Kyle's friends bristled as the shocked audience riveted their collective, peeved attention at Kyle, standing defiantly amid the packed audience.

"Hey, Kyle," one of his friends shot irritably, "sit down and shut up."

"No!" Kyle held his ground. "What he's doing is wrong."

The comic stood at the microphone, angry about this interruption of his well-greased patter. The club's bouncer lumbered across the floor, heading toward Kyle. The comic tried one more entreaty against his recalcitrant critic. "Say, man, like just sit down, I don't want any trouble here."

"Then stop the retard jokes," Kyle responded flatly. The bouncer reached Kyle and laid his beefy hand on Kyle's upper arm.

"Come on fella," he said grimly, "You're outta here." Kyle's friends groaned and twisted in their chairs as the confrontation deepened. Kyle did not resist the bouncer.

He was about to be walked toward the door when the comic spoke, "No, let him be. He's right." The bouncer stopped and stared at the man at the microphone. "Let go of him, he's right." The bouncer released Kyle's arm.

Stunned, Kyle stood momentarily, then returned to his table and sat down, waiting for the comic's next move. The comedian began a new routine, using no retard jokes whatsoever. But Kyle felt the tension cling like a toxic residue at his table. His friends had not shared his outrage or his principled willingness to disrupt the comic's routine. They didn't move past the incident. Frosty silence settled over the table.

In subsequent weeks, Kyle would feel that chill crystallize into permafrost that froze him out of contact. His calls were not returned as he was systematically excluded from the group. We spoke about the situation and my heart ached for my son. He had lost an entire group of previously welcoming friends. With that dislocation from his peers, went his sense of belonging. When the shunning was fresh, his emotional pain and social isolation was very difficult.

It was some time before Kyle was able to gain the perspective needed to recognize that the value difference, between him and the other guys, was so great that there was no real chance for deep and binding friendships. The late Rev. Ralph W. Sockman wrote, "The test of courage comes when we are in the minority. The test of tolerance comes when we are in the majority." Kyle has continually faced the test of being the minority who take offense at the glib majority's intolerance of the difference of disability. He has often spoken out against ridicule, insult, and exclusionary humor. His advocacy has taken place in cyberspace, with potential musical collaborators, friends, co-workers, and in other spheres within which the casual vernacular has become noxious with its dull acceptance of hate speech in the form of retard jokes. The proudest moment for me is when I witness his character, his courage, and his willingness to sacrifice his comfort and his place in community for this difficult principle. Courage comes at the moment when one is tested: putting oneself in the path of real danger, as the price consciously paid to protect another.

Chapter 19: Oral and Aural History

Lest We Forget

In 1970, after a particularly painful visit with Mark, I became disoriented and quickly lost on the sprawling grounds of the Institution. I had given Mark my prized, faded blue jean jacket after he had shaken and wept, clinging to me. Chilled, I wandered for many minutes, finding myself away from the residential buildings and in the unfamiliar area of equipment barns, utility trucks, and heavy machinery. Seeking a way out of the woebegone maze, I crossed an open field and stumbled over the uneven ground. Stopping in the weedy field, I realized with horror that I was walking over the institution's graveyard. The irregular, sunken rectangles were unmistakable, although no stones marked individual graves. Here and there, a rock had been laid flat at the head of a grave, someone's lasting monument to an individual in this potters' field of buried neglect. In the late afternoon's deepening cold, I finally found a service road that led to a side street that bordered the vast institution's grounds. From there, I expected that I would find Broad Street and the bus line returning to Columbus. As the emotional wound bled, I swore to myself that I would do something to bring down the Institution. I lived in California, not Ohio. I wouldn't know where to start. Surely, whatever draconian bureaucracy oversaw this unknown prison, for those locked away for the crime of being different, would not respond to me. But unbelievably, over the next decade, the chains were broken and the place did change. I didn't expose the entire state institution system–others did. But I did, after many years of unbroken advocacy, vault my brother into the community and supported living. I have talked about Mark's circumstances and his powerful impact on me, to audiences, everywhere I have performed. I have recorded many songs about Mark. I told his story in an NPR commentary on Morning Edition, and have published essays about him, including a Chicken Soup story. But I think that my most lasting contribution will be the oral history project I conducted and produced called, *Lest We Forget*.

Lest We Forget was a collaborative project with Judy Leasure. Judy and I first met in 1996. I was working for her agency, The Montgomery County Board of Mental Retardation and Developmental Disabilities, serving Greater Dayton Ohio. We were planning how my time would be used, during an upcoming artist in residence week. Judy was managing public relations for the County Board, and was structuring how my performances could serve their mission for educating and supporting inclusion of people with cognitive disabilities. One outcome of our collaboration was a multi-media presentation at a staff recognition event. I sang my songs about my brother's institutionalization, and photographic images from Christmas in Purgatory were projected on the auditorium's big screen. The photojournalism classic is a powerful and bleak glance at the timeless, hopeless, and despairing life within institutions. The images morphed into scenes from the Board's community wide impact, as my songs opened to Mark's return to the community and my appreciation for the people whose work makes community integration possible. Judy had strung together a wonderfully busy week–five full days' worth of performances, staff events, and workshops that ranged from pre-school and college audiences to a concert Friday night at a downtown Dayton coffeehouse.

I returned to work in Montgomery County three times, always working with Judy. For Judy's retirement evening, I wrote her an original song lifting high the impact of her career. A few years later, she called me one winter afternoon with a general concept. The familiar synapse between us began to spark and a two-and-a-half year long project began. Judy was concerned about the generation of parents dying out–those who were forced to institutionalize their children without a record of their memories. Their stories needed to be preserved. She wanted to collect the memories of all of those suffering family members, as well as the early advocates and pioneers whose struggle began the long road back to community integration. Judy wanted a "legacy" project to document their life experience, and this unknown, dark epoch of American history. I had been conducting oral histories and expanding my work roles as an audio producer. I suggested that I might conduct a series of interviews and then weave them together with elements of my music into an audio production.

Judy liked the idea and detailed a plan for her employer. Judy then worked for Partners in Community Living, a consortium of non-profit residential service providers in the Dayton, Ohio area. Pairing their efforts with organizations in Akron, the title, *Lest We Forget* was adopted and funding was gathered from several sources. Five full days of interviews were scheduled in Dayton and Akron. I arrived in Dayton for three and a half, densely-compacted, days of oral history taking. I was armed with a new recording system that my son, Kyle, had selected for me due to its accessibility, portability, and quality. I had a DAT (Digital Audio Tape) recorder, high-end stereo microphone, studio grade headphones, and boxes of ninety-three minute, digital tapes. A retired colleague and friend from The Sight Center served as my recording engineer and road assistant. The first days of the interviews were held in the basement recreation room of one of the supported living homes run by Partners in Community Living. Judy had arranged to have the oral histories digitally video recorded as well. The technician stood behind his camera, my road assistant sat at my audio station, and I sat in a chair off camera, facing the interviewee. Each was seated on the sparse set consisting of camera lighting and microphones on overhead booms. I conducted the oral histories in an unbroken chain of interviews for seven hours every day. We repeated the process again in Northern Ohio.

My format was straightforward. I asked for the interviewees' names, what was their first-hand experience with state institutions, and then for descriptions of what they saw, smelled, heard and observed. I pursued a series of topical questions of the individuals, different for each subgroup, including those who had lived within institutions, parents, siblings, attendants, supervisors, and advocates who had worked to establish community-based housing and services. Interviewees were men and women, black and white, from middle aged to elderly. Common attributes were complete clarity of memory, candidness, and deep emotion as they revisited a chapter in their life that was wrought with the common denominator of pathos and remembered suffering.

I held my brother's remembered agony within institutional walls from 1963 until 1981. That penitential epoch had prepared me well for my task. I had seen such terrible misery and abuse, such dehumanizing, grinding conditions and years of unbroken violence, that, as I began, I imagined that I had nothing to learn and that nothing could shock me. But as I interviewed those survivors, although much was painfully familiar, some was unknown to me.

A citizen member of public oversight committees for years had heard accusations about ongoing staff brutality. Her outrage was visceral, beginning with her contemptuous recollection of a large concrete sign that read, "Columbus State Institution for Idiots, Imbeciles and Morons". Forty years before, my mother recoiled when she had beheld the very same heartless brutal sign.

A plain-spoken aging woman, with a southern accent, spoke with spitting disgust about the doctor's advice to immediately institutionalize her newborn daughter, born with a severe cognitive disability. Two other mothers remembered with contempt, that their doctors proffered the same advice. They raised a chorus of outrage and fiercely stated, like my own parents, their initial refusal to send their children away and the heartbreaking circumstances that forced them to surrender their offspring to the medieval prisons. During a lag between interviews, I commented on my brother's history. The video engineer suggested I tell Mark's story. So I sat in the other chair and provided my brother's oral history from my perspective. I recalled my parents being told that the hospital would let my brother die by not feeding him. I grimly told Mark's story, including aspects of his tortured experience not addressed through other speakers.

A lifelong father advocate spoke of his physical revulsion when first seeing institutional conditions. His leadership, along with many others, had helped to close or reform Ohio's institutions. Siblings, inside staff, and community advocates all spoke, but it was the survivors, themselves, who most darkly described the belly of the beast.

A middle-aged, African American man provided a straight-talking interview. At the time of the interview, he owned his own home, was an active community member, and had worked as a custodian for the County Board for thirty years. He had been institutionalized as a teenager. He remembered his incorrigibility and his mother's heartbreak with her failed attempts to control her son. He recalled his mother marking his name in all of his clothes just as my own mother had for my brother. Then he was seen before a judge, handcuffed, and driven to the institution in the back seat of a police car. He viscerally recoiled and shuddered as he remembered his time in isolation within the prison building, where he was locked in a cell in total darkness, with a hole in the floor as a toilet, for weeks at a time. He witnessed six attendants viciously beat a defenseless resident for twenty minutes and then send him, senseless, to the institution's disgustingly inadequate hospital. One summer afternoon, as he and others sat in the yard, they saw a resident who had run away being dragged by his feet across a rocky field on the way to the prison building. His and all the interviewees' unvarnished memories were stark and unfazed by time.

A friendly mother told the same story about how her son was remanded to the institution in police custody. A tireless and effective advocate, she had refused to leave the superintendent's outer office when she was confronting him about an inhumane policy. During a summer of unusually oppressive heat, all residents were being locked on their wards without the rudimentary breaks of alternating periods in the yard. They had recently all been placed on Thorazine, a drug with the side effect of

345

potentially-extreme sunburn. Her one-woman sit-down strike brought the superintendent to his office after hours. At her demand, to avoid sunburn, all residents were provided wide-brimmed, straw sun hats so that daily, outdoor breaks could again be taken. A soft-spoken, middle aged woman said that she had been institutionalized because she had become pregnant. She shuddered as she recalled the tiny isolation cell so small that she could not even sit, where she spent a month at a time, coming out only to eat and sleep.

Another woman reported that she had been institutionalized because she had been orphaned. While in the institution, she provided uncompensated childcare for a staff woman who was taking college courses. She also remembered how she bled and bled, when all of her teeth were pulled by the institution's primitive dentist.

An articulate fellow reported that he had been institutionalized after high school when the principal's adherence to rigid graduation guidelines had denied him a diploma. He experienced what he described as "a near nervous breakdown". He recalled, trembling with fresh sorrow, how the principal kicked him out and how his parents wanted a place for him where he could be happy. He signed his own papers to be institutionalized when he realized its inevitability. Once inside, he was selected to work sorting laundry because he could read. While institutionalized, he taught others to read as well.

A nervous man with savant ability spoke at length, with an exacting calendric memory, about his life inside. He was one of the "bright boys" who worked cleaning residents on a unit for "low grades" after they had soiled themselves. He remembered how he would "clean them up with green buckets and green rags." He gave graphic and detailed accounts of violent abuse, including a thirty-minute beating he endured. He remembered the exact time because of a television show that ran in the background. His savant-exact reports cited specific dates and times, throughout, such as: "On Pearl Harbor Night, 1969, at 6:15 p.m., my friend Eddie Powell got hit in the head with a baseball bat by our attendant Bob, last name redacted. Eddie went to the hospital and Bob was fired, and couldn't be an attendant anymore." His mother told of her son's working, cleaning other residents and not getting paid. She had seen the same telephone booth size, one-person cell that had caged another interviewee.

I blended the thirty-five hours of stories into a quilt of voices, each speaking on the common theme I had developed during the interviews. No one was identified by name during the production. Their names, in order,

346

could be referenced within the text of the CD print insert. The result is the recounting of the common experience of degradation, crowding, violent abuse, isolation, heartache, and a tortuously slow return to the community. I embedded relevant verses of my songs and poetry into the production, divided into chapters and sections. The listener is taken on a two hour and fifteen minute, spoken word odyssey. *Lest We Forget* captures a slice of American disability history that was repeated at multiple sites in every state for a century. Since its release in 2004, I know of three of the interviewees that have passed away.

After the completion of *Lest We Forget*, I was presenting on accessible design at The National Automobile Museum Association in Bowling Green, Kentucky. One evening, we were invited to the historic plantation home of the director of The National Corvette Museum, our host. His family had owned the place for nearly fifty years. He suggested that we explore the grounds, particularly the cemetery of the original family that had owned the place for one-hundred and forty years. Burials began in 1817 and ended in 1954. The graveyard was chock-a-block full of large, tilting monuments of many styles, reflecting changing design tastes, but all showing the lasting craft of the day's stone carvers. Perhaps fifty yards away, was another, smaller burial ground, the slave graveyard. That barren boneyard rose and fell in sunken, humble rows of uneven, unmarked graves. A flat river stone, sunk deeply on its side, with faded scratch marks suggesting a name, had marked one grave. Another had been memorialized with a broken chunk of cemetery stone, an unadorned cast-off fragment from the owner's monument makers. The graveyard was chillingly familiar. It was the same class of disregard I had witnessed at the Columbus State Institution for the Mentally Retarded, when I had become lost and stumbled onto that shocking burial ground that reflected no more regard for the humans buried there than this master's family had held for their slaves who had served them throughout their degraded lives. Thanks to national advocacy movements, the cemeteries on institutional grounds have changed. State institutional administrators were forced to begin the slow process of identifying the names of the poor souls buried there, and having name markers set in place. In many cases, birthdates were not known.

In 1999, I was invited by Dr. Katherine Ott to a behind-the-scene tour of the medical collection of the Smithsonian Institution's National Museum of American History. In addition to feeling some truly remarkable, historical artifacts, I was shown one particularly gripping item. I was directed to a small, earth-encrusted, concrete marker with the number seven stamped in the middle of the stone-like piece; it was going to be used in a planned exhibit on the Disability Rights Movement. The marker was from an institution which had been replacing such numbered markers with the name of the person buried there. Such institutional "reform" is symbolic and ironic. Posthumously, it is finally honoring, by this humble means, those so anonymously debased in life. During that visit, Dr. Ott had asked me if I would donate the guitar I had played during the San Francisco 504 Demonstration in 1977. She wanted the instrument for the exhibit on Disability History and for the Smithsonian's permanent collection. I was profoundly honored, but sadly, that Martin D-18 had been traded in for a better guitar in 1989.

Interdependence

I have lost my vision over nearly sixty-five years and counting, in an inexorably slow, lifelong deterioration. A decade of stable vision ended in the late seventies; my fragile shreds of sight slid and then cratered during the first decade of the twenty-first century. As loss crept on, subtle changes would go unnoticed until a threshold was reached. Through the years, specific visual tasks have stood as grim bellwethers of the slow stealing of vision by the cone-rod retinal dystrophy disease process that would not be denied. I recall the morning when I was forty, when, in the shower, the label on the shampoo bottle, familiar and commonplace, became unreadable. I realized that I had really taken joy in glancing at and being able to read, albeit slowly, the large, black block letters on the lime green shampoo bottle. They were nothing special, just jumbo letters giving the product name. But now they appeared to me as fragmented dark marks, not discernible as letters. When I asked my wife if the label had washed away, Sandy reported that it was intact and readable as usual, confirming that I had lost a critical mass of threads in the tapestry of the visual field and that my retina's genetic misprint had claimed new blinding zones. There have been other times when I have shockingly perceived a powerful difference between a visual perception and my memory of vision within that specific environment. When back in the same setting or type of place, after a considerable hiatus, the difference between my stored visual memory and my current ability to see can be gripping. I call it the snapshot phenomenon. Memory's snapshot compared to the picture of what now can be seen will bracket the extent and degree of loss over time. Once, at a cocktail party in

1987–a very occasional setting for me–I realized that I could no longer recognize people at the typically-close standing distance. The snapshot phenomenon informed me with a jolt that I had reached a gateway at which I could no longer recognize faces.

While walking down Berkeley's renowned Telegraph Avenue with my family in 1989, I was struck by my inability to see the cityscape around us. After not having been there for a decade, the amount of vision I had lost in the intervening years hit me with a familiar cold bolt of recognition. I couldn't see anything across the street. I could remember seeing well enough to ride a bicycle, which I did in traffic, while appreciating colorful Berkeley. While scuba diving in 1990, after not diving since 1974, I was panicked when I realized that I could no longer see my dive partner's hand gestures. It was disturbingly different from my last memory of my vision under water, through a diving mask.

Complex public settings that require accurate orientation began to inform me that my vision was disappearing. Cleveland Hopkins Airport became my reference environment. Accessing its familiar signs, corridors, gate numbers, and restrooms were required for independent travel. My vision had changed dramatically. When I began to fly extensively, I could read the giant gate numbers at close range with my eyes alone. Then, I could only read them with my powerful pocket telescope. Then, the slow erosion of vision blocked my ability to read the giant numerals with my monocular. Finally, I could not read them at all. For years, I had prided myself in my ability to walk independently through the airports and hotels, as required, to work on the road.

In 1975, I could ride a bicycle but could not read signs. I began to use a newly developed type of telescope to augment my severely reduced vision. It was a giant leap forward in distance optical aids. The straight barrel, spyglass type telescope was based on a fifteenth-century design by Galileo. The innovation opened a thrilling focal range from 18' to infinity. The telescope enabled me to see everything at ten times magnification. I could see photographs and bathroom scales, objects within museum cases, and most importantly for independent travel, signs in public environments. So armed, employing my new optical capability and relishing its attendant freedom, I stood against one wall of the Dallas-Fort Worth Airport, working to focus in on the restroom signs across the broad hall. In those days, all signs were placed in the middle of the doors. I could see people going in and out of two doors, but I couldn't tell which said "men" and which said "women". As I got the sign into focus, but had yet to begin the laborious process of weakly reading it, the door opened; I was looking into the eyes of a very angry woman who was looking down the barrel of the telescope of a man she could only assume to be a voyeur.

During the 1990's, my vision slipped beyond my finger-hold on independence, and I then began to require a sighted guide in unfamiliar locations. In Tennessee Williams' *A Streetcar Named Desire*, Blanche Dubois uttered the line summarizing her tragic fall to personal ruin, "I have come to rely on the kindness of strangers." In our common parlance, there is, perhaps, no more familiar statement suggesting the threadbare life with its attendant dependence. But I think that there is an alternative meaning that can be drawn from Blanche's observation. During my frequent forays through shared, complex public spaces like airports, I have required the assistance of strangers. Even for seasoned and skilled blind travelers, unfamiliar environments necessitate others' help for navigation to desired locations. In differing ways, people with disabilities often experience such reliance on "the kindness of strangers".

The movement into situational dependence did not come easily for me. I have not "gone gentle into that good night". Darkening with embarrassment, when having to request assistance, I have inwardly railed against being on the constantly receiving end in that exchange of giving and getting. I came to dread having to ask for guidance, and I could feel myself tighten when others' aid was required. One afternoon, I was coming home after speaking at both Guide Dogs For the Blind facilities in San Rafael, California, and Boring, Oregon. I was changing planes, on a layover in Minneapolis. I sat in the gate area for a crowded flight to Cleveland that was late. Every seat was taken and luggage, including my guitar and backpack, crowded the floor space. The update announcement was made by a tired and tense gate agent to tell us that our already-delayed flight was not going to depart for another four hours. A collective groan rose from the assembled passengers. Cell phones snapped open and toned their varietal, ready-for-action signals as the news was sent far and wide to colleagues, spouses, and secretaries.

I had been guided from my arriving gate to a seat in this boarding area, about an hour before, by a vested helper–an airport employee providing assistance to travelers with disabilities. This time, the guide was a woman of retirement age. Guides tend to be recent immigrants, students, single moms, or retirees trying to make ends meet. All serve in the minimum wage, no benefits, underclass position that so many of us depend upon. I always tipped such guides–a minor courtesy. These guides hoof miles every day, walking travelers through vast and complex airports. My mood dropped into anticipatory exhaustion, as I considered the number of people whose help I was going to require during the next few hours. One possibility was to request and official airport guide from the counter. Then an interminable wait would ensue. I preferred the support of the public, although I didn't look forward to the number of chance interactions I would have to initiate. I would need assistance finding the pay phones, someone else to help me locate the door of the men's room, and then guys, young or old, inside, to locate the desired plumbing. That last process had resulted more than once in gaining a well-meaning volunteer, a personal guide who took it upon himself to wait for me regardless of what I said. Sometimes, when hyper-responsible volunteers' own time has run short, they have recruited a new guy to take over and wait for me. Loud vocal exchanges have, more than once, made my toilet use a communal and participatory event.

Such tag-team hand-offs of Good Samaritan responsibility, have gone like:

"Hey buddy–I got a blind guy in this stall and I'm waiting for him but I gotta catch a plane. Can you help him?"

"Thanks, really, I don't need any help."

"I don't know anything about helping the blind."

"There's nothing to know. Just help him."

"Seriously. Nobody needs to wait for me. I don't need any help."

"You gotta go, huh?"

"Yep, he's in there."

"Hey blind man; I'll wait for you out here, okay?"

Quietly, "Please don't wait for me."

"You okay in there?" etc.

Meanwhile, back in the Minneapolis boarding area, I debated about whether getting a sandwich–a complex and non-essential stop–was going to be worth the extra effort. Finally, after trips to the payphone, to the restroom, and maybe to get a sandwich, I would need help to return to the boarding area and to find an available seat.

As I sat in my dark reverie, I unexpectedly perceived a new, different, and clear point of view. Every time another human being assists me, they have the opportunity to have a meaningful interaction that validates their humanity. The world of travel has become increasingly anonymous. An opportunity to actually help somebody else, even in a simple and minor way, is rare and worthwhile. Guiding me helps the guide feel good about providing a genuinely needed service to another in the human family. We all need to be of service to others. Anyone's act of selfless giving provides an immediate experience of being validated as a human being. I am being assisted, as is the guide who assists me. This was, for me, a revolutionary idea. With this simple shift in perspective, my disability's attendant dependence provides a social good and a potential boon to the one offering assistance. A true win-win! With that alteration in point of view, I relaxed and stopped feeling conspicuous and dependent. I was 54 years old and had been battling with my sense of self, about vision loss, for nearly half a century. At that airport gate in Minneapolis, I felt a new lightness, an inner peace, and even happiness. With relief, I prepared to set off. I slipped on my backpack, hung my guitar case's strap over my shoulder and took out my telescopic white cane. I began to pick my way through the clutter of oversized carry-on bags. Gratefully and fully engaged, I sought and greeted the first volunteer, who quickly understood my orientation dilemma and offered assistance. What had been a one-sided, fretful dance of essential, unwanted, need had morphed into an interdependent, fluid exchange of give and take. Once I had sensed that the giving and receiving of simple kindnesses was a gift to both parties, I was able to accept assistance in a positive light and appreciative attitude.

What an amazing thing, that equilibrium. Yes, I, and many of us, have come to rely on the kindness of strangers. Thanks to all of you kind strangers, and thanks Mr. Williams for giving us such a universal and elegant idea. However, it requires some mental gymnastics to move it from the pathos of *Streetcar* to the sweet equilibrium of human need, and to the universal desire to be of service.

Film Festival

In 1990, while I worked at The Cleveland Sight Center, I commented to the counselor in our adult rehabilitation program, that I had noticed a slight loss of hearing in the higher register. It was a troubling development as I grappled with progressive blindness. Several blind friends had reported a similar problem and we had speculated that years of earbud listening, to computers and books, might have been causal. The counselor suggested that I have my hearing tested by the audiologist who regularly came to The Sight Center to test clients in rehab. At the appointed hour, I walked down the hallway to The Sight Center's sound-proof recording booth, where hearing tests were administered. The audiologist gave me the simple instructions required, and I set to work hitting the button as I heard the range of tones at varying amplitudes and frequencies. When the test was finished, I was informed that I had a moderate hearing loss in the high-frequency range–just as I had suspected. He said that as we get older such a pattern of hearing loss can develop. However, at forty-two, I was a bit on the young side for the extent of the loss that he had documented. The loss presented no real problems and I took the news in stride.

As the years tumbled on, I found it more and more difficult to understand conversation in noisy places. I often had to ask people to repeat themselves. The telephone conversation was never quite loud enough, and I began to buy phones with amplifiers in order to boost the sound level to a more understandable volume. Then I developed tinnitus, a high-pitched constant tone in both ears. My hearing was definitely slipping. I arranged for an updated hearing evaluation. The test showed a worsening of my hearing in the high-end range. The loss had deepened to severe loss in the high end and moderate loss overall.

The audiologist reported that the problem can cause difficulty with conversation, due to trouble perceiving consonants accurately. The resulting inaccurate hearing of words due to consonant misunderstanding had become an on-going problem. I was busy doing the dishes one evening with National Public Radio providing the background. It was the winter fundraising season and the announcer was pressing on in that manic hyper drive that is the style of such marathon entreaties. I had paid up the previous spring, so my guilt was not being pricked. I was absently enduring the pledge pitch, waiting for the resumption of normal programming. Then, I heard the announcer say something that struck me as very odd. She happily informed me that with my public radio membership card, I could get in, free, to the upcoming "porn film festival". I stopped scrubbing the pan I was focused on, and I wondered what in the world she had just said. While I knew that NPR stations are always attempting to broaden the net of subscribing listeners, I thought that the porn film market would not be one of their targeted niches. I disassembled the sounds in "porn" and tried to figure out the auditory gaff my brain had inserted. After the exercise of swapping sounds, I finally figured that the announcer had likely said "foreign" and not "porn" film festival. This was a funny moment, but also trumpeted trouble's advance. Throughout my fifties, I continued to sadly note the slowly devolving, partial disconnection with the hearing world.

Two more audiograms confirmed that my hearing was becoming worse, year by year. An extensive diagnostic process came up empty-handed, after ruling out several potential conditions, the worst of which was described to me as being "moderately fatal". The good news was that, although the root cause was unknown, new, digital "open fit" hearing aids could greatly help. Assistive technology again to my rescue! These miniature marvels are held in place atop the ear and send the amplified sound down a thin stem and into the ear canal. There, a tiny speaker provides the exact sound increase needed. Ambient sound is mixed naturally with the amplified signal, and a remarkable restoration in hearing results.

The day I walked out of the clinic, wearing my new, digital hearing aids, I was overjoyed to hear the thin hiss of tires on the wet streets, scraps of conversation by passersby, and best of all–music!–in all of its frequency-rich glory. I listened with rapture to my own guitar, enthralled by its full, dynamic sound, and to the richness of familiar recordings that had become muted and dull as hearing had been blunted. Hearing, even everyday sounds, was an ongoing pleasure. After the first year of wearing the hearing aids, I noticed the dampening of the crisp and clear hearing world I had so appreciated. It felt like the volume on my life's sound track was being gradually turned down. I went back to the audiologist to learn that I had indeed lost more hearing, particularly in the left ear. She boosted the amplification of the left ear's hearing aid to the maximum. The audiologist summarized that I needed a 100% boost in volume to achieve the same level of hearing that I had the year before.

Recently, at a noisy luncheon, a tablemate was telling me that "We have forgotten that we all eat wool." Eat wool? I suspected that my audio perception had been wrong, since eating wool seemed like an idea not likely to gain wide acceptance. I told her my mishearing and asked her to repeat. She laughed and re-stated, "Not eat wool–We have forgotten that we are all equal!" That made a lot more sense. As always, assistive technology provides a tool that vaults capability to a level of much-appreciated increase. However, the limitations of human ingenuity applied to the reality of disability leave a gap that must be filled with acceptance and good nature.

At the writing of this chapter, I now wear even more powerful hearing aids that have programs for quiet settings, noisy restaurants, and music. There are six volume settings–at first I placed the amplifier on level three. In the very few years since I have had these new aids I have already seen some disquieting changes as I now use level four or five. Sometimes in noisy places I can boost my hearing aid signal to the max-and it is still not enough. The time may well come for my relationship with hearing aids when I will need bittersweet acceptance and release of expectation. That winding down of hope for the best assistive technology has to offer is not an unfamiliar reality for me. And if that day comes, I will have to remember that, with or without good hearing, I still eat wool.

Chapter 20: Higher Ground

Multiple Wisdoms

My brother has been one of my best teachers. Mark is a humble man with a life circumstance that no one would willingly want to take on. Yet my brother has experienced obvious personal growth through his hardships, deprivations, and victories. In recent years, Mark has increasingly demonstrated moments of what I see as our universal wisdom. Mark is able to sustain peaceful relations with staff with whom he bonds. There are a few evolved souls among us who have achieved and can maintain a state of consciousness that, unfailingly, reflects wisdom. But if we are observant, wisdom can be glimpsed in any of us. There are multiple forms of wisdom—each a universal capacity.

Looking for these multiple wisdoms allows us to see each other, using a different paradigm, beyond the measurements and labels upon which we typically rely. This viewpoint transcends categories of difference or disability. They unite. Whatever we call them, we each have the capacity to act in accordance with them. In my discernment, multiple wisdoms include: forgiveness, compassion, service, courtesy, kindness, generosity, humor, courage, and acceptance. I believe that the concept is rooted in high-minded spiritual and secular teachings. Multiple wisdoms are a healing, comforting, centering, and empowering perspective. They can elevate our perception of each other. Anyone can demonstrate wise and transcendent moments, worthy of our attention, appreciation, and affirmation.

My brother's life story, as portrayed in this book, reflects a complex, occasionally difficult, and deeply loving man. But in spite of his mercurial nature, Mark has also provided me with many demonstrations of multiple wisdoms, since his circumstances have been lifted from the misery of institutional life to the normalcy of integrated community living. That freedom has given him the opportunity to demonstrate his inner wisdom. Here are a few illustrative thumbnail examples.

Forgiveness: In spite of Mark's decades in institutional prisons, he lives as a man without rancor toward anyone. He laughs easily and enjoys the little pleasures that his life affords. Although he can't articulate it, Mark seems to have forgiven all of us for the social contract that led to his prolonged abuse and suffering.

Compassion: During a dinner out with Mark, at a local restaurant, I became overcome by a fresh constellation of losses. Mark reached across the table and took my hand. "Don't cry, brother," he comforted. "I'll help you." Mark's compassion for a beloved family member's suffering is not unlike anyone else's, no greater and no less. It is intact and was never diminished by his disability. Once, in another restaurant, a diner in the next booth began to choke. Recognizing the crisis, my wife applied the Heimlich maneuver and dislodged the piece of meat creating the obstruction. As the crisis developed and resolved, Mark's attention was riveted on the drama. When things returned to normal, Mark put his hand on the man's arm and asked if he was all right.

Service: Mark attended occasional church services and activities at the small church to which I belonged. We were enjoying a potluck dinner, at the end of which people were visiting across the tables. Without being prompted, Mark got up and began to clear the plates and silverware from the tables. I asked if there was a suitable tray that he could use. A deep tray was provided and Mark happily moved throughout the room, clearing tables and taking the dirty dishes into the little kitchen. Like anyone, Mark shares the desire to be of service. When visiting in my home, he enjoys taking out the trash, drying dishes, and otherwise pitching in.

Courtesy: Mark is courteous–almost courtly. He will open doors and allow others, albeit strangers, to pass before he enters. We frequently take Mark for breakfast at McDonald's, one of his favorite gastronomic experiences. Sometimes, slightly bowing and gesturing a sweeping inward arc, he holds the door for everyone and says, "Ladies, gentlemen, come on in," as if he owned the establishment. He delights in the use of "please" and "thank-you". One Christmas Eve, driven by an impulse that was not a very sound idea, I had taken Mark to an 11:00 p.m. candle lighting service at a large church. By the end of the service, Mark had been asleep for over forty-five minutes. While pulling himself out of the medicated sleep, brought on by the cocktail of pharmaceuticals he takes, he wordlessly held the coats of strangers sitting around us as we all prepared to go back into the frigid December night. Only when everyone else around us had gotten ready, did he put on his own coat.

Kindness: Many of the examples cited in this section are imbued with kindness in addition to the other wisdoms that Mark has demonstrated, in the illustrations provided. Mark is quick to apologize and his interest in others' well-being is always colored by genuine kindness. A man who lives without rancor and who is not hide-bound by ego and conceit is open to the expression of one of the most gentle of human sentiments–kindness. Because Mark is not concerned about status, and because he does not measure himself or others by any yardstick of mundane success or accomplishment, he is free to approach everyone and all situations from a sweet viewpoint, under the control of a kind and good heart, unimpeded by the shackles of intellect. Kindness is not a soft and flabby emotion–rather one in the highest rank of human capacity. The world would be different and more joy-filled if all people approached each moment of their life armed with kindness as the guiding principle. In my work in schools, I boil down everything to one single aphorism: It is not important to be cool. It is important to be kind.

Generosity: Mark is kind and generous, some might say, to a fault. He cannot measure relative value, and there have been times when he has been taken advantage of by nefarious individuals. Mark also is just plain generous when no barter or exchange is involved. While living at House Five, in 1985, Mark received a wallet for his birthday, and he had asked for money to carry in it. I gave him a few dollars. While I was walking him back into his home, another resident was on the porch. Mark excitedly showed him his new wallet and cash. The guy told Mark that he needed some money. Although Mark had loved the idea of having folding money, upon the request, he immediately handed the contents of his wallet to the man with the quick comment, "You can have it." Martin Brokenleg's Circle of Courage, a "medicine wheel", has taught the western world about the Native American concept that communities are responsible for teaching children the principles of Belonging, Mastery, Independence and Generosity. Although Mark was denied belonging to any normal community until later in life, and although his mastery and independence can only be defined as negligible, he clearly has leaped over those stages to become a generous and open spirit.

Humor: Mark has a keen sense of humor. Once I was taking on a persona, with Mark and my wife, pretending that I was their boss. I was barking orders and everyone was laughing and enjoying the pretense. I asked Mark what he thought of my direction and he replied–quite aware of the humor–"I quit."

Courage: Courage is both engaging in those acts of heroism that few of us will ever have to face and stepping up to defend those principles of justice and dignity that demonstrate the inner steel of a person's character.

358

Consider Mark's courage through the lens of this quote by E.F. Schumacher, author of *Small Is Beautiful*: "Any intelligent fool can make things bigger, more complex, and more violent. It takes a touch of genius–and a lot of courage–to move in the opposite direction." Mark's natural way is the path of peace, non-violence, and love. However, when necessary, Mark will stand on principle, placing himself in harm's way. Once when I was performing at Mark's sheltered workshop, I witnessed a man intimidating another with harsh words and name calling. Although roundly enjoying himself, singing into a microphone with me, Mark saw the aggression and left his privileged place to intervene. I stopped singing but played quietly to overhear what was transpiring.

"Hey buddy," Mark began. "No name calling. Peace, brother. Peace."

Although the aggressor might have turned his verbal or perhaps physical violence toward Mark, instead he stopped and Mark quietly returned to our performance.

Acceptance: My brother was torn from the bosom of his family when he was a small child. He lived for over thirty years in dehumanizing, degrading, and violent places. Yet he lives today with a deep acceptance of his life's circumstances, forgiveness for the past, and love for those who care for him and provide him family support. Mark's life's success is not measured in rank, accomplishment, or wealth. One must step entirely beyond the normative values with which we are all inculcated and look deeply at what this man has accomplished. Mark has achieved a pinnacle of success because he lives with a deep and abiding acceptance of what is. Arthur Rubinstein, one of the twentieth-century's great pianists wrote, "Of course there is no formula for success except perhaps an unconditional acceptance of life and what it brings."

Thanks to Mark's acceptance, he brings me joy, opportunities for learning, patience, and frequent flashes of wisdom, demonstrated within the burbling stream of consciousness that comprises his unique perspective. Thanks Mark. Your wisdom, manifest in multiple ways, lights my way.

Critical Tools

In March 1980, two months before my father's death, following an eight-year heroic losing battle against cancer, we stood in his garage. I was visiting from California for the weekend, on a business trip to Washington

D.C. The early spring, Cleveland evening was cold as we looked out of the open door of Dad's garage at his naked trees, the neighborhood, and the deepening purple-gray sky. He smoked a cigarette and the silence between us was peaceful and expectant. He dragged on his Viceroy and exhaled long columns of smoke, giving a familiar and comforting aroma to the cool night air. I had always associated the smell of cigarette smoke in the fresh air with my dad. After he had finished his smoke and a paroxysm of coughing, he began to speak. My father was of a generation of men who didn't talk much about their feelings, and Dad had never addressed his approaching death. But that evening, he spoke the humble burden of his heart. Dad's speech was thin and whispered, emanating from a shred of larynx and a missing jaw. He placed his index finger over his trachea opening, to smoke, or to speak, in short, forced whispers.

"You know," he began, "I haven't made much money in my life. About all I will leave you, Bonnie, and your mother is this house, and I want to leave you my tools. It is just a shame that you live so far away. If you lived here you could take them, but there is no way for you to get them to California."

My father could fix, build, fashion, repair, or restore anything. Electrical, plumbing, carpentry, metalwork, motors, wall papering, concrete, tree gardening and yard maintenance, house painting, plastering–my father had tools and workshop supplies that filled cabinets and shelves with well-ordered and organized collections of hardware and tools of graduated sizes. From X-ACTO knives to machetes, from the delicate tools of the model ship maker to the power saws required to cut lumber, Dad's extensive craftsman's skill and knowledge of the manual arts was reflected in his vast tool collection. Dad knew all the trades, and his meticulous workshop, itself, had always been a source of pride for him and a ready resource for me when projects arose. Standing by his side, I learned as he taught me to strip wire, repair a dripping faucet, and pound a nail straight and true. But most of Dad's extensive knowledge could not be transferred, due to my limited vision and his lack of understanding about how to teach a son who couldn't see his demonstrations or diagrams. His motivated and intense instructional sessions were thwarted by circumstances neither of us could change. That evening, Dad was grieving that I would not be able to inherit his tools–the only thing he had, that he considered to be of worldly value. I felt the continental distance between us in a most poignant and painful way. I told him that his tools were important to me, and that I would find a way to take them. We walked back inside the house.

Dad died on May 23, 1980. After his passing, I reverently looked through his tools and took a few select pieces back West with me. Mom remarried the following year, and I moved back to Cleveland in 1982. A couple of years later, Mom phoned to say that her husband did not want Dad's tools around, and she offered me the entire collection. I phoned a friend with a truck, and we accomplished Dad's fondest wish. Dad's collection had been picked over by Mom's new husband, who had selected a generous, general workbox of my favorite of Dad's tools for his own use. Those were not available, but the project at hand was considerable, and upon that I focused. The basement workshop smelled of a dead mixture of old sawdust, oil, turpentine, and the dust of years. Manual, circular, jig, and a chain saw, drills, pipe wrenches of all sizes, socket sets, regular and automotive wrenches, brushes, rollers, squares, straight edges, electrical outlets, electrical outlet boxes, saw horses, and trouble lights–the collection of tools was dumbfounding. There were the sorted nails, nuts and bolts, screws, fasteners, pull chains, tacks, brads, washers, tape, toilet tank hardware, and a dizzying array of things I couldn't identify. I took it all and created a solid cube, five feet square, on a wooden pallet in my basement by my workbench. As I moved Dad's beloved tools, I picked out the screwdrivers, pocket knives, crescent wrenches, and other simple hand tools that I knew how to use. The master's tools and collected accouterments were carefully stored.

A few years later at Christmas, Mom gave me a small, well-used pocket knife that she had found in a utility drawer. I recognized it at once. It had been Dad's everyday pocket knife. The two small blades were sharpened to a fine edge, stained and worn by years of use. It was still well-oiled and clicked cleanly when the blades were snapped closed. I held the treasure in my hands and realized that I could not have been given a more useful nor valuable gift.

In 2007, I moved to a historic, old home in Cleveland Heights, after twenty-four years in the suburban ranch house where I had lived since three years after my Dad's passing. The move required an archeological dig through the detritus of two marriages, my children's childhoods, my lifetime accumulation of cassettes, DAT's, CD's, VHS tapes, hundreds of small and large folk and world instruments, cast off junk from the family that lived in the house before us, plus abandoned layers of encyclopedias, rolls of tar paper, and lawn furniture. The requirement of pitching or packing everything in the place took eighteen months of increasing work and was an exercise in pure tenacity. I had moved many, many times when I was younger and when I could still see. This time, I began by handling every tool and supply. I sorted several full boxes from the scattered tools that had migrated to many sites in the house. I planned to give my son a complete toolbox from the collection. The exacting process of going through the volume of tool tonnage was exhausting. Below the universal smell of a long forgotten workshop, the distinct smell of nearly everything was muted. Time had slowly wiped clean the musty, earthy, manly and mechanical smells of the tools. They were just old now–not alive anymore. I found myself just packing everything and labeling it, designating what the box generally contained and where it was to be placed in the new house. I would carefully write in block letters with a heavy marker, hoping that the movers would be able to read my printing.

The move went off on schedule and over three weeks, our new house was becoming more and more functional and clutter free. But the garage and the basement work area were still clogged with box upon box of random workbench flotsam and jetsam. On a Sunday afternoon in mid-September, I busied myself opening numerous boxes and digging into their contents. Perhaps it was the sheer repetitiveness of the task and the quality of what was there. Shortly before I moved, a disreputable workman had stolen many of Dad's best and oldest tools. Others had been used up or ruined by misuse by many hands over the years. Still others had been given to my sister Bonnie's husband and our children. But there still remained a vast collection of Dad's tools and hardware. I had opened an automotive socket set, a serious soldering gun, and a box containing two jigsaws. The workbench was littered with bags and assorted containers of random connectors and fasteners of all kinds. My heart was heavy as I handled item after item, some beyond my knowledge and some beyond my sight. Some people who are blind are wonderful craftsmen who can design and build electronic circuitry or who operate power tools with safety and skill–but I am not one of them. Then it occurred to me. These are not my tools. My tools are musical instruments, audio recording gear, my computer's Braille keyboard, and the power of ideas. These are my father's tools and I have been a good steward of them. I can release them into the hands of someone who can really benefit from them as tools, not stored museum pieces that only bring me heartache.

Some years after my father died, I dreamed of being in his workroom and searching for something of his that I wanted, but had been lost. The missing tools had been beloved links to my father. My father came to me in the dream and said, "Don't you know that the things that I gave you, that are of real value, can never be taken from you? They will always be with you?"

In the quiet of my basement, I heard his words again and I reflected on what he had given me. My father had demonstrated great strength in the face of overwhelming adversity, humility, good humor, patience, an ironclad will, courage in the face of pain and suffering, and tender compassion. When I consider those immutable gifts, those priceless tools for effective living, the wooden, metal, and wire collection on my bench now seemed of interest, but not of value to me anymore. Beyond those things that I can hold in my hands, greater than the tools of my own trade, my father had passed on to me–those tools which I genuinely need most of all. Thanks, Dad. It took me a while, but I think I finally figured out why you were so insistent about my inheriting your tools. And you are right; they can never be taken away from me. This collection that you handled, and that served you so well, is valued in my memory's scrapbook as I see you selecting the exact implement you needed for the task at hand. With these tools you completed every project you started and never excused yourself for not having the right one. I will select a few more for my son's toolbox and my own, and then I will be able to let go and release the rest to be used by some young artisan who will be grateful for the gift of this quality collection of well-loved and well-used tools.

Mark's Friends

In the neighborhood where we lived until Mark was four, parents, siblings, and children his age all knew Mark. Kathleen was the mother of the Sullivan family of six children who lived next door. Her children and Bonnie, Mark, and I played together. Mark was protected and nominally included. But things worsened for Mark when we moved three blocks away. In spite of the many children in our new neighborhood, Mark lived as a boy with nearly no friends, and he yearned for the companionship of other children. Annie was his only occasional friend. Younger than Mark, she would knock on the door from time to time and invite Mark to come outside and play. When Annie and Mark were alone things were fine, but often their play was overtaken by aggressive older children who would abuse Mark in ever-evolving diabolical ways.

Bruce was the only other child of Mark's age, with an obvious difference, within our church community. Bruce had a serious surgical scar on his forehead. He was kind and patient with Mark. A boy in my brother's kindergarten class was also named Mark. I knew Mark's older brother through Scouts. His family lived on the other side of our community.

Also Mark's classmate, Becky, was a shy, pretty little girl. She was the younger sister of two of my friends whose father was the scoutmaster for our Boy Scout troop. My brother's presence, as a classmate, was short lived. After traumatic bullying a few weeks into first-grade, Mark refused to go to school, and his world shrunk dramatically. Mark was eight years old when he was sent to the institution. It happened suddenly–the call came on Thursday–Mark was gone on Monday. For his young acquaintances that still had occasional contact with him, he must have seemed to have vanished. Death would have been no more separating. No doubt the word of Mark's fate spread, and some explanation was given to those children. But through the years, Mark's horrific circumstances were not shared beyond our struggling family. Nineteen years after Mark's institutionalization began, I moved from California back to Cleveland. During the past fifteen years, I have had contact with Kathleen, Becky, Bruce, Mark, and Annie. I was pleased that all of them had remembered and been touched by Mark's life.

Our old neighbor, Kathleen, had read a newspaper feature after one of my essays about Mark had been published in a Chicken Soup book. Kathleen's reminiscences about her friendship with my mother, and her fond memories of, and compassion for Mark were heartwarming. A few years before, I had seen her eldest son, Billy, after a concert during which his third-grade daughter had sung in my one-hundred-thirty voice, backup chorus, comprised of ten students from each of the district's thirteen, third-grade classes. When I mentioned to Mark that I had heard from Kathleen, I named all of her six children, except for Billy. When I paused, Mark inserted his name. After forty-five years Mark still remembered Billy, one of the children who had been kind to him.

Becky grew into a community leader and, as a mother, was very active in her daughter's education. She learned of my performance work, promoting inclusive schools, and twice hired me to present to organizations with which she was involved. I didn't remember that Becky had known Mark, but she tenderly remembered Mark's lonely wanderings as a child, pulling his tricycle behind him, back and forth, on the sidewalk in front of our house. I shared that memory. It had been preserved in a black and white, Brownie snapshot I had taken of my little brother. He preferred to pull his trike rather than riding it. Becky and her brother's company also underwrote the publication of my school musical, *How Big Is Your Circle?*

I was taking a break during a performance at a local Very Special Arts Festival when a polite, middle-aged man approached me and introduced himself. It was Bruce. He had become a patient and kind, special education school bus driver. He had driven a bus full of children to the festival. Bruce asked with sincere interest about what had happened to Mark. He shared his empathy and sad memories about Mark having been sent away when they were boys.

Mark, my brother's kindergarten classmate, developed diabetes as an adult. During dinners out, we would often see him eating with his mother, who lived in an assisted living home nearby. Our supper times coincided, and several times we were seated in booths across from each other. Although Mark's diabetes caused pain in his feet, he would always slowly walk over, greet us, and open a warm hug to my brother, calling him his old friend. My brother would joyfully embrace him. This was a new experience. Mark was the only adult who shared my brother's childhood, who encountered him as an adult.

But the most poignant reconnection was Annie. I had believed, and written in an earlier chapter, that Mark's first broken leg was a result of bullying, leading to Mark being struck by a car. A neighbor reported to my parents that she had seen the children forcing Mark to retrieve their balls thrown into the street. I referenced the misinformation and it was included in a newspaper feature about Mark's life. Following its publication, I received a beautiful letter from Annie. She told of her genuine fondness for

365

Mark and how that summer evening, the two of them had been practicing crossing the quiet street, holding hands. The car that struck Mark turned the corner quickly and was suddenly coming toward them. Annie jumped back to the curb, but Mark did not. I now understood, after over half a century, that Mark's broken leg had resulted from reckless driving and an innocent childhood mishap–an accident–not a result of mean-spirited bullying. Annie also wrote that her friendship with Mark touched her deeply and had led her to a career in special education.

Mark has directly and indirectly touched many lives. I have told his story in recorded songs, from many stages, and on many pages. But these caring adults turned the tables, and each shared Mark's story with me, from their unique vantage point. They all had known Mark in those short years of childhood before his institutionalization; they had not forgotten him.

Created Equal

I stood unmoving at the microphone, guitar in hand, waiting for my audio cue from the video being projected on the giant screen next to me. The historic tape showed the crowded White House lawn, eighteen years before, on July 26, 1990, at the signing ceremony for The Americans with Disabilities Act. The video was opening a national forum that was witnessed by a large and diverse live audience. It was being web cast to sites nationwide. Broadcast from Columbus, Ohio, The Presidential Candidate's Forum on Disability Issues was an unprecedented event, conceptualized by a few Ohio disability rights advocates and ultimately sponsored by over seventy national disability organizations. I had been asked to provide the music. During the planning process, I suggested that the "ADA Anthem" would be a good song for the event since the forum simultaneously celebrated the ADA's eighteenth anniversary and, most importantly, gave the presidential candidates a chance to address the concerns of the disability community. Moved by the importance of the occasion, I had also written a song that I thought would articulate the nature of what the forum was about. The new song, "Created Equal", was to be performed later in the three and a half hour program. As the recording of the historic event began, I listened again to President George H. W. Bush's short and moving statement before he signed the Act into law, and, as rehearsed, I started to finger pick the

"ADA Anthem". Then the recorded applause quieted and I began to sing. I ended and left the stage.

Ironically, the forum was being held in close proximity to The Columbus Developmental Center, formerly The Columbus State Institution for The Mentally Retarded. This landmark event was within easy reach of the site of my grim pilgrimages. In the twenty-seven years, since I had returned to Ohio, I had not been able to go to Columbus for any purpose without feeling the visceral clench of knotted memory from the nineteen years of Mark's imprisonment there. Thanks to decades of hard advocacy and reform, how many people had been freed from the sort of suffering my brother endured?

The ADA's majestic weight, through the Supreme Court Olmstead Decision, had been driven like a battering ram through the closed gates of remaining institutions. Olmstead established that residents' Civil Rights for community living were violated by institutional confinement. President Bush had said at the signing, "Let the shameful wall of exclusion finally come tumbling down." Although the ADA had been bruised and battered by The Supreme Court in the intervening years, Olmstead remains a towering ADA victory.

Later that afternoon, I returned to the microphone to sing "Created Equal" and was introduced by the moderator for the event, Judy Woodruff of The PBS News Hour. After the song, Judy thanked me and noted that I had played at a United States Senate reception following the ADA's signing. She then introduced Senator John McCain, whose image was projected on a giant screen, broadcast through a video feed from his home in Arizona. Judy noted that Senator McCain had been an ADA sponsor and was responsible for the Telecommunications Title, creating the operator-assisted relay service linking hearing telephone users with the deaf community. The Senator began his remarks by saying that he remembered and appreciated me from the day of the signing. I was thrilled and honored by his mention. I had served on Senator Obama's, (the Democratic Candidate's), disability advisory committee, although he was unable to be at the Forum.

At a break, I was in the lobby of the facility when I met Senator Tom Harken, Senator Obama's august proxy, and a principle ADA sponsor. Senator Harken is one of the true legislative lions on Disability Rights. Although his office communicated that blindness would not be included in the specifics of the law or its regulations, I still respected the man for his leadership. After Senator Harken and I had spoken about the impact that having a brother with a disability had had on us, a photo was snapped of the two of us. Backstage, after my final performance, another was taken with Judy Woodruff, after we had spoken about her son's disability and my brother's. There is a bond that is formed between people when the mutuality of disabilities, either of oneself or of family members is shared. What a day! The forum ended with my playing half a dozen of my disability rights songs, as credits ran, and the head of the American Association of People with Disabilities thanked the host of people responsible for the historic broadcast. Then I took my stage gear apart and packed my guitar. We squeezed everything back into my driver's two-seat, hybrid hatchback, and drove back North to Cleveland Heights and home.

CREATED EQUAL

By our hallowed Declaration
Created equal are we all,
A sounding for the ages,
A stirring, sacred call.
Not a promise, not reality
Did Jefferson inscribe,
For its want so many suffered,
For its want so many died.

And it's on toward our common dignity,
In a land whose great promise we now keep.
Civil Rights and an equal open door,
As we pass where so many trod before.

Lincoln guided toward that yearning,
With the slaves' emancipation,
But a bloody road still lay ahead
For those freed within our nation.
And then women took their rightful place
Sweet suffrage hard won,
Two thousand eight's historic milestones
See how far we've come!

And it's on toward our common dignity,
In a land whose great promise we now keep.
Civil Rights and an equal open door,
As we pass where so many trod before.

With civil strife and native rights,
Freedom's flames burned ever higher.
Then movements aimed at access,
A torch of truth's own fire.
Out of bleak and barren shadow lands,
Through the wailing of the storm,
The winds unfurled our banners,
A better day, a brighter morn.

Bridge:
Equal, we are created equal.
Given life, given liberty and more,
Equal, we are created equal.
Our Creator gave us rights none can ignore!

Yes, we are created equal,
Intrinsic rights endowed.
All the same beneath the surface.
Gifts bestowed on one and all.
And these battered truths self-evident,
Passed through time from hand to hand,
May our leaders join our purpose
For true access must expand.

And it's on toward our common dignity,
In a land whose great promise we now keep.
Civil Rights and an equal open door,
As we pass where so many trod before,
As we pass where so many trod before.

© Jeff Moyer 2008

Chapter 21: Donation

Ward Bond, my Talking Signs partner's email arrived in early January 2010. It was a plea on behalf of his adult daughter Julie. The email was sent to his circle of friends, requesting that it might be posted widely. I knew that Julie had lupus. Now she needed a kidney. She had just gone onto the national wait list for transplant candidates. He gave her blood type and I was a match. For a very intense hour I pondered the decision, looking in vain for a possible valid excuse with which I could live, not to offer myself as a candidate to donate a kidney to save the life of this mother of a thirteen-year-old daughter and wife of a husband in chronically poor health. I supposed that there would be a pool of donors, likely friends or family, perhaps someone who lived in Julie's community in Michigan. I figured that my age, nearly sixty-one, must put me in a less-than-optimum category. How many more, good years could be expected of one of my kidneys? While I anticipated that I would not be selected as the perfect donor, I knew that by throwing my hat into the ring I was opening myself to the possibility that I would undergo abdominal surgery to remove one of my kidneys. The prospect of the pain itself was chilling, and I frankly did not want to volunteer although, after I had focused in depth on the matter, I considered it a spiritual imperative and a moral commandment to do so. My pain would be the price I would pay, but I knew that that too would pass. All I had to do was live through the pain. A lesson that my father had repeatedly taught me came to mind. Although Dad died in 1980, he remains one of my life's great teachers. He had faced down sixty-three grim operations over his eight years of trench warfare with cancer and the ravages of over radiation. At one juncture, Dad was facing a protracted gauntlet of grueling procedures. He knew that at least six operations would be needed and would occur, like clockwork, every six weeks. I asked if he wished that the upcoming surgeries were behind him. He thought for a moment and then shook his head. "No, I wouldn't want to wish my life away." My father's courage and indomitable spirit provided me with a personal and potent model of strength of character. I also remembered that day, over half a century in the past, when Dad had told me that he and his mother had asked my eye doctor if they could each give me one of their beautiful brown eyes. Although such surgery was impossible, then or now, with that unimaginable gesture they had demonstrated real selflessness. In the light of those memories, I considered the possibility of transplant surgery with its nearly certain return to perfect health. The comparison gave me needed perspective. It was a decision that made itself. I would volunteer to be evaluated as Julie's donor. I knew that if I was selected I would have the greatest opportunity in my life to do something of lasting value for the human condition–to save a young mother's life and ensure her teen daughter that her mother would be on hand, with full, vital energy, to serve in the most critical years of a young woman's life.

That evening, I told my girlfriend about my decision, and I was met with angry resistance. She said that I wasn't considering her and the inconvenience this would no doubt present in her life. During my deliberation, I pictured the scales of justice weighing a mother's life against my pain and the recovery period. Now I pictured the same scales balancing a mother's life against my girlfriend's inconvenience. There had been disconnections growing in our relationship, but now I realized that ultimately we could not endure this terrific distance of values. Knowing that I was truly alone in my decision, I moved ahead as I had planned.

The next morning, I phoned The Cleveland Clinic transplant center's donor office, and I was told that indeed, because of my age, they would consider me a marginal donor candidate. In any case, the usual blood and medical evaluation to determine my eligibility would be required if I volunteered.

That day I also phoned The University of Michigan Transplant Center, where the surgery was to be performed. A nice young fellow took down my initial information and stated that, at his center, my age was not considered a problem. With that interview, we had begun the donor evaluation process. What followed was months of extensive evaluative blood tests and an exhaustive series of medical examinations including a nuclear stress test of my heart's functioning–all conducted at Cleveland's University Hospital, Michigan's long distance partner for this undertaking. On April 15th, I learned that I had been accepted as Julie's transplant partner. At my initiation, the surgery was scheduled for June 24th when Julie would be on summer vacation from her work as a school speech pathologist and her husband and daughter would be able to care for her during her recovery period. I had proposed to my NPR editor that I present bookend commentaries before and after the donation surgery. She agreed and the first commentary was recorded to air the Monday of surgery week. I had done my homework and I knew a functional amount about what to expect. Other details I learned after the fact. The left kidney would be removed using a process called hand-assisted laparoscopy. Three incisions would be made in the abdominal wall to provide lights and camera, a surgical tool port, and a port to inflate the abdominal cavity with gas so that the organs could be cleanly separated from each other. A "hand port" was cut in a question mark pattern around the navel and down toward the pelvic bone, through which the surgeon's hand would be inserted to manipulate the instruments and bag the kidney. The hand went under the stomach muscles and the surgery, while invasive and serious, promised a relatively short period for healing and a return to work within two to four weeks.

However, when I met my surgeon on Monday morning, June 21st, he informed me that because of my anatomical structure the left kidney could not be taken; the right kidney would have to be used. He dourly informed me that this was to be much more difficult surgery–for the surgeon. My research had disclosed that right side nephrectomy or kidney removal was rare and included forebodings about its difficulty and pain in recovery. I asked if this didn't mean a far more difficult surgery–for the patient. I didn't ask details, although I was between the rock of reality and the hard place of my acceptance of this new and unwanted development.

Regardless, everything was in motion and when the big day arrived, I went willingly into the pre-surgical area. I would learn later that the team of surgical residents and medical students in the rotation had their hands, up to the forearm, within my abdominal cavity for over three hours. The surgery was a success and Julie's new kidney began to produce urine for her while she was still on the operating table. Although she required two blood transfusions the day after surgery, she went home on schedule and returned to work with normal kidney function at the beginning of the school year. I, on the other hand, did not bounce back. The surgeon had sliced through four inches of stomach muscle and separated my spleen, stomach, colon, and liver, from their myofascial web, in order to shove them out of the way so that the right kidney could be harvested. The extensive surgery left scar tissue wherever the surgeon's scalpel had cut, and over a period of months, I learned that my new normal was to live with chronic and severe neuropathic pain and the shocking denial of the transplant center that it was a result of the "far more difficult surgery" that I had endured. So although I had intended to save Julie's life and be inconvenienced in the short term, instead I became a member of the vast number of wounded donors who are left to fend for themselves by a medical transplant complex that denies their existence and turns a deaf ear to their entreaties for assistance. In short, I have become an advocate for yet another one of humanity's cast off sub-groups, but I have been able to use all of my life's lessons in advocacy, rehabilitation, and assistive technology to meet my own needs. At a reception thrown in my honor, when I returned as a volunteer musician at my local hospice, I discovered that I was eligible for assistance through their palliative or pain management team. They worked with my reluctant general practitioner to provide me with a host of pain medications that make my pain manageable, and my life livable, although quite debilitated, regarding most physical activities. Thanks to my volunteering at hospice, I was not charged at all for their palliative services. The University of Michigan transplant center, in violation of Federal law, has refused to pay for expenses such as pain medication, my reclining wheelchair, or the massage table that I now use to give my "core", or center of my body, relief during many hours of the day.

My relationship ended several months after my surgery, as foreshadowed by my girlfriend's anger over my decision to donate. At Christmas 2010, I flew to California to visit my daughter Laura and her husband Eric, and to meet my new grandson, Scott, who had been born on October 13th of that year. I was driven from the airport to their home by a woman named Cris with whom I had worked in 2000. A mutual friend reunited us and suggested that Cris do me the favor.

We fell in love during that vacation. Having just retired after a half century of Special ed teaching , and realizing that we were meant to join our lives as one, wonderful, resilient Cris began her journey. She drove her truck, loaded with furniture and possessions, racing ahead of a winter storm, from San Diego to Cleveland in sixty-one hours–arriving in my driveway at 6:30 a.m., on January 6, 2011. We spent forty-eight hours of those sixty-one, connected by phone. She slept a scant eleven hours of short cat naps along the way. Cris and I were married, and we enjoy what can only be called a later-life storybook romance. Rather than resenting the inconveniences my chronic pain causes us, Cris honors my willingness to have given a kidney to Julie and lovingly helps me with the unintended consequences of that decision. Her background in special education and her great and good heart were a natural fit with my brother Mark. Quickly, he too fell in love with her. Saturday morning breakfasts at McDonalds and visits to our home for holidays and occasional Saturdays, became the pivot points around which our calendar regularly moved. Finally, I had a life mate who truly loved Mark and considered it in the natural order of things to love and serve him and me. Together we gave Mark a quality of life he had never before enjoyed. In 1970 I wrote a song to Mark, during the darkest days of his ghastly thirty-three years of institutionalization. A few lines read:

> If I could break these shackles
> That tie up time and space,
> I'd free us both from bondage
> And find a quiet place–
> Where we could live as family,
> Whole and well and free.
> If there is truth or a living God
> This time will come to be
> You shall be free.

That hope was realized fully by Cris. For what I desired for Mark went beyond a home in the community–it included a loving family. Kyle, Mark and I needed Cris to fill the feminine role. She gave me the flexibility to provide a real family life for Mark. But our life also goes beyond Cleveland into the wider world where three of our four grown children and their children live.

Cris introduced me to recreational vehicles. For a time we owned a comfortable trailer we hauled behind her big Dodge truck. To visit our children, grandchildren, and families, we drove to Texas, California, and Colorado. We also traveled to Buffalo to visit my elder uncle, to other locales to see extended family, and to speaking and performing jobs as they arose. But we still wrestled with my need to lie down so much of the time. We had a platform built under the back seat of the king cab, but it was too short to be really comfortable, and my old arthritic knees began to complain mightily. Our solution was to trade in our truck and travel trailer for a lightly-used, elegant, converted Chevy van that now gives us a compact mobile home and a vehicle within which I can recline while on the road. Our new van serves as our home away from home for our annual trips visiting our far-flung kindred, and to get to jobs as they develop around the country.

Beginning in 2002, I volunteered to play a weekly concert at Hospice of the Western Reserve for patients and their families. When in Cleveland, we continued my hospice concerts. As I sang, Cris spoke to patients and their families and gave them my hospice CD. It was a gratifying and meaningful part of our lives and another example of how we live a life within which our spirituality, vocation, and community service interweave.

Chapter 22: Loss and Release

Mark's Death–The Brush of Wings

It was the anniversary of my mother's birth; she had been dead for nineteen years. November first, 2013 was chilly. It had already snowed in October, providing a foretaste of a long and snow-dense winter. Cris and I had married that June, in Evergreen, Colorado. But back in Cleveland Heights, I had finally convinced her to buy a dishwasher; now we were in an appliance store selecting one, when my cell phone rang. Mark was being taken to the Emergency Room due to an elevated temperature and heavy coughing. The workshop nurse suspected that he had pneumonia. Cris and I climbed into our second-hand Subaru and drove to the hospital. But once there, Mark was nowhere to be found. I began speed dialing the numbers for Mark's support staff. With growing anxiety, I left numerous messages and gathered scraps of information. Mark had left his house over an hour ago with his favorite service provider, but it was only a ten-minute drive from Mark's House to Hillcrest Hospital. We eventually learned that she had bribed him with a McDonald's Coffee Frappé, in order to have him cooperate about going to the hospital. Finally, Mark walked into the ER lobby. He took a few steps, recognized where he was, spun on his heel and started booking back the way he came. Cris called his name in a voice that expressed concern, authority, and urgency.

Mark saw her, hurriedly shuffled toward her, and through choking sobs called, "Mommy, Mommy." Wrapping her arms around him in a loving embrace, while gently rocking and stroking, Cris exuded genuine mother love. Of all of the women in Mark's life, outside of Mom, Bonnie, and our grandmothers, only Cris loved Mark with such depth and compassion. Mark cried, choked, and coughed, as he wept out his jumble of sorrows. But in addition to this–his normal mode of communication–he was also speaking through a fog of fever, misery, and congestion. Cris & I turned Mark toward the intake window, which he immediately began to resist. I bent close to my brother and, speaking slowly and confidently, urged him onward toward the inexorable goal of becoming a patient of the fine suburban hospital. Five exhausting hours later, Mark finally climbed into his hospital bed in the emergency room. He reluctantly, with my full-court, supportive press, accepted blood withdrawal and IV port insertion. He would not, however, take off his sweatpants or his socks. I had gently wrestled Mark up every step of the emergency room's spiral staircase, but he had made it clear that Mark Smith Moyer did not want to be there. But, as he relinquished his status as a civilian and collapsed onto the rubber-sheeted hospital bed, he was battling exhaustion, sleepiness, and a very serious illness.

Soon, Mark was transported by a nice young orderly. He pushed Mark's bed through the halls, onto the elevator, and ultimately to a room at the end of a wide hall across from the nurse's station. Mark was in a private room within a newly-completed, exclusive-feeling, hospital tower. These floors had the ambiance and beauty of an art museum, with none of the standard hospital clutter that made walking through the halls of a typical hospital quite difficult for a person who is blind. Mark's room was spacious and included a reclining chair that would suit me perfectly for the long hours I knew were ahead of me. We had asked for round-the-clock nurse's-aid support for Mark, which the doctor, who managed intake, had agreed to provide. Shortly after we were settled, a nurse's-aid appeared. Mark and she got along pretty well, so Cris and I took our leave. On the elevator we encountered Mark's house manager who was delivering his medications. She hurriedly, and nearly happily, rattled off a long chain of actions she had taken to support Mark's unexpected hospitalization. I found her style of manic enthusiasm difficult, just then. But then it hit me that there were numerous aspects of this experience which were remarkable. The ER doctor had spent a long time with me, recording Mark's medical odyssey. His room was as clean, well-appointed, and private as that which would be extended to heads of state. Mark was receiving twenty-four-hour, personal nursing aide support. Many other professionals were involved in his care and concerned about his well-being. This state-of-the-art medical picture could not have presented any sharper contrast with his world of thirty-three years before.

Back in 1981, Mark was caged within a barbaric institution, where real medical care was non-existent. There, over the years, he had suffered from hepatitis, an untreated leg wound from being thrown down a fire escape, and no dental services whatsoever. What had wrought these utterly profound changes within the life of one man? Mark could be seen as an example of the new social order. My brother was benefiting mightily from the changes in public law and hospital policy that had come about through Section 504 of the Rehabilitation Act of 1973, and, subsequently, The Americans With Disabilities act of 1990. We, the thousands of Disability

Rights activists, had changed America. I set that reverie aside; Cris and I had a mountain to climb. Mark was very sick. Yes, fine medical services were in place, but we knew that Mark's illness, wherever it might lead, was going to require complete family support.

By the time New Year's Eve rolled around, Mark had been hospitalized twice, for over two weeks, and had been under the care of a pulmonologist, with a proactive community-based nurse. She had taken a portable X- Ray of Mark's lungs and had seen a disturbing shadow. She suspected lung cancer. Mark had agreed to quit smoking during his first hospitalization in early November and had since been wearing a nicotine patch. But it was far too late. Introduced as a cruel behavior control tool in the institution, when Mark was nine, fifty years of hard and deep smoking had taken its dire toll. Now it was probable that Mark's life was about to end. He was released on January 5th, under the care of Hospice of the Western Reserve–the same hospice for which I had been volunteering for thirteen years.

Two months later Mark was admitted to Hospice House with stage-four lung cancer which had resulted in a bowel obstruction that was causing terrible pain and the inability to eat without becoming violently ill. Although Mark received twenty-four-hour a day care within the hospital and in the community, maddeningly, no organization was willing to provide Mark with the services that he absolutely needed, now that he was dying. Hospice of the Western Reserve did not provide one-on-one care. The county program, responsible for Mark's community care, ceased providing any services once he entered Hospice House. The direct care provider, which had organized Mark's county funding for twenty-four-hour care for over twenty-four years, also suddenly withdrew services. Cris and I were going to have to provide constant bedside support. Mark's final days were spent in a private, lovely room with a picture window capturing the ice-bound expanse of Lake Erie– an infinite view of winter's primacy over air and water. But it was not an easy few days for any of us, and Mark endured the unintended incompetence of professionals and our unending but ineffectual advocacy. A cot was wheeled in, upon which I napped throughout the nights, as my brother's needs continued day and night. Mark was patient and as gentle as a lamb while enduring an onslaught of pain that he could not communicate and which hospice professionals could not intuit. Mark had never been able to anticipate his toileting needs, so, throughout his life, suddenly and urgently he would announce his emergency-level need to urinate or defecate–using the ubiquitous pronouncement: "I have to go to the baffwoom."

From the moment it was spoken, a waiting period ensued after I hit the nurse's call button. During that time, Mark would agonize and often, despite wearing Depends, helplessly wet his bed. Several times I attempted to position the urinal myself, usually also soaking the bed. The staff would have to strip and remake the bed. One night this had to be done three times. Hospice was just not set up for a person with Mark's extensive needs. In spite of the many, maladaptive aspects of Mark's hospice care; the direct care staff was competent, heart-centered, and kind.

Throughout the period of Mark's decline, I would speak to him about the end of life as we know it. Sometimes he would listen openly, and sometimes he would resist and not want to hear what I had to say. Mark could stall the story, but not stop its progress. But Mark did hear the story many times that when he died–when his body was used up and when he no longer wanted to be in his body–the angels would lift his spirit up, and he would have wings and would be able to fly. At the beginning of Mark's decline, I asked loved ones to send angels, and cards with angels and hearts. How everyone responded! His bedroom, within his supported living house, had become surrounded by cards we had hung on fishing wire, angel statues, and even full-sized angel wings.

He went to Hospice of the Western Reserve early in the morning of Tuesday, March 4, 2014. The next day, Mark's hospice physician told us that, although it was hard to say, Mark might have as long as three more weeks to live. That night he again became violently ill, emptying the contents of his terribly distended stomach. Throughout Mark's time with hospice, he was under medicated. Afraid of doctors, he would tell them he felt fine. Although I begged them all to ask me how he was doing, only now, near the end, were they listening to me and providing adequate pain relief. By Thursday his pain medication was finally properly in place, and he slept in a recliner, opening his eyes to speak to his many visitors. No one had visited at Hospice House up to that point, but on that day many friends and loved ones came by. A woman from Jewish Family Services, Mark's care provider, who Mark called his sweetheart, came to visit. So, also, did other dear friends of his. For each visitor Mark would open his eyes, say hello, wave, and then drift back to badly needed sleep. A wise, elder friend of ours came too, who Mark had met at my church, twenty years before. He looked at her and said, "I know her." Then Kyle came to relieve us, as we ran home for a bite and to pick up my needed pain medication. Kyle and Mark were always very close. They had three hours together.

Thursday night Mark was fitful and again became very ill. At one point, he was talking quietly and I leaned over to hear him. He said, very peacefully and distinctly, "Jesus Christ."

Mark became ill again and received more morphine. He became peaceful. Then, Mark crossed his hands at the wrist, across his body, in the same pose as is depicted in the Shroud of Turin. He had never seen that image. The nurse who was caring for him at night was a lovely woman with a kind and gentle manner. She considered Mark for a long moment. Her years of experience lead her to say that Mark was preparing to leave. I had the opportunity to speak to him, stroke his hands, sing his name, and tell him how much I loved him. Then his breathing slowed and stopped, and his heart slowed and stopped. The nurse said she had never seen a patient strike that pose, wrists crossed below the belly before approaching death.

Cris awoke at home at two-thirty AM and could not go back to sleep. She was in and out of a shallow sleep when she felt a warm wind and the brush of wings. It was at two-forty-eight, the precise minute that Mark had left his body. I called a few minutes later to say Mark had passed on, and Cris shared her remarkable fly-by.

There were a few things I knew I wanted to do. I washed Mark's body with the nurse's assistance. Then I shaved him and brushed his hair. Although I wanted to put Mark's favorite clothes on him, the nurse convinced me differently, and we dressed him in a clean gown and clean Depends. I touched his body and stroked him until he was as cold as stone. Cris arrived and we waited for the hearse limousine which would carry Mark to the same funeral home that had taken care of Mom and Dad. This is the announcement which we sent to our broad circle:

Mark Smith Moyer made his spiritual transition at 2:48 AM, on Friday, March 7, 2014 with his brother Jeff by his side. During the last few days of his life, he lived at the David Simpson Hospice House, in a beautiful room, beholding the ice-bound expanse of Lake Erie. Mark's final days were difficult as he suffered from lung cancer, an impacted bowel, and pneumonia– but the loving attention of Hospice staff brought him pain relief and rest. At the end, Mark serenely folded his hands across his body in elegant repose and finality. A brilliant dawn lit a sky-blue heaven as Mark was moved with dignity, through Hospice House, into a morning, rich with the promise of spring.

Everybody who knew Mark appreciated his spirituality, joyful élan, sense of humor, creativity, deep love for his family, and the tender friendliness of this gentle, generous man. For over three decades Mark was forced to live in violent institutional conditions, however, Mark did not carry resentments or anger about his chilling past. He appreciated the love and kindness of his direct care staff, his friends and teachers at the Euclid Adult Activity Center (EAAC), his Sunday school class at First Baptist Church, and visits from family and friends–surely the sustaining lifeblood for all of us. Mark's life will be celebrated during two memorial concerts performed by his brother Jeff–one at the EAAC, Mark's workplace, and another at the home of Jeff & Cris Moyer. Gifts of memory may be sent to Mark's housing provider, North Coast Community Homes, www.ncch.org, which provides high-quality housing for people with severe disabilities.

On May 17th, I performed a concert of the ten songs which I had written for Mark since 1970. We had printed the words to all of the songs and stapled a booklet for each of Mark's circle and for our friends who had honored Mark by coming to our home that Sunday afternoon. I sat at my lovely Yamaha upright piano, with my road-worn, Taylor guitar in a stand nearby. My scroll-carved mandolin and loaded harmonica brace were also within reach. As family, friends, and Mark's Sunday school teachers arrived, every seat was taken in our living room, hallway, and dining/music room; stragglers sat on the staircase. For ninety minutes, through reflection and song, I told Marks life story. The songs' stories began with his institutionalization in 1963, celebrated his joyful return to community, and traveled to his preparation to die. Songs were sung about how he prepared to cross over, our release of his body to cremation, and our release of his soul. Several times I wept as the fresh wound of Mark's painful death seeped uncontrollably. Kleenex boxes softly rustled throughout the house. Everyone was moved as the slow, long saga of how Mark had been brutalized, first by the neighborhood, and then by the medieval institution, and how these circumstances had punched and scarred his years. But the redemptive story of Mark's ebullient spirit and the return to his home community, through supported living, gave heartfelt relief to all, as more tears flowed. Two hard-boiled friends said, with a new genuineness and gentleness, that it was the most meaningful service they had ever attended. One fellow said he didn't know Mark's story, although he thought he had known me well. The other had grown up with us and remembered Mark,

382

both as a little boy and, as my adult brother who lived in his neighborhood. When the service ended, a lid slid quietly into place over an epoch of my life.

THE BRUSH OF WINGS

My brother loved the Bible
Though he couldn't read a word,
At the name of Jesus, he'd call "Amen!"
The sweetest sound he'd ever heard.
He gave a humble table grace,
Repeating time and again,
The names of God and Jesus
"Everybody loves God, Amen!"

But he didn't want to face the end of life,
He didn't want to see it ebb away.
He didn't want to hear about the end,
When the angels come and then you fly away.

My brother, he died slowly
Lung cancer stole his breath away.
I talked to him about the end
Not what he wanted me to say.
He got angel cards and angels;
In statues and full-sized wings.
Wherever in his room, he looked
He would hear the angels sing.

But he didn't want to face the end of life,
He didn't want to see it ebb away.
He didn't want to hear about the end,
When the angels come and then you fly away.

My brother died at hospice,
I was by his loving side,
They said he was getting ready
Peace filled him–then he died.
At home, my wife awoke from restless sleep
A warm wind blew–his soul to bring
The very moment that he died,

She felt the brush of wings.
She felt the brush of wings.
She felt the brush of wings.

© Jeff Moyer, August 30, 2014

Lives Worth Living

"A life unconsidered is not worth living."
–Socrates

"If invention comes to the aid of memory, it does not betray it."
–Olivier Philipponnat, Patrick Lienhardt: *The Life of Irène Némirovsky*

Every memoir is important in some way. My belief is that this book is valid for several reasons. My family has endured and healed from multiple profound losses–the true equalizer. Unlike memoirs that address one life with one disability, we have lived with ten distinct disabilities impacting four men–the most profound being my brother's severe cognitive disability. It is not that the sheer number of disabilities makes this a book of value; it is, rather, how our family, collectively and individually, rose above those circumstances. Further, this book tells two largely unknown chapters in American history. *Grit* follows the arc of monumental social change, for which my family can be seen as a bellwether. These stories span the half century during which families with individuals with severe cognitive disabilities, moved from lives of anguish and sorrow to lives of advocacy, hard-won inclusion, and acceptance. I think this book offers something to the broader community as well. All of us face adversity and this memoir, fundamentally, is about resilience, perseverance, and the power of

385

championing one's and other's rights and keeping a positive attitude. Although weakened, the jackals of ridicule and intolerance remain, but the certainty of prisons for de-valued societal members are fading into the mist. They are still present in our great nation, but they are shackling far fewer individuals. Both assistive and general technology, have given us powerful tools which can help us vault the barriers of communication and mobility. Consumer-driven legislation has changed much for many, but not much for some. Yet it is our own point of view that is the engine of our attitude and which holds the key to our success! This book has been written to provide solace, example, history, and hope. If I have accomplished any of these goals for even one family, then this writing has been a success. I hope that its reading has been an exercise of some consequence for you.

As I wrote these interlocking stories, I attempted to squeeze nectar from the laurels of victory and to distill bitter brine from the brackish toxins of suffering. In all lives, there are defining moments. These stories are of those moments in my family's life; no invention was needed. Sometimes we know those life moments immediately because we taste the honey of hard-won success. Or, at other times, we understand as devastation knocks us down and only a shift in outlook can get us back on our feet.

The latter was my experience as a five-year-old, during that distant summer of 1954. In less than two weeks, I began to lose my vision, unknown to my grieving parents, as my little brother was born with a severe cognitive disability. The birth of Baby Mark triggered a chilling radiation that was social, educational, and societal. Its poisonous impact was ultimately fatal for my heroic parents. Mom and Dad knew that they could not control the course that life demanded they follow. They were subject to the powerful winds that buffeted our stunned family and blew us into uncharted waters.

When Mark was born, my folks were courageous in their determination to bring their little son home and into the bosom of their family. They did not follow the doctor's advice to let him die or to doom him to an anonymous life in an ominous institution. But, after all, the perfect storm of unchecked, childhood thuggery, and the lack of educational opportunities, forced the heartbreaking decision to condemn their youngest child to life within the dungeon of the institution. I lived the long years of that trail of tears, but during my teens was schooled in the activism of the sixties. My parents' generation had a narrower sense, than mine, of their personal ability to impact society.

The last quarter of the twentieth century saw one of the most profound periods of expanding civil rights opportunity in American history. Families, with members who have severe disabilities, now have greater freedoms which, although not perfect, were unimaginable in 1954. Within less than twenty years of Mark's birth, The Children's Defense Fund would lead a powerful political surge, marshaling the current of parents' advocacy. A major tenet of the sixties was that an individual could change society; a major tenet of Disability Rights is that every individual has value. Through effort and fortune, I found myself on the rising crest of unprecedented disability empowerment–an ongoing upheaval. Stories in this book have focused on points along the zigzagging path that began with the tumult and crises of that summer, long ago. Some of these essays document how my battered family struggled to rise on the zephyrs of resilience. Others cover my personal odyssey with civil rights, disability, disability rights, assistive technology, and the critical power of perspective.

This book has been fifteen years in the writing, requiring ten edits to make it a more readable volume. I am deeply in debt to Harriet Slive, the late Pam Venables, the late Lisa Terrazzino, Casandra White, Donna Urban, Kathy Talalay, Molly Danzinger, Anjuli Lochan, Judy Gillett, Patti Lott, Tarsha Ebbern, Liz Reimers, Ed Gain and Cyndi Price–my talented administrative assistants, editors, and loyal friends–who have served through assisting me and aiding in the refinement of this text. Particular gratitude is extended to author and friend, Gair Linhart, whose edit tightened the manuscripts form and structure, pulling it over the finish line. The diverse elements, herein reviewed, have a common weave–the evolving story of members of my family's lives, as each has walked through the valley of suffering and emerged, having integrated their disability into the undiminished totality of themselves. Of course, the overarching perspective is my own blend of activism and spirituality. My life's goal has been to become an integrated man, within whom there is not compartmentalization or separations between head and heart, vocation and spirituality, mind in prayer, and mind at work. When that oneness has been reached, song lyrics, emails, and all speech and writing flow from the same inner source.

My evolving personal goal has always been to be of service to others. I began my compassionate action by being with my lonely little brother. Imperfect and irregular, I stutter stepped into the practice of giving to others. As a youngster, I imagined becoming a minister–a man who spoke as others listened–a man for whom acting compassionately was vocation. Rightly or wrongly, that goal changed when, as a rebellious teenager, I observed hypocrisy within my beloved church. With work experience, I honed my vocational direction beginning with my work as a VISTA volunteer. Although progressive blindness made education and all of life's undertakings a harder slog, I also recognize that it has given me the distraction-free focus to draw on my inner landscape and become a writer. My encroaching disability and my brother's suffering opened my empathy to a growing circle of others with losses and de-valued differences.

Attitudes and beliefs about the nature of disability vary wildly. Some state that disability is nothing more than a nuisance. For some independence should be the only goal for everyone with a disability. My belief is that a disability is a medically-measurable fact that requires accommodation in its many forms and that we must each work through the emotional pain of the loss itself. To me disability is a fundamentally concentrated loss. As I lived for decades with progressive blindness, and then progressive hearing loss, the task was much harder because the floor of ability continued to drop away, leaving me in a sort of free fall, having to constantly adjust to new losses. For my family, during the long years when my brother lived in brutal institutions, the emotional jolt and fresh wound of loss began anew with every visit. I perceive that all souls are touched, peppered, struck, or overwhelmed by varying types and degrees of loss.

Living effectively with loss requires recognizing that we must find a way out of our misery by working our way through our unmarked, common maze, saturated with heartache. Then we are required to begin the lonesome work of struggling over the labyrinth's barriers, only made easier by the companionship of others who share our plight and those who have empathy for our circumstance. And if circumstances re-open the wound, we may channel our anguish into the righteous anger that may drive advocacy for change. At all times, disability and all profound losses may chain us to a bludgeoned self-image and to a broken identity, wherein we feel that we are somehow less than others. Ultimately, we may recognize that we are all truly equal. That realization may come through the company of others who share our loss, books and music, the kindness of strangers and friends, or from our own solitary work of compassion, spiritual growth, and love. It has been said that there is no hierarchy of loss. Whether or not that is true, we may recognize that we can empathize with other's losses because we have fully felt our own. The human heart is tuned to a collective great chord. Our common humanity is connected in part by our losses, along with the gifts that we have been given to overcome and to heal.

While our losses may differ, our Spirit and resilience are the same.

GRATITUDE

I'm grateful to my grandparents
Whose love had follow-through
Who bore the grief and gave the time
That helped to see us through.

I'm grateful to my father
For his courage and his steel,
For decades of our lifetimes' wounds
Were tended and did heal.

I'm grateful to my mother
Whose patience didn't fail,
Her resilience and her ardor held
And Mom's humor helped us bail.

I'm grateful to my brother
Though circumstances spare
I felt his sorrow like my own
I always met him there.

I'm grateful to my sister
Who shared our common load
And whose support–that joined my own,
Gave courage on the road.

I'm grateful to my children
Who never turned nor shunned,
Who held the line and did sustain
Though, often not much fun.

I'm grateful to my spouses
Each helped to move along

The progress of my brother's life,
The journey rough and long.

But of all of these the best was Cris,
She loved Mark like a mother.
And he would call her Mommy,
When fear his heart would smother.

I'm grateful for the family
Who never dipped the torch
Though cold of night and fire of hell
Did darken and did scorch.

I'm grateful to my blindness
Though not an easy way
Has opened up the inner path
That brought me here today.

I'm grateful for my donation
A choice that led to strife.
My cost in life's great balance–slight
Against a mother's life.

And for the countless others
Whose leadership and heart
Did call my name and hold my hand
And helped each chapter start.

Dear Life for all you've given
This way now still compelling
The writing here is now complete
The story in its telling.

© 2018 Jeff Moyer

THE END

AFTERWORD

Here is the summary of my family's lives. I did not ask for anyone to proofread these, so any omission or error is mine alone.

Mark Smith Moyer: 1954-2014. Mark lives on through my extensive published work concerning his life and multiple wisdoms. In 2017, I began work on a one man show entitled *Brotherman*, which integrates the songs that I wrote for Mark, published commentaries, essays, and elements from this book—all of which delineate this man of sorrow, triumph, and celebration.

Grandma Jane–Jane (Moyer) Rasnick: 1901-1985. My grandmother Jane died in 1985 after two heart attacks. Her love and devotion to her family continues to serve as a grounding beacon of love for generations of her progeny. Her selfless love for her grandson Mark was unending, along with the heartache that she shared with our parents. I once performed a concert of family-related songs in a suburb of Cleveland, miles away from East Cleveland where she worked in a drug store for thirty-seven years. I played the song, "Jane", which told the story of her beaming personality and generosity within that community. After the concert, a woman my age approached and told me that she had known my grandmother, from her drug store role, as a child growing up in East Cleveland. Many, many other families did, as well.

Ruth Hildebrand Smith and Cyrus Abel Smith: Mama and Daddy Smith, my mother's parents, played a significant supportive role during Mark's early years. They would take care of him when we went on family vacations and supported us in many mundane ways not detailed in this memoir. They moved to Florida in 1969, where Cyrus died of emphysema in 1975. Ruth then moved to North Carolina to be near her sister Bonnie Ledford. Ruth died of Alzheimer's disease in 1994.

Louise Smith Moyer: 1923-1995. My mother retired from General Electric in 1988 after twenty-seven faithful years of service. Mom remarried after my Dad's death and learned to enjoy opera. She traveled to Italy and New York, annually, for the opera season and died of pneumonia in January 1995. Despite the burden that she carried on her heart, Mom was known as a very funny person whose sense of humor and fun was enjoyed by all. Mom's lifelong commitment to Mark was unbroken until her death at seventy-one. As she was dying, I promised her that I would continue to care for Mark. With that assurance, she was able to release her finger hold on life and slip away.

John Welsh Moyer: 1921-1980. My father's valiant story continues to be read in Laura Greenwald's book, *Eye of the Beholder: True Stories of People with Facial Differences*–Cleveland Clinic Press. It was written of FDR that a man's greatness can be known by those things of his creation that live on after him. Excerpts of my father's dictated memoir can be read in Greenwald's book. Dad's chapter documents his later life's grim odyssey with mouth cancer and the ravages of over-radiation, all faced in his sobriety. He endured sixty-three operations to remove necrotic tissue and to attempt to rebuild his face. He lost his lower jaw and the ability to swallow and speak. The inclusion of Dad's saga, amid the other stories of successful face re-building in Greenwald's book, raises him as an exemplar of the power of the human spirit, when facial disfigurement cannot be mediated. Although trained as a chiropractor, upon graduation he could not afford to begin a practice while being the sole breadwinner for his family. Dad then worked selling industrial machinery. When the steel industry collapsed in Cleveland, he humbly went to work driving a school bus. My father was beaten down by life but never bowed.

Bonnie Householder (née Moyer): My sister Bonnie is retired from a career in human resources and Life Insurance Administration and lives in Jekyll Island, Georgia with her husband Dan. Bonnie volunteers serving several elders in her community, is extremely active with; the Jekyll Island Arts Association, Jekyll singers, Jekyll Island United Methodist Church and was chair of the Shaw High School 1965 fiftieth reunion committee. Bonnie is actively pursuing an avocation as a weaver and jewelry creator. Bonnie's two children, Bill and Dawn, live in Dripping Springs, Texas, and Corvallis, Oregon, respectively. Bill is married to Mica and they have two sons, Jackson and Truman. Dawn Moyer Schumaker is married to Nathan and they have two daughters, Sophie and Sadie, both adopted from Thailand.

John Kyle Moyer: Kyle earned a degree in acoustic engineering, from Full Sail University. His career has been in banking and management. My son now lives in Lakewood, Ohio and works as the Vice President of a call center company. In 2018 Kyle ran for and was elected to public office, unseating an incumbent as precinct leader and Cuyahoga County Central Committee member. He continues as a gifted experimental musician, photographer, and artist and he serves as the creative director for my publishing company Music from the Heart. Kyle is also the other half of Moyer & Son. We have produced *Moyer & Son,* an album incorporating original music by both of us. Our songs have been used in numerous advocacy efforts.

Laura Elizabeth (née Moyer) Angell: Laura earned a degree in Engineering from Harvey Mudd College. My daughter Laura now lives with her family in Poway, California. Laura and her husband Eric have two sons, Scott, born in 2010 and Jeremy, born in 2012. At the publication of this book, we have moved closer to them, returning to Cris's home in Chula Vista, near San Diego, California. Laura is an engineer, currently working in project management for an electrical engineering firm.

Cris (Cristina) Rose Moyer: Cris retired following fifty years in special education. Cris taught students from early childhood through college, acted as a mentor of teachers, coach, supervisor, and active union member. Cris's vitality, enthusiasm, sense of adventure, spirituality and willingness to work hard have given both of us in these later years a life of constant change, stimulation, and growth. She loved Mark like a mother and loves all four of our combined adult progeny and our five grandchildren. My love for Cris is available on the CD: *Love Songs*, presenting the twelve songs which I have written and recorded for her. Cris's daughter Kelli and her husband Mick have two daughters, Gabi and Chloe–they live in Austin, Texas. Her son Andrew lives in Denver, with his wife Cheryl and his daughter, Vana.

Julie Bond Stinsen: When I donated my right kidney to Julie, she was dying with only twelve percent of kidney function. My kidney began producing urine for her on the operating table. With her new kidney, Julie bounded back to robust health, even taking overnight trips with her daughter's marching band. Julie developed tongue cancer, joining the one-third of kidney recipients who develop cancer, as a result of the fierce anti-rejection medications they must take. But a miraculous cutting-edge surgery transplanted wrist muscle and a skin graft to her tongue, allowing her to return to her work as a speech pathologist. Her daughter is now in college, and her husband, Michael, a beloved professor of computer science at Central Michigan University passed away in 2018.

Sandy Moyer: After we divorced, Sandy attended The Pacific School of Oriental Medicine in San Diego, where she graduated with a four-year advanced degree in acupuncture and Chinese medicine. Sandy, my first wife and mother of our grown children, is now an acupuncturist in Atlanta, Georgia. She specializes, both, in women's reproductive health and in ameliorating the side effects of cancer treatment. Her heart's desire had always been that field; she now is a bona fide healer, fulfilling her great career destiny.

Maggie Lash (Moyer): Maggie, my second wife, continues to work as a physical education teacher and coach at the now-combined Philips Osborne/Andrews School. Maggie's sense of humor, and love of her family and students, is matched by her commitment to swimming, biking, and rollerblading.

Lefty (Fred) Pastorius: 1909-1975. Lefty worked for the railroad and it was through the Railroad Retirement Administration that I tracked down his vital statistics. Lefty played professional baseball for the Cleveland Indians for less than a full season, his career ending suddenly, due to an injury incurred while catching a line drive. The baseball broke many of the bones in his middle and ring fingers, his hand and his wrist. Lefty told me that he had broken twenty-seven bones, playing baseball professionally in those hard-scrabble years. Lefty's importance in my life could only be seen after decades had elapsed. Lefty befriended me and spent time with me during years when my father was consumed by his work, his grief concerning my brother's plight, my progressive blindness, and his resulting alcoholism. I wrote "Lefty", a song capturing this man's role in my life and his faded baseball career. It remains a favorite of friends who share a love for the Cleveland Indians. Lefty was survived by his daughter Barbara, his grandson, and his second wife.

Guitars and other instruments: Guitars become living things to their owners. For the sake of those who love guitars, I include the following.
I began playing guitar in 1963. After three, very low-end, student guitars, I played two Harmony twelve-string guitars, both of which failed due to bowed necks. I then bought a dreadnaught Gibson which had been

battered terribly and rebuilt with roofing paper and Bondo. In 1968, thanks to the generosity of a local guitar store owner, I bought a Martin D-18. This was the guitar that was heard, coast to coast, on the CBS evening news with Walter Cronkite on April 15, 1977, at the historic 504 demonstration which changed American Disability Rights history. In 1999, Dr. Katherine Ott, curator in the Division of Science and Medicine at Smithsonian's National Museum of American History, requested that I donate the instrument for their collection on disability history. Sadly it was no longer in my possession and untraceable. I played that guitar for twenty-one years, within churches large and small, and at my father's memorial service. Upon it, I wrote birth songs for both of my children. I traded it in on a bottom of the line, large body (dreadnought) Taylor. That instrument, just two years later– in an even trade–was bartered for a fine Bart Writer 5-string banjo. I bought a used Guild 12-string guitar that had belonged to John Hammond Jr.

In 1986, I founded Music from the Heart and began to play out professionally. When my hands and arms developed chronic tendonitis in 1991 and I could no longer play a dreadnought, I bought the best small-body guitar in the store. It is a grand classic-sized 912 Taylor with lovely sculpted abalone shell inlays, in increasingly-complex design up the neck, a delicate Florentine cutaway, and a sound that is evenly-balanced, full and warm. That guitar has a finish that is crazed with many crescent-shaped finish cracks from uneven warming, after being subjected to Arctic cold during a long night in a Wisconsin garage–a mistake made by a well-meaning host, while on the road. But the honey-golden age of the spruce represents the decades I have played it, and I wouldn't think of having it refinished and removing the wood's tone. I had a two-acoustic microphone system added, terminating in a stereo output jack. A stereo guitar chord then transmits the signal to a stereo Fishman pre-amp that creates a warm acoustic sound before the signal is sent to an amplifier.

Instruments have braided their sounds, charm, and character throughout my life. Guitar and harmonica has been my mainstay and have been the foundation of my recordings beginning with *Do You See Me as an Equal?* I have maintained my love of the five string banjo and recorded songs on *Maxwell the Dancing Dog* using it. I began playing the world's most ancient instrument, the Aborigines' didgeridoo, after my trip to Australia with Third Street Kids. I now have half a dozen and have used them on two songs on my children's album *Maxwell*. I began playing bamboo flute in 1970. Sandy gave me a silver flute in 1975 which can be heard on *How Big Is Your Circle?*. The late Kevin Stockton a member of the

Lakota Sioux Tribe gave me a fine Native American wooden flute which can be heart on *Peace Sweet Peace*. For my sixtieth birthday I bought a fine used clarinet, taught myself to play it, and have recorded with it on my *Love Songs* album. The minor key harmonica is one of my favorite small instruments along with the classic five octave chromatic harmonica that can be heard on *We're People First*. I have numerous ukuleles; my favorites are a baritone uke given to me by my daughter Laura and an eight string instrument by my son Kyle. The baritone uke can be heard on *Maxwell*. Kyle also gave me a Yamaha Digital Piano who's numerous synthesized voices are recorded on *Love Songs* and *Thunderhead*. My long time benefactor Jim Storer died in 2012. Upon his death, his widow Dede gave me his wonderful Yamaha upright piano. It can be heard on *Moyer & Son*. I have a handmade autoharp which I used on *Love Songs*. My mountain dulcimer, a gift from Sandy, can be heard on *How Big Is Your Circle?* My fabulous bass dulcimer, a gift from Cris, is the solo instrument on several tracks on *Love Songs*. I have numerous bamboo flutes and ocarinas. My favorite, the smallest, was crafted by friends Sandy and Richard Schmidt of Clayzeness Whistle Works. I play it as the closing track on *Special Ed Ranger*. It is one of 300 made for the 1992 Earth Summit in Rio, to be played homeless children as they opened and closed the Summit. In 1975 I found a two chamber, lemon-sized, volcanic rock on a beach in northern California. After I learned to play the didgeridoo, I discovered I could play that rock! Most remarkably, it has a two octave range, terminating five steps below the lowest note on the piano. I played it on *Maxwell* and in numerous concerts including several at Severance Hall, home of the Cleveland Orchestra. I fabricated clay versions of the rock, that I call the pocket tuba, or the pocket didgeridoo.

When my piano lessons terminated with the encroachment of progressive blindness, I thought I would never be able to play an instrument. However, subliminally, I learned that I could play by ear. I now play twenty instruments and have taught myself each of them by listening. I am not unique. Half of the musicians in the world cannot read music. My advice to you all is learn to play any instrument. Don't be afraid of playing it badly at first, just play it. Your musical instruments will be your friends, source of expression, joy and solace. It has been so throughout time. It has been theorized that as a species we sang before we spoke. We all can sing and my life has been about opening choruses to singers of all ages without exception. My albums can be found on all music services without cost.

Make music, sing and open your hearts to the expansive and wondrous, diverse human family.

J.M. December, 2018

50402121R00238

Made in the USA
Columbia, SC
06 February 2019